The Floating World Revisited

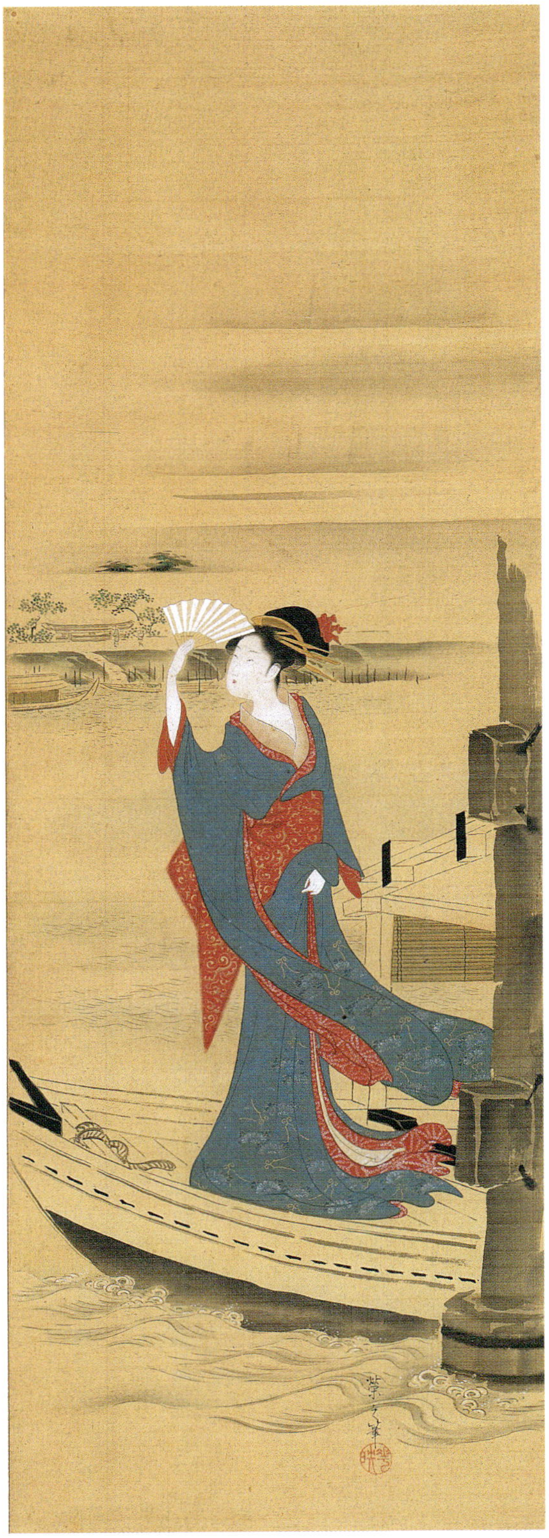

The Floating World Revisited

Donald Jenkins

WITH THE ASSISTANCE OF

Lynn Jacobsen-Katsumoto

WITH ESSAYS BY

Henry D. Smith II

Haruko Iwasaki

Laurence Kominz

Tadashi Kobayashi

Portland Art Museum
in association with
University of Hawaii Press

Library of Congress
Cataloging in Publication Data

Jenkins, Donald
The Floating World Revisited / Donald Jenkins, with the assistance of
Lynn Jacobsen-Katsumoto; with essays by Haruko Iwasaki . . . [et al.].
p. 253.
Exhibition catalog.
Includes bibliographical references.
ISBN 0-8248-1612-9 (cloth).
ISBN 0-8248-1614-5 (paperback).
1. Arts, Japanese—Edo Period, 1600-1868—Exhibitions. 2. Ukiyo-e—Exhibitions. 3. Tokyo (Japan)—Civilization—Exhibitions.
I. Katsumoto, Lynn Jacobsen. II. Title.
NX584.T65J46 1993
760'.0449952135025'07479549—dc20
93-38081 CIP

Copublished by
Portland Art Museum and
University of Hawaii Press
2840 Kolowalu Street
Honolulu, Hawaii, 96822

Text editing by Philippa Brunsman
Design and layout by John Laursen at Press-22
Color separation and printing by the Irwin-Hodson Company
Binding by Lincoln and Allen Company
Printed and bound in the United States of America

Exhibition Schedule for *The Floating World Revisited*

Portland Art Museum
October 26 through December 30, 1993

Cleveland Museum of Art
February 2 through April 2, 1994

Preface

More than five years of planning and preparation have gone into the exhibition recorded in this catalogue. It has been a major undertaking for a museum of Portland's size and has occasionally taxed the institution's resources to the limit. Yet it is with mixed emotions—an undercurrent of regret as well as feelings of relief—that I send this final page of typescript to the printers. It is hard to turn away from the many avenues of inquiry this project has opened. During the course of our work we have come across a great many leads, only a few of which we have been able to pursue to satisfying conclusions. Exhibition schedules and publication deadlines run on tracks of their own, however, to which everything else must yield. The time has come to share the results of our work with others.

The chief purpose of our efforts has been to encourage a fresh look at ukiyo-e, those images of the Floating World that were among the first works of Japanese art to attract the interest of collectors and scholars in the West and that continue to fascinate many Europeans and Americans. Indeed, probably no other aspect of Japanese art has received greater exposure outside the country of its origin. This may well prompt questions as to why yet another exhibition should be devoted to such familiar material. Our answer is that these images only seem familiar to us; that, in fact, we know less about them than we imagine; and that, in particular, we know precious little about the world that produced them for its own purposes.

This is why we have called our project "The Floating World Revisited." It is a reexamination of a world that has never been fully explored. As such, its purpose is not so much to reach conclusions as to raise questions and suggest possibilities. If what we present here stimulates additional investigations and more focused inquiries, we will feel that our efforts have succeeded.

Acknowledgments

Neither this book nor the exhibition could have been completed without help and support from many quarters. The many institutions and private collectors who have so generously lent work to the exhibition are listed on the following page. Those who have contributed their time and expertise to the project are too numerous to be thanked individually. They include Haruko Iwasaki, Tadashi Kobayashi, Nyx Lyman, Andrew Markus, Kozō Sasaki, and Henry D. Smith II, all of whom took part in the initial planning, and several of whom have continued to be involved. Many others have come to our aid at critical stages along the way. In particular, I would like to thank David Newman for directing us to several important paintings; Iwao Nagasaki of the Tokyo National Museum for consulting with us on textiles; Kate Boninsinga for her research on lacquer, Louise Wilson for her work on the glossary; Richard Brown for his editorial advice; and Aaron Bess, Karin Kaneps, and Laura Weinberg for their clerical and organizational assistance. Several people helped us in deciphering inscriptions, including Misa Yoshioka, Toemon Hashimoto, Mary Mast, and Yoshimi Uchimura, and Peter Navratil aided us in our communications with France. Finally, my heartfelt thanks go to the past and present members of the museum's Asian Art Council whose faith in this project gave it the start it needed.

This exhibition has been supported by a major grant from the National Endowment for the Humanities, a federal agency. Additional support has been received from the Asian Art Council of the Portland Art Museum, the Japan Foundation, Delta Air Lines, Pacific Power, the Maybelle Clark Macdonald Foundation, the Metropolitan Center for Far Eastern Art Studies, the Kaneko Foundation for International Research and Education, SEH America, Inc., and Synektron. Individual contributors include Mrs. James Castles, Mildred Schnitzer, Andrée Stevens, Jean Vollum, and Mr. and Mrs. Alan Green, Jr.

Lenders to the Exhibition

Art Gallery of New South Wales, Sydney
The Art Institute of Chicago
The Azabu Museum of Arts and Crafts, Tokyo
The Chester Beatty Library and Museum of Oriental Art, Dublin
Comune di Genova, Museo d'Arte Orientale Edoardo Chiossone
The British Museum
The Mary and Jackson Burke Collection
The Cleveland Museum of Art
East Asian Library, University of California, Berkeley
Harvard University Art Museums, Cambridge, Massachusetts
Honolulu Academy of Art
Idemitsu Museum of Arts, Tokyo
Indiana University Art Museum, Bloomington
Kimbell Art Museum, Fort Worth
Los Angeles County Museum of Art
The Mann Collection, Highland Park
The Metropolitan Museum of Art
Minneapolis Institute of Arts
Musée National des Arts Asiatiques-Guimet, Paris
The New York Public Library
Albert Odmark
Peabody Essex Museum, Salem, Massachusetts
Portland Art Museum
Joe and Etsuko Price Collection
Gerhard Pulverer, Cologne
Robert Ravicz
Mearl and Kazue Snell
Spencer Museum of Art, The University of Kansas, Lawrence
Tiger Collection
Takoyakushi Temple, Tokyo
Tobacco & Salt Museum, Tokyo
Tokyo National Museum
Tsubouchi Memorial Theater Museum, Waseda University, Tokyo
Tsuyama City Museum, Tsuyama
The University of Michigan Museum of Art, Ann Arbor
Walters Art Gallery, Baltimore
Waseda University Library, Tokyo

Contents

The Floating World

INTRODUCTION

Donald Jenkins

The Floating World Revisited deals with an aspect of Japanese art which, though it has received considerable attention in the past, still remains ill understood in several key respects. Its subject is twenty years in the history of what the Japanese call *ukiyo-e*, a term that embraces, but is not limited to, what we in the West simply call "Japanese prints." The twenty years in question are roughly 1780 to 1800, a span of time that has been described as the golden age of ukiyo-e. These were the years when masters like Kiyonaga, Utamaro, Sharaku, and Eishi were creating their most memorable images, works that have been so widely reproduced that they are now familiar to those with only the most passing interest in Japanese art. Yet to most people these images remain nothing more than arresting compositions—curious, largely indecipherable icons of another time and place. That they once reflected the interests and enthusiasms of real people and expressed at least some of their values seems hard to imagine. As a result, no matter how striking they are compositionally, they seem doomed to a certain bloodlessness.

This need not be their fate. The purpose of this exhibition is to restore the flesh and blood to these works of art—or, to use what is perhaps a more appropriate metaphor—to plant them once again in the soil that originally nourished them. For most of these works were never intended to stand alone. They grew out of, and contributed to, a culture that gave them meaning, and divorced from which they become mute. They are like half of a conversation, unintelligible unless the other half is also heard. A *surimono*, for instance—a print in which an image is combined with poetry to celebrate a special event—loses much of its resonance if we cannot read the poems and are ignorant of the purpose for which the print was commissioned. An actor print may well seem merely grotesque if we are unfamiliar with the conventions of the kabuki stage.

In what follows, we shall do our best to provide "the other half of the conversation." To do so, we will first need to describe the physical and cultural environment in which ukiyo-e was rooted. Along the way we will have to say something about Japan's history and traditions in general. Later, when we get to individual works of art, we will explain (wherever possible) why, and under what circumstances, they were produced. This will sometimes make for tough going. We will be dealing with concepts, beliefs, and practices that are often without any parallels in the West and with a language that frequently seems all but untranslatable. However, the material has an inherent fascination, which will quickly reward the extra effort required. Once the viewer pushes past the initial strangeness, the art will shine through with even greater brilliance.

Ukiyo-e Defined

The Japanese word *ukiyo-e* is a compound made up of two parts: *ukiyo*, "Floating World," and *e*, "pictures," and is usually translated quite literally as "pictures of the Floating World." But this translation is not particularly helpful in and of itself. The problem has to do with the meaning of the expression "Floating World," which is no longer used in everyday Japanese. To get some real sense of its meaning, we have to turn to the late seventeenth century, when the term "ukiyo-e" first began to gain currency. At that time the word "ukiyo," which had originally been a Buddhist term expressive of the transience of life, had begun to take on different, more positive connotations. Instead of "this (transient) world of sorrows," it became "this (transient) world of pleasures." And the pleasures referred to were not just any pleasures but, rather, those associated with a certain extravagance and high living. The art depicting this world of pleasure, and those involved in it, quite naturally, came to be called "*pictures* of the Floating World."

In short, originally at least, ukiyo-e was defined in terms of its subject matter. Seen from that point of view, it was a *genre* of art, and, as such, could be produced by artists of different schools. This was probably true of the earliest ukiyo-e. Before long, however, particularly in Edo, ukiyo-e became a school, with all the stylistic interdependences and master-pupil relationships that such a definition implies. It is hard to say just when this development occurred, but it had certainly already taken place by 1700, by which time the Torii family had begun to emerge as the preeminent artists associated with the kabuki theater, a position the family would retain for generations.

Prints, Painting, and Book Illustration

Though most people associate the term "ukiyo-e" exclusively with prints, its actual meaning, as suggested by the literal translation given above, is much broader, and includes paintings as well. To be sure, some ukiyo-e artists did concentrate primarily on printmaking. Others, however, never designed prints at all. Fujimaro, for instance, who is represented in this exhibition by two works (Catalogue nos. IV-3 and IV-4), seems to have devoted himself solely to painting. But his was an unusual case. Most ukiyo-e artists seem to have been equally at home in either medium.

To say that an ukiyo-e artist designed prints does not mean that he actually made them. Ukiyo-e prints were commercial products sold by publishers, and the artist's role was limited to providing the publisher, at the publisher's request, with a design. The designs were transferred to blocks by special craftsmen and printed by yet other craftsmen in a primitive form of mass production. The artist might or might not be called in to consult on the process.

The term "ukiyo-e" also embraces book illustration, which was another important form of expression—and source of income—for many ukiyo-e artists. Here too, however, the artist's role was limited, with only occasional exceptions, to providing designs for the illustrations. In most cases, the idea for the book was the publisher's, and it was the publisher who oversaw the production. This probably explains why greater prestige was associated with painting than with designing prints. In painting, an artist was more of his own master. This became a matter of pride to some artists, and it is easy to understand why some of them may have chosen to give up print designing when they had an opportunity to do so. Two artists included in the exhibition, Kiyonaga and Eishi, did just that.

Yet the publishers of the late eighteenth century seem to have been interested in more than merely catering to the market. Much of what we admire in Japanese prints and book illustrations of the 1780s and 1790s depended on their taste, inspiration, and standards. It is hard to imagine what the history of ukiyo-e would have been like if the publisher Tsutaya Jūzaburō had not discovered and encouraged the young Utamaro or had not come up with the idea for the extraordinary series of books that culminated in *Momochidori kyōka awase* (Catalogue no. IV-15). And Tsutaya was not alone in his insistence on quality and willingness to take chances. His competitors, Nishimuraya Eijudō and Tsuruya Kiemon, have prints to their credit that are every bit the equal of his.

Most ukiyo-e exhibitions in the past, in this country at least, have focused exclusively on prints. This is unfortunate, because it has given rise to a skewed notion of what ukiyo-e is. There are many glorious images among the prints; of that there can be no doubt. But the prints *were* commercial products, after all, and, as such, tended to be limited in both subject matter and style. In their paintings, ukiyo-e artists could work much more spontaneously. They could choose their own subjects and explore effects according to whim. As a result, some of their paintings are so unlike their prints that it is hard to believe they are by the same artists. Eishi is a case in point. Though some of his paintings parallel his prints quite closely (Catalogue no. II-7), others (Catalogue nos. I-3 and IV-2) employ techniques and expressive effects never seen in his prints. The same may be said of Hokusai. If our knowledge of his work were limited to his prints, we would consider him only half the artist he actually was.

Yet it is the prints that have shaped much of what we know about ukiyo-e—perhaps inevitably so. There are more of them, for one thing, and they constitute a more consistent, more comprehensible body of work. They are also easier to date, in part because of the huge number of actor prints that can be linked to specific, dated performances, and in part because of the evidence provided by illustrated books, which almost always bear the date of their publication. Paintings, too, occasionally bear dates—there are several examples in this exhibition—but more often they do not; and the features mentioned above, their spontaneity and the greater variety of their subject matter, make it harder to subject them to the kind of comparative analysis needed to date them on stylistic grounds. These inherent difficulties have been compounded by the fact that the paintings are widely scattered in various collections around the world and have only recently begun to receive much serious scholarly attention.

The Golden Age

The prints and paintings of the "golden age" of ukiyo-e display a confidence and maturity that clearly set them apart from the charming but more tentative, and compositionally less sophisticated, work of the previous two decades; and they achieved a level of refinement and consistency of taste that was rarely equalled after 1800. However, there was nothing static about the art of this so-called golden age. There are important differences between the work of the 1780s and that of the 1790s.

The 1780s were dominated by Katsukawa Shunshō and his followers, who specialized in actor prints, and Torii Kiyonaga, who excelled in depictions of beautiful women. Both Shunshō and Kiyonaga approached their work with a certain sobriety. Even in his more dramatic prints, Shunshō seemed to favor the most straightforward presentation possible, and there is often something rather matter-of-fact about Kiyonaga's treatment of his subjects. Their work is too competent, too ingeniously crafted, to be dull, but it rarely has the edge of excitement that is found in the prints of the 1790s. What it offers instead is composure and dignity. This is particularly true of the majestic compositions in some of Kiyonaga's more ambitious diptychs.

When Kiyonaga gave up print designing around 1790 and Shunshō died in 1793, their places were already being taken by other artists with different temperaments and sensibilities. By 1795, print styles had changed markedly. The striking "large-head" (*ō kubi-e*) type of print had been introduced (a development as radical for its time as the introduction of closeups in the movies was for ours), together with the use of brilliant mica backgrounds. The stately compositions of the previous decade had fallen out of favor, to be replaced by designs in which dramatic or evocative concerns were paramount. There was a new sophistication in the handling and framing of blank space: what was not shown but merely implied often became as important as what was actually depicted—as in Catalogue no. II-30 (a).

The images themselves became more sensuous and playful. A bamboo blind, a mosquito net, a diaphanous gauze kimono—anything that might simultaneously obscure and reveal—was seized on to tease and tantalize the viewer. The figures of courtesans became taller, their garments more flamboyant, their coiffures more striking. A similar pushing to extremes is apparent in the portraits of actors, which reach a high point of intensity and caricature in the work of Tōshūsai Sharaku. Only one print genre seemed to escape the prevailing taste for exaggeration, and that was the surimono, where restraint and delicacy remained the norm.

Most modern viewers probably prefer artists of the 1790s like Utamaro, Eishi, and Sharaku to their more sober predecessors, Shunshō and Kiyonaga. Something in their intensity and willingness to take chances probably accords better with our own sensibility. But their work may well have harbored the seeds of its own destruction. Collectors and scholars have long noted that there was a precipitous decline in the quality in ukiyo-e after 1800, and there can be no doubt that the early years of the nineteenth century constitute a major fault line in its history. Though ukiyo-e would survive for the remainder of the century, and even go on to produce some of its best-remembered images in the landscape prints of Hiroshige and Hokusai, it would never again recapture the particular brilliance of its golden age.

What happened? All we can say is that the great flowering of ukiyo-e in the 1780s and 1790s was the product of an exceptional milieu; when that milieu vanished, the art it produced was bound to vanish with it. It is time to look at that milieu more closely.

Ukiyo-e as an Edo Product

By the mid-eighteenth century, ukiyo-e had become almost exclusively identified with Edo. This was particularly true of the prints, which, after the introduction of full-color printing in 1765, came to be called *Azuma nishiki-e*, "brocade pictures of the East" (i.e., eastern Japan). They were considered an Edo specialty, the kind of thing visitors to the capital might pick up as a souvenir, and were not produced elsewhere until the early 1800s. But in painting and book illustration, too, ukiyo-e was essentially an Edo phenomenon, which means that it can be fully understood only when seen within the context of the peculiar social and cultural conditions that obtained in that city.

Each of the three major cities of eighteenth-century Japan—Edo, Kyoto, and Osaka—had its distinct character. Kyoto, the ancient capital and still the residence of the emperor, the hereditary nobility (the *kuge*), and many of the leading Buddhist prelates, was more steeped in tradition than the other two, yet it was also a thriving industrial center specializing in book publishing and the production of woven silk and other luxury goods.

The economic life of nearby Osaka, on the other hand, revolved around commerce, particularly the storage and transshipment of rice and other foodstuffs—so much so that the city came to be called the "kitchen of the nation." Its citizens had a reputation for being no-nonsense businessmen with a developed respect for the value of money. At the same time, they were great fans of *ningyō shibai* (puppet theater, or *bunraku*) and related forms of narrative music, many of which originated in Osaka.

Edo, the residence of the shogun and the administrative capital of the nation, lay some four hundred kilometers (approximately 250 miles) to the east of Kyoto, in the Kantō (i.e.,"east of the barrier") region. With a population close to—or perhaps even exceeding—a million people, it was not only the largest city in Japan but one of the largest cities in the world. For all its size, however, it was not an industrial or commercial center. Nearly half of its population consisted of samurai and their families who were either direct vassals of the shogun or in the service of the regional lords (daimyo), all of whom were required to maintain residences in Edo. With so high a proportion of its population in official or ceremonial service, Edo inevitably became a net importer of goods, where economic activity revolved around the consumption, rather than the production or accumulation, of wealth. This focus on consumption eventually affected even the merchant classes. The typical Edokko (literally, "child of Edo") was regarded by other Japanese as a spendthrift, much too apt to splurge on fashion or other forms of outward show.

But the position of the *chōnin*—the "townsmen," or non-samurai residents of Edo—was very different vis-a-vis their overlords from that of their counterparts in Kyoto and Osaka. In Edo, the number of samurai was so much larger, and the visible reminders of their privileged status so much more in evidence, that the chōnin could easily have ended up feeling like second-class citizens. They refused to do so, however, and sometimes even assumed a certain swaggering air of defiance toward their nominal superiors, an attitude that came to be exemplified by one of Edo's favorite fictional heroes, Sukeroku.

Ukiyo-e as a Social Phenomenon

In the West there has been a tendency to see artists as independent creators who work for themselves rather than in concert with, or at the behest of, others. We recognize, of course, that this was not always so—that in the past even the greatest artists often worked on commission and were obliged to heed the whims of their patrons; but the ideal of the artist as free agent is so strong in our culture that it makes it hard for us to imagine other possibilities. It also colors our value judgments. With only occasional exceptions—a Toulouse-Lautrec, for instance—we think of posters and illustrations as something barely worthy of the serious artist, and the notion of finding worth in a sketch playfully dashed off at a party would never occur to us. Yet it is precisely in these forms of artistic activity that ukiyo-e found its most natural expression. Most of the works in this exhibition were created for specific persons or in connection with a specific occasion, and many of them were created in collaboration with others. In this respect, the closest European parallel to an ukiyo-e artist might be the eighteenth-century court composer, who was expected to provide appropriate music for occasions as diverse as a Te Deum or a lighthearted summer garden party.

The Linkage with Literature

Writing began as a form of image making. This is as true of the West as of the East. But where contemporary Chinese ideographs (which are used by the Japanese as well as the Chinese) still often show direct links, in both form and meaning, with their pictographic origins, the same is not true of modern western alphabets. We have forgotten whatever connections these alphabets may once have had with image making, and now think of writing and drawing as totally separate, unrelated kinds of activities. This is less likely to be the case in either China or Japan. It is revealing in this regard that the Japanese use the same verb, *kaku*, to mean both "to write" and "to draw" and use a compound form of the same verb, *egaku* (literally, "picture writing"), to denote painting.

None of this is to suggest that the Chinese and Japanese make no distinction between writing and drawing—they do—but merely to point out that they are apt to see the two activities as more closely allied than is the case in the West. As a result, they are more likely to think it natural to create works of art that combine words and images; in both China and Japan there is a long tradition of creating such works. That tradition was nurtured in both countries by a strong belief that writing was as much an artistic as a utilitarian activity, that it was meant to be expressive visually as well as semantically. Writing and drawing, in other words, were seen as kindred, readily compatible, functions.

A similar belief may once have prevailed in the West, among the monks who created illuminated manuscripts during the Middle Ages, for example, but our views today are quite different. Our attitude toward illustration, for instance, is often distinctly pejorative. We tend to think of illustrations as something added on to a text and therefore subservient to it.[1] The Japanese, on the other hand, are more apt to see text and illustrations as integral to one another. The illustrations in certain Japanese narrative handscrolls (*emaki*), for example, virtually become part of the text, amplifying and extending its evocative range to such a point that the text would be diminished without them.

In this regard, it is important to remember that for centuries much of Japan's classical literature was preserved and disseminated almost exclusively in the form of illustrated handscrolls. This was certainly true of *The Tale of Genji* (Genji monogatari), the eleventh-century novel by Lady Murasaki Shikibu, which is generally considered to be Japan's greatest literary masterpiece. Fragments of illustrated handscrolls of the novel survive from as early as the first few decades of the twelfth century, and there are hundreds of later examples.

From the start, illustrations of *The Tale of Genji* seem to have followed certain well-established conventions. Invariably courtly and stylized, they tended to be understated rather than explicit, and more concerned with nuances of feeling than with depicting action. As time went on, the conventions seem to have become more rigid and the expressive latitude allowed the artist more restricted. Even the specific scenes to be illustrated and the iconography associated with each came to be determined by tradition. The result was that, over time, images dictated by this iconography came to be so closely identified with certain incidents in the novel as to become a virtual code for them. This progressed so far that for many people—particularly the growing number who found the language of the *Tale* itself increasingly inaccessible—these images virtually *became* the novel. As such, they took on a life of their own and began to appear on screens and in album paintings with no accompanying text. They also became a rich source of motifs for artists wishing to evoke the elegance and refinement of the courtly past. Motifs derived from illustrations to *The Tale of Genji* appear repeatedly in Japanese art, not only in paintings and prints but incorporated into the designs of textiles and the decoration on lacquer.

Something similar happened with another of Japan's great literary classics, *The Tales of Ise*. This mid-tenth-century work is essentially a collection of poems, loosely linked with brief prose passages dealing with episodes in the life of a fictional nobleman thought to be modeled on the courtier-poet Ariwara no Narihira (825-880). *The Tales of Ise* was also a popular subject for illustrated scrolls and, like *The Tale of Genji* (though to a lesser extent), provided artists with a rich stock of images evocative of ancient court life. These were not, it should be pointed out, the only literary classics to be handed down in the form of illustrated handscrolls. Many other literary works were treated in the same way. These were simply the most often copied.

By the time of the period covered by this exhibition, writers and artists could look back on, and draw upon, a lengthy tradition of combining words and images in ways that mutually strengthened both. It seemed only natural to them that the written word should be embellished and enhanced with visual imagery and that images should take on additional meaning from the words they accompanied. But the last two decades of the eighteenth century were enormously creative, and though artists and writers continued to collaborate on handscrolls and in other traditional ways of combining pictures and words—such as "party pictures" (*sekiga*)—they also came up with entirely new ways of doing so.

Perhaps the most original of these was the surimono—a privately published, exquisitely produced print in which poems and images were combined with a degree of creative interplay unique even within the Japanese tradition. In a surimono, sometimes even the most subtle allusions in a verse are picked up and toyed with by the artist, and sometimes the image adds unexpected poignance to what seems like only a passing reference in a poem; the interplay is constant, and the resulting work makes nonsense of the usual boundaries between art and literature. Though an occasional surimono-like print may have been produced earlier, the genre became popular only in the late 1790s, and there can be no doubt that it was a late-eighteenth-century Edo invention. The extraordinarily effective combination of poems and images in illustrated albums such as Utamaro's *Momochidori kyōka awase* (Catalogue no. IV-15) may have provided the inspiration for the genre, which was closely asssociated with the *kyōka* movement. (Kyōka was a form of humorous verse that became widely popular in Edo in the 1780s.)

Meanwhile, the inventive people of Edo had come up with a different way of combining words and images. This was the *kibyōshi*, a kind of illustrated novelette in which essential parts of the story—much of the action and details regarding the setting—were told through the illustrations. The narrative was not printed separately but along the tops and sides of the illustrations, and snatches of dialogue were printed near the speakers. The resemblances to modern comic strips are striking.

The Political, Social, and Economic Background

With the consolidation of power under the Tokugawa family during the first years of the seventeenth century, Japan entered a period of unprecedented unity and prosperity that was to last some 250 years. The contrast with the previous strife-torn century, during which regional lords competed for dominance, could hardly have been more striking. Yet the unity imposed by the Tokugawas was—for all its seeming strength—based on a system that incorporated fundamental inconsistencies, which would only become more marked with time.

The most basic of these had to do with the importance placed on the role of the samurai, the caste of hereditary warriors who served as vassals to the shogun and the regional lords. Though their primary reason for existence had been to serve in battle, and practice in the military arts was required by their code of conduct, there was little or no need for them to function as warriors during the protracted peace of the Tokugawa era. Indeed, the regime felt so secure after putting down the Shimabara rebellion of 1638 that it never felt obliged to mobilize troops in any significant number thereafter until the arrival of Commodore Perry in 1853. Under such circumstances, the military exercises enjoined on the samurai must have come to seem increasingly pointless. The samurai had become a caste without a mission, and the hypocrisy of their position must have been obvious to many of them.

Another inconsistency in the Tokugawa system, which would also have negative consequences for samurai morale, had to do with the fact that taxes were collected and feudal stipends were paid in rice,[2] even though the country was rapidly moving toward a full-fledged money economy. The only way the samurai could acquire cash was by selling their rice allotments, but this exposed them to the vagaries of a market in which prices often varied markedly from year to year. The resulting fluctuations in a vassal's monetary income could only become a source of considerable anxiety for him. The system was bound to cause a certain degree of samurai resentment toward the chōnin, whose incomes were based on money to begin with. That resentment was further inflamed by the sharp practices of rice merchants who took advantage of the samurais' money troubles by lending them cash at exorbitant rates of interest.

There were other sources of potential weakness in the Tokugawa system. One of these had to do with the way in which power was divided between the shogun's central government (*bakufu*) and the governments of the various regional domains (*han*). In theory, the latter were virtually independent, their only connections with the central regime being those required by their lord's, or daimyo's, feudal relationship to the shogun. The han were, in other words, fiefs, which the shogun had granted to the daimyo in exchange for their loyalty and whose internal administration—to the extent that it did not affect national security—was a matter left to the han themselves. The Tokugawas were clearly aware that this aspect of the *bakuhan* system, as it is called, presented a possible threat to their authority, and early on they took extraordinary measures to counter the threat.

One of these was to require all daimyo to spend alternate years (or, in some cases, half-years) in Edo, in nominal attendance on the shogun, and to leave their wives and children in the capital as hostages when they were in residence in their home castles. The introduction of this so-called *sankin kōtai*, "alternate attendance," requirement was an extremely clever move on the part of the Tokugawas. Its primary purpose, of course, was to keep the daimyo under surveillance and make it difficult for them to conspire against the regime, and it served this purpose admirably. But it also served Tokugawa policy in other, less obvious, ways. The costs of maintaining a suitably impressive residence in Edo were a substantial drain on a daimyo's finances and made it less likely that he would be able to accumulate the resources to oppose the shogun. The residences of the more important daimyo were surrounded by extensive grounds and had adjoining housing for numerous retainers. Such establishments required the services of a sizable staff even when the daimyo himself was not in Edo. Another result of the alternate-attendance requirement was one that even the Tokugawas had probably not foreseen, and this was the extent to which prolonged residence in Edo tended to urbanize (and, in a sense, make Edokko of) even some of the most provincial daimyo and their retainers. The growing cultural dominance of Edo during the eighteenth and nineteenth centuries was probably due as much to this as to any other cause.

The alternate-attendance requirement was only one of the strategies the Tokugawas used to consolidate their power. Other policy decisions were equally effective and, in some cases, even more far-reaching in their consequences for the nation's cultural life. Probably the most extreme example of these was the seclusion policy, which prohibited all contact with the outside world, with the exception of only the most minimal, highly regulated trade with China and the Netherlands. The motivation for this drastic policy almost certainly lay in the Tokugawas' fear of the unsettling effects of foreign ideas, particularly religious (i.e., Christian) ideas that might undermine loyalty to the established order. The fact that what negligible foreign trade did take place was rigorously confined to a single port, Nagasaki, which was as distant from Edo as possible, supports such an assumption. It was as though the regime sought to seal off a source of possible infection.

The shogunate had already ruthlessly suppressed whatever vestiges of Christianity had survived from the brief period (ca. 1555-1612) when the country had been completely open to the West and Catholic missionaries had made thousands of Japanese converts. At the same time, it began actively promoting Confucianism, in which it found an ideology ideally suited to its purposes. With its emphasis on service and social responsibility as expressed through the obligations owed by vassals to their lords, sons to their fathers, and pupils to their teachers, Confucianism proved to be a powerful force for strengthening the authority of the government and promoting social stability in general. Though not strictly speaking a religion, it was still capable of inspiring men and women to a life of self-improvement and sacrifice for the sake of others. Among the virtues it promoted were industriousness, learning, and respect for tradition. At the same time, there can be no doubt that it also encouraged authoritarianism and excessive regard for the proprieties.

As formulated in Japan under the patronage of the shogunate, Confucianism also provided the intellectual justification for the way society was organized. The hierarchical division of society into four tiers, with the military caste at the top, farmers next, craftsmen after them, and merchants at the bottom, was interpreted as an immutable state of affairs, any disruption of which would be considered not only inappropriate but contrary to the natural order. It was this view of things that lay behind the moral opprobrium evident in the bakufu's frequent resort to sumptuary legislation: the idea that a merchant might aspire to live in a style befitting someone of higher rank smacked of perversion.

The rationale behind this hierarchical division of society was simple. The samurai were seen as the natural rulers, serving as the metaphorical head of the body politic. Farmers owed their relatively high status to the fact that they carried, in effect, the rest of society on their backs, producing the basic food and materials needed by everyone. Craftsmen came next because their work modified and added value to what the farmers had produced. Merchants came last because they were thought merely to profit from the work of others, adding nothing of value themselves.

One's place in this rigid hierarchy depended on one's birth, and movement from one class to another was virtually impossible. The behavior appropriate to each class was carefully prescribed, and any activity that might blur the distinctions thus created was frowned upon. Though this did not make contact between the different classes impossible, it did set up barriers to free and easy communication. The fact that such barriers were frequently disregarded or overcome during the years covered by this exhibition is one of the features that makes the period so remarkable.

The Rise of the Merchant Class

One of the most significant features of the Edo Period was the phenomenal growth experienced by the major urban centers. This growth, which was fueled by an extraordinary increase in trade and merchant activity, transformed Japanese society in countless ways. It is one of the ironies of Japanese history that the merchants, the class most responsible for these changes, were looked upon at the time more as parasites than as productive members of society.

The scope for mercantile activity in Edo, particularly, was immense. First of all, there had been the building of the city itself, with its huge drainage and construction projects; then came the constant rebuilding necessitated by the city's frequent and often quite extensive fires; meanwhile there was always the need to provide food, clothing, housing, and entertainment for the huge samurai establishment serving the shogun and the regional daimyo. Under these circumstances, it is hardly surprising that merchants prospered. Some of them even accumulated sizable fortunes. But none of their wealth could buy them status, and the system placed severe limits on the ways in which they could express themselves or spend their money. Ostentation—anything that gave the appearance of setting them above their superiors—was strictly forbidden. Participation in government, other than through their guilds and neighborhood associations, was also out of the question. One of the few avenues of self-expression left open to them, apart from scholarship or devotion to their work, was pleasure.

This probably explains the intensity with which so many Edo chōnin pursued pleasure. They spent vast amounts of money and creative energy on pursuits that to us often seem frivolous. Yet they also attended the theater, took part in poetry contests, followed the latest trends in music, and purchased paintings. They became, in short, patrons of the arts; and the arts responded by increasingly reflecting the interests of their new patrons. The result was a burgeoning of new forms of expression: kabuki, ukiyo-e, and the proliferation of amusing literary genres known collectively as *gesaku.* The chōnin, the merchants, were not the only patrons of these new art forms, as we will learn later, but there can be no question that they constituted the primary market for them, that it was their money that stimulated their development.

The Exercise of Power

Unlike some of their predecessors, the shoguns of the last half of the eighteenth century had little taste—and even less talent—for leadership and were content to leave the actual governing of the country to others. These others were the Council of Elders (*rōjū*) and its president or chairman, whose role in overseeing the bakufu's elaborate bureaucracy was not unlike that of a prime minister.

Under the Tokugawas, the idea that policy decisions might be subject to public debate was unthinkable. There were no newspapers, or even anything resembling them, and it was illegal to publish information about current events. The deliberations of the Council of Elders took place behind closed doors; few on the outside were aware of the extensive political maneuvering—or the occasional palace intrigues involving the shogun's concubines—required to reach major decisions. Decisions directly affecting the public were promulgated through the guilds and neighborhood associations concerned or posted on public signboards (*kōsatsu*).

During the first part of the period covered by this exhibition, the most powerful person in the government was Tanuma Okitsugu. Though he seems to have been a capable administrator with rather far-sighted economic ideas, his venality was notorious and his regime was riddled with corruption. Moreover, his relaxed attitude toward the Confucian proprieties (he fraternized openly with powerful merchants and turned a blind eye to infringements of the sumptuary laws) earned him the enmity of conservative moralists.[3] None of this might have mattered had a series of natural disasters not caused widespread starvation and seriously weakened the bakufu's own finances. Several years of abnormally cold weather, combined with the devastation caused by the eruption of Mt. Asama some seventy-eight miles northwest of Edo, resulted in a series of failed harvests and spreading famine. Unrest spread to the cities as the price of rice climbed out of the reach of whole segments of the populace. When his protector, the Shogun Ieharu, died in 1786, Tanuma fell from power. A year later riots broke out in Edo itself, and the authorities found themselves unable to control them. Pressure for reform mounted.

The man who emerged as the champion of reform was Matsudaira Sadanobu, the scion of a daimyo family closely related to the Tokugawas who had been groomed for high office since childhood. When he finally received official backing in 1787, he moved swiftly to put an end to official corruption, stabilize the price of rice, and restore the bakufu's depleted finances. He also reinstituted enforcement of the sumptuary laws and made it clear that he expected the samurai to turn away from their involvement in the less seemly aspects of the Floating World. A firm believer in the power of ideas, he initiated a thorough reform of the government-supported Confucian Academy and issued ordinances discouraging the teaching of unorthodox schools of thought. These collective actions, which were taken over a period of several years beginning in 1787, are usually referred to as the Kansei Reforms, after the name of the era in which they were promulgated.

There has been a widespread belief that these reforms had an immediate and chilling effect on the intellectual and cultural life of Edo. Certainly the tolerance and laissez-faire fiscal policies of the Tanuma years had provided a stimulating environment for the arts. Free spending and a relaxed attitude toward unconventional modes of expression had encouraged artists and writers to apply their imagination in new directions. More importantly, perhaps, educated samurai had felt themselves at liberty for the first time to take part openly in the cultural life of the Floating World, and the knowledge and cultivated tastes they brought with them had profoundly affected the way that world viewed itself. By putting a sudden end to such a tolerant era, the Kansei Reforms must inevitably have had some effect on cultural life.

But was their effect as great as is often maintained? Much has been made of the punishment, described elsewhere in this catalogue, meted out against the writer Santō Kyōden and the publisher Tsutaya Jūzaburō. The punishment does seem to have been unusually harsh—the authorities apparently wished to make examples of the two—and Kyōden's later work did become much more circumspect as a result. But the people of Edo had experienced censorship and sumptuary regulations before and knew all kinds of ways to get around them. Though authors may have momentarily avoided certain subjects or prudently decided to dull the edge of their satire for a while, little seems to have changed in the publishing industry otherwise that would not have changed in all likelihood anyway. As far as prints were concerned, it is difficult to discern that the reforms had any effect. The prints of the 1790s are much more flamboyant in design and luxurious in their effects than the prints of the 1780s.

There was one area, however, in which the Kansei Reforms did have a serious—and perhaps lasting—impact on the art and literature of the Floating World. When Sadanobu came into power, he quickly made it clear that he regarded samurai involvement in gesaku literature and the like as inappropriate. Ōta Nampo, perhaps feeling particularly vulnerable because of his close association with one of Tanuma's officials, lost no time in getting the message. Other samurai writers soon followed his lead.

The samurai contribution to the Floating World has often been overlooked. To be sure, the Floating World was essentially a chōnin creation; but samurai participation, even if only marginal at first, was important from the start. It became even more so in the 1760s, when a group of samurai dilettantes unwittingly initiated the vogue for nishikie-e by commissioning the first full-color prints. Thereafter, for the next thirty years, samurai played a central role, both as creators and as patrons, in defining the sensibility of the Floating World. Their key contributions to the development of gesaku literature in the 1770s and 1780s are detailed elsewhere in this catalogue.

The loss of some of its most influential participants was bound to have consequences for the Floating World. Nampo became somewhat involved again later, as the exhibition will show, but never as actively as before. Others died or chose not to return. In any case, the samurai never regained the level of influence they had enjoyed earlier. Their departure came at a crucial moment. The public for ukiyo-e and popular literature was growing. Tastes were changing. The sophisticated circles who constituted the Floating World of the late eighteenth century would hardly recognize what that world was to become a mere decade later.

The Two Poles of the Floating World

These art forms described a world of pleasure and aspiration, a world that was at once both real and imaginary, a world that in its expensive glamour suggests comparisons with Hollywood. The Japanese called it *ukiyo*, the Floating World. Earlier we gave a preliminary definition of this curious term; now we must look at the word more closely, giving particular attention to its meaning in the late eighteenth century.

First, it must be pointed out that the Floating World was not a place but a way of life. As such, it fostered its own code of behavior and set of values. These were definitely not those espoused by the prevailing Confucian morality of the time but, in some cases, the very opposite. In the Floating World, the notion of style was preeminent. It was for their style that one admired the leading actors, the celebrated courtesans, and the legendary *tsū* (sophisticates) who were the stars of that world. And style did not come cheaply; it almost always entailed some extravagance. At the same time, it was not something that could be bought; it had to be acquired, often at the cost of years of discipline and training. The extent to which this was true will became apparent when we consider some of the leading exemplars of the Floating World.

In Edo, the life of the Floating World gravitated around two poles, the theater district and the Yoshiwara. The theater district was in the Sakaichō-Fukiyachō area, a few minutes' walk from Nihombashi, the teeming heart of Shitamachi, with its crowded fish market and rows of masonry storehouses. The Yoshiwara, on the other hand, lay to the north on the very outskirts of the city, surrounded by paddy fields. Each of these two poles constituted, to some extent, a world unto itself, with its own rituals, its own seasonal observances, and even, in the case of the Yoshiwara, its own private language. Each also offered a seductive reward for the price of admission: escape, if only for a time, from the rigid obligations imposed by the "real" world outside.

The Yoshiwara

One corollary of the alternate-attendance system was an imbalance in the population of Edo in favor of men. This was because men formed the greater part of the numerous retinues that accompanied the daimyo to and from the capital. It therefore comes as no surprise to learn that prostitution was ubiquitous. It flourished at every level of society and took many forms, from the homeless streetwalkers known as "night hawks" at one end of the spectrum to the devastatingly expensive "castle breakers" at the other. The authorities, whose attitudes were decidedly puritanical in most other respects, seem to have taken a relatively tolerant view of the phenomenon. Though, strictly speaking, prostitution was supposed to be limited to the so-called licensed quarters of the Yoshiwara, the government rarely cracked down on the practice elsewhere—much to the disgruntlement of the brothel owners in the Yoshiwara, who would just as soon have been rid of what they considered unfair competition.

With their lower prices and relative lack of formality, the *okabasho*, or "hill places," as the unlicensed centers of prostitution were called, probably did pose a growing threat to the Yoshiwara during the years covered by this exhibition. Yet for glamour and spectacle the Yoshiwara remained unrivalled. Its leading courtesans partook of a mystique that, however theatrical or contrived, still exercised a powerful hold over the imagination of artists and writers. Throughout our period, the name of a celebrated courtesan like Hanaōgi or Segawa remained something to conjure with.

For the first half-century of its existence, the Yoshiwara was near the heart of Edo, not far from Nihombashi, but the disastrous fire of 1657 caused its move to the city's outskirts. It is this Shin (i.e., new) Yoshiwara that concerns us here.

The relocation meant that the Yoshiwara could no longer be visited on the spur of the moment. Getting there became a serious undertaking—enjoyable enough in itself, but time-consuming as well. The usual route was by boat up the Sumida from Yanagibashi, near the Ryōgoku Bridge, to the Sanya Canal (a distance of over two miles), and thence by land along the Nihon Dike. Over time, the various landmarks along the way came to be so closely identified with visits to the Yoshiwara that the slightest reference to them in art or literature was sufficient to evoke a whole train of pleasurable associations. For the true Edokko, the image of a boat being poled past the overarching branches of the "Pine of Fate," or of the torii gate of Mimeguri Shrine barely visible above the dike at Mukōjima, were tinged with an aura of adventure and romance that made them much more than the mere genre or topographic details they seem to us.

The Yoshiwara was rectangular in shape and enclosed by walls surrounded by a shallow canal. The only entrance was through the Ōmonguchi (Great Gate), which was manned by guards and closed each night. The gate opened directly into a broad street, the Nakanochō, which divided the enclosure into two equal halves. Other, narrower, streets met the Nakanochō at right angles. The strict regularity of the street plan, totally unlike anything else found in Edo, was one of the many features that set the Yoshiwara apart from the rest of the city.

The Nakanochō served as a kind of main street or public square for the Yoshiwara. It was lined on either side by teahouses, known as *hikitejaya*, whose primary function was to arrange appointments with courtesans in the more prestigious brothels. The brothels themselves were on the quieter side streets. The Nakanochō was at its liveliest during the early evening hours when the *oiran*, the highest-ranking courtesans known as *yobidashi* or *chūsan*, appeared in full regalia, accompanied by their apprentices and attendants, for their nightly promenade, the *dōchū*, which was one of the distinctive customs of the licensed quarters.

The Yoshiwara had many customs found nowhere else. We have already mentioned that it had its own dialect (called *arinsu kotoba*), but it also had its own festivals and its own special ways of observing more general holidays. Perhaps the oddest custom associated with the licensed quarters, however, had to do with its observance of closing hours. By law, the brothels were supposed to close at the beginning of the fourth hour, which was 10 PM by our reckoning, but, since this would severely curtail business, it was tacitly agreed that the fourth hour would not be sounded until an hour later. Since Edo-period "hours" lasted more or less 120 minutes, this meant that the brothels could stay open until midnight. As a famous poem of the time put it, "In the Yoshiwara, even the clocks tell lies."

The yobidashi were the stars of the Yoshiwara and their presence was essential for any brothel of status. As a result, owners were willing to go to great expense to maintain them, and resorted to all kinds of stratagems to enhance the mystique surrounding them. Only the costliest garments were good enough for them; master teachers were brought in to give them lessons in skills such as calligraphy or the tea ceremony; and their customers were expected to observe the most elaborate protocol in engaging their services. The mystique extended even to their names, which were jealously guarded as the exclusive property of the house, to be bestowed only on the most promising candidates of successive generations. The bearer of one of these names might enjoy her transitory celebrity, but the prestige of her house depended on her, and she was probably never allowed to forget that. She could not afford to lose any of the claims to distinction listed in detail in the *Yoshiwara saiken*, the guidebooks to the Yoshiwara that were sold to visitors. And for all her status, even a yobidashi needed special permission to leave the licensed quarters. This applied to the most innocent-seeming outing.

An evening with one of these high-ranking courtesans was expensive. The basic fee (which was doubled on festival days) ranged from the equivalent of $450 to $750 in 1993 American money, and this included none of the tips that had to be paid to the hikite-jaya, the entertainers, and the courtesan's attendants. It has been said that the real cost of an evening's entertainment at the high end of the spectrum was probably closer to $3,000.[4]

The lives of lower-ranking courtesans were even more restricted than the yobidashis'. They could not enjoy even the relative freedom of the nightly promenade, but had to sit on public display in a custom known as *harimise*. Several works in the exhibition show these unfortunate women sitting behind their cage-like windows on full view to passers-by. A scene in Eishi's *Journey to the Yoshiwara* (Catalogue no. I-3), showing the two protagonists "window shopping," makes clear how the harimise was intended to function.

Behind the glittering surface of life in the Yoshiwara lay the ugly social reality that most of the women living there had, in effect, been "sold" to the brothel owners—usually by parents who felt they were too poor to raise them. Though the sale was more akin to indentured service than slavery as such, and life in the brothels was not excessively harsh by the standards of the time, there is no overlooking the fact that the women were virtual prisoners. It is a side of the Yoshiwara that tends to be glossed over in the art.

Most women were sold into prostitution when they were sixteen or seventeen years old, and since the standard period of service was ten years, this meant they could "retire" when they were in their mid- to late twenties. This was well past the usual marriageable age, however, and many women, discovering that after ten years in the quarters they were ill-equipped for life on the outside, decided to stay on to work in some other capacity—if they were lucky, perhaps as a courtesan's manager (*yarite*). There was always the chance that one of a courtesan's customers would offer to purchase her freedom, but this was costly—brothel owners preferred to get a full return on their investment—and happened only rarely. This makes it all the more unusual that a relatively impecunious samurai like Ōta Nampo (one of the writers featured in this exhibition) should have purchased the freedom of a courtesan in order to make her a concubine. His fellow writer, Santō Kyōden, found both his first and second wives in the Yoshiwara but, at least in the case of the first wife, prudently chose not to marry her until after she had retired.

Kabuki and the Theater District

Even though it has elements that might remind us of classical Greek drama or nineteenth-century opera, kabuki is totally unlike any form of drama with which we are familiar in the West. A few of its distinguishing features are that its stories are told only in part through the actions and dialogue of the actors, while other, essential parts are sung or narrated by a chanter or small chorus; music is played throughout, sometimes merely serving as accompaniment to the chant, sometimes as an element of importance in its own right; the plots are often extremely complicated, and the action can alternate in the same play from the most stylized to the most realistic; the costumes, scenery, and stage sets are as apt to be designed for their visual effect as for their usefulness in providing a convincingly realistic setting; a revolving stage allows for dramatic and rapid changes of scene; and all the roles, whether female or male, are played by men.

It is often said that in kabuki the actors are paramount. This means that the plays are more likely to be seen as vehicles for the actor than as inviolate works of art in their own right, and was particularly true in the eighteenth century. Then, actors could—and quite often did—cut or add lines as they saw fit. The whole attitude toward play writing was quite different from ours. Entire sections of earlier plays were seized on to be used, with only minor changes, in later productions. Much of the dialogue, rather than being written down, was left to be filled in by the actors.

As mentioned earlier, much of the action was stylized, some of it to the point of exaggeration. What was admired in an actor was not so much the degree of realism he brought to his role as the amount of control and finesse—the attention to detail—that he put into the stylized moves and poses connected with it. Most admired of all was his ability to strike, and hold, a stylized pose (*mie*) at a particularly dramatic moment in the action. Such poses are depicted in the majority of actor prints.

Most kabuki actors belonged to one or another family, or lineage, of actors, and each family had its own hierarchy of names that it awarded to its members, based at least in part on their talent and skill. An actor, in other words, was expected not just to inherit his name but to earn it; he might go through a number of different names during his career as his skill and reputation increased. These were a matter of public record as theater critiques (*hyōbanki*), published annually, carefully recorded the varying degrees of an actor's success.

The chōnin of Edo were passionate playgoers and adulated their leading actors. Actors like Ichikawa Danjūrō and Nakamura Nakazō had avid fan clubs whose members followed their every move onstage, and wealthy patrons held expensive parties for them between acts. Prints depicting them in popular roles were eagerly snapped up and stored away as precious mementoes.

The three officially sanctioned kabuki theaters of Edo were the Nakamura-za, the Morita-za, and the Ichimura-za. Although the Nakamura-za was considered the most prestigious of the three, they all shared the same general features, and competition between them, for both audiences and actors, was strong. The buildings themselves were unusually large and, with the curious, marquee-like drum towers (*yagura*) on their roofs and their facades covered with posters, were quite unlike anything else in Edo. Crowding in against them from either side were rows of lantern-festooned teahouses, the *shibaijaya*, which catered to wealthier theatergoers by reserving box seats for them and providing a place for refreshments between acts.

Seating in the theaters was divided into two sections—a pit or orchestra, which filled the bulk of the hall with mass seating, and two tiers of boxes along either side for more exclusive parties. Most pictures of the period show the audience behaving more as though they were at a baseball game than at a serious play. Vendors hawk their wares and people eat and chat, seemingly oblivious of the action taking place onstage. However, it is important to remember that performances went on all day, and some of the acts probably served more as interludes or fillers than anything else. Plays were presented only during daylight hours because the number of lanterns that would have been required for evening performances would have posed a serious fire danger.

As we have mentioned, the theater district, like the Yoshiwara, had it own rituals and conventions. Many of these centered around the formal opening of the theater season in the eleventh month. This was known as *kaomise* (literally, "face showing"), and was when the theater publicly announced, with much fanfare, the year's lineup of actors. Since kaomise was, in effect, the beginning of the theater year, the observances connected with it borrowed heavily from customs associated with the New Year's holiday.

The Japanese Courtly Tradition

Though the Heian court, with its highly developed esthetic sensibility and dignified rituals, belonged to a remote past (the traditional dates of the Heian Period are 794-1185), it was still very much alive to the educated samurai and chōnin of Edo. Much of classical Japanese literature was either a product of the Heian court or, like the Imperial anthologies of poetry, reflected its refined standards. Albums, screens, and even the decorative arts evoked the past through images associated with *The Tale of Genji* or *The Tales of Ise*. It would have been impossible, therefore, to grow up in an educated milieu in eighteenth-century Edo without becoming thoroughly familiar with a whole range of poetic and visual imagery relating to the courtly tradition, which could be alluded to or drawn on at will. A Japanese author of the time would refer to Lady Murasaki or Ariwara no Narihira as naturally as Shakespeare or Milton would refer to Ovid or Homer, and would do so with a frequency that is apt to take a modern reader by surprise.

What was true of literature was also true of art. Many of the references in the art escape the modern viewer unfamiliar with the subtle iconographic clues employed, but in the Edo Period, when familiarity with the classics of the courtly tradition was taken for granted, viewers could be counted on to discern even the most cryptic allusions in what might otherwise seem a relatively mundane representation. Many examples of such allusions may be seen in this exhibition. When a courtesan is portrayed with loose, flowing hair, for instance, we are expected to be reminded of the long, trailing hair worn by Heian court ladies. When a woman is shown seated at a writing table on a veranda, with a full autumn moon in the sky, the reference is almost certainly to Lady Murasaki writing *The Tale of Genji*. References of this sort were all-pervasive in the art.

The classics of the courtly tradition could never have played such an important role in the art and literature of the time had it not been for the extraordinary spread of literacy that was one of the earmarks of the Edo Period. The level of literacy had already begun to climb in the seventeenth century and continued to do so steadily thereafter—a phenomenon that was clearly related to the growing prosperity of the cities and the ensuing increase in leisure. As a result, what was once the exclusive province of a courtly elite became accessible to an ever-widening public as printed versions of the classics, many of them extensively illustrated, became more available. It was only natural that this new public would bring its own point of view to its reading and use of the classics. How else could it stake out its claim to something that did not belong to it by birthright?

One thing seems almost certain. Some of the ways in which the writers and artists of Edo used the classics would have scandalized the courtly writers of previous generations. The Immortals of Poetry became the subjects of charades and mimicry; extravagant comparisons were made between courtesans and court ladies; and some of the most widely read classical poems were subjected to outrageous parodies. Yet, as hard as it may be for many of us to understand today, no iconoclastic intent lay behind this seemingly cavalier treatment of venerated icons of the past. The writers and artists of the Floating World were not interested in repudiating the classical heritage; they simply wanted to make it their own; they wanted to have fun with it and at the same time demonstrate its relevance to their own lives.

When a kyōka poet compared himself humorously to one of the "hundred poets," for instance, he seems to have done so more out of self-mockery than any desire to break with tradition, and seems, in fact, to have felt genuine affection for his classical model. It was as though, by playing at being one of the classical poets, he could actually take on some of that poet's qualities. And when an artist endowed a courtesan with the attributes of a court lady, he was clearly attempting to imbue the present with some of the luster of the past. Even when a kyōka poet came up with what seems a highly sardonic parody of a classical poem, his intent was not to put down the original but to demonstrate his wit in applying it to the present.

The Chinese Classics

For more than a millennium—from the late sixth century until well into the nineteenth century—educated Japanese were as likely to write in Chinese as in their own language. (For background on the relationship between the Chinese and Japanese written languages, see the section on the subject in this catalogue.) For certain types of writing, in fact, Chinese was the preferred language. Though the idea of a people's expressing themselves in a language other than their own may seem strange—perhaps even perverse—to us today, we should remember that something rather similar happened in Europe. For many centuries, scholars and poets in Europe routinely wrote in Latin rather than their respective vernaculars, and their reasons for doing so reveal some interesting parallels with the Japanese experience.

In many respects, what ancient Greece and Rome were to Europe, China was to Japan. In both instances, contact with a powerful, more mature civilization had had a transforming influence on a marginal, less developed society. And in both instances, language was the key to gaining access to the more powerful civilization and its accumulated stock of knowledge. The parallels can be pushed only so far, however. Rome was already in a state of decline when the people of Northern Europe first came into contact with it, while Tang Dynasty China was at its most glorious when the Japanese were visiting there in greatest numbers during the seventh and eighth centuries. Moreover, Latin had become a dead language to all intents and purposes by the Middle Ages, while Chinese continued to be spoken.

For much of its period of use in Japan, however, Chinese could as well have been a dead language. The official contacts with China that had been so intensive during the seventh and eighth centuries gradually tapered off, and after the mid-ninth century ceased altogether. For many years thereafter, only the most sporadic contacts occurred. Chinese never ceased to be read and written, but the way it was pronounced began to deviate more and more from spoken Chinese. While the spoken language gradually changed in China itself, the Japanese continued to try to pronounce the characters in the old way, though with growing concessions to Japanese speech habits. The end result is a language that, when read, is an artificial construct, neither Japanese nor Chinese.

None of this, however, has much relevance to the Japanese use of Chinese as a literary language. There is a long history of Chinese verse by Japanese poets (the *Kaifūsō*, the first collection of such verse, was produced in 751), and several of Japan's most celebrated authors wrote extensively, if not exclusively, in Chinese. The resulting body of work is impressive by any standards and deserves more attention than it has generally received. Unfortunately, it now exists in a kind of literary limbo. Its language is accessible to only a dwindling number of Japanese, yet, since the work is not truly Chinese—i.e., it is not by Chinese authors—it is of little interest to Chinese literary historians.

During the Edo Period, growing literacy, the bakufu's increased emphasis on Confucian studies, and an influx of new publications from China stimulated a fresh surge of interest in Chinese writing. New styles and genres were introduced, and the sheer volume of work written in Chinese was huge. All of this should be borne in mind when we look more closely at one of the authors featured in this exhibition, Ōta Nampo.

In Conclusion

An introduction of this sort presents the writer with several dilemmas. How can he strike a balance between giving too much information and not enough? How can he be as clear and succinct as possible without stating things too baldly? How can he be accurate without burdening the reader with distinctions of interest only to the specialist? Considerations of this kind are perhaps inevitable in any work aimed at a general public; they become particularly troublesome in dealing with a culture as foreign to our own as that of Edo-period Japan.

If the information presented so far seems cursory, I can only ask the reader to bear with us. The essays that follow will expand on some of the points that have been made and will reinforce others. The glossary will provide definitions for many of the unfamiliar terms, while the section entitled "Names, Dates, and Hours" should help throw light on some of the Edo-period customs and practices that westerners are apt to find most baffling.

The real heart of this catalogue, however, lies in the discussions of individual works that follow these introductory essays. It is there that the reader will make the discoveries that matter. The ultimate purpose of this catalogue and the exhibition it records is to open people's eyes to works of art that (as pointed out at the start of this essay) have not been fully understood in their own terms before. If at least some of our readers and viewers come away with an enhanced appreciation of what the art of the golden age of ukiyo-e was really about, we will count our project a success.

NOTES

1. Recent developments in contemporary art suggest that this attitude may now be changing.

2. In earlier periods, most samurai had been attached to the land—that is, they had possessed their own estates from which they received rice directly, but by the sixteenth century this system was already being replaced by one in which samurai were required to return their lands to their lords and live in castle towns, in trade for which they would receive fixed stipends. It was a change that, by severing the samurai from any direct connection with the land (and, therefore, from any independent source of income), obviously made them much more dependent on their overlords.

3. There is reason to believe that Tanuma's "fraternization" with the merchant class may have reflected a rather modern (certainly not "Confucian") attitude toward the need for commerce and capital if a society were to expand economically. He supported several ventures of the sort that we would call "economic development" projects.

4. Cecilia Segawa Seigle, *Yoshiwara, The Glittering World of the Japanese Courtesan* (Honolulu: University of Hawaii Press, 1993), 67-68, 112-13.

The Floating World in Its Edo Locale 1750-1850

Henry D. Smith II

True to its name, the Floating World of Tokugawa Japan was constantly shifting in location. It had its origins in Kamigata, the Kyoto-Osaka region, where it was given its classical definition by Asai Ryōi in *Tales of the Floating World* (Ukiyo monogatari, 1661), as a world of "singing songs, drinking wine, and diverting ourselves just in floating, floating. . . like a gourd along with the river current."[1] Its quintessential locale was the pleasure quarters, the rigidly enclosed districts of prostitution that had been set up under official license, first in Kyoto in 1589 and in Osaka a few decades later. The classic Floating World of the Kamigata region took shape in the Genroku era of the later seventeenth century and powerfully influenced a parallel culture in Edo in the same years, centered in the Yoshiwara pleasure quarter, which had first been licensed in 1618.

The leadership in cultural innovation then passed from Kamigata to Edo in the course of the eighteenth century, and the Floating World took on a coloring distinctive to the shogun's capital. It emerged in full form in the last decades of the century, in the ukiyo-e paintings and prints and in the playful *gesaku* literature that are the foci of this exhibition. Its primary locales were the Yoshiwara pleasure quarters and the three downtown kabuki theaters, the sites that set the rigorous standards for the quickly changing and fastidiously enforced styles of the day. Many other venues of urban life make their appearance in the prints and fictions of the era, but it remains the *akusho*, the "bad spots" of official and commonsense opinion, that provided the essential self-definition of the Floating World in the Edo culture on view here.

Where does this fulfillment of a truly Edo-esque Floating World begin, and where does it end? Among modern historians of Edo culture, certain standard narratives have evolved, although the chronology differs with the specialty. Scholars of ukiyo-e see the 1780s and 1790s as the classic golden age of the genre, with the death of Utamaro in 1806 serving as a common demarcation of the end of the era. From this point, "pictures of the floating world" enter a dismal phase of decadence and decline in which any artist of interest (among them Hokusai, Kuniyoshi, and Hiroshige) is qualified as either exceptional or of superior decadence.

In literature, the accepted story line hangs on the names of eras by which years—and hence history—were arranged (and continue to be arranged) in Japan. The golden age of Edo literature is seen as An'ei-Temmei, the seventeen years from 1772 to 1789, with the Kansei Reforms of the early 1790s interpreted as the crushing blow that destroyed the sophisticated wit and subtle rebellion of gesaku literature in its prime. The narrative then skips over the years of the succeeding Kansei-Kyōwa eras (1789-1804), which are thus relegated to a historical vacuum, and homes in on the combined Bunka-Bunsei (sometimes reduced to the shorthand of "Kasei") period of 1804-30 as the time in which an utterly different literary regime emerged, now commercialized, popularized, and vulgarized (although again with apologetic exceptions, in this case particularly for Takizawa Bakin). At this point, the story line merges with that of ukiyo-e in a general judgment of "decadence."

The burden of this essay is not to challenge these established story lines, which remain persuasive in their own ways, but to suggest a different way of looking at what was going on in Edo culture, in the context of the broader social and cultural history of the city itself. The basic argument is that in the transition from the eighteenth to the nineteenth century, the Floating World was expanded and relocated so that it became more of a generic "floating world," much less attached to the particular locales of the Floating World (as a proper noun) anchored in the pleasure quarters.

In a way, this relocation of the floating world was a return to the more elementary meaning of *ukiyo*, a sense that had never been abandoned in common usage, of the floating world not as a place of escape and release from everyday life, but precisely as daily life *itself*. Despite the clear change in emphasis that typified its Genroku usage, the word "ukiyo" had never lost either its original Buddhist meaning of the world as experienced in the here and now, nor the sense of ultimate pessimism about that world as ephemeral. As one Japanese scholar has suggested, the medieval ukiyo as a "world of sorrow" was simply the other side of the coin of the early Tokugawa ukiyo as a "floating" world (using a different character for *uki*) of pleasure and release: both were rooted in an essentially religious faith in the meaningfulness of an afterlife or "other world" (*anoyo, gose*).[2]

This shift of emphasis from the world of escapist fantasy to the world of life-as-lived represents a major change in the cultural history of late Edo, with the year 1800 as a convenient benchmark. The most revealing example of the newly relocated floating world is *The Bathhouse of the Floating World* (Ukiyoburo, 1809), the most famous work of the gesaku writer Shikitei Samba, followed by *The Barbershop of the Floating World* (Ukiyodoko, 1814). What a change in the locale of the floating world! The theater and the brothel, places where huge sums were expended to purchase fantasies of escape from everyday life, were now replaced by the bath and the barbershop, the places of ordinary community that every common citizen could (indeed, was obliged to) afford.

What were the dynamics behind both the efflorescence of a truly Edo-like Floating World in the Temmei era, and its evolution as a more generic "floating world" into the Bunka-Bunsei era? I wish to explore three areas of change, of which the first is the social structure of the city of Edo, particularly the relationship between samurai and non-samurai: it is precisely the interaction between the two estates that helps explain the emergence of a truly "popular" culture, one that is the exclusive property of no specific social grouping.

The second dynamic of change is the emergence of "Edo nativism," a cultural ideology that sought to define what was special about the city, particularly as personified in the self-image of the Edokko, the Japanese counterpart of London's Cockney. The best single tag for the phenomenon of Edo nativism, however, is "Great Edo" (Ō-Edo). It differs essentially (although phonetically only in vowel length) from "O-Edo," Edo with a simple honorific prefix that marked it as the capital of the shogun. Great Edo was a boast of the prosperity and vitality that was the city's lot from the middle of the eighteenth century until the 1860s. In deference to the impact of the two great famine-and-reform cycles, I would most narrowly date Great Edo as the city between the two major famines, 1787-1833, a period of about half a century.[3] Most of the works in *The Floating World Revisited* date from this era.

The third ingredient of this broad change in Edo culture is the role of print culture brought about by the steady evolution in Edo of the technologies of printing and publishing, and the increase in literacy. Of particular interest is the way in which restrictions on what could be printed led to a special role both for private printing and for orally transmitted culture.

The Political Economy of Edo

Many descriptions of Tokugawa society begin with a recitation of the official hierarchy of "four classes": samurai, farmer, artisan, merchant (*shi-nō-kō-shō*). However, this is an artificial formula adopted from Chinese Confucian ideology, and distorts the real processes of social change. The most basic distinction was between samurai and everyone else, a distinction enforced by elaborate rules prescribing the marks of samurai status (most visibly, the wearing of two swords), the places of samurai residence, and special procedures for samurai inheritance, marriage, and punishment. The samurai did not constitute a "class" in any economic sense, because it was such a large and diverse group, reaching from the true political elite at the top to the majority of samurai who were either unemployed or at best held jobs as guards or petty functionaries. It is best to conceive of the samurai as an "estate" rather than a class, set apart from "commoners" by special status and privileges but highly differentiated within.

The essential nature of the city of Edo was determined by its two political functions, one as capital of the Tokugawa domain, the other as national capital. The site itself lies at a strategic point on the Kantō Plain where the Sumida River flows into what is now Tokyo Bay, and had been the location of a substantial castle of a local lord in the fifteenth century. It was chosen by Tokugawa Ieyasu in 1590 as the site of his new capital for control over the Kantō Plain, and work was begun immediately on the construction of the great castle and the adjoining commoner settlement. Building on the remains of the earlier castle, vast earthworks were carried out, digging moats and rechanneling rivers to provide the foundations for the massive stones of the castle walls, which may still be seen in Tokyo today. The castle was finally completed in the 1630s under the third shogun, Iemitsu, and was resplendent with the gilded roof ornaments and azure walls of the main keep (*tenshukaku*), which towered more than 250 feet above the city below, the tallest such structure ever erected in Japan.

As capital of the Tokugawa domain, which came to encompass about one-fourth of the agricultural production of the entire country, Edo had by far the largest assembly of direct retainers of any castle city in Japan—about two hundred and fifty thousand in all (including families and servants). What set it apart from any other city was its function as the national capital, enforced by the critical institution of *sankin kōtai*, which required most of the 260-odd daimyo to maintain permanent residences in the city for their families, and to reside themselves in Edo every other year. Growing out of older feudal practice, the sankin kōtai had become an intricate system of requirements by the time of the completion of Edo Castle. These rules specified that each daimyo must maintain at least three separate estates in Edo, one for official domain business and for the residence of the daimyo himself, one as permanent residence for the family, and one as a suburban retreat in case of fire. Each daimyo was assigned a particular month for entering and leaving the city, and a set number of samurai to accompany him. These military processions, the largest of which numbered in the thousands, were a constant feature of life in the city, particularly in the peak months from spring to early summer.[4]

The effect of the sankin kōtai was to double the samurai population of the city of Edo, and to multiply the goods and services required by such an immense consumer population. Although the domains made efforts to supply the Edo mansions directly from their own provinces, they were still dependent on the local Edo economy for a wide variety of goods (especially perishable produce) and services. As a result, the costs of both the permanent Edo mansions and of the processions themselves consumed up to half of all domain income, working as a powerful engine to recirculate the wealth of the nation to the advantage of Edo. The system worked just as powerfully to circulate culture, making Edo a microcosm of the products and habits from all Japan, and in turn carrying Edo back to the provinces in the form of memories and souvenirs.

A Social Map of Edo, Circa 1800

A "social map" of the city, a simple list of the groupings into which it might be divided, is a way of getting at the complexity of social change in later Edo. It is a more complex rendering than conventional conceptions of Edo as polarized between samurai and *chōnin*, but it remains only a crude scheme of the highly complex society the city had become by about 1800. The population figures need to be taken with several grains of salt: the only official enumerations that we have are for the total population of the commoner *chō* (known collectively as the "*machikata*") alone, which was about five hundred thousand in the middle years of the eighteenth century, dropped to a low of four hundred and fifty-seven thousand in 1786, and then grew at a slow but steady increase to a high of five hundred and seventy-four thousand in 1854.[5] The samurai class, however, was never enumerated, nor do we have any clear sense of the dimensions of the large servant population of the city, much of which was probably excluded from the commoner census.[6] The estimations offered here are, at best, educated guesses at rough orders of magnitude for around the year 1798, when the machikata population was 492,449, with a ratio of 135 males per 100 females.[7]

Direct shogunal retainers. About two hundred and fifty thousand. These were the true natives of Edo, for whom the political city was created. By the end of the seventeenth century, virtually all of this group had been born and bred in the city, and they played a role in the creation of its higher culture that has yet to be properly assessed; one stellar example in this exhibition is Ōta Nampo. The shogunal retainers were broadly divided into the two categories of *hatamoto* (bannermen) and the lower-ranking *gokenin* (housemen), numbering respectively perhaps six thousand and twenty thousand. The larger of these would themselves have a number of retainers, so that the average household size has been estimated as about ten persons.[8] On maps of Edo, such as the one in this exhibition, the higher-ranking shogunal retainers, who were given individual house lots (as opposed to the row-house barracks in which most gokenin lived), are recorded with their individual names. This minutely detailed inscription of personal names, totalling in the thousands, is visible witness to the local presence of this crucial group.

Proper chōnin. About one hundred and twenty thousand. The great majority of non-samurai in Edo lived in the residential units known as chō (also read *machi*), typically consisting of all houses (including the back-lot tenements) along each side of a block-long section of a street. In the later Edo Period, the chō numbered about seventeen hundred, with an average population of about eighty households each. Although the word chōnin (person of the chō) is often used to refer to all residents of the machikata, in official *bakufu* usage it designated only those who owned real estate, whether land (*jinushi*) or buildings (*ienushi*). Most of these "proper" chōnin ran businesses as merchants, and represent the political and economic elite of the city. Of the total of almost twenty thousand household heads who constitute this group, a certain number were the Edo branches (*Edo-dana*) of merchant houses from west Japan, which provided the all-male staff of clerks and apprentices and dealt in imported finished goods, primarily from the Kyoto, Osaka, Ōmi, and Ise regions. The majority, however—increasingly so as the Edo Period progressed—were merchants of local origin who dealt primarily in goods from the Kantō region and helped nurture the Edo nativist sentiment that emerged in the eighteenth century.

Property superintendents. About eighty thousand. In a pattern that was probably first set by the absentee merchant owners of Edo branches, many of the landlords of Edo came to hire superintendents to watch their properties and collect rents. Known as *yamori* (also more formally as *ienushi* and less formally as *ōya*), this group of about sixteen thousand men came to serve also as the agents of the bakufu in maintaining public order at the local level, and hence were increasingly treated as "proper" chōnin, even though they owned no property (receiving housing as one of their perquisites). They generally held jobs as small merchants and artisans, and, though not wealthy, were a crucial middling group in Edo life, likely to be Edo natives with a strong sense of urban identity.

Petty merchants and artisans. About two hundred and twenty thousand. These were the lower middle class of Edo, who lived in rental housing, whether on main streets (important for those with shops) or in the back alleys. Some were artisans who sold their wares from their own homes, while others were craftsmen who moved from job to job, such as carpenters (the elite of the group), masons, or gardeners. Some (although certainly a minority) were recent immigrants from the provinces who probably came to the city as apprentices. This group tapers off into the lowest social levels, of entertainers, menial workers, and coolies. The majority were married with families, with an average household size of about four. As we shall see, this group provided the class base for the Edokko of the late Tokugawa Period.

Daimyo mansion staff. About fifty thousand.[9] These were the domain samurai known as "resident in Edo" (*jōfu*), as opposed to those who accompanied the daimyo in alternate years. Chief among these were the daimyo heirs, who were typically born in Edo and remained there until succeeding to the domain headship. Beneath them were the substantial staffs needed to conduct ongoing domain business in Edo and to maintain the various residences. Since such samurai lived in Edo for years at a time, with some posts even becoming hereditary, they lived with their families and were intimately familiar with the city. Among the leading lights of eighteenth-century Edo culture in this group was Hōseidō Kisanji, a principal retainer on the Edo staff of the Akita domain.

Domain samurai on sankin kōtai duty. About three hundred thousand. Whenever a daimyo came to Edo for his year of alternate attendance, he was required to bring a number of soldiers appropriate to his rank. These were almost all single men, most of whom had very few official duties to perform in Edo. For many, the stay in Edo seems to have been a once-in-a-lifetime experience, in the course of which they would consume the savings brought from the domain on the many pleasures of the city. This was an exclusively consuming class in Edo, and a pivotal group in the recirculation of culture throughout Japan. Domain samurai were also the most common target of ridicule by Edo natives, who stereotyped them as provincial bumpkins, a tone reflected in such epithets as *asagiura*, *buza*, and *shingoza*.

Male contract laborers. About eighty thousand. Several of the above categories already implicitly include a variety of servants, such as hereditary servants of bakufu retainers, male and female live-in servants of chōnin families, and daughters of chōnin families who spent a period of service in the samurai mansions as a form of training. Other than these, however, was a male population, many of them single, who worked as contract laborers in two rather different capacities. Some were hired by the domain mansions while the daimyo were in residence in order to fulfill the required quotas of guards. They were, in effect, "rent-a-samurai," men who were given two swords and the lowest of samurai status for their term contracts of one year or less. Of a different sort were unskilled day laborers who worked primarily in construction trades. This contract labor market was under the control of employment agencies, and the men they handled tended to be rowdy and prone to gambling in the eyes of the bakufu, which periodically devised measures to control them.

Priests. About fifty thousand. About two-thirds of this number were Buddhist priests who staffed the very large number of temples scattered throughout the city. Most were celibate, and well known for their enjoyment of the pleasure quarters, both male and female. In addition, this number includes Shinto and Shugendō priests, as well as such priest-like categories as doctors and diviners.

Shin Yoshiwara. About ten thousand. The Shin Yoshiwara brothel was a self-contained community, headed by the wealthy owners of the teahouses and brothels, who often were active figures in the making of Edo popular culture. About one-third of this population were actual prostitutes, the remainder being largely male servants and entertainers.

Outcastes and vagrants. About twenty thousand. The outcaste class was divided into a small community of *eta* in a ghetto northeast of the Asakusa Kannon Temple and a larger number of *hinin* (whose status, unlike that of eta, was not hereditary) scattered in small groups on riverbanks and in temple precincts throughout the city. Not too different in social status were a sizable number of "homeless" (*mushukunin*) people, mostly men, who had no legal place of registration and hence difficulty in finding regular work. These groups formed the underclass of the city of Edo, and their numbers swelled in times of famine.

These ten categories yield a total of about one million two hundred thousand for the population of Edo in about 1800, a figure that should be taken only as a rough estimate. The figures for the enumerated machikata population, as mentioned before, increased by about 15 percent over the following half-century, but the samurai population may well have declined as the domains made efforts to cut back on Edo expenditures. Apart from considerable variations by season and year because of the vagaries of weather and natural disaster, the population of the city remained fairly stable throughout the era we are discussing, from the mid-eighteenth to the mid-nineteenth century.

The Blurring of Chōnin and Samurai

To understand how this population structure worked as a dynamic system in the formation of Edo popular culture, we need to look more closely at how different groups were arranged geographically, and how they interacted. Of particular interest is the interaction of the samurai and chōnin estates.

In early Edo, samurai and chōnin territories were sharply segregated. The chō were laid out in a long belt along the Tōkaidō highway as it entered the city, about five hundred yards wide from Shimbashi on northward to Nihombashi. North of Nihombashi, the belt of chō extended in two directions, northeast toward Asakusa and highways to the north, and northwest through the Kanda district in the direction of the Nakasendō highway. The chō were arranged with geometrical regularity into blocks, a pattern that remains evident in downtown Tokyo today. This initial center of chōnin Edo came in time to be known as "Shitamachi," particularly the area around Nihombashi where the oldest and wealthiest merchant houses stood. To the west of the Shitamachi lay the grounds of Edo Castle and the surrounding area devoted to samurai residence. Another block of samurai land lay southwest of Nihombashi along the banks of the Sumida, intended primarily for warehousing, while clusters of temples were placed in the interstices.

This neatly arranged plan gradually gave way to a pattern of sprawl as time passed. A great fire in 1657 destroyed almost two-thirds of the city, including the great donjon of Edo Castle (which was never rebuilt), and led to various measures to deconcentrate the population. Temples were moved to the edges of town, firebreaks were opened at major road intersections, and the low-lying area east of the Sumida was opened to both samurai and chōnin settlement.

At the same time, new chō began to sprout like mushrooms along the more travelled roads of the city, particularly in the hilly area to the west that had formerly been almost entirely samurai settlement. As a result of this continuing sprawl, Edo tended in the direction of a patchwork of alternating samurai and commoner settlements. Some 70 percent of the city's land area remained in samurai hands, with the remainder split evenly between chō and religious lands, but the central arteries all tended to be lined with commercial activity. This was particularly conspicuous east of the Sumida, where commoner lands lined the various canals, and samurai estates filled in the area between.

Residential segregation was nevertheless a key fact of life in Edo, and the elites of both estates lived in fundamentally contrasting forms of housing. In the chō, the great merchant houses faced directly on the main streets, set adjacent to one another with almost no space between so as to maximize the commercial frontage. The front part of the structure was the *mise*, devoted to the display and selling of wares, while the back part provided living quarters for family and servants. In the samurai neighborhoods, by contrast, the residences were sharply separated from the streets by encircling walls that cut out all views of the inside except for the garden trees that protruded above. Inside, a detached dwelling with space all around was laid out in the classical *shoin* style, with reception areas in front and living quarters behind. The single-family form of the elite samurai dwelling, as best seen in the hatamoto ranks of shogunal retainers, was the prototype for the twentieth-century Japanese ideal of the detached single-family suburban home.

At the sub-elite level of both samurai and chōnin, however, one finds a convergence of residential style in the row-house form. The majority of chō dwellers, for example, lived in the back-alley rental units known as *nagaya* (long houses), structures with thin common walls separating as many as eight small single-family units in a row, sometimes back-to-back with another row. Not too different were the row-house units (*kumi-yashiki*) in which many of the lower shogunal retainers lived. Such quarters were scattered throughout the city, and, like the back-street nagaya, were provided with entrances direct from narrow side streets. Most of the samurai residents of the great daimyo mansions were quartered not in the mansions proper, but in row units built into the surrounding walls. Some were larger than others and designed for the families of the regular staff, while others accommodated groups of single samurai on sankin kōtai duty.

In these ways, both samurai and chōnin at the middle to lower levels tended to live in dense clusters of row housing. The two also came to resemble each other more closely as many lower samurai of the shogun were obliged to take on handicraft jobs such as the making of umbrellas or clogs in order to make ends meet. In general, contact between samurai and non-samurai at the lower class levels was regular and familiar, increasingly consolidated by the emerging common language of the city.[10] The visiting domain samurai, as provincial transients, were not part of this process.

The most important realm for the forging of what might be termed the "common culture" of Edo, however, was in the world of leisure and entertainment. The enclosed realms of the pleasure quarters and the theater were perhaps the starting point for this common culture, but as time passed a far broader and more public realm extended the scope of interaction among the citizens of Edo on a basis of anonymity and social equality. This was the realm of the "famous places" (*meisho*) of Edo that were celebrated in growing numbers of landscape prints from the later eighteenth century. Many of these were religious or scenic sites, visited on ritual or seasonal occasions. A complex landscape of dozens of these covered the city, offering certain pleasures for each season, whether cherry blossoms on Gotenyama or wisteria at Kameido, summer fireworks at Ryōgoku, or autumn insects at Dōkanyama.

Perhaps the greatest of the popular "famous places" was the combined area at either end of Ryōgoku Bridge, the premier center of street activity in Edo. Vast throngs of people would gather there on summer evenings to enjoy boating, sideshows, and an endless variety of stalls for food and shopping. Ryōgoku Bridge was depicted more than any other single place in woodblock prints, and finds its classic literary description in Hiraga Gennai's humorous tale *Nenashigusa* of 1763. After an exhaustive list of all the sideshows and street-vendors at Ryōgoku, Gennai turns to a sketch of the people who gather there:

> Where there are priests, there are laymen, and where there are men there are women. For every countrified samurai there is a stylish townsman wearing a long comb and a short *haori*. The Young Master's attendant carries along a goldfish in a glass bowl; the noblewoman's followers dangle pipe cases of gold brocade; the buxom maid-in-waiting hauls her buttocks along; the overweening bodyguard-for-hire, rather than wearing his two swords, seems himself to be an appendage to them.[11]

And so the list continues, through many other social and occupational types, constituting a veritable catalogue of all Edo, high and low, samurai and commoner.

The Emergence of a Regional Kantō Identity

Cementing and consolidating the common culture of Edo was a strong consciousness of the special identity of the city and those native to it. This identity had two dimensions, that of the city itself and that of the Kantō region in which it was situated. The broader regional identity set the parameters of Edo's urban identity. To begin with, Edo was in east Japan, beyond the line (roughly from the current prefectural boundaries between Shizuoka and Aichi on the south, and Toyama and Niigata on the north) that bisects Japan into two distinct cultural zones, differing in speech, customs, and social organization.[12] Historically, west Japan was always more advanced, the east relatively undeveloped. From the Kamigata standpoint, all of eastern Japan was considered a remote and provincial backwater. The Kantō Plain in particular was seen (not without good reason) as a place of deep-rooted military tradition, dominated by the samurai class and symbolized by the Kashima and Katori shrines, which were near the mouth of the Tone River and were dedicated to gods of war. The typical man of the "East" (*Azuma*) in medieval times was thus a warrior, rough and uncultured but with a certain directness of manner.[13]

In the early decades of Edo's history, however, most of its higher culture was directly transplanted from the Kamigata region, including the early culture of the Floating World. This naturally created a certain tension with the older "eastern" traditions of the Kantō, and by the final decades of the eighteenth century a self-conscious Edo identity had begun to assert itself. The critical development was the emergence of the form of kabuki theater known as *aragoto*, or "rough stuff," describing the blustery style of acting developed by the Ishikawa Danjūrō line and explicitly set off against the softer style and more domestic preoccupations of the Kamigata *wagoto* (soft stuff) kabuki. The origins of the Danjūrō line are said to have been in Narita, east of Edo, where the great Fudō temple of Shinshōji was center of a Kantō-wide cult that, abetted by Danjūrō patronage, became a popular pilgrimage site for Edo residents.

In time, Danjūrō—of whom nine generations were to span the Edo Period from Genroku on—became the superhero of the city, the "flower of Edo," in many ways its symbol. The importance of Danjūrō was the way in which the tradition could encompass both commoner and samurai Edo. On the one hand, Danjūrō as an actor was very much a commoner and in many roles (such as the famous Sukeroku) was often set in contemptuous opposition to samurai. Yet the bravado that was part of the Danjūrō style was itself well suited to the rough-and-tumble military self-image of the Kantō region, reinforced by the Danjūrō enactment of such eastern samurai legends as the revenge of the Soga brothers. Danjūrō could serve both as symbol of resistance to samurai, and as the samurai spirit itself.

Another crucial aspect of the regional character of Edo lies in the long-term process by which the city became ever more deeply integrated with its local hinterland through economic development. Over the years, the initial backwardness of the Kantō region was gradually overcome, thanks in large part to the immense consumption demands of the city. As the hinterland developed economically, the city was able gradually to decrease its reliance on products imported from west Japan by way of Osaka. In such commodities as soy sauce and seed oils, by the end of the Tokugawa Period the Edo region had reversed the initial pattern of reliance on the west. In the process, the Edo branches of west Japan's merchant houses declined in influence within the city, while the wholesalers of native origin grew in wealth and local pride.

A turning point in Edo's economic and demographic history came some time in the first half of the eighteenth century. Until then, the city had grown so rapidly in population that more than a million people were living there within a century of its founding. No real census was conducted for it until 1721, at which point the population had already stabilized, so there is no way of knowing the exact pattern of its early population change. Such rapid growth inevitably required a steady in-flow of migrants, such as to warrant the proverbial characterization of Edo as the "dumping ground of the provinces" (*shokoku no hakidame*)—an expression that could also refer to the constant circulation of domain samurai through the sankin kōtai.

At any rate, in the eighteenth century, Japan as a whole entered a period of population stability and mature economic development. It was an era of generally stable prices and gradually rising real wages, with a decline in wage differentials between skilled and unskilled, urban and rural.[14] This is not to say that all was easy for the city. On the contrary, the era of the 1770s and 1780s in particular was one of frequent natural disaster, as fire, epidemic, and famine followed one another.[15] The great famine beginning in 1783 in Edo culminated in a large riot in the early summer of 1787 in protest against the spiralling rise in the price of rice. Apart from these difficult years, however, Edo generally knew peace and prosperity from the 1730s for a full century until the Tempō famine of the 1830s.

Edo Nativism and the Birth of the Edokko

Regional character and development provided the context for the growth of a specifically Edo identity, but ultimately it was the cultural dynamics within Edo itself, as a city distinct from the countryside and the provinces, that was critical in the birth of the Edokko, the "child of Edo," in the course of the eighteenth century.

Japanese historians have carefully traced the various inflections of "Edo" used to characterize Edo and its residents.[16] In the seventeenth century, for example, we find the early appearance of the term "O-Edo," with an honorific prefix added to Edo to indicate respect for the city as the capital of the shogun. Clearly such a top-down conception was weak in potential for commoner urban identity, and although "O-Edo" was often used in formal ways, such as in the titles of maps of the city, it had little power to stir local emotions.

The earliest textual usage of the word "Edokko" yet discovered is in a *senryū* (a form of short comic verse, about which more below) that may be dated to the year 1771, although the term had likely been around for a while already in common speech. After that, the word appears with increasing frequency in comic verse and gesaku fiction, with a classic definition of Edokko qualities coming in a 1787 *sharebon* by Santō Kyōden, *Tsūgen Sōmagaki*. From this complex and punning passage, the historian Nishiyama Matsunosuke has distilled four broad characteristics of the prototypical Edokko, of whom Kyōden clearly considered himself a fine example: a sense of pride in being born in the capital of the shogun, looking up at the gold roof finials of the castle and taking his first bath in water supplied from the city aqueduct; an irresistible urge to part with his money as soon as it is earned, by spending a fortune to taste the first bonito of the season or selling a fine downtown house for a single fling in the Yoshiwara; having a classy upbringing, complete with a wet nurse under an umbrella and the best toys; having as his base the very center of the city, near Nihombashi.[17]

As these features suggest, the Edokko of this era was a well-to-do type, a big spender at the Yoshiwara, and perhaps best represented, Nishiyama has argued, by the "Eighteen Great Tsū." A person with *tsū* was one versed in all the ways of the world and the heart, particularly in the Yoshiwara pleasure quarters, and the "Great Tsū" were the ultimate in this urbane quality. The "eighteen" did not refer to any fixed number of individuals, but, rather, to a loose and shifting group of leading playboys of the sort celebrated in gesaku literature of the 1770s.

Of the historical figures recorded as "Great Tsū," the most common single occupation was that of *fudasashi*, the merchants who brokered the official rice stipends of the shogunal retainers for cash. Their shops were near the great bakufu granaries along the Sumida River north of the confluence with the Kanda River, the area known as Kuramae ("in front of the warehouses"). These were merchants whose livelihood was indissolubly linked with the bakufu itself, and whose daily dealings were not with ordinary chōnin, but with bakufu retainers. In other words, they occupied a special position precisely at the intersection of the samurai and merchant classes, knowledgeable about the ideals and cultural practices of both.

Gradually, however, the image of the Edokko began to change: in essence, this quintessential representative of the city began to move *down* in class and status, until in the early decades of the nineteenth century he came to be personified as a small merchant or craftsman. (The same seems to have been true of the Cockney, London's counterpart of the Edokko, who was originally among the "merchants and first-rate tradesmen" but who in time became the more familiar plebeian type we know today.[18]) The callings most characteristic of this new Edokko were firemen (temperamentally given to living for the moment and always busy because of the many fires in the city),[19] carpenters (just as busy as firemen, for the same reason), and fishmongers (who dealt in the most perishable of daily foodstuffs).

The vast and varied literature on the Edokko tends to deal exclusively with this later evolution of the type rather than its elite origins.[20] By the mid-nineteenth century, the essential Edokko came to be typified by the "Three Men of Edo": the Danjūrō line of actors, the commoner firemen, and the young fishmongers of Nihombashi.[21] This transformed Edokko has been particularly encouraged by the patterns of modernization in Tokyo, where the old artisanal and petty merchant class was left as the only bearer of true Edo traditions in the commoner part of the city. The "Shitamachi," as the place of Edokko residence, similarly underwent a transformation, from the elite merchant district around Nihombashi to the entire vast sprawling flatlands to the north (Asakusa), the south (Shiba), and across the Sumida (Honjo, Fukagawa).

As the Edokko broadened his class base, his ideology took on an increasingly nativist cast, with an exclusivist bias against all who came from the outside. This was seen in the emergence of such stereotypes as "Sagami maids" (*Sagami gejo*, single women from the countryside south of Edo, known for their lust); "Shinano types" (*Shinano-mono*, single men from the mountainous region of Shinano Province who came to Edo as servants, known for their big hearts and appetites); and "yellow-liners" (*asagiura*, from the unstylish light-yellow cotton lining of their jackets), provincial samurai hicks on sankin kōtai duty who were considered inept dressers and shameless lechers.

According to the proverb that is widely repeated today as one of the essential attributes of the Edokko, it is necessary to have lived in the city for three generations. In effect, native Edo birth of native Edo parentage became the definition—a constraint that in reality would have drastically limited the actual pool of Edokko. This tendency should be seen, however, in light of a crucial change in the demographic reality of Edo throughout the last half of its history: the sex ratio of the commoner population was moving steadily in the direction of parity. The figures we have are scattered but consistent: for 1733-47, the ratio moved from 173 (males per 100 females) to 169; in 1798 it dropped to 135; and in the period 1832-67 it continued a steady decline, from 120 to virtual parity on the eve of the Meiji Restoration. This is a remarkable feature of late Edo society, the causes and consequences of which remain little studied.[22]

One great imponderable is the death rate of Edo compared with that of the countryside. Until quite recently, studies of European cities have assumed that all premodern cities had much higher death rates than did rural areas, which necessitated a constant excess inflow of population to make up for the loss. This was doubtless true of many cities, but may not have been the case for Edo, which had one of the cleanest and most reliable public water-supply and waste-disposal systems of any large premodern city in the world.

The water-supply system was constructed in the seventeenth century, first with the Kanda Aqueduct (built in the early Edo Period) and then with the Tamagawa Aqueduct of 1653-54. The Tamagawa Aqueduct in particular, lined with cherry trees and lovingly maintained, was a true lifeline for the city and served as its major water supply until the 1960s. Both these major aqueducts (various other minor ones came and went) passed into Edo through a remarkable underground system of stone and wooden conduits, linked in turn to the countless "wells" of Edo, which were found both in samurai mansions and downtown commoner chō. There were true wells in Edo, but on the whole the ground was too unsettled and close to the bay to yield good drinking water.

The waste-disposal system was based on the practice of all East Asian cities since ancient times of recycling the city's organic wastes back into the soil of the hinterland. In Edo, human waste was systematically collected by farmers from the surrounding area, who in turn paid the landlords for this by-product of their tenants. So precious an urban crop was human excrement that its sale provided as much as one-half of the total income of Edo landlords from their properties.

Thanks in large part to these appropriate technologies for dealing with urban water and waste, Edo was spared any truly devastating attacks of disease.[23] Smallpox, measles, influenza, and dysentery were all part of the calendar of epidemic disease in Japan, but none posed sudden or drastic threats to the health of the city until the arrival of cholera from the West in 1858. Most disastrous in any premodern society is not disease alone, but disease in combination with the weakness occasioned by famine or poor diet. In the case of Edo, this phenomenon was clear in two great famines of late Edo, Temmei (1783-87) and Tempō (1833-37). Even then, the problem was less acute in Edo, whose people could somehow contrive to get the rice they needed (although in Temmei it required violent action to achieve).

Even if the death rates in Edo did not differ greatly from those in the countryside, it is certain that the birth rate was lower, partly because of the sex ratio and partly because of a later average age of marriage. By the same token, however, the gradual equalization of the sex ratio in the later Edo Period means that the birth rate must surely have been rising, a tendency further supported by late Edo statistics for the percentage of native-born residents of the city, which grew from 70 to 78 percent in the period 1843-67. These trends mean that the picture commonly drawn by Japanese historians of late Edo as a city increasingly besieged by swarms of rural immigrants is misleading. On the contrary, it was a city that was steadily *less* reliant on immigrants to make up for any deficit in the natural rate of increase.

In these ways, Edo was becoming in a sense more "Edo-like" as a growing native population continued to evolve its own sense of a distinctive identity, and as the social base of the prototypical Edokko continued to move downward into the working-class masses. The term that best captures this new and broader sense of identity is "Great Edo" (Ō-Edo), suggesting the boastful sense of superiority of the Edokko. The earliest usage the historian Takeuchi Makoto has found for the term was in a 1789 sharebon of Santō Kyōden.[24] The term nicely conveys the sense of prosperity that characterized Edo's popular culture from the late eighteenth to the early nineteenth century. The attitude is well expressed by the words of a character in Shikitei Samba's *The Bathhouse of the Floating World* who criticizes a fellow Edoite for not saving money: "You're not determined enough, that's all. That's why you can't manage to put anything aside. How can anybody not build up a little capital in this bountiful city of Edo? It's such a wonderful place—money just seems to accumulate naturally here. Isn't that why so many people can come here from all over the country and make successes of themselves?"[25]

Indeed, as suggested earlier, *The Bathhouse of the Floating World* itself, published in 1809, is indicative of the broadening conception of the floating world in late Edo. The work consists of a loosely connected series of vignettes of the diverse customers who make their way into an Edo public bath, and is constructed largely through colloquial conversation. In his introduction on "the larger meaning" of the bathhouse, Samba puts forth a theory of the bath as a place of absolute social equality: "It is, after all, the way of Nature, and of Heaven and Earth, that all are naked when they bathe—the wise and the foolish, the crooked and the straight, the poor and the rich, the high and low."[26] The bath is where all members of society come together as equals, a floating world not of the most up-to-date and sophisticated pleasures, but of ordinary, everyday Edo.

The Dynamics of Print Culture

Printing and publishing were of fundamental importance to the emergence of the popular culture of the Temmei era and its transformation into Bunka-Bunsei in ways that can only briefly be suggested here.[27] It seems clear that in scale, early modern Japan had a culture of print in every way comparable to that of many European countries of the time, working through the power of reproduction to circulate Edo culture far more broadly than ever before, stimulating a rapid increase in literacy, and moving in the inexorable direction of a mass culture.

Commercial woodblock printing in Japan grew rapidly in the seventeenth century, first in Kyoto from the 1630s and then in Osaka from the 1660s. Publishing in Edo, which in the seventeenth century was little more than a market for books produced in the Kamigata region, expanded dramatically from the mid-eighteenth century, surpassing both Kyoto and Osaka by 1800. Whereas Kamigata publishing was distinguished by its large number of serious classical, Buddhist, and Confucian texts, Edo was notable in the realm of popular literature of all sorts, a category known as *jihon* (local books, that is, not imported from Kamigata).

These "local books" of Edo were sold through bookstores known as *ezōshiya*, "picture-book stores," a term that conveys the pervasive importance of illustration in much Edo publishing. Pictures were central to the print culture of Edo, whether in the form of single-sheet ukiyo-e, or the dominant comic-book-style lineage of fiction, from the simple "red books" or "black books" that began in the later seventeenth century to the sophisticated *kibyōshi* (yellow-cover books) from 1775, which were such a pivotal genre of the ensuing decades, and then to the successor *gōkan* from the early nineteenth century.

Publishing was not limited to pictures, of course, but served as a crucial vehicle for many other networks of literary production. One particular example of special significance for the evolution of a distinctive Edo culture was the short verse form known today as *senryū*.[28] The form itself is easily enough summarized as a kind of comic haiku that endeavors to capture a slice of everyday life in only seventeen syllables. Like haiku, it evolved from the practice of comic linked verse (*haikai*), but came to exist as an independent form, free of the initial stanza to which it was intended to be a sequel.

Both as a literary form and a social practice, the roots of senryū, as of much Edo literature, are to be found in the Kamigata area, but it was in Edo that it took on the form of a true movement by way of print. The movement coalesced around a single man by the name of Karai Senryū (1718-1790), whose name would become synonymous with the verse form itself long after his death. Professionally he was a judge (*tenja*) of a practice known as *maeku-zuke* (first line links), whereby the judge would pose fourteen-syllable (7, 7) first lines (*maeku*) that amateur poets would then use as inspiration for their own seventeen-syllable (5, 7, 5) creations. For such judges, this practice was a way of making money, collecting submission fees for each poem in return for a grade and the chance for a cash prize. In early-seventeenth-century Edo a number of judges were active in promoting such competitions, known as "ten-thousand-verse rankings" (*manku-awase*).

For such a judge, print was an essential medium. He would announce a competition of maeku-zuke by posting printed notices around the city. The aspiring poets would then compose their own contributions and submit them, together with a fee of about twelve *mon* (eventually, in Senryū's case, sixteen mon—about the price of a bowl of noodles), at any of a number of shops that, just like American lottery vendors today, served as "intermediaries" (*toritsugisho*) for the judge. The judge would then have printed on loose sheets a list of all the prizewinning verses from those submitted. The first *Ten Thousand Verse Rankings, Judged by Senryū* (Senryū-hyō manku-awase) appeared in summer 1757 and offered only thirteen prize verses from a meager pool of 207. Within five years, however, submissions were up to over ten thousand in the regular contests, and Senryū had far outstripped all his competitors in popularity.

In 1765 Senryū's growing movement was given a new boost with the publication of a distillation of the best from previous competitions, entitled *Yanagidaru*. A second followed two years after, and then became an annual event. The main innovation in these compilations was the selection of only those verses that could be understood without reference to the opening maeku, a decisive break from the linked-verse origins of the form. The verses were all anonymous, identified rather by the name of the submitter's senryū club, the social groups that were the bottom-level source of creativity for such poetry. Although originally intended to avoid favoritism in the competitions, such anonymity worked to ensure the populist quality of the poetry. It was a local and up-to-date, even newsy, form of art, revealing Senryū's own well-honed ability at keeping up with his times and providing a marketable outlet for insights on those times. By his death in 1790 his publications accounted for eighty thousand out of some two hundred thousand surviving Edo senryū.

Senryū are pivotal examples of the way in which the commercial culture of print worked to encourage the formal celebration of ordinary life in later Edo. They were appreciated not as individual literary creations, as was the case with the more elite forms of poetry, but as incisive vignettes into the life of the city. As such, they are a precious resource for social historians of the city, and also serve to reflect one crucial way in which the social basis of Edo nativist identity was moving rapidly in the direction of an anonymous and commercial mass culture.

Other Outlets: Private Printing and Public Storytelling

An important negative characteristic of publishing in Edo Japan was the bakufu prohibition of any books or pictures dealing with current events, or even with historical events that were considered to reflect adversely on the Tokugawa polity (a notable example being the prohibition of any mention of Hideyoshi). This meant, for example, that there were no newspapers in Tokugawa Japan, since the very idea of "news" was prohibited by the regime. Enforcement was achieved as much through the self-restraint of publishers, fearful of the consequences should they be punished, as through effective bakufu scrutiny. Still, the threat was always present, as the crackdown on gesaku writers by Matsudaira Sadanobu in 1789-91 vividly demonstrated.

One pervasive consequence of such a regime was the tendency of writers to use the oblique techniques of allusion and satire to disguise discussions of current events. This was widely seen on the stage, for example, in the displacement of current events to the medieval period, a classic case being the transposition of the story of the Akō *rōnin* from 1701-03 to the Kamakura Period when staged as *Kanadehon Chūshingura* in 1748. Not that anyone was particularly fooled, of course, when the historical Ōishi Kuranosuke became "Ōboshi Yuranosuke" onstage: the bakufu seemed to be satisfied by this transparent avoidance of any literal references. Yet this constant habit of "distancing" the political present by way of puns and historical transposition helped to enhance the popular culture in late Tokugawa Japan as a sort of never-never land.

Another consequence of the state control of publishing was the creation of a thriving market in illegal and private printing. Erotic books and pictures, for example, were produced in great numbers and circulated with apparent ease, if we are to judge from the large numbers that have survived today. Another subterfuge was to avoid printing, and to circulate works on current affairs known as *jitsuroku* (true accounts) in multiple manuscripts through the lending libraries that grew rapidly in number in the late Edo Period. The jitsuroku recorded tales about the private affairs and family trials of both the Tokugawa shoguns and various daimyo, much of it based on rumor and embellished to give it a fiction-like quality.[29]

The private circulation of information was by no means limited to politically sensitive materials. Far more important in the transition from the eighteenth to the nineteenth century was the proliferation of private printing in a wide variety of innocent sociable contexts. Such works were known generically simply as *surimono*, or "printed things," and have their origins in the calendar prints of 1765-66 that gave rise to the multicolor printing technique known as *nishiki-e*, "brocade pictures," which almost overnight transformed the history of the Japanese woodblock print.[30] The impetus behind these prints was an earlier bakufu prohibition of the public production of calendars. The only information actually offered by the calendar prints was the identity of the long and short months for the coming lunar year, which everyone knew anyway, so the government refrained from taking measures against the practice as long as it remained a private game.

Such private printing of New Year's greetings, whether in the form of calendar or other motifs, saw the greatest burst of activity in the wake of the Kansei Reforms, which imposed restrictions on the public production of excessively decorative printing. From the 1790s into the nineteenth century, it became a veritable boom among men of culture to distribute privately commissioned surimono to their friends. Most common were New Year's prints, combining the sender's poetry (usually *kyōka* or haiku) with a picture done by an ukiyo-e artist, but such private prints were also issued for all sorts of other celebrations and parties, whether as invitations or as gifts for the guests. Haikai masters ordered printed collections of their students' work, practitioners of the musical and performing arts would print announcements of the conferring of an art name to a pupil, and merchants would send out printed placards for the opening of a shop. In this way, printing of high quality was important in cementing and spreading networks of cultural sociability in late Edo life.

Still another and quite different consequence of the formal prohibition of open political discussion on current issues was the encouragement it offered to the formal elaboration of oral culture. At the simplest level, this meant that, since people were prohibited from writing and publishing about politics, they tended to talk about it instead. Oral performance has provided a central dynamic in Japanese cultural evolution since medieval times, giving rise to what Barbara Ruch has called a "national literature" by the end of the Muromachi Period. (Ruch emphasizes that "oral" should not be thought of as being opposed to "literate," since written texts were often performed for literate audiences, and recommends the term "vocal literature" as preferable.)[31]

Late Edo witnessed a further expansion and refinement of oral performance, seen in the proliferation of commercial vaudeville establishments known as *yose* that offered a wide variety of recitation and storytelling. The typical Edo form was the monologue storytelling that came to be known as *rakugo*, which was reinvigorated with the arrival of the Osaka raconteur Okamoto Mansaku in 1798 and grew rapidly in the early decades of the nineteenth century.[32] Reflecting in particular the increase in popularity of rakugo, the number of yose establishments rose steadily, from 75 in 1815 to over 200 by 1840. Rakugo joined with senryū as an art form that served to express the sense of solidarity in everyday Edo life that was central to the transformed floating world.

The acute sensitivity in rakugo to inflections of the evolving Edo dialect—and to the speech of those provincials who had not mastered it—reflects one important way in which urban identity came to be intimately linked with the spoken language. This kind of sensitivity is evident in *The Bathhouse of the Floating World*, in which Samba strives to capture the precise inflections of Edo speech. It should come as no surprise that the author's "oldest and most constant friendships seem to have been with people associated in one way or another with the vigorous revival of rakugo and allied storytelling arts that coincided with his most active years as a writer," as reflected in the strong influence of storytelling on his fiction.[33]

The Case of Kuwagata Keisai

By way of summary, a single artist appearing in this exhibition, Kuwagata Keisai, serves as a particularly revealing example of the dynamics at work in transforming Edo culture in its last century.[34] He was born in 1764 as Akabane Sanjirō, son of a tatami-maker, squarely within the petty merchants and artisans class that would become in time defined as the source of the quintessential Edokko. He became a student of the ukiyo-e artist Kitao Shigemasa, and from as early as 1778 began the illustration of kibyōshi, the genre most central to the emergence of Temmei gesaku literature. Over the next two decades, under the name of Kitao Masayoshi, he became the most prolific of all kibyōshi illustrators, credited with some two hundred titles.[35] In this way, his career was built by work for commercial book publishers.

But then a remarkable transformation took place. In 1794, the lowly ukiyo-e artist Masayoshi was appointed official painter of the daimyo of Tsuyama, Matsudaira Yasuchika, and took the new name of Kuwagata Keisai. By this, he was effectively made a samurai, and would have been given the right to wear two swords. Albeit a unique case, Keisai's crossing of estate lines suggests the importance of the borderline between samurai and non-samurai in stimulating much of the creativity of this era.

Keisai's career also provides a particularly interesting case of the growth of Edo identity in his depiction of the "famous places" of the city. In the 1780s, he followed in the footsteps of Utagawa Toyoharu in designing a series of *uki-e* "perspective prints" illustrating the greatest centers of Edo pleasure and entertainment: Ryōgoku Bridge, Nakasu, the theater district, the main street of the Yoshiwara, Shinobazu Pond, the Takanawa shore, and the Sumida embankment at Mimeguri. In 1785 he designed an elegant printed handscroll entitled "Views of the Famous Places of Edo" (*Edo meisho zue*), presenting fifty different scenes (Catalogue no. I-13).

His most imaginative leap in landscape came later, after his entry into the service of Tsuyama, when he designed a large-size print showing the entire city of Edo in panoramic perspective. The print may be dated to about 1803, and served as the model for various similar paintings executed by Keisai, notably the magnificent large work displayed in this exhibition, which was originally designed as sliding-door panels for Tsuyama Castle (Catalogue no. I-2). Probably shortly after making this print, Keisai indulged in an even more radical leap of the imagination and produced a view of the entire archipelago of Japan as if it were a continuous landscape, looking east to a distant silhouette of the Korean peninsula. This kind of expansive vision is suggestive of a breaking away from the narrow confines of the older Floating World.

Keisai's work also reveals the shift suggested at the beginning of this essay, toward a heightened interest in the daily life of ordinary Edo. His work as an illustrator for kibyōshi, many scenes of which are rich in elaborate details of daily life, had prepared him for the task. His greatest achievement in this area, and perhaps his masterpiece as a painter, is a set of three handscrolls depicting scenes of various Edo artisans at work, which may be dated to 1806. Executed in a rapid but highly animated and expressive manner, the work is now in the Tokyo National Museum, and is known as the *Kinsei shokunin-zukushi e-*

kotoba (Illustrated scroll of modern artisans). Each scroll includes an inscription by one of the leading stars of Temmei culture: Yomo no Akara (Ōta Nampo), Hōseidō Kisanji, and Santō Kyōden. Particularly revealing is the patron, who appears to have been none other than Matsudaira Sadanobu, the very person who is assigned conventional responsibility for bringing Temmei gesaku to a crashing halt. This suggests that the impact of the Kansei Reforms may have been not so much to bring an end to an era but to deflect its energies in new directions, away from politics and toward the depiction of ordinary life.

Keisai's later paintings also reveal another critical dimension of the broad change in Edo culture, along the axis of history. In retrospect, we can see the transition from the eighteenth to the nineteenth century as marking a pervasive growth of interest in the past throughout Japan. On a national scale, this clearly reflects the growing strength of "national studies" (*kokugaku*), the scholarly movement calling for the systematic investigation of Japan's indigenous literary tradition. Harry Harootunian's translation of kokugaku as "nativism" captures the note of concern for national identity fostered by the movement, and suggests a natural linkage with what I have called "Edo nativism" at a more local level.[36] In Keisai's later paintings, from the turn of the century until his death in 1824, the regard for the past is seen in his frequent depictions of beautiful women in archaic styles, and in the adoption of the scroll format for his vignettes of artisans.[37]

In popular literature, we find similar manifestations of a growing interest in the past in the figure of Ryūtei Tanehiko, a popular writer of fiction in the Bunka-Bunsei Period. As detailed in a revealing recent study by Andrew Markus, Tanehiko was driven by an antiquarian obsession with the past, which in his case centered in the Genroku era.[38] We begin to see that the transformation in Edo culture at the end of the eighteenth century was not simply a movement downwards and outwards in the space of the city, but a movement backwards in time as well. In these ways, the Floating World so beautifully crystallized in this exhibition was dispersed throughout the city neighborhoods and their histories, so that by the time of the critical confrontation with the West from the 1850s, the floating world was everywhere.

NOTES

1. Richard Lane, "The Beginnings of the Modern Japanese Novel: Kanazōshi, 1600-1682," *Harvard Journal of Asiatic Studies* 20 (December 1957), 672.

2. Hashimoto Mineo, *"Ukiyo" no shisō—Nihonjin no jinseikan* (Tokyo: Kōdansha Gendai Shinsho, 1975), 94-95.

3. This essay does not deal with the Temmei famine, the Kansei Reforms, or the Tempō crisis of famine-and-reform: the undeniably great impact of these events, particularly at the level of bakufu policy, has been outlined in detail by Herman Ooms, *Charismatic Bureaucrat: A Political Biography of Matsudaira Sadanobu, 1758-1829* (Chicago: Chicago University Press, 1975), 77-104, and Harold Bolitho, "The Tenpō Crisis," in *The Cambridge History of Japan* (Cambridge, England: Cambridge University Press, 1989), 5:116-67.

4. The panoramic screen of Edo by Kuwagata Keisai in this exhibition shows numerous such daimyo processions; these, however, appear to represent the lords on their way to and from the offering of official new year greetings at Edo Castle, and not the larger processions that entered and left the city. One can get a sense of the complexity of the seasonal pattern of sankin kōtai movement by

analyzing the data for 1853 provided in Toshio G. Tsukahira, *Feudal Control in Tokugawa Japan: The Sankin Kōtai System* (Cambridge, Mass.: Harvard University Press, 1970), 140-73.

5. The only surviving official figures for the machikata are for the periods 1721-47 and 1832-67; see Koda Shigetomo, "Edo no chōnin no jinkō," *Shakai keizai shigaku* (April 1938), reprinted in *Koda Shigetomo chosakushu*, 7 vols. (Tokyo: Chūō Koronsha, 1972-74), 2: 263. For the eighty-five-year interval between, the era of most interest here, I have accepted the sexennial figures reported in Katsu Kaishū's *Suijinroku*, in *Katsu Kaishū zenshū*, ed. Katsube Mitake, Matsumoto Sannosuke, and Ōguchi Yūjirō (Tokyo: Keisō Shobō, 1978), 10: 227-38.

6. The variety of types of servants in the Edo population, and their place in the machikata population statistics, present many difficult problems. Gary P. Leupp, *Servants, Shophands, and Laborers in the Cities of Tokugawa Japan* (Princeton: Princeton University Press, 1992), offers useful data on Tokugawa servants, but fails to pursue various crucial distinctions among service types. For various insights on this issue, see Saitō Osamu, *Shōka no sekai, uradana no sekai: Edo to Ōsaka no hikaku toshi shi* (Tokyo: Riburopōto, 1987). Saitō suggests in particular (p. 72) that many short-term male domestic servants may not have been included in the machikata population figures.

7. The 1798 figures, which are the only evidence for the sex ratio between 1747 and 1832, were reported by Ōta Nampo in his miscellany *Ichiwa ichigen*; see *Nihon zuihitsu taisei*, 1st ser. (Tokyo: Yoshikawa Kōbunkan, 1928), 2: 45-47. For further discussion of Edo's demography, with emphasis on the end of the Tokugawa Period, see my "The Edo-Tokyo Transition: In Search of Common Ground," in *Japan in Transition: From Tokugawa to Meiji*, ed. Marius Jansen and Gilbert Rozman (Princeton: Princeton University Press, 1986), 347-74.

8. Naitō Akira, "Edo no machi to kenchiku," supplementary volume to *Edo zu byōbu,* ed. Suwa Haruo and Naitō Akira (Tokyo: Mainichi Shimbunsha, 1972), 24, gives an estimated range of 9-13 for average household size of the shogunal retainers. I suspect that this may be too high a figure.

9. I have accepted the estimate of Naitō Akira, ibid.

10. For a wonderfully revealing account of the life of a lower samurai of the shogun and his frequent dealings with non-samurai in late Edo, see Katsu Kokichi, *Musui's Story: The Autobiography of a Tokugawa Samurai*, trans. Teruko Craig (Tucson: University of Arizona Press, 1988).

11. David Asher Sitkin, "An Edo Satire: Hiraga Gennai's *Nenashigusa*" (Master's thesis, University of Hawaii, 1977), 89.

12. For a summary of this issue in English, see Kazuo Nakamura, "Eastern and Western Japan," in *Geography of Japan,* ed. Association of Japanese Geographers (Tokyo: Teikoku Shoin, 1980), 184-96.

13. See my "*Kyo ni inaka ari* versus *Rus in urbe*: City and Country in Japan and England," *Senri Ethnological Studies* 19 (1986), 34.

14. Saitō Osamu, "Scenes of Japan's Economic Development and the 'Longue Durée,'" *Bonner Zeitschrift fur Japanologie* 8 (1986), 15-27.

15. For an account of these disasters in the era of Tanuma, see John Whitney Hall, *Tanuma Okitsugu, 1719-1788: Forerunner of Modern Japan* (Cambridge, Mass.: Harvard University Press, 1955), 119-22.

16. I have drawn here on Nishiyama Matsunosuke, "Edokko," in *Edo chōnin no kenkyū,* ed. Nishiyama Matsunosuke (Tokyo: Yoshikawa Kōbunkan, 1973), 1:1-93, and Takeuchi Makoto, "Edo no chiiki kōzō to jūmin ishiki," in *Koza Nihon no hoken toshi*, ed. Toyoda Takeshi, Harada Tomohiko, and Yamori Kazuhiko (Tokyo: Bun'ichi Sōgō Shuppan, 1983) 2:291-316.

17. Nishiyama, "Edokko," 42-46.

18. Julian Franklyn, *The Cockney—A Survey of London Life and Language* (London: André Deutsch, 1953). For more on the comparison of the Edokko and Cockney, see my "Tokyo and London: Comparative Conceptions of the City," in *Japan: A Comparative View*, ed. Albert Craig (Princeton: Princeton University Press, 1979), 82-87.

19. For the important role of firemen in building Edo's identity in the early nineteenth century, see William Kelly, "Incendiary Actions in Edo: Fires and Firefighting in the Shogun's Capital and the People's City," in *Edo and Paris: The State, Political Power, and Urban Life in Two Early-Modern Societies*, ed. James L. McClain, John M. Merriman, and Ugawa Kaoru (Ithaca: Cornell University Press, forthcoming).

20. In putting forth this argument, Nishiyama provides a useful summary of different interpretations in the literature on the Edokko; see idem, "Edokko," 3-14.

21. Nishiyama Matsunosuke et al., eds., *Edogaku jiten* (Tokyo: Kōbundō, 1984), 580-81.

22. For more on this issue, see my "From Edo to Tokyo," 365-67, and Saitō, *Shōka no sekai, uradana no sekai*, 124-32.

23. For a study of epidemic disease in Tokugawa Japan, see Ann Bowman Jannetta, *Epidemics and Mortality in Early Modern Japan* (Princeton: Princeton University Press, 1987).

24. Takeuchi, "Edo no chiiki kōzō to jūmin ishiki," 295.

25. Robert Leutner, *Shikitei Sanba and the Comic Tradition in Edo Fiction* (Cambridge, Mass.: Harvard University Press, 1985), 158.

26. Ibid., 137.

27. For a fuller discussion of Edo publishing in a comparative context, see my "The History of the Book in Edo and Paris," in McClain, *Edo and Paris*.

28. Many senryū have been translated into English by R. H. Blyth; see *Senryū: Japanese Satirical Verses* (The Hokuseido Press, 1949) and *Japanese Life and Character in Senryū* (The Hokuseido Press, 1960). For an outline of the history of Edo senryū, see Hamada Giichiro, *Edo senryū jiten* (Tokyo: Tokyōdō, 1968), 507-37.

29. On jitsuroku, see Peter Kornicki, "The Enmeiin Affair of 1803: The Spread of Information in the Tokugawa Period," *Harvard Journal of Asiatic Studies* 42 (December 1982), 503-33.

30. For details of this process, see Kobayashi Tadashi, "Daishō-goyomi to egoyomi no kōansha," in *Genshoku ukiyo-e dai-hyakka jiten* (Tokyo: Taishukan Shoten, 1982), 3: 109-18.

31. Barbara Ruch, "Medieval Jongleurs and the Making of a National Literature," in *Japan in the Muromachi Age*, ed. John W. Hall and Toyoda Takeshi (Berkeley: University of California Press, 1977), 286.

32. For the origins of *rakugo*, see Nobuhiro Shinji, *Rakugo wa ika ni shite keisei sareta ka* (Tokyo: Heibonsha, 1986).

33. Leutner, *Shikitei Sanba*, 11.

34. I have written in greater detail about Keisai and his work, particularly his panoramic views of Edo and all Japan, in "World Without Walls: Kuwagata Keisai's Panoramic Vision of Japan," in *Japan and the World—Essays on Japanese History and Politics in Honour of Ishida Takeshi*, ed. Gail Bernstein and Haruhiro Fukui (London: Macmillan, 1988), 3-19.

35. For a list of all Keisai's book illustrations and paintings, see Ozawa Hiromu, "Tsuyama-han kakae-eshi Kuwagata Keisai Shoshin no kenkyu josetsu," *Chōfu Nihon bunka* 1 (March 1991), 100-14.

36. Harry Harootunian, *Things Seen and Unseen: Discourse and Ideology in Tokugawa Nativism* (Chicago: Chicago University Press, 1988).

37. These points are emphasized in Uchida Ginzō, "'Kinsei shokunin-zukushi e-kotoba' o megutte," *Ukiyo-e geijutsu* 104 (1992), 3-12.

38. Andrew Markus, *The Willow in Autumn: Ryūtei Tanehiko, 1783-1842* (Cambridge, Mass.: Harvard University Press, 1992), ch. 4.

The Literature of Wit and Humor in Late-Eighteenth-Century Edo

Haruko Iwasaki

To appreciate fully the popular art in Edo of the Temmei (1781-89) and Kansei (1789-1801) eras, we must first come to grips with a paradox in the cultural world of the time. At the mid-point of its 260-year history, the Tokugawa regime still held firmly to its hierarchical system, based on Neoconfucian principles. Yet in the diverse range of social and cultural activities, an unprecedented degree of interaction was taking place, especially in large cities. As a result, any study focused on one area of culture alone—be it a visual, literary, or theatrical art—seriously undercuts its effectiveness.

This interaction involved almost all forms of popular arts, entertainment, and scholarship. The visual and literary arts, in particular, developed an almost symbiotic relationship. The kabuki theater and the licensed pleasure quarters of Yoshiwara exerted a dominant influence over the rest of the cultural world. Various disciplines of scholarship, especially the newly rising "national studies" (*kokugaku*) and western studies (*rangaku*), enriched the popular culture with whole new sets of ideas and materials.

Such interaction among the arts was paralleled by an equally vigorous interaction among the people who produced them. Central to this ferment were writers and poets of the samurai class, including some leading scholars of the time. Participation of the ruling classes may also be found, albeit in discreet ways, in the occasional presence of daimyo family members and of high-ranking officials of both *bakufu* and domain governments, as well as members of such great merchant houses as Mitsui. On the lower end of the strata were commoners from all walks of life. Publishers, ukiyo-e artists, actors, and entertainers were most visible, and around them flocked pornographers, speculators, and small-business owners of all sorts. Wives and daughters of these men also joined in. Renowned courtesans of the pleasure quarters often graced the various cultural scenes. The participants in this culture also varied widely in age. While those in their twenties and thirties were the most active, teenagers and the elderly were involved as well.

Despite such discrepancies of rank, gender, age, occupation, and artistic persuasion, these men and women mingled freely in a remarkably egalitarian atmosphere. The primary locus of their activities was in the frequent "theme parties" that centered on a multiplicity of arts. The scale of the gatherings varied. More traditional parties, such as *waka* competitions or *haikai* gatherings, tended to involve a relatively small group of like-minded participants, whereas *kyōka* parties, which often served as the umbrella for multi-generic parties, mobilized a far greater crowd. In the Temmei years, when kyōka became the rage of Edo, popular hosts could attract over a hundred participants from all forms of the popular arts. This diversity and freedom led to fruitful exchanges of all sorts. Ideas, topics, and themes were tossed back and forth among the guests. Connections were made and business deals struck. Verses, prose, and sketches produced during the event were often collected, edited, and published. The parties and other gatherings thus came to function as the marketplace of talents and ideas in literature, the performing and visual arts, scholarship, business, and even politics.

Two traditions played major roles in promoting such interactions. One was that of group art. From the earliest eras of Japanese history, many forms of the arts, including literature, were produced and consumed in a group setting. The exchange of waka poems constituted an essential means of communication among lovers, friends, and families. From the Heian Period on, verses were also produced in poetry competitions known as *uta-awase*, in which poets divided in two groups engaged in the game of poetry matches. In medieval Japan, the group composition of linked verse, or *renga*, became the dominant poetical practice, often combined with another form of group art, the tea ceremony. By the Edo Period, the group mode of composition was again reinforced by the rising popularity of the casual form of linked verse known as haikai.

Popular arts in late-eighteenth-century Edo incorporated many of the practices of group poetry, especially haikai. Most gatherings were held on a specific occasion, at a specific time, and at a specific location. Clear demarcation of time and space helped to separate the event from the quotidian world outside. During the event, constant efforts were made to promote the group spirit and fusing of minds. Avoidance of socially differential language, names, and clothing all helped to create the feeling of egalitarianism.

Another tradition that encouraged cultural interaction in late Edo was the literati (*bunjin*) life-style, adapted from the Chinese tradition of *wenren*. The idea of a broadly cultivated gentleman-ruler appealed first to samurai intellectuals, who were generally underutilized and bored. The increasingly fashionable bunjin pose then spread to literate members of the townsmen class, who by then had attained a high level of urban sophistication and literacy. One key bunjin qualification that profoundly influenced the popular culture of late Edo was versatility. The primary area of learning was, of course, Confucianism. To qualify as a bunjin, however, one also had to be accomplished—or at least knowledgeable—in any number of arts. A classic example is the high-ranking samurai bureaucrat Yanagihara Kien (1706-1758), who, while serving the daimyo of Kōriyama Province, boasted "professional expertise" in as many as sixteen different arts. In addition to Neoconfucian learning, these included Buddhist studies, herbology, calligraphy, drawing, and seal carving.

By the late eighteenth century, the image of a diversely talented, smoothly polished intellectual had gained much popularity, while the once-admired ideal of the samurai as single-mindedly devoted to the martial arts had become a popular target of ridicule. At the same time, the spheres of operation for the self-styled Japanese literati expanded to include the popular urban arts of townsmen, such as kabuki, *jōruri*, popular music, and parodic poetry. Diversity of talent, sometimes bordering on reckless dabbling, thus became a norm rather than the exception among sophisticated urbanites in the Temmei Period. An ukiyo-e artist, for example, may well have been bred in haikai poetry and have dabbled in kyōka, and was likely to be a connoisseur of popular theater and music. By the same token, a well-known samurai scholar could also write novellas on courtesans and compose pornographic classics, while demonstrating his artistic skill with occasional illustrations. Needless to say, such diverse expertise contributed much to the interaction among the arts and artists. It gave rise to the creativity of the individual artist, while a broad interest in and knowledge of so many arts fostered cross-disciplinary exchanges among the artists themselves.

Another impact of bunjin culture is seen in the proliferation of pseudonyms. It was customary for a bunjin to use a different name (or names) for each art he practiced. In composing poems in classical Chinese, for example, the poet usually signed a sinified pen name, consisting of three Chinese characters. When composing in comic mode, he would prefer a humorous and often self-mocking nom de plume. Names for painting and music usually indicated the artistic lineage of the artist or composer. The pseudonyms and genres of art thus tended to be matched and kept apart. This also meant that practitioners' proper names, whether as samurai or as owners of well-established shops, were neatly segregated from their "playful" activities.

Such compartmentalization of lives through pseudonyms seems to have helped their users to escape temporarily the constraints of a tightly controlled society. In some cases, pseudonyms were a real necessity. Men and women of high standing needed them to conceal their official identities. More frequently, however, people seem to have engaged in a kind of collusion for the duration of an artistic event. Although fully aware of one another's real identity, each member of a group acted as though he or she occupied no other place than the one activated at the time. Through this process of pretending, the participants were able to protect their formal identity and engage fully in the artistic exchange regardless of their relative social status, age, and sex.

Literature and the Visual Arts

From early times, Japanese literature maintained close ties with the pictorial arts. Famous works of fiction, such as *The Tale of Genji*, continued to inspire pictorial versions in scrolls and prints. Poetry, too, formed a part of visual art by the insistence on the use of elegant paper and accomplished calligraphy. In the communal culture of the late Edo Period, this interdependence deepened to create some hybrid genres, in which text and images are inseparably fused.

The growth of ukiyo-e was the single most significant factor in this symbiotic development. Prints by Suzuki Harunobu (1725?-1770), for example, owe much to the interaction within one particularly prolific haikai group in Edo, which often met at poetry gatherings in the 1760s. Affluent samurai poets of the group provided the financial backing, while the haikai technique of *mitate* (parody or allusion, as described below) added a new complexity to Harunobu's art. In addition, the samurai technologist and poet Hiraga Gennai reportedly advised Harunobu in developing the technique for his famous multicolor prints (*nishiki-e*, or "brocade pictures").

Increase in such group activities in the cultural world of Edo eventually led to an extraordinary degree of mutual innovation among various arts. In art and literature, the technical advances in woodblock printing expanded the significance of illustration. Haikai poets, for example, showed an increasing interest in *ebaisho* (illustrated haikai collections), a hybrid genre that gained popularity in the early eighteenth century. Before long, pictures gained as much significance as the accompanying verses, sometimes even surpassing them. The luxuriant *Treasures of the Sea* (Umi no sachi, 1762), for instance, is known today not so much for the quality of its verses as for its elegant illustrations by Katsuma Ryūsui. Talented artists thus cultivated and profited from the patronage of haikai groups.

In addition to the well-known case of Harunobu, the senior artist Toriyama Sekien wove similar ties with another haikai group, formed in the Edo residence of a daimyo. The founder of the Kitao School and prolific illustrator, Kitao Shigemasa (1739-1820), was also known under his haikai pen name of Karan, evidence that he himself had tried his hand at haikai composition. Given such barrier-crossing interests, it seems no accident that artists like Sekien and Shigemasa spawned disciples deeply involved in hybrid arts. Sekien's most illustrious student, Kitagawa Utamaro, later produced the *Picture Book of Selected Insects* (Ehon mushi erami, 1788) and other exquisite illustrated collections, not of haikai but of kyōka. Sekien is also known to have taught Koikawa Harumachi, the creator of the major hybrid art of *kibyōshi*. Shigemasa's foremost student, Kitao Masanobu, came to be better known as the brilliant writer and illustrator Santō Kyōden.

In prose literature, the emergence of the genre of fiction known as kibyōshi ("yellow-cover books," after their appearance) was doubtless the most important event in combining the arts of text and pictures. As an artistically inclined samurai youth, Koikawa Harumachi enjoyed haikai with his master and his colleagues, occasionally attempting pictorial illustration. In the mid-1770s, he began exploiting the format of illustrated storybooks for children to offer a lighthearted satire of the fashionable scene in contemporary Edo. The resultant kibyōshi, *The Dreams of Glory of Master Glitter* (Kinkin-sensei eiga no yume, 1775), instantly captivated urban readers with its effervescent mix of contemporary satire and elegant new style of ukiyo-e illustration. Kibyōshi quickly grew into a major genre in Edo, eventually comprising over two thousand titles in its thirty-year history.

The attraction of kibyōshi, which closely resemble modern comic books, lies in the complex interaction between the text and the illustrations. In conventional illustrated fiction, pictures and text occupied separate spaces, and told essentially the same story side by side. In kibyōshi, however, pictures and text are entwined. Spatially, the narrative text fills any convenient patch left by the images, while the dialogues are wrapped around the speakers. The stories told in the text and those represented by the pictures supplement and enhance each other. At times, details in the pictures conceal satirical messages that would have incurred censorship if articulated in the text; at others the pictorial story might subtly conflict with the narrative to create ironic or satirical effects.

Such mingling of language and images required the closest possible collaboration between writer and artist. It is not surprising that some of the best kibyōshi writers, such as Harumachi and Kyōden, were also professional artists who could do their own illustrations. Another witty kibyōshi writer was Nandaka Shiran, who doubled as the popular ukiyo-e artist Kubo Shumman. In the majority of the cases, however, kibyōshi writers and illustrators were separate people who depended heavily on each other. The writer needed to commission artists to illustrate their texts, while many artists—especially beginners—needed the patronage of writers to get experience in the big kibyōshi market.

In the collaborative process of creating kibyōshi, the writer provided sketches for the illustrations and indicated the layout of the accompanying text. After close consultation with the writer, the artist turned both image and text into the finished product. The implication of such a practice is that competent kibyōshi writers had to have a visual imagination with which to calculate the total effect of the layout on the story. Artists, for their part, needed to be reasonably well versed in literature, theater, and many other areas of popular culture. Through experience and practice, the translation of literary elements into visual composition must have become a mental habit.

In poetry, a similar confluence with visual art developed. We have already noted that haikai and ukiyo-e were weaving an ever closer relationship. In the 1780s, when a boom in kyōka exploded in the city of Edo, a comparable phenomenon occurred in an even more intensified form. Just as haikai poets had evocative sketches grace their anthologies, so various groups of kyōka poets collaborated with ukiyo-e artists and publishers to bring out luxuriously illustrated collections. Many were bound in book format (*kyōka ehon*), while still more appeared as single-sheet surimono. These publications, especially those in the surimono format, served as handsome gifts for New Year's and other special occasions. Today, the best of them—by Utamaro or Masanobu, for example—rank among the priceless legacies of Edo culture.

Shukō: The Organizing Device of Edo Art

The newly created hybrid arts of late-eighteenth-century Edo shared a certain brand of light humor. Wit, irony, and a parodic stance marked the product, so that the humor had a definitely cerebral quality. In many cases, the humor lay in riddles that demanded a considerable degree of sophistication on the part of readers and viewers. Such characteristics must be understood in relation to a distinctive underlying structural strategy found in many works of the era. Typically, this involves a doubling structure, whereby the main story or image represents the current scene, but almost always has some classical tale or situation superimposed over it. The audience's pleasure derived from identifying the disparate elements and appreciating the skill with which this fusion was executed and the ironic juxtapositions it occasioned.

This dual structure did not emerge overnight in the Temmei era, but was deeply rooted in a well-established artistic convention known as *shukō*. No single English word can translate its meaning, since shukō takes widely varied forms in different kinds of art. Roughly speaking, however, shukō is a way of amplifying the dimension of the contemporary elements by connecting them in some way with the old. A wide range of creative devices were used to connect a new verse, story, image, or other artistic production to well-known stories, events, situations, or other pre-existing elements.

Having its origin in waka and haikai poetry, shukō found its way into puppet and kabuki theaters, where it became the major organizing device. The given element from the past to be exploited through shukō became known as the *sekai*, or "sphere." About 150 famous tales and events entered the list of appropriate sekai. Once every fall, the producer, the star, and the scriptwriter for a given theater gathered for "sphere-setting" (*sekai-sadame*)—selecting specific tales to serve as sekai for the following year's productions. A scriptwriter would take the larger-than-life background of sekai and bring it to life by using his new stories in ways that would please current taste and make the most of the stars' talents.

Since a shukō was meant to create novelty and surprise, the actual linking contrivances tended to be extremely diverse. It may be helpful, however, to distinguish the following major types: *naimaze* (or *hamemono*), *mitate*, *fukiyose*, and *jiguchi*. Most commonly used in fiction, drama, and other storytelling genres, naimaze entwines two or more unrelated stories. Usually, a situation taken from an old story serves as sekai, while the other story treats the contemporary world. If the new tale is entwined with a Chinese story, the technique is called hamemono, or "fitting in." Whatever the sources, many naimaze and hamemono fictions freely resorted to the trick of double identity to connect the disparate tales. Thus a thoroughly contemporary hero might suddenly elevate his petty street scuffle to a higher level at an opportune moment simply by declaring, "Well, in fact, I am really... (*Jitsu wa*...)," revealing that he was carrying out the vendetta in a famous samurai saga of centuries past. Total lack of plausibility presented no problem to an Edo audience who willingly accepted this expedient convention.

Another popular shukō, mentioned earlier, was mitate, which exploited the convention of double identity even more fully. However, in contrast to the plot orientation of naimaze, mitate is essentially a visual technique (the term itself meaning "view and construct"), which evokes the duality through images. Needless to say, mitate was the technique of choice for many ukiyo-e artists. As Tadashi Kobayashi's essay in this catalogue richly demonstrates, mitate became one of the most fruitful conventions for Suzuki Harunobu and later artists. The overt image of the figures in such works is contemporary—a courtesan or actor, for example—but some clever detail in the scene connotes another, more classical, identity. Here again, the most unlikely combinations of identities were preferred in order to create a sense of surprise.

While naimaze and mitate brought together only two or three tales or images, fukiyose was a "blowing together" of a number of well-known but again totally unrelated tales or characters. This was done by finding and highlighting one little element shared by them all. The impulse to take a handful of independent items and assemble them into a set may also be seen more broadly in late Edo culture. Since its structure differs somewhat from that of fukiyose, we might tentatively call this approach "packaging." The process may simply consist of presenting people or objects in numbered sets, such as "A Competing Duo of Eastern Beauties," "A Triptych of Eastern Scholars," or "One Hundred Views of Mount Fuji." In a similar vein, the names and images of a well-known classical grouping could be superimposed on the corresponding number of contemporary people or items. When presented visually, most "packaging" overlapped with mitate.

In part for marketing advantage, packaging with or without mitate conceits became a great favorite in the visual arts. The popular groups favored by ukiyo-e artists for mitate prints were the Four Devas (*shitennō*), the Six Immortals of Poetry (*rokkasen*), the Seven Gods of Good Fortune (*shichifukujin*), and so on. Kibyōshi mobilized all of these, as well as many variations of the drama *The Storehouse of Loyal Retainers* (Kanadehon Chūshingura, 1748), and the newly popular Nagasaki style of Chinese cuisine (*shippoku ryōri*), which was set for four guests. Some ambitious non-mitate series in ukiyo-e prints are such masterpieces as Hokusai's book *One Hundred Views of Mount Fuji* (Fugaku hyakkei, 1834-35), and Hiroshige's single-sheet series *One Hundred Famous Views of Edo* (Meisho Edo hyakkei, 1856-58).

Of other nonvisual groupings, the Japanese obsession with ranking found a congenial format adopted from ranking lists of prostitutes (*hyōbank*i) and sumō wrestlers (*banzuke*). These tongue-in-cheek and often irreverent extensions of the ranking-list format were devised for a great variety of groups—scholars, officials, poets, popular writers, entertainers, restaurants, fashionable foods, clothing, insects, plants, and coins, among others. Ranking lists of females included, in addition to the predictably numerous listings of beauties, such surprising categories as wives of actors and female restaurateurs.

The last major group of shukō were those that parodically engaged themselves with language. *Jiguchi* consisted of puns and other forms of language play, while *kojitsuke* involved the provision of outrageously distorted etymologies for words or tongue-in-cheek explications of the origins of place names, commercial products, virtues, and so on, mostly through language play. They could work as grouping devices by assuming the form of a dictionary or glossary.

All told, shukō was a diverse and freely overlapping group of conventions that present great challenges to scholars of Edo literature and art today. The main difficulty is in its fluidity. Precisely because each one has to be a new twist on the old, it is useless to try to impose a single definition over the constantly shifting manifestations of shukō. The important point to bear in mind is its basic structural principle, in order to be able to anticipate its presence underlying so many of the various cultural patterns of the late Edo Period. This is why narrow scrutiny of one genre or aspect often proves futile. Far more profitable is an interdisciplinary approach in which images, tales, and language of many genres may be instantly recalled and cross-matched to deepen the appreciation of specific artistic products.

Ōta Nampo

This exhibition pays special attention to two cultural figures active in turn-of-the-century Edo, Ōta Nampo (1749-1823) and Santō Kyōden (1761-1816). Here, we shall outline their backgrounds and the particular contributions they made in bringing such brilliance to Edo's distinctive urban culture.

Anyone interested in the many-faceted popular culture of late Edo soon becomes aware of the somewhat puzzling preeminence enjoyed by the popular kyōka poet Ōta Nampo. His name comes up in countless places in the cultural history of the time. Journals and essays by his contemporaries are filled with admiring references to this samurai member of the literati; his deft prefaces and postscripts and, at times, his own brief but elegant contributions grace sundry contemporary works in verse, prose, the visual arts, or their hybrid forms; while the comments he made on a vast range of topics have been regarded as major sources for the era by generations of scholars. Without doubt, Ōta Nampo was a towering figure, even "a cultural hero of Edo," as one of his biographers put it.

Yet the exact nature of Nampo's fame remains elusive. His total literary output, as we can see in the recently published *Collected Works of Ōta Nampo*, does not seem to add up.[1] Nampo was an excellent kyōka poet, but not necessarily unequalled. Most of his prose consists of many fragmentary pieces, such as forewords and postscripts, composed on behalf of his numerous friends. Throughout his life he composed a large number of verses in classical Chinese, but most of them remained unpublished until recently. The remaining bulk of his copious writings consists of mere records of events.

I believe we can find the answer to our question when we look at Nampo's literary productions in context, rather than as isolated works. We must focus on his function in the network of relationships, both personal and artistic, that he wove around himself. To do this, we should consider the nature of the kyōka groups and try to understand how Nampo and a small group of friends sparked an explosive current among all aspects of popular culture of their time.

As Nampo himself later reminisced with irony, his involvement with popular culture began almost accidentally, through his teenage experiments with kyōka. Talented and ambitious, he had been studying at the academy of the poet-scholar Uchiyama Gatei, in the hopes of rising above his obscure station as a bakufu bureaucrat to become a true scholar. But the publication of his first parodic anthology when he was eighteen and its instant success effectively derailed Nampo from the proper path of a samurai scholar. As his samurai career stagnated, he became ever more deeply involved with other parodic poets and writers, and then with actors, artists, and various entertainers. He quickly found himself at the center of what was to become the popular-culture movement of the Temmei era.

The initial circumstances surrounding the young parodist and his friends largely determined the nature and the function of the cultural networks Nampo would later organize. The heterogeneity is clearly traceable to the early kyōka group, a handful of samurai students in Gatei's academy. When Nampo joined them, he brought with him a few lively *chōnin* poets, who in turn recruited more of their kind. This merging of classes created the particular mix of erudite humor and colorful street wit that would develop into the effervescence of the Temmei cultural scene.

A freewheeling pattern of activity was also set early, mostly by Nampo. In the beginning, the samurai student group followed the genteel traditions of poetry parties. The small group met among themselves and competed in composing poems—in this case, kyōka—around a set theme. Nampo and the more frivolous members of the group, however, took to reinventing the format. They combined these gatherings with other less scholarly activities, injecting an intensified parodic element, and expanded their operation by inviting artists of many other genres. Most of these events ended in merriment, each merrier than the one before.

Nampo's "Treasure Competition" (*Takara-awase*) of 1774 reflects this transformation in its early stages, when the scale of the group remained small. He and a handful of friends gathered in a temple on an appointed day in full ceremonial costume and each in turn recited a learned explication of a particular "miraculous treasure" that he had brought along. These reverently presented treasures were, in truth, worthless junk, and the explications were wild parodies of time-honored texts from diverse sources—fiction, poetry, dramas, legends, and even religious scripts. The pious format of the exhibit was in itself parodic. No less than three types of gatherings were lampooned: the ancient format of poetry competitions (*uta-awase*); the lucrative exhibits (*kaichō*) of "holy treasures" held by Buddhist temples in Edo; and the trendy "exhibits of natural resources" (*bussankai*) that had been developed by Nampo's friend Hiraga Gennai, a student of western science.

The other participants also deserve our attention. While all shared an interest in literature, these samurai and chōnin intellectuals held various occupations and specialties in real life. In addition to low-ranking samurai like Nampo and his schoolmates, the group included a distinguished scholar of Japanese classics, a minor bookseller who published the *Record of the Treasure Competition* (Takara-awase no ki, 1774), and a neighborhood pharmacist who doubled as ukiyo-e artist, joke writer, and pornographer. There was also a town marshal and possibly a Shinto priest. As the *Record* relates, the motley crowd spent a languid spring day playing the congenial parody game they had invented.

Another important aspect of the party was the new role played by the publisher. Judging from his preface in the *Record*, he seems to have taken an active part in conceiving, preparing, and executing the event. Afterward, he gathered all the "explications," commissioned an attending artist to sketch all the exhibited items, and published the material in a slim, elegantly illustrated volume as a record of the entire proceedings. Such participatory involvements by publishers and artists were to become a basic pattern in many kyōka parties over the following decade.

With the passing years, Nampo's off-duty life in popular culture grew ever busier, while his rank in the bakufu's lowest group of retainers remained exactly the same. Now widely known as one of Edo's most popular kyōka poets, Nampo enlarged his circle of friends to include people of status and fame. Sons of daimyo and highly placed officials of both bakufu and domain governments often invited the wit to regale them at their table. Nampo's new friends also came from the two glittering worlds of entertainment, the kabuki theater and the Yoshiwara pleasure quarter. The glamour of such figures as the leading Edo actor, Ichikawa Danjūrō, and renowned courtesans of the major Yoshiwara houses drew ever wider attention to Nampo's kyōka parties. By the Temmei era, various cultural events promoted by his group could mobilize over a hundred participants.

Throughout this process, Nampo was always at the heart of the movement as its indisputable leader. Contemporary comments on him explain at least a part of this preeminence. The depth and breadth of his learning, evident even in his most flippant poetry, commanded respect from many elite intellectuals in many different fields. His convivial warmth, so free of affectation, attracted men and women of all classes, from the most humble of chōnin to the members of daimyo families.

The most essential element of Nampo's power, however, was his ability to deal with the group. He was a uniquely talented organizer. He not only attracted people, but happily made efforts to strengthen and enrich the ties among them. At the same time, he valued spontaneity. Unlike many of his friends who eagerly formed their own sects, he never attempted to bind his fans and followers into formal groups. Instead, his networks thrived on his creative orchestration. Extant notices, letters, and records of various parties indicate that this process was a complex one. It consisted first of devising an event for a specific occasion. Next, the appropriate theme and location had to be set, and genres and arts specified. After the guests had been selected, food and drink had to be arranged and funded. The guests also needed to be coordinated to balance spontaneity and cohesion, creativity and form. After the party, the host usually collected whatever artistic products it yielded, whether verses, prose, or pictures. More efforts at coordination followed when the results were edited and illustrated for publication.

The exact nature and extent of Nampo's contribution to particular events are difficult to ascertain, since so much of this process was carried out in the name of a group of people. But the record of some early parties show that when Nampo was chiefly in charge, he managed all aspects of the events with great energy, competence, and creativity. Even during later parties, at which he tended to remain in the background, the hosts often indicated how essential his presence was in formulating and executing the events. But the most eloquent testimony of his talent comes from the parties themselves. Many of the ones presided over by Nampo were remembered as phenomenal successes, and many resulted in multi-art anthologies, often illustrated by major ukiyo-e artists. Clearly he had the special talents necessary to turn the stilted tradition of poetry parties into great cultural events.

Santō Kyōden

A generation younger than most of Nampo's early kyōka friends, the popular writer Santō Kyōden (1761-1816), known as an ukiyo-e artist under the name Kitao Masanobu, represents the second wave of urban talents who joined the ever widening circle of popular Edo culture. Mostly of chōnin class, these aspirants were taking proud notice of what had always been their own culture, now glamorized by the playful involvement of eminent samurai intellectuals. As the indulged son of a comfortably affluent townsman, Kyōden was steeped from childhood in the rich cultural mix of kabuki theater, ukiyo-e prints, popular music, and fiction. Heavy involvement with the Yoshiwara, which began in his teens and lasted a good part of his life, added the ultimate polish to this artist in language, clothing, manners, and the subtle arts of human relationships.

Kyōden's artistic career began early and developed rapidly. A teenage apprenticeship with the leading ukiyo-e artist Kitao Shigemasa soon led to a minor involvement with kibyōshi, first as an illustrator and then as a writer. These efforts yielded affiliations with a few of the humorists in Nampo's camp. Then, at the age of twenty, the neophyte delighted the world of popular fiction by his subtly constructed kibyōshi, *Your Favorite Mer-*

chandise (Gozonji no shōbaimono, 1782). He took an old format of the "battle of books," but projected over it a tongue-in-cheek sketch of contemporary events in publishing, notably the increasing dominance of the Edo literary world over its traditional competitors in Kyoto and Osaka. Nampo's generous praise for the work gained Kyōden's admission into the Nampo coterie, and established him as the most promising talent in contemporary popular fiction.

Once in the Nampo circle, Kyōden quickly absorbed the artistic values and practices of the group and, throughout his spectacular career as a writer-cum-artist, proved to be its most creative proponent. With the apt kyōka name Migaru no Orisuke (The Nimble Servant), Kyōden joined the major festivities of Nampo's group in 1783, including a birthday party for Nampo's mother and the second Treasure Competition. Thereafter he became a most faithful and productive participant of numerous theme parties hosted by the coteries of Nampo and others.

One memorable theme party that Kyōden himself helped to produce in 1784 illustrates the style that dominated the life of the young artist. Presided over jointly by Kyōden's teenage sister and by a famous Yoshiwara courtesan, the "Hand-towel Competition" (*Tanagui-awase*) drew nearly eighty participants from many areas of cultivation—kyōka poets, writers of popular fiction, publishers, ukiyo-e artists, kabuki entertainers, denizens of the Yoshiwara, and their princely patrons. The diverse cultural and social backgrounds of the participants converged in the witty designs of hand towels (a common accessory in Edo life, often dyed with indigo patterns). While visually striking, these patterns were in effect built as riddles. Many bridged image and language by way of visual-linguistic associations. The guests included several members of daimyo families, but their aristocratic identities were hidden in their aliases and in coded details of their towel designs.

This impulse toward diversity and confluence, so elegantly demonstrated in the Hand-towel Competition, would mark all aspects of Kyōden's career over the next three decades. He moved nimbly from one genre to another, from one medium to the next. Even when he was working in one medium or genre, he would incorporate elements from others. Being a writer-artist, he was a natural in all hybrid art forms, some of which were his own making. Just as he established himself as a major writer of kibyōshi, he renewed his emphasis on the visual, often combining it with literary, social, journalistic, and other interests. In 1784, for example, Tsutaya published Kyōden's seven-sheet set of portraits of famous courtesans, "A Competition Among the New Beauties of the Yoshiwara, Mirrored in Their Writing" (*Yoshiwara keisei shin bijin awase jihitsu kagami*, 1784), which is included in this exhibition. In this luxurious oversized album, Kyōden marked an early peak in his artistic career and also demonstrated his finesse as a reporter and promoter of Yoshiwara culture. Mobilizing details available only to an insider, he told the viewers tantalizing tales of the courtesans and their retinues in their own opulent surroundings. Even more effective were the New Year's poems that surround the portraits. These felicitous verses were all the more captivating for having been handwritten by the courtesans themselves.

Experiments with witty textile designs opened yet another realm of possibilities. The Hand-towel Competition of 1784 was just one example of this effort. In the same year, Kyōden also published a booklet entitled *Scraps of Patterns* (Komonzai), a playful collec-

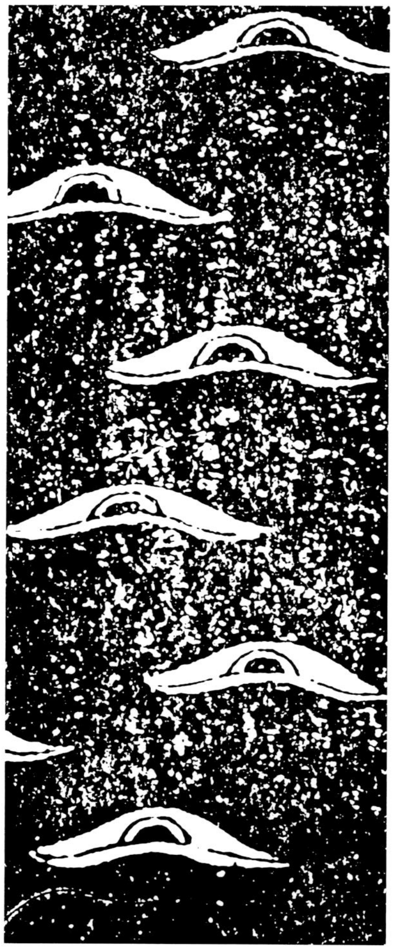

FIGURE I

tion of over a hundred textile patterns similar to the hand-towel designs. Evidently popular, similar collections of Kyōden patterns continued to be published in years to come. Bold and simple, these stylized patterns could serve as striking textile designs even today, but when combined with the title and brief explications, they revealed complex riddles about the city's culture.

Let us take a single example from *Scraps of Patterns*, the "Kumano Pattern" (Figure 1).[2] It is a design of squirming white objects on a black ground, accompanied by the comment, "This material is a piece of whale sash (*kujira-obi*) worn by the courtesan Nanasato." From this evidence, the viewer can begin the game of associations. In contemporary Edo fashion, a "whale sash" was a garment of black silk with white lining, so called because, like certain whales, it was black on top and white below. Kyōden goes one step further, however, and imposes a paisley-like pattern of small whale eyes. This in turn brings to mind the word "whale eye" (*kujira-me*), which any connoisseur of the kabuki theater would have known as the term for the small slits in the stage curtain that allow the backstage staff to spy on the audience. The sense of curious peeping evident in the eye pattern serves to strengthen this association. But then our vision can expand still further to imagine the pattern as a band of whales themselves, swimming in the ocean. This helps explain the title, "Kumano Pattern," since the Kumano area on the southern Kii Peninsula was the great center of whaling in those days, the Japanese equivalent of Nantucket or New Bedford. Finally, the image has the owner of the sash, the courtesan Nanasato. Those in the know would realize that she was from the house known as Yotsumeya, or "Four Eyes," while her name, literally "Seven Villages," recalled the proverb "When one whale is caught, seven villages profit." And, given Kyōden's expertise, it is likely that the real Nanasato in fact favored wearing a "whale sash."

In these years of the mid-1780s, Kyōden's work as a portrait artist expanded into the literary world to which he now belonged. He produced two works, *A Bookcase of Edo-style Kyōka* (Azumaburi kyōka bunko, 1786) and its expanded sequel, *A Sackful of Kyōka, Old and New* (Kokon kyōka bukuro, 1787), copies of both of which are included in this exhibition (Catalogue nos. III-10 and III-11). They constitute an illustrated Who's Who of the kyōka poets of the day, produced by the cooperative efforts of Nampo's circle. The calligraphy was in Nampo's own hand, and his ardent follower Yadoya no Meshimori took care of the editing. Predictably, the publisher was Tsutaya Jūzaburō. The fact that young Kyōden took the major role as the illustrator attests not only to his skill as an artist but also the centrality he quickly achieved in the kyōka community.

This new portrait project bore a resemblance to Kyōden's previously mentioned album of courtesan portraits, *Competition Among the New Beauties*, published two years earlier. Just as the one promoted the Yoshiwara, so the other promoted the world of kyōka, revealing and establishing its hierarchy. The format, too, was similar, both works containing a poem for every person depicted. In the *Bookcase*, these poems were kyōka—one for each of the fifty poets, a number that was doubled in the sequel of the next year. In execution of the portraits, however, these two volumes of kyōka poets appear to have closer ties to the textile designs in their coded details. Although the faces seem to have been realistically portrayed, curious aspects of hair styles, clothing, and accessories suggest the presence of mitate riddles. Many of these hinge on in-jokes and are now obscure, but well-informed contemporaries undoubtedly enjoyed identifying the disguises and deciphering the allusions.

In the latter half of the 1780s, Kyōden shifted his emphasis again. His productivity and popularity as a writer surged, and to keep up with the rising demand he all but ceased to illustrate other writers' works. His stronghold remained kibyōshi, in which he exposed human follies with one new shukō after another. *Playboy Grilled in Edo Style* (Edo umare uwaki no kabayaki, 1785), for example, is a comedy of human vanity that drives the protagonist, a self-appointed gallant by the name of Enjirō, to absurd extremes. Born with the face of a good-natured piglet, this spoiled son of a millionaire launches an all-out campaign to fulfill his singular ambition of becoming the greatest lady-killer in the Yoshiwara. He braves the tattooer's needles, suffers the tantrums of his wife (actually a woman hired for the purpose), becomes the theme of a current love ballad, and experiments with eloping with a courtesan. But all is for naught. The world detects that all the evidence of superior dandyism had been elaborately staged by Enjirō himself. This story line is given added punch by the illustrations, which are integral to the work, showing on every page the outrageous efforts of Enjirō being betrayed by his ever-present pig nose.

In a slightly later kibyōshi entitled *The Three Stripes: Patrons Styled in Fashionable Ueda Fabric* (Misujidachi kyaku no ki Ueda, 1787), Kyōden engages in his favorite technique of grouping. Three frequenters of the Yoshiwara try to outdo one another in devising novel tricks (shukō) for the game of love. One brings his small son to the Yoshiwara in order to appeal to the motherly instincts of his courtesan. The scheme works too well: the courtesan is so taken with the bed-wetting urchin that she promptly dumps his father, while the boy quickly falls for the luxuries of the Yoshiwara and soon bankrupts his dad.

The second man's trick is to spread his fame as a tragic lover. He selects and cultivates a courtesan whom a physiognomist has claimed to bear "signs of an impending early death." The man proceeds with elaborate preparations for her memorial, engraving a deluxe tombstone, printing memorial surimono, employing top singers to rehearse heartrending ballads, and even planning the menu for the wake. On the predicted day of her demise, just after he has added the final touch of himself taking the tonsure, he discovers that the woman has eloped with her young lover.

These disasters of the first two induce the third man to make artless devotion itself the "trick." But again things are carried to a ludicrous extreme. Although he could ransom his courtesan lover from the brothel at any time, he shuns such an easy path and continues to brave rain and snow to visit her—for decades! His grown children finally get fed up with the wrinkled lovers' quarrels and force the octogenarian prodigals into marriage.

As Kyōden established himself as the leading artist-writer of kibyōshi, he added another proof of versatility by easing into the other, relatively new genre of prose fiction known as *sharebon*, "books for the chic." Derived from published guides to the pleasure quarters, novellas of this genre coolly exposed the vanity and conceits of the patrons of the Yoshiwara, relying chiefly on dialogue. Here Kyōden proved himself as adept with his ears as with his eyes. Even in his early sharebon, such as *The Son's Room* (Musukobeya, 1785) and *The Great Houses of the Yoshiwara* (Sōmagaki, 1787), we see how his gift for visual detail is turned into vivid verbal descriptions of the manners and appearance of his characters. His finely tuned use of language, especially in dialogues, enhanced the sense of the reality of the men and women he portrayed. Toward the end of the 1780s, Kyōden had come to command as great a reputation in sharebon as he had already established in kibyōshi.

The Kansei Reforms and After

The death of the Shogun Ieharu in 1786 and the series of natural disasters that struck Japan in the mid-1780s culminated in the dismissal of Tanuma Okitsugu as the leader of the government, and the appointment of Matsudaira Sadanobu to the post of senior councilor. The stringent reforms that Sadanobu launched, and their impact on a wide range of Temmei culture, are a familiar part of Tokugawa history. The devastation took a particular toll on the samurai participants in popular culture. By summer's end in 1788, under increasing pressure from the bakufu authorities, Nampo had already announced his retirement from kyōka. Harumachi, who was apparently summoned in 1789 by Sadanobu for questioning, declined to appear and died shortly afterward, a possible suicide. Other major samurai writers, too, disappeared from the scene, never to resume their vigorous leadership over a broad range of popular culture.

The suppression soon extended to chōnin as well, although here the effects were less permanent than for samurai. Kyōden was fined in 1789 for illustrating a kibyōshi that lampooned Sadanobu's reforms. Although the sentence was light, Kyōden was intimidated enough to forswear all works of illustration thereafter. In 1791, however, he and his publisher, Tsutaya Jūzaburō, came into far more serious conflict with the law for trying to sell sharebon, which were now forbidden. Tsutaya had half of his property confiscated, while Kyōden was sentenced to fifty days in manacles.

The shock and pain of the suppression did not stop Kyōden or other chōnin artists from producing, but, in concert with changes in readership and the market, they helped to alter profoundly the nature of popular literature in the years to come. The lighthearted and cerebral kibyōshi gave way to thicker "combined volumes" (*gōkan*), which preserved the technique of integrated text and illustration, but now featured humorless and drawn-out tales of vendettas. The generally patronizing and didactic tone worked well with an increasingly popular audience, among whom numbered many women. Gōkan thus thrived as the mainstay of popular fiction until the very end of the Tokugawa regime. The other genre of fiction that came to popularity in the post-Kansei world was the more serious *yomihon*, "books for reading," which relied much more heavily on Chinese characters and were directed more toward a better-educated male audience.

Kyōden held on to his position as senior popular novelist in this new literary era, producing an impressive array of both gōkan and yomihon. But the tide was clearly turning. The grim, powerful world of the fantastic created by the gifted younger writer Takizawa Bakin slowly eroded the more delicate world of Kyōden. As though to compensate, Kyōden turned more and more to antiquarian studies—the ultimate gesture of this man who so longed to be a true bunjin. His *Collection of Antiques* (Kottōshū, 1815), which was completed shortly before his fatal heart attack in 1816, earned high words of praise from Nampo, who had himself returned to his scholarly origins. The age of Temmei wit and humor had come to an end.

NOTES

1. Hamada Giichirō, editor-in-chief, *Ōta Nampo zenshū*, 20 vols. (Tokyo: Iwanami Shoten, 1985-90).
2. From Tani Minezō, *Asobi no dezain: Santō Kyōden "Komon gawa"* (Tokyo: Iwasaki Bijutsusha, 1984), 142-43.

Ichikawa Danjūrō V and Kabuki's Golden Age

Laurence Kominz

In the eleventh month of 1770 a promising thirty-year-old actor received from his father the name Danjūrō. It was the most prestigious name in Edo kabuki, a name that assured its bearer fame and fortune, but also conferred upon him a heavy burden of expectations. An actor-evaluation book (*hyōbanki*) from 1771 describes Danjūrō V's first play, *Nue no mori ichiyo no mato* (A ray of sunlight illuminates the target in the forest of the chimera). The title alone suggests a magical time and place, and reading the hyōbanki entry transports us back to the splendor of kabuki in its golden age:

> It was a marvelous scene. On opening day the whole row of box seats on the west side of the theater shone brightly with lanterns adorned with Danjūrō's family crest. Danjūrō's well-wishers and supporters provided a lavish feast, and Danjūrō looked resplendent in his persimmon-colored robes, samurai cap, and bearing his great, long sword.[1]

In the first act Danjūrō played a superhero in the "Shibaraku" (Wait a moment) scene, a scene replete with bombast and swordplay. It was a scene first done by his great-grandfather, celebrational kabuki passed down to him through four generations of ancestors. The description of the play in the hyōbanki takes the form of a dialogue between the theater manager and a Danjūrō fan:

> *Manager*: When he shouted "Wait a moment!" twice, and rushed in, saving Yorimasa from that forced ritual suicide, it was very well done.
>
> *Fan*: Yes, we were worried before he shouted those critical lines. It was, after all, his biggest moment ever onstage, but when he pulled it off we were so relieved.
>
> *Manager*: And then the way he took out the brocade banner, sliced off the evil minister's head with a single sweep of his sword, and rescued Yorimasa—it was fabulous, just fabulous. Later, when Lady Tokiwa fell in love with him, he danced superbly in the drum-song duet. Next, he broke into Kiyomori's mansion when the tyrant was about to rape Tokiwa, beat up Kiyomori and killed Kiyomori's henchman. And it was a joy to behold Danjūrō retrieve the magical jewelled flute when it rose mysteriously up from the depths of the water.
>
> Yes, his acting was totally transformed from the days when he was Koshirō. The people all loved him, and presents and gifts rained down on the theater. There is no way to find fault with him for what he did in this show.[2]

Kabuki in the 1770s and 1780s: The Glory Days

The 1770s and 1780s are often called kabuki's golden age. In fact, more than any other time before or since, it was an age when kabuki penetrated every corner of Edo life. It was the age when Danjūrō came into his own as the cornerstone of the kabuki edifice in Edo; he himself not only created but was shaped by his times. As is evident in the above description of his debut, the kabuki stage of that era was a glorious world of fantasy, romance, intrigue, and villainy, of lavish costumes and innovative and imaginative stage tricks, a showcase for the best and newest forms of music and dance, and, above all, a place to commune with fabulously popular actors. Plays would change considerably during the last decade of the eighteenth century, primarily because of a new attack mounted on kabuki by Japan's samurai rulers, but the ingenious actors and playwrights of kabuki found ways to avoid the retrenchment that the government sought to force on theater, and instead expanded in new artistic directions.

During kabuki's golden age, playwrights were stage magicians whose job was to enable fantasies of the mind and the page to be converted into corporal reality onstage. Namiki Shozō (1730-1773) set the precedent, creating plays on a grand scale and inventing mechanisms that brought flights of imagination to life in the plays: the revolving stage; cables and hoists that enabled actors to fly; hinged roofs that opened to reveal action inside buildings; huge trapdoors that made whole scenes appear or disappear almost instantaneously.

FIGURE I
Courtesy of Honolulu Academy of Art

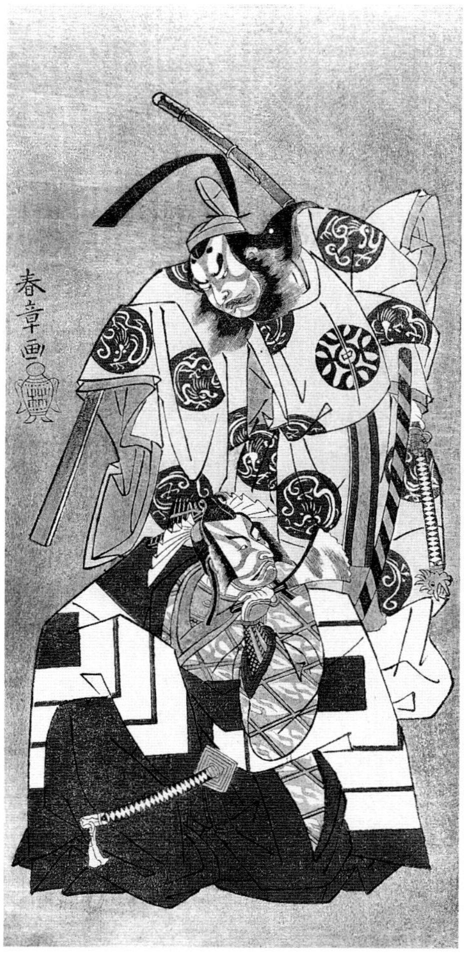

Plays moved at a fast pace, with frequent changes of scene, tempo, and mood. Leading actors usually played two or three roles in a single play, and characters sometimes had to shed one or more disguises before their true identities were revealed. Scripts were crafted with a light touch; plots abounded in love affairs, intrigue, and martial conflict; and plays were written to facilitate the presentation of virtuoso performances of music and dance.

In the mid- to late eighteenth century, Edo abounded in musical talent. Singers and *shamisen* players teamed up to present long romantic ballads and short love songs. The best of them developed their own styles and attracted crowds of devotees who came to listen or to learn to sing and play themselves (Catalogue no. V-21). These groups founded schools of music that might endure for many decades, or might pass away with the death of the master. In late-eighteenth-century Edo, the two most popular musical styles were *tokiwazu* (still performed today) and *tomimoto*, and kabuki playwrights included dance scenes in their plays to be accompanied by the leading musicians of the two schools. These musicians were so popular they were placed on center stage, on a dais just behind the actors. In these *degatari* scenes (Catalogue no. V-11), musicians were more prominent than ever on the kabuki stage.

In early kabuki, dance had been the province of the *onnagata*, the actors who specialized in playing women's roles, but that changed during the golden age. Nakamura Nakazō (1736-1790; Figure 1, standing), kabuki's greatest rags-to-riches success story, turned dance into an art that could establish the popularity and enhance the reputation of leading actors of male parts. Long and complex dance dramas then became possible.

The gala event of the year-long Edo kabuki calendar was *kaomise*, or the "face showing," when each of the three Edo theaters organized a special performance to exhibit the new actors they had hired for the coming year. It took place in the eleventh month (midwinter), which was the kabuki new year. Kaomise shows were a splendid interweaving of drama, dance, and ceremony. Group dances and pantomimes put large numbers of actors onstage together, creating a rare spectacle, and leading actors were given scenes that displayed their looks and talents to extra advantage.

It was during the kaomise season, more than any other, that Danjūrō V stood head and shoulders above his peers in Edo kabuki. It did not matter which theater had hired him; almost every year, in the eleventh month, he would paint his face with bold red stripes and don the immense persimmon-colored robes that in Ichikawa family tradition represented a samurai superhero. This was for the playlet "Shibaraku," which he had done for the first time in his Danjūrō debut. Every year he performed a different character in a different play, but the essence of the "Shibaraku" scene was always the same (Catalogue nos. V-5 and V-7). It was so archetypal in its popularity that its appeal seemed inexhaustible, as unfailingly popular to Edoites as car-chase scenes are to American movie audiences.

In the "Shibaraku" scene, a powerful and high-ranking villain and his grotesque henchmen have captured a powerless and virtuous victim (or victims). The innocent victims are about to be tortured or executed when a great voice bellows "*Shibaraku*! (Wait a moment!)" from behind the *hanamichi* curtain. Danjūrō, as the hero, enters on the hanamichi and stops just short of the stage. His presence freezes the villains. The hero presents a bellicose monologue, which serves as a self-introduction for both the actor and the character in the play. The monologue usually included references to Danjūrō's exalted ancestry, often contained humorous puns and jokes, and sometimes mentioned other actors and real-life events. Finally the hero moves onto the main stage. He prepares for action by pulling off his upper garment, then, drawing his seven-foot long sword, lops off the heads of the villains' henchmen in a single sweep. His ferocious glare cows the main villain into inaction, and the victims are saved. All strike a climactic pose and the playlet comes to an end.

"Shibaraku" was one of a number of plays and scenes in the *aragoto* tradition, first performed by Danjūrō V's ancestors, Danjūrō I (1660-1704) and Danjūrō II (1688-1758). *Aragoto* means "wild acting," and all aragoto heroes are valiant fighters: some, like the Shibaraku hero, are powerfully martial in appearance and demeanor, others are romantic swashbucklers, and some are imbued with the power of fierce Buddhist deities. Danjūrōs I and II had established their dominance of Edo kabuki by performing aragoto roles extensively, but in the 1750s and 1760s, in the time of Danjūrō V's father (Danjūrō IV), this was no longer possible. Kabuki had entered the age of the *kaneru yakusha*, the "versatile actor" who could dance and act and play villains, amorous young men, and samurai heroes to equal acclaim. Danjūrō V was a man of his times and a consummate kaneru yakusha. He played in far more numerous and more varied roles than any of his Danjūrō forebears, and prided himself on his versatility and flexibility as an actor. The only role he performed regularly was his kaomise "Shibaraku" hero.

The golden age of kabuki saw similar trends in the development of the onnagata's art. Again the public demanded both virtuosity and versatility of its great stars. The result was a move toward greater professionalism—training, study, and research of roles became paramount where in previous generations leading onnagata had written that the most important form of preparation was to live and act like a woman in one's daily, offstage life.

The twin grand champions of the Edo onnagata world were Iwai Hanshirō IV (1747-1800) and Segawa Kikunojō III (1751-1810). Hanshirō vastly broadened the range of female types that a leading onnagata could use to build his career. He invented the art of playing evil and scheming leading women, and was the first leading onnagata to play a low-class whore.[3] Kikunojō made his reputation in dance and in playing multiple female roles. His popularity was immense and he became fabulously wealthy. At his peak he made fifteen hundred *ryō* a year at the theater, an unprecendented sum for an onnagata, and supplemented his salary with endorsements of cosmetics, fabric dyes, hair ornaments, tea, and other consumer products.[4]

The onnagata of the era reflected the trends and fashions of the Yoshiwara courtesans and the newly popular geisha, and sometimes portrayed popular contemporary woman entertainers on stage. But onnagata were believed to epitomize feminine beauty and charm, and were themselves often leaders of women's fashion. This perhaps seems incongruous to westerners, but the Japanese have always admired dedication and effort, and none in Edo-period Japan had to work harder at being beautiful and charming women than did the men who played them on the kabuki stage, under the gaze of thousands of critical eyes. By the same token, from the Edo Period on, Japanese consumers have been of a practical bent. They want evidence that products will work for them. This partially explains the popularity of onnagata endorsements for beauty and fashion products. If a certain brand of make-up could help make even a paunchy middle-aged man look like a charming young maiden, women consumers had every right to expect splendid results when they used the same brand. The beautiful courtesan Hanaōgi needed less artistic enhancement than did Kikunojō.

Product endorsements such as Kikunojō's were only one of many ways that kabuki penetrated the daily lives of Edoites at the end of the eighteenth century. Kabuki had a visual presence all over the city, thanks to the black-and-white play advertisements (*tsuji banzuke*) pasted on building walls, and to the newly invented multicolor ukiyo-e prints (*nishiki-e*) that shopkeepers and private citizens used in decorating interiors. Print collecting was a burgeoning hobby, and theater fans would leaf through each other's collections of theater prints, reminiscing about favorite actors and plays. At temples and shrines in the city and in the countryside, worshippers and merrymakers could view paintings of kabuki actors done by leading ukiyo-e artists; these paintings on wood were commissioned by private individuals or groups and were donated to religious institutions as illustrated votive tablets (*ema*) (Catalogue no. V-2).

Kabuki had entered the world of popular literature as well. Poets composing light verse (*haikai*, *kyōka*, and *senryū*) often referred to kabuki actors and kabuki events and plays in their poetry, and *gesaku* fiction writers frequently borrowed plots and characters from kabuki plays. Even in stories with no ostensible connection to the theater, illustrators often turned characters' faces into likenesses of top kabuki actors, in a practice known as *mitate*.

Mitate pictures created new associations between fictional stories and characters, and actors' personalities and stage plays. Sometimes fiction writers even featured popular actors as the heroes of fictional tales.

While theater-going and print collecting were important pastimes for Edoites, many hobbies derived from kabuki called for more active participation. Edoites played and sang the music of the kabuki theater. Their daily practice filled the streets of the commoner neighborhoods with music, and their amateur recitals enlivened the restaurant districts of the city (Catalogue no. V-21). Professional and semiprofessional teachers, not kabuki actors, tutored amateurs in these arts. Devotees of kabuki assembled to imitate kabuki dialogues in a hobby known as *kowairo*, and others studied and presented kabuki dance, or performed *chaban*, improvisational skits parodying kabuki, at parties, or larger-scale plays at home (*zashiki kyōgen*).[5] Instructional books were published and specialty stores were established to provide the properties and costumes necessary for the devotees of these theatrical hobbies.[6]

Kabuki aficionados in the commoner classes ranged from lowly shop clerks to the large-scale rice brokers and financiers who were the multimillionaires of the late eighteenth century, and kabuki had many samurai patrons as well. From the beginning of the Tokugawa Period the central government had permitted kabuki theaters to operate as a form of distraction for the urban commoner classes, the artisans and merchants. Many samurai thought of kabuki actors as little better than outcastes, and they were often called "riverbed beggars" because in the medieval period performers had lived and worked on the river flats in Kyoto. In theory samurai were not supposed to attend kabuki theater. They had their own theater, the lofty, austere, and edifying No theater, a product of Japan's medieval age. Commoners were almost entirely restricted from attendance at No plays, most of which were performed on private stages within the grounds of feudal lords' mansions and estates. However, by the late eighteenth century No theater apparently seemed archaic and boring to members of the samurai class, many of whom, like the commoner citizens of Edo, were enthralled by kabuki.

Men and women of the samurai class flocked to the kabuki theaters, usually disguising their faces so as not to be recognized. Reed blinds concealed the identities of audience members sitting in the expensive box seats lining the sides of the auditorium. Kabuki actors were as erotically appealing to samurai of both sexes as they were to commoners. An affair in 1714 between a leading actor of romantic male roles and a senior lady-in-waiting to the shogun had led to the permanent closure of one of Edo's four kabuki theaters.

In his memoir, *Shizu no oda maki* (1802), the government official Moriyama Takamori (1738-1815) criticized eighteenth-century samurai enthusiasm for imitating kabuki actors' speech and staging kabuki skits:

> The shamisen became extremely popular from 1740 to 1760. Eldest sons of good samurai families and even other sons all took lessons; from morn till night shamisen sounds were always to be heard. Eventually they began to perform other kabuki music and dramas, and the like, and followed this depravity to the extent of performing amateur kabuki plays in residences. High *hatamoto* officials mimicking riverbed beggars, aping female impersonators and stage heroes! But with the Kansei Reforms [in the 1790s] all this ceased and society returned to normal.[7]

The greatest samurai patron of kabuki may have been Yanagisawa Nobutoki, a wealthy feudal lord who "hired ladies-in-waiting according to their acting and dancing talents, creating a small kabuki troupe within his household. Directed by Nobutoki and assisted by Nakazō, the women's troupe performed once or twice a year in plays Nobutoki wrote himself. For these shows he had a stage—complete with hanamichi—built within his residence."[8]

Popular fiction made fun of lowbrow samurai lords who were infatuated with kabuki. One example is the humorous illustrated book, or *kibyōshi*, *Kyōgenzuki yabō daimyō* (The boorish daimyo who loved kabuki), published by Kishida Tohō in 1784.[9] In it, a country daimyo, nicknamed "Horseface," takes to imitating kabuki in his everyday speech and bearing. He summons courtesans and actors to his mansion to be his supporting cast in a kabuki play starring himself.[10] To men like Moriyama Takamori and other members of the government's highest elite, samurai participation in the Floating World, and especially in kabuki, was not amusing, but was part of a general blight of bureaucratic corruption, financial mismanagement, and declining moral standards among the samurai that had run rampant for decades. It was a situation that had to be remedied.

The Kansei Reforms and Kabuki "Realism"

The Kansei Reform decrees that affected kabuki were promulgated over a period of six years, from 1789 to 1795, and had two main goals: to remove the overt and extravagant samurai presence from kabuki patronage, and to limit the splendor and popularity of kabuki actors and shows by restricting theaters' production practices and financial resources.

The first goal was already largely achieved, because punishments for samurai misconduct were administered entirely within the ruling class. Samurai continued to attend kabuki and to participate in the culture of the Floating World, but concealment became even more important, and the samurai presence in kabuki was considerably reduced.

The government addressed its second goal with a series of edicts, restricting the running time of plays, banning licentious behavior and prostitution in the theaters and theater environs, outlawing sumptuous costumes and lavish gifts to actors, and limiting actors' salaries to a maximum of five hundred *ryō*. At that time a salary of between eight hundred and a thousand ryō was the mark of a superstar, and there are occasional references to higher salaries—two thousand ryō for Danjūrō II might be the highest salary ever for a kabuki actor. It is hard to estimate the equivalent income to one thousand ryō today, but it would probably be close to half a million dollars.

The decade of the 1790s was a time of financial crisis for the Edo theaters. In 1794 the three Edo kabuki theaters were half a million ryō in debt. One after another they changed to new management, under a system whereby the permanent producers sold their rights to produce kabuki for a certain number of years to other managerial families. Although the multifarious causes of the crisis are still debated by theater historians, most agree that one likely source of debt was the failure of ticket prices to cover rapidly rising costs of production and escalating actors' salaries. Ticket prices increased considerably in the latter part of the eighteenth century, and by the turn of the century kabuki had become a theater for the wealthy. Poorer townspeople enjoyed plays performed at considerably smaller theaters, which tried to seem as much like large-scale kabuki as they could manage. These theaters, too, operated under government license and were subject to numerous restrictions.[11] Ticket prices at the small theaters were much lower than for kabuki, the shows were much less elaborate, and the actors were paid low salaries and were less skilled.[12]

At the kabuki theaters, even with increased ticket prices and a decrease in the material splendor of the shows, good plays and great performers were able to fill the Kansei-period halls. It would be a decade or less before samurai administrators began to slacken in the enforcement of their zealous decrees, but in the meantime kabuki's artistic response to the Kansei Reforms was to move in the direction of so-called realism. The contemporary term was *shō utsushi*, or "re-creating the truth," or "the facts," and, as *The Floating World Revisited* exhibition demonstrates, the Kansei-period vogue for realism influenced many of the arts of the Floating World. Ukiyo-e prints of actors backstage and offstage were very popular (Catalogue nos. V-12, V-19, V-22, and V-23), and Kansei is the age of the close-up, true-to-life actor print (Catalogue no. V-18). Sharaku's portraits, which were considered highly unflattering when he published them, are the most extreme example (Catalogue no. V-13).

Onstage, popular actors' *kōjō*, speeches delivered to the audience with the actor in standard formal dress and wearing little makeup, were becoming more important draws. In 1791 Iwai Hanshirō removed his makeup onstage, left to change into normal dress, and then returned to the stage, where he simply sat and watched the rest of the play. Apparently the audience loved it.[13]

It is clear that some artists in the Floating World had little taste for such changes, and Danjūrō V was probably among them, though the closest he came to saying so publicly was at the Ichimura-za in the eleventh month of the same year, when he gave a kōjō speech announcing his passing of the Danjūrō name to his son, and his assumption of the name Ebizō. He came to realize that his kōjō was the major attraction to the month's program, and stopped presenting it four days into the run. He explained his action, saying it was embarrassing to the actors doing the real work if his speech was the main reason that people were coming to the theater.

Santō Kyōden (1761-1816), Danjūrō's friend and the leading fiction writer of the day, was more open in his criticism of the new realism. In 1791, in a kibyōshi entitled *Sejo share mie zu* (A stylish posed picture book of current affairs), he exaggerated and satirized the wrong turn he thought kabuki was taking:

> If people like offstage actor pictures so much, they'll get more and more up-to-date, until they won't need plays at all. If the theaters just re-create actors' houses and families onstage, in detail, *reproducing the facts* (shō utsushi), they'll always have big hits and won't have to worry about attendance. I can see it now, the interior of Danjūrō's house running the full width of the stage. Danjūrō wears no makeup, he is in ordinary clothes, and he is sitting at his desk, correcting some of his poetry. Okame, his real-life wife, enters from the back, and says, "Hey Ebi, what're you doing?" She seems worried.[14]

It is ironic that what Santō Kyōden imagined in jest as the death of the theater he loved is just the sort of realism that early-twentieth-century Japanese converts to Ibsen and Chekhov struggled for decades to achieve. In fact, Kansei kabuki never came close to the level of realism depicted in the Kyōden caricature, but in 1791 it seemed to be moving in that direction.

Kansai audiences had always preferred more rational play plots and more believable characters than their Edo counterparts, and in 1794 Namiki Gohei (1747-1808) came from Osaka to become Edo's leading playwright. His characters, and their actions and dialogue, were more true to life than had been the case in earlier Edo plays, and he presented aspects of *chōnin* life not yet seen on the kabuki stage. In 1795 a realistic conversation in a restaurant kitchen among cooks, maids, and geisha created quite a stir among up-to-date lovers of realism.

For many years realism in kabuki had meant borrowing "realistic" puppetry from the *bunraku* puppet theater. In the puppet theater, "realism" usually consisted of challenging feats of manipulation that reproduced complex human actions. Namiki Gohei, like Namiki Shozō, was a special-effects innovator, and he drew inspiration from the Osaka puppet theater. In his last two years in Osaka, Gohei took realism to new extremes in kabuki when he paraded two real horses down the hanamichi in one play and used real fireworks onstage in another.[15] In the former a horse bolted, trampling some customers, and forcing a three-day suspension of the play, and in the latter the fireworks so frightened women viewers that many fled the theater.[16] One wonders whether these mishaps occasioned Gohei's sudden departure for Edo. In any case, his arrival must have reassured Santō Kyōden that kabuki was not in immediate danger of degenerating into unadorned living-room scenes.

It was not long before Gohei and Kansei kabuki were experimenting with new forms of spectacle. If sumptuous costumes could not be worn, less lavish ones could be changed onstage at such speed as to dazzle the eyes of spectators. Bizarre plots and remarkable character transformations had long been staples of kabuki plays, but, from the Kansei Period on, scenes of the macabre and the grotesque became more and more frequent. In Gohei's hit play of 1795, *Go dairiki koi no fūjime* (The five strong men and the seal of love), the hero kills his geisha lover, whom he mistakenly believes has betrayed him. Her hand clings to him after she has died, and continues to do so even after he cuts it off her arm. The hand is clutching her farewell note to him, and, after he pries the note out of the hand, the note still sticks to his kimono.[17] Doing such scenes in a realistic manner attracted customers to kabuki. The term *kizewamono* ("living" or "raw" domestic play) was first used for Gohei's plays; the genre would be perfected a few decades later by Tsuruya Namboku IV, whose plays are characterized by convoluted plots, low-life heroes, frightening scenes of brutality, and amazing occult and macabre occurrences.

Kabuki was more than holding its own against the government restrictions. The foundation of its staying power at the turn of the century was the enormous popularity of its leading actors. Of them all, Danjūrō V stood paramount. He was Japan's first multimedia celebrity. Not only did his presence ensure a sold-out theater, but every year booksellers stocked new fictional and factual stories about him, histories of his family, volumes of poetry dedicated to him, and books of his own poems. As *The Floating World Revisited* exhibition shows, his face, and his figure in costume or in street clothes, were visible all over Edo. In the next part of this essay, we will enter the life of the man who was the "flower of Edo" in the city's golden age of popular culture.

Ichikawa Danjūrō V: The Man and His Art

Unlike Danjūrō V, his father, Danjūrō IV (1711-1778), had fought his way to the top. Officially he had no blood relationship to the eminence who had dominated Edo kabuki for almost half a century, Danjūrō II, but widely accepted rumor held that Danjūrō IV (called Matsumoto Koshirō II for most of his career) was Danjūrō II's illegitimate son. When Danjūrō III died suddenly in 1742 at age twenty-two, Koshirō, then a skilled portrayer of villains, asked old Danjūrō II for the right to take the Danjūrō name. He was refused, and for twelve years Edo had no Danjūrō. Finally, in 1754, at the advanced age of forty-five, Koshirō was rewarded for his persistence.

In his younger years Danjūrō IV was an energetic and abrasive man who had a love-hate relationship with kabuki audiences. In a 1748 kaomise, when the audience applauded other actors enthusiastically but were decidedly cold in their reception of Danjūrō IV, he stopped the show and addressed the audience directly, telling them that this was a ceremonial occasion and that their rudeness had deeply offended him. He challenged any one of them to come to his house and fight him after the play. Apparently no one was brave enough to accept the challenge.[18]

For several years after he assumed the name and responsibilities of a Danjūrō, he received frequent poor acting ratings in the hyōbanki. One entry went so far as to call him "a disgrace to the Ichikawa family name."[19] Since Danjūrō IV had spent the previous decade playing villains, his portrayal of aragoto heroes seemed heavy-handed to audiences who still remembered Danjūrō II. But Danjūrō IV worked hard at his art, and by the 1760s he had become one of Edo's most popular and respected kabuki actors. He lived in Kiba, near the lumber yards east of the Sumida River, and other actors called him "the Lumberyard Boss" (*Kiba no oyadama*).

Danjūrō IV was a pioneer kaneru yakusha who lived and breathed kabuki onstage and off. After he became Danjūrō, he held training workshops (called *shugyō kō*) for actors at his Kiba home. He broke with tradition and encouraged participation by actors who were not his official disciples. He enjoyed helping younger actors, and it was he who discovered Nakamura Nakazō when he was a bit player, and helped him become one of the great actors of the age. Much of the time in Danjūrō IV's training sessions was spent in free and open discussion, and one historian has called them "remarkably democratic workshops."[20] Danjūrō V describes these workshops as follows:

> Even after my father got home from the theater, all he would talk about was acting. He would bring Nakazō, Koshirō IV, and Yaozō II over to his training sessions and they would talk about how they would approach this and that role, about how they would love to play this or that role, and they would debate acting styles and techniques.[21]

Danjūrō V's gently rebellious attitude toward his father is revealed in the continuation of the above passage, when he tries to present his father with an insoluble acting problem:

> At that time all I did was drink sake and amuse myself composing haikai. One day my father told me that I should work harder on my art and he ordered me to attend the sessions. Once I asked him how he would handle a play where he had to enact Akamatsu Norisuke possessed by the dead spirit of Musashibō Benkei. He laughed, and said it's best to have people read plays like that to you, you don't actually do them.[22]

What made this an impossible challenge for Danjūrō IV was the fact that Akamatsu is a traitorous villain and Benkei is the epitome of a loyal retainer. In kabuki the spirits of evil characters often possessed virtuous people, but the reverse never occurred.

Danjūrō V was sickly as a child, and began reading literature and writing poetry during his convalescences. As a youth he was instructed by Danjūrō II, whom he called his grandfather, and the image of Danjūrō II, an eminent and gentlemanly actor-poet, would remain with Danjūrō V to counterbalance the example of his father, a fighting actor turned teacher, who lived for the theater alone.

Danjūrō IV had his son follow in his footsteps as a young actor. Danjūrō V began his mature acting career as Matsumoto Koshirō III, and although he played all sorts of roles, he focused primarily on the art of playing villains. Danjūrō IV, remembering his own difficulties, was careful not to let his son become too entrenched in such parts. Danjūrō V later wrote:

> Once, at a training session, I asked my father how I should play Sadakurō [an important villain in *Chūshingura*]. Father said, "Sadakurō is the epitome of a samurai turned bad. A Danjūrō should not play him," and he ended the discussion.[23]

Danjūrō V obeyed his father's injunction, and later told Nakazō that, as his father had forbidden him to play Sadakurō, Nakazō should take the role and do what he wanted with it.[24] Nakazō turned the Sadakurō role into a virtuoso portrayal of a villain that remains with us in today's kabuki.

The hyōbanki seem objective in their evaluation of Danjūrō V in his pre-Danjūrō days. He was good, but he never received the fulsome praise that he received for his Danjūrō debut. For example, in a 1768 kaomise he played a villain and a concubine, and a 1769 hyōbanki commented that "he was very good when he learned that he was the son of the tyrant Kiyomori and then turned evil in nature but his female role was poorly received. It is too bad, because that role gave him an excellent opportunity to display his skill."[25] This is admittedly one of his worst reviews, but before his Danjūrō debut the hyōbanki usually describe him as, at best, a promising young actor. Theater historians call him a "late bloomer."

Inheritor of the Danjūrō Tradition

In late 1771, at age 31, just a year after his Danjūrō *shumei* (the assumption of his new name), Danjūrō became the *zagashira*, or production director, at the Morita-za Theater. Zagashira was the highest official rank that an actor could hold, and Danjūrō would maintain his zagashira status until his retirement. The zagashira consulted with the producer and with playwrights on new plays to be written, and made final casting decisions for plays. Zagashira could have the kinds of roles they liked to play written into scripts, and could arrange casts so that they worked with actors they liked and respected. Producers hired zagashira on a yearly basis, as they did all actors, but the fact that Danjūrō was hired as a zagashira every year from 1771 meant that he was in control of his own destiny.

Danjūrō II had been a powerful, long-term zagashira, and had reserved for himself and for designated successors the choice aragoto roles that he and his father had pioneered.

Danjūrō IV was more of an interloper and had less authority, but the Lumberyard Boss was a strong-willed man who had special roles and scenes of his own that were to go only to his son. One such was Shibaraku; another was Danjūrō IV's best scene, "Kagekiyo Smashing the Prison," which featured the darkest, most villainous aragoto hero of all.

Immediately after his shumei, Danjūrō V began doing the important Ichikawa family aragoto roles. In his next performance he played Soga Gorō, alias Sukeroku, Danjūrō II's ever-popular romantic swashbuckler. Sukeroku is the aragoto hero most like a townsman, but he is a townsman who can beat any samurai in combat. Sukeroku epitomized chōnin pride, gallantry, and vicarious wish-fulfillment.

In plays in 1771 and 1772, Danjūrō V enacted the fierce Buddhist deity Fudō. In the 1771 kaomise at the Morita-za—Danjūrō's first as zagashira—Fudō was the fourth role that he played. In the climax of the show, his ferociously glaring Fudō saved all the lost souls in the play (see Figure 2). The Morita-za kaomise was the biggest success of the 1771 kaomise season.

The Fudō of the Shinshōji Temple in Narita (forty-five miles northeast of Edo) was the Ichikawa family's tutelary deity, and Danjūrō I had played Fudō on numerous occasions, with Fudō usually making a spectacular appearance in the last act as a deus ex machina. Danjūrō II had made his stage debut playing Fudō. The official Ichikawa family history tells us that after Danjūrō I performed one week of austerities at Shinshōji, Fudō appeared before him and bestowed upon him the famous "Fudō glare" to use onstage. The glare became a trademark of Ichikawa aragoto acting. Danjūrō I and Danjūrō II drew heavily on esoteric Buddhist iconography, ritual dance, and sutra chanting when creating the costuming, makeup, choreography, and vocalization for their aragoto roles. All members of the Ichikawa family went on pilgrimages to the Narita Temple and served as official greeters when the Shinshōji Temple displayed sacred images in Edo at festive events called *kaichō*.

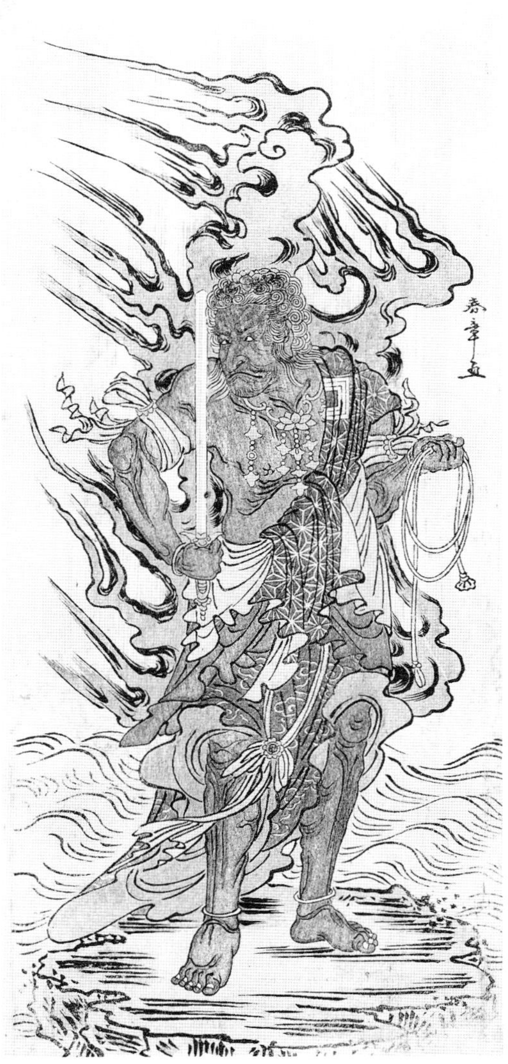

FIGURE 2
Courtesy of the British Museum

Danjūrō V played Fudō again several times, and often played heroes who were possessed by, or imbued with, the spirits of Buddhist and Shinto deities. Although he wrote little about it, it is evident that he followed in the family tradition of belief in, and service to, the Narita Fudō. In 1789 he served at the Narita kaichō in Edo,[26] and presented his second "Ya no ne Gorō" (Gorō sharpening arrowheads) scene as a gift to Fudō (Catalogue no. V-2). Soga Gorō was a young avenging hero in a popular medieval epic, and Danjūrō I had converted him into a minor deity for Edoites by associating Gorō with Fudō in his kabuki plays. Danjūrō II's Gorō in "Ya no ne" came to be used to represent ferocious deities in disguise—in Danjūrō V's 1789 play, Gorō was an incarnation of Fudō.

By the late 1700s Fudō worship was one of the most popular cults in Edo. The early Danjūrōs had been instrumental in propagating the cult, and Danjūrō V's continued close association with Fudō was a major factor in Edoites' adulation of him. When Danjūrō V played Fudō and other powerful characters onstage, many members of the audience saw him as imbued with divine strength.

Danjūrō V played Kagekiyo often. In 1778 he did a Kagekiyo play with a special twist—it had a new, heartrending parting scene between Kagekiyo and his daughter, derived from the No play *Kagekiyo*. Six weeks into the play Danjūrō IV died; Edoites said that the parting scene had been a harbinger of his death. The play was quickly rewritten to memorialize the departed actor. The playwright added a prison-smashing scene to remember Danjūrō IV's best kabuki, and a Fudō scene to ensure the Lumberyard Boss's safe journey to Buddha's paradise. Kagekiyo became the character Danjūrō V always chose to perform in plays memorializing his father.

Because Danjūrō V performed so many new roles, and so many multiple roles, the roles invented by his ancestors do not dominate his stage record. Danjūrō V was not an authoritarian by temperament, and therefore was less proprietary toward the Ichikawa plays and characters than his forebears had been. While he was a zagashira no other actors performed "Ya no ne" or "Kagekiyo Smashing the Prison," but other actors performed many other roles that had once been the exclusive province of the Danjūrōs. "Shibaraku" remained a Danjūrō V scene through and through, essential fare at his kaomise show almost every year. Danjūrō V would allow that role to be performed by only one other actor: the son who would become Danjūrō VI.

Family Tragedy and a Scandal

In 1777, a year before his father died, Danjūrō V's only son, eight-year-old Momotarō, died of a disease. The little boy had already made his stage debut, and his death was a terrible blow to Danjūrō and his wife, Okame. In his diary Nakamura Nakazō describes the old Lumberyard Boss as racked by grief over the loss of his precious grandchild.[27] A 1777 hyōbanki expresses all of Edo's sorrow at the loss: little Momotarō had not only danced beautifully for thousands to see, but was already reading Chinese poetry and the *Analects* of Confucius. Now there was talk that Danjūrō would take Koshirō IV's son as his heir, and rumor had it that Okame was again living with Danjūrō after a period of estrangement.[28] It is clear that celebrities' broken marriages and family tragedies were just as fascinating to eighteenth-century Edoites as they are to today's citizens of Tokyo.

It turned out that both rumors were false. Danjūrō's marriage was in a worse state than ever. Husband and wife were still living separately. In 1778, six months after his father's death, Danjūrō V appeared onstage during a performance at the Nakamura-za to denounce his fellow actor Matsumoto Koshirō IV, for slandering him and intriguing with Okame to force Danjūrō V to retire and pass the Danjūrō title to Koshirō's son. Danjūrō declared that he had to expose Koshirō's perfidy and stop the rumors about his retirement.

Koshirō had apparently accused Danjūrō of betraying his wife by having an affair with the widow of a recently deceased actor. According to Nakazō's diary, which scholars regard as a generally accurate source, this accusation was true—the widow had, in fact, already moved into Danjūrō's home. Danjūrō left the Nakamura-za in the middle of a play, and audiences stopped coming to the theater. He also walked out on his zagashira post with two months left on his contract. For eight years he would have nothing to do with Matsumoto Koshirō.

Hiraga Gennai (1728-1779), a fiction writer and devoted Danjūrō supporter, wrote that "Danjūrō's speech in his own defense was very manly. The scandal has made him a more interesting person and his popularity will increase."[29] Danjūrō was not out of work for long. Nakazō helped him secure the zagashira position for the forthcoming season at the Morita-za, the least prestigious of the three theaters. Danjūrō wrote Nakazō a grateful poem of thanks. A year later Danjūrō was back at the Nakamura-za, kabuki's top theater, and the theater's patience with him paid handsome dividends. His three-role kaomise (one role was, of course, the "Shibaraku" hero) ran for over forty days—a long run for a kaomise show—and the theater had to add temporary seating for the ever-increasing number of spectators. Danjūrō earned the highest rating he had ever received in a hyōbanki for the show. It would seem that Hiraga Gennai had been correct.

Danjūrō's affair with the widow evidently did not last long, and after a few years he and Okame were again living under one roof as man and wife, although theirs was never a stable and harmonious relationship. Danjūrō did not frequent the pleasure districts or engage in affairs with other actors. This was apparently so remarkable for a kabuki actor that it merited frequent comment in the hyōbanki. Theater, literature, and the social whirl seem to have consumed all of his time and energy.

There was, however, one mystery woman in Danjūrō's life. All we know about her is the name with which she signed her poetry: Ume Asahiko. She was a fellow member of a kyōka poetry circle called the Sakaichō Group, and was either Danjūrō's mistress or poetry disciple, or both. It is possible, but not certain, that she was the mother of Danjūrō's illegitimate son Tokuzō, born in 1778, who would become Danjūrō VI. Because Danjūrō V never officially recognized Tokuzō's mother, her identity remains a mystery. Danjūrō's relatives raised the baby, and Danjūrō formally adopted him when he was four years old. The only evidence supporting the idea that Asahiko was Tokuzō's mother is a particularly fine poem she wrote commemorating Danjūrō VI's shumei. The fact that this is considered to be any evidence at all shows how much import Japanese read into poems, even light verse like kyōka.

Danjūrō V Writes on How to Be a Virtuoso and a Versatile Actor

As a young man Danjūrō V may not have been the most highly motivated participant in his father's workshops, but we know that in his mature years he gave serious and careful thought to his work. He recorded his insights in the form of random jottings and essays, called *zuihitsu*, a genre with a long and distinguished history in Japanese classical literature. The greatest medieval work in the zuihitsu tradition, Yoshida Kenkō's *Essays in Idleness* (*Tsurezuregusa*), was one of his favorite books. He wrote his own commentaries to the work, and modelled the preface to his first book on the earlier work's preface. Since many of his jottings are very personal and some are highly critical of other actors, he probably never intended them to be published, and they never were. Some were carefully rewritten after his death—perhaps by a family member or one of his literary friends—but others remained as he first wrote them on the margins of play texts.[30] Taken together, Danjūrō V's zuihitsu provide an excellent insight to his personality and his approach to the actor's craft.

We do not know when he wrote his essays and jottings, but they are certainly from his post-Danjūrō shumei years, because the danger of fame concerns him greatly:

> As you become more famous people will stop criticizing you. This is when you have to make the effort to arrange for someone to watch you rehearse, someone you can ask about your work, and who will tell you if it is bad.[31]

Danjūrō V followed in the tradition of Zeami, the great master of Nō drama, in his conviction that perceptions of performance from the outside, not the actor's own subjective feelings, were the real measure of artistic quality. This did not mean that actors' attitudes about their art were unimportant. Danjūrō again followed in the path of Zeami and Kenkō in his belief that humility was essential to self-improvement: "It is best always to think that you are unskillful. You should have this attitude all of your life. Once you start thinking you are good, then it is all over."[32] In another entry he wrote, "Actors should think highly of themselves, but they should not be conceited."[33] On the other hand, excessive humility in an actor of high stature was affectation, and onstage there were times when an attitude of overweening pride was essential:

> In "Shibaraku" and the like it is no good if an aragoto master is weak. It is weak if you think, "I want the audience to like me. I hope they will support me." The right feeling is, "It is only because I am appearing that the audience is enjoying itself." You should feel that you are the greatest of actors. You should look down on all and sundry. They are mere insects compared to you.[34]

The approach to playing an aragoto superhero has never been better stated.

Danjūrō V wrote that to be a successful kaneru yakusha, actors should be flexible and ready to try anything: "There should be no role that does not suit an actor's character. If an actor says that a role or action does not suit him, he is saying he is a bad actor,"[35] and, "When one cannot do things that do not suit one's body, then one cannot do anything."[36] Clearly, Danjūrō V loved artistic challenges, and he was the first Danjūrō to play women's parts after his Danjūrō shumei.

"Approach good roles and bad roles in the same way," he wrote; "concentrate hard on bad roles too, and make them part of yourself."[37] Even he, a zagashira, sometimes played a "bad role." He chose to exert a light influence on staff playwrights, and enjoyed the challenge of performing the roles they created. He even enjoyed performing an occasional subordinate role. In 1775 he played the spirit of a white tapir that was trampled underfoot by a character played by a lower-ranking actor. The hyōbanki were critical, saying a zagashira should not allow himself to be humiliated in this way,[38] but Danjūrō had served notice that he was going to be his own man.

Danjūrō wrote that first and foremost an actor had to understand himself: "My body is small, I am short and thin, and I am not strong. Recognizing these defects, how do I act in accord with or in opposition to my natural gifts?"[39] With this basic understanding, he next advocated flexibility and balance in one's approach to the stage, and to life:

> Sometimes one does things that do not suit one's body. Because they do not suit, one manages on spirit and courage.
>
> Sometimes one does things that suit one's body. Because one does them so well, nothing one does seems to ill-suit one's body.[40]

> Don't have personal quirks in everything you do. Having too many personal quirks is as bad as not having enough.[41]

> There are times to imitate others and times not to, times to accept others' advice and times not to, times to flatter and cajole, and times not to, times to be ostentatious, and times not to be.[42]

Danjūrō wrote many entries like this last one—fascinating bits of opposing advice that leave the reader to ponder when specific actions are right or wrong. These entries would have made excellent points of departure for discussion, and perhaps he used them as such with his disciples and with his son.

He was less obsessive than his father had been about his stage career. He wrote, "You should have two big successes a year. If every time you get a role you rack your brain with strategies on how to achieve a great success, life will be unbearable."[43] In other jottings, however, he seemed to be reprimanding himself for his interest in offstage pastimes: "All should be focused on the stage. If you devote yourself to things offstage, your performances will become poor, and you won't be there onstage."[44]

Many of Danjūrō's zuihitsu jottings are technical bits of theatrical advice: how to apply makeup skillfully, how to glare ferociously, when to use large or restrained gestures, and so on. It is clear from his writings that he saw life onstage and off as a whole. An actor's offstage bearing and demeanor, and even habits like sniffling and fidgeting, would inevitably appear onstage. The actor who is large-spirited and in control of his life offstage would be that way in his plays. Danjūrō's writing is as much about life as it is about the stage, and, like *Essays in Idleness*, his zuihitsu entries may be culled and organized to form a code of gentlemanly conduct. If a title were to be given to the body of his writing, a good one might be "The Way of the Gentleman-Actor."

Ichikawa Danjūrō, Nakamura Nakazō, and the Legacy of Temmei-Era Kabuki

From his writing we know that Danjūrō was concerned about a man's entire life as an actor. He wrote that it was important to live a long life and to have a balanced stage career, with successful performances from youth through old age. How could an actor remain forever at the top of the highly competitive Edo theater world? Danjūrō put it simply: "Don't ever let audiences tire of you, and don't let them forget you."[45] It is a simple prescription but a formidable challenge for an actor to achieve over a span of four decades, yet by all accounts Danjūrō V managed to do just this. His writings and his performance record suggest how he managed to remain unforgettable but always fresh to Edo audiences, and they show why the playlet "Shibaraku" was so important to him.

Beginning with his shumei, Danjūrō always won acclaim in "Shibaraku." It was sure to be one of the two successes he felt he needed every year. To do a fine "Shibaraku," first and foremost an actor needed vocal virtuosity and wit, and these were Danjūrō's two strongest suits. For Edo audiences the high point of most "Shibaraku" scenes was not the killing of the villains, it was the hero's delivery of the *tsurane* monologue at the end of the hanamichi. We know this from the number of "Shibaraku" tsurane that were excerpted and published in special anthologies. Danjūrō typically wrote new tsurane for every play, leaving the rest of the script to the playwrights. In addition to his vocal and writing skill, he excelled at aragoto histrionics and glaring, and the play's costume made his skinny body look as burly as a sumo wrestler's.

The large number of Danjūrō V "Shibaraku" prints demonstrate that this was his "unforgettable" role. To maintain his audiences' interest, Danjūrō experimented with a variety of techniques and roles during the other seasons—seasons in which he could try out things that did not suit him. He played every sort of male hero and every sort of villain, he played gods and Buddhas, and he played women. He danced frequently, but we see him less often working in the subdued style used to portray wise samurai retainers (a style called *jitsugoto*). He clearly enjoyed histrionic acting. He often played old, favorite Ichikawa family aragoto roles, but would occasionally surprise his fans by doing something outlandish or unprecedented.

Nakamura Nakazō finally came into his own in the 1780s, the Temmei era. After many years as a fine dancer and Edo's leading villain actor, often playing opposite Danjūrō's hero, Nakazō had become one of Edo's three zagashira, and was making more than eight hundred ryō a year. It had been a long and hard journey for a bit actor orphan who had eked out a living with a ten-ryō salary, had been tormented by higher-ranking actors, and had twice come close to suicide. Nakazō was never the all-around actor that Danjūrō was, but he knew his strengths well, and when he became zagashira he used his position to collaborate with playwrights and musicians in creating long romantic dance dramas. A few of them are still performed today and are our only living testament to kabuki's golden age.

Danjūrō V has not left kabuki such a legacy. Gunji Masakatsu, Japan's leading kabuki historian, believes that the reason for this is that he was *too good* an actor. Nakazō worked repeatedly in a form he invented, the long dance drama, creating masterpieces like *Kurama Jishi* and *Seki no To* through a process of accretion and refinement. Danjūrō V never focused his time and energy on one kind of role or one play, other than "Shibaraku." If "Shibaraku" had ever failed him, it might have forced him to do so, but that did not happen.

If Nakazō has left us the only Temmei legacy on the kabuki stage, Danjūrō V has bequeathed to us the glorious picture of Temmei and Kansei kabuki that remains in art, in popular literature, and in history books. Nakazō was admired, but Danjūrō was a figure of adulation. Exposed to Danjūrō's charm and elan, Edo's most creative men of culture behaved like star-struck adolescents, adorning entire houses with Ichikawa family-crest decor, and filling their houses with Danjūrō memorabilia. They celebrated their idol in art, praised him in poetry and prose, and used him as a hero in fictional tales.

Actor or Writer? From Danjūrō to the Shrimp and the White Monkey

In the early 1780s Danjūrō V became an active member of the ukiyo literary and art worlds. He met and established friendships with many artists. Among his closest friends were Santō Kyōden, the kyōka poet Ōta Nampo, the fiction writer Utei Emba, and the illustrator Hokusai. Considerably younger than Danjūrō, these four men were in awe of his celebrity and honored to have him as a member of their social and literary circles. Many exciting literary and artistic collaborations were first conceived at their parties and poetry gatherings. Danjūrō began his publishing career with an anthology of his grandfather's best poetry in 1781, and Nampo's first published kyōka book was created as a gift to five-year-old Ichikawa Tokuzō on the occasion of his stage debut in 1782.[46] Danjūrō participated in several poetry circles, and by 1786 was the leader of his own social and literary society, the Mimasu Group (*mimasu* means "three rice measures," and was the design of the Ichikawa family crest), which met regularly at the Musashi-ya restaurant. Throughout the 1780s Danjūrō's poetry appeared in print in piecemeal fashion in anthologies compiled by other poets, but he was collecting a body of his own work that he intended to publish. One of his better poems captures the energy of the Temmei stage, but shows that, at the age of forty-seven, Danjūrō felt he was beginning to lose the stamina necessary for a great aragoto actor:

> For the kaomise play at the Kiri-za I played two roles, requiring quick costume changes, and I composed this poem in the third-floor dressing room.
>
> It's only natural that getting to the third floor is painful
> After doing spinning, life and death, costume changes.[47]

In 1790 Danjūrō stunned Edo when he took several leading actors, including the onnagata star Kikunojō, and went to the provincial town of Kōfu, where they performed for five months. They set out for Mt. Fuji from the suburban town of Meguro (the site of an Ichikawa family villa), and were followed on the whole journey by a crowd of fans and well-wishers. Edo kabuki aficionados were aghast: never before had a Danjūrō performed openly in the provinces. They thought that "Mount Fuji, the Asakusa Temple, and Danjūrō were three things that were immovable."[48] Utei Emba, Danjūrō's closest friend and supporter, wrote a hyōbanki in 1790 that both voiced Edoites' criticism and gave Danjūrō an opportunity to explain his action. In it Danjūrō stated that it was no disgrace to perform in the countryside, and added he would go anywhere in the sixty provinces of Japan where people wanted to see him and where there was a place to perform. He concluded with a poem of thanks to the people of Kōfu.[49]

Indeed, in 1790, all of Japan *did* want to see Danjūrō. His family crest graced products for sale all over the country. According to a proverb, he was known "even in towns where they eat horse"[50]—probably a reference to far-off Kyushu. After returning to Edo for a kaomise, Danjūrō spent the next season performing in the provinces around Mt. Fuji. It was the time of the peak of the "realism" boom, and his conspicuous absence from Edo is further evidence that it was a trend he did not like. His provincial fans wanted to see good old-fashioned superhero kabuki, and he obliged them. At Kōfu in 1790 he performed *Kagekiyo*, *Sukeroku*, and *Narukami*, and then gave the stage to Kikunojō in *Musume Dōjōji*, the most exciting dance drama for onnagata.

When Danjūrō returned to the Edo stage in late 1791, it was for a double shumei. He was giving the name "Danjūrō" to his fourteen-year-old son. The boy was still too young to bear the burden of responsibility of a Danjūrō. Danjūrō V wanted to begin decreasing his own responsibilities in the kabuki world, but he would have to spend at least a few more years nurturing the young Danjūrō VI. Perhaps he hoped that an early Danjūrō shumei for his son would force the boy to mature more rapidly than he himself had. The fifty-one-year-old Danjūrō took the family's other hereditary name, Ebizō, but changed the ideograph for "ebi" from "lobster" to mean "little shrimp." He also assumed a new poetic name, "Hakuen," the same pronunciation as the poetic name his father and grandfather had used, but changed the characters to mean "white monkey." The reason he gave for his modifications of old family names was that he wanted meanings more diminutive than the names of his exalted ancestors. His elegant and poetic speech celebrating his son's rise and including explanations of the name changes was the fabulously popular *kōjō*, which he discontinued after only four days. His immense fame was running at cross-purposes with his notions about the directions that kabuki should take and his sense of what his own place should be in the theater world.

By 1793 Danjūrō V (now Ebizō) was rated as "incomparably the best actor in Edo,"[51] but he was an incomparable actor who wanted to leave kabuki. When Santō Kyōden visited him in his dressing room for the first time, it was in the second month of that year. Ebizō was playing a woman's role and the crowds were pouring into the Kawarazaki-za Theater. Ebizō was in the third-floor dressing room and was wearing the white makeup of an onnagata. He told Kyōden that he wanted to retire from the theater. It was due to bad kharma that he had been born a lowly actor and had to suffer the humiliation of being an old man who dressed and acted like a young woman. Ebizō wept at his predicament. He sensed that his ability as an actor was declining, and he sighed, saying he had only a little time left on the stage.[52]

Ebizō wanted 1795-96 to be his last season as an actor, and when he did what was to be his final "Shibaraku" his fans were chagrined. To them it seemed he was leaving the theater while he was still in his prime. One fan's poem expresses their sentiment: "I too cried out, 'Wait a moment!' / That's how much I'll miss the boss."[53] But for the same event Ebizō saw himself in a different light. His poem goes: "Bent over at the waist, beard long and straggly / The Shrimp gazes back at his past life."[54]

So the "old man" gave up his last stage name, Ebizō, and retired to a small, austere house in Katsushika, on the eastern fringe of Edo, resolved to live the rest of his life as the poet Hakuen, The White Monkey. In his first year in retirement he published the first book of his own work. Entitled *Tomo nashi zaru* (The friendless monkey), it consisted mainly of poems he had written in the previous decade, but included some zuihitsu, and two of his own watercolors. His choice of poetic name and title were in tribute to the great haiku poet Bashō (one of whose great works was *The Monkey's Raincoat*), and signalled that Danjūrō V intended to take his light verse seriously.

The most frequently cited poem in *The Friendless Monkey* expressed the author's desire for a life of retirement spent in literary pursuits and contemplation,[55] but the White Monkey was not to enjoy this luxury. Friends, relatives, and fans clamored constantly for him to return to the stage, and when their arguments were compelling enough, he did. In 1798 he gave a kōjō speech (he refused to act in a play) to help twenty-one-year-old Danjūrō VI celebrate his first kaomise as a zagashira. In his speech he presented a new kyōka poem every day of the run.

Only a year later Danjūrō VI was gone; the old man had lost his second and last son to sudden illness. The prospect was grim for the Ichikawa family. There were many popular and talented actors in Edo, and if too many years went by without a powerful Danjūrō or Ebizō the family might never regain its position of authority. The White Monkey would not make a total return to the theater, but he decided that his ten-year-old grandson had to be promoted right away. The boy was the son of Danjūrō V's second daughter and a part-time theater musician turned teahouse owner. Danjūrō had staked his hopes on his own son and had not had this grandson groomed to be a successor to the Danjūrō name, but the Danjūrō shumei took place in 1800, and once again the old man, now sixty, was onstage for a kaomise. Twice more he gave in to the pleading of friends and relatives who told him there would be an artistic or family crisis without him. He was getting a little rusty as an actor. In 1801 he forgot his lines in a "Shibaraku" scene. Looking across the stage at his counterpart playing the villain, he shouted, "Well, shall we glare at each other a little bit?"[56] The audience loved it, and the line was added to the play and repeated for the duration of the show. Even at the end of his stage career, Danjūrō V could do no wrong.

No kabuki actor had ever retired as early when in good health. Danjūrō V's withdrawal from kabuki in 1795 had jeopardized his family's future. Why did he do it? Was he truly embarrassed by the actor's status and calling? Was acting a distraction to a man bent on being a poet? Was he simply tired of theater politics and family responsibilities? Or was he a wily and clever old actor who knew that as his skill and stamina decreased the only way to maintain his popularity was to play the "reluctant old lion of kabuki"? Probably each of these considerations played a part in Danjūrō's decision to retire, but it is certain that poetry was an important activity for him during his retirement. As evidence, there remains a large body of work published between 1795 and 1804: four anthologies of his own poems, a hyōbanki satire, and numerous shorter works and poems chosen for anthologies compiled by other editors. Many of his books are illustrated by the finest ukiyo-e artists of the age. Some of his poems written after he had at last truly retired in 1803 show a man at peace with himself, able to look back at the world of the stage and the adulation of thousands as things of the past, now sources of poetic images, no longer binding him to the world of emotions and desires:

> During my leisurely retirement I use my aragoto long sword as a fishing pole.
>
> Has it been painted with *sujiguma* [striped, superhero makeup]?
> The narrow lane adorned in the first frost of autumn.[57]

In late 1806 the sixty-six-year-old White Monkey was ill, and during his convalescence composed one hundred poems dedicated to Buddha. One day in early winter he invited his friends to his hermitage to celebrate his recovery. According to Utei Emba, that was the day he died. His last poem was: "Where are the rain-laden clouds bound / Borne on the wintry wind?"[58] Of the memorial poems written by the friends who were with him that day, my favorite is by Hokusai, the ukiyo-e master: "Composing one hundred poems to the Buddha / White Monkey outpaces the magical Monkey King on his Journey to the West."[59] Onstage, as Danjūrō V, the White Monkey had performed as many exploits, and had used supernatural powers as great, as the heroic Monkey King of *Journey to the West*, China's most bombastic adventure tale. In his farewell poem Hokusai had created a wonderful image: the two magical monkeys hurtling through the heavens in a race to the Buddha's paradise.

The great actor-poet was dead, and the current Danjūrō was just a boy. In the first decade of the nineteenth century, Edo learned that it could live without a great Danjūrō, and without a fabulous "Shibaraku" every year. Other gala shows were invented to regale kabuki audiences at the kaomise. Was Danjūrō V to be the last of the great Danjūrōs? At this critical juncture, the literary elite of the ukiyo who had been Danjūrō V's last and best friends moved to support young Danjūrō VII. They continued to publish works celebrating the Danjūrō line, and transformed the young actor into "the heir to the grandest tradition in the history of kabuki." Their tireless service in publicity and promotion would culminate in the creation of the "Eighteen Great Plays," which would solidify Danjūrō VII's position as one of the pillars of Edo kabuki, and which have maintained the family's stature to this day.

NOTES

1. "Yakusha Saitanchō," *Kabuki hyōbanki shūsei*, 2d ser., 10 (Tokyo: Iwanami Shoten, 1992), 104.
2. Ibid., 104-5.
3. Tsuda Rui, *Edo no yakushatachi* (Tokyo: Perikansha, 1987), 61.
4. C. Andrew Gerstle, "Flowers of Edo: Eighteenth-century kabuki and its patrons," *Asian Theatre Journal* 4 (Spring 1987), 61.
5. Ibid., 66.
6. Ibid.
7. Ibid., 64.
8. Ibid., 65.
9. Ibid., 63.
10. Ibid.
11. There were two kinds of small theaters: small commercial theaters (*ko-shibai*) and small theaters operated by temples or shrines (*miyachi shibai* or *hyakunichi shibai*). The latter were regulated by the Bureau of Religious Affairs.
12. Many of the actors in small theaters were kabuki actor disciples who could not make a career on the kabuki stage. Once an actor had appeared on a small theater stage he was prohibited from ever appearing in kabuki.
13. Tsuda, *Edo no yakushatachi*, 61.
14. Santō Kyōden, "Sejo share mie zu," in *Gose Ichikawa Danjūrō shū*, ed. Hino Tatsuo (Tokyo: Yumani Shobō, 1975), 613.
15. Tsuda, *Edo no yakushatachi*, 163.
16. Ibid.
17. Gunji Masakatsu, *Kabuki mon Gunji Masakatsu santei shū* (Tokyo: Hakusuisha, 1990), 1: 229.
18. Ihara Seiseien, *Ichikawa Danjūrō no daidai* (Tokyo: Ichikawa Sōkezō, 1917), 41.
19. Tsuda, *Edo no yakushatachi*, 102.
20. Ibid., 103.
21. Utei Emba, "Yakusha konote kashiwa," in *Gose Ichikawa Danjūrō shū*, 626.
22. Ibid., 64.
23. Ichikawa Danjūrō V, "Tsurezure azuma kotoba," in *Ichikawa Danjūrō no daidai*, 63-64.
24. Ibid.
25. "Yakusha chibiki no ishi," *Kabuki hyōbanki shūsei*, 2d ser., 9, 246.

26. Evidence for this is the wooden tablets that Danjūrō V gave as offerings to the Shinshōji Temple during a *kaichō*, and the fact that he later described himself in a kōjō as a "helper [*torimochi*] at the kaichō." For an account of the gifts, see Asahi Jūzan, *Naritasan to Ichikawa Danjūrō narabi ni geinōjin no shinkō* (Narita City: Narita-shi Bunka Zaidan, 1968), 32-33. The only Shinshōji kaichō held in Edo when Danjūrō was head of his family took place in 1789. Hiruma Hisashi, *Edo no kaichō* (Tokyo: Yoshikawa Kobunkan, 1980), 152.

27. Ihara, *Ichikawa Danjūrō no daidai*, 43.

28. "Yakusha sensaku ron," in *Gose Ichikawa Danjūrō shū*, 598-99.

29. Hiraga Gennai, "Tonda uwasa hyō," in *Gose Ichikawa Danjūrō shū*, 600.

30. The Danjūrō V zuihitsu that were carefully recorded after his death are in a handwritten volume entitled *Tsurezure azuma kotoba*. The book is reproduced in facsimile form in *Gose Ichikawa Danjūrō shū*, 71-180. Many entries from *Tsurezure azuma kotoba* are reproduced in *katsuji* print, with commentary, in Ihara, *Ichikawa Danjūrō no daidai*, 64-68. The zuihitsu that Ihara discovered written on the margins of play texts appear as "Danjūrō V gigeiron," in Ihara Toshirō (Seiseien), *Danjūrō no shibai* (Tokyo: Waseda Daigaku Shuppanbu, 1934), 181-91.

31. Ichikawa Danjūrō V, "Tsurezure azuma kotoba," in Ihara, *Ichikawa Danjūrō no daidai*, 66.

32. Ibid.

33. Ibid.

34. Ibid.

35. Ichikawa Danjūrō V, "Gigeiron," in Ihara, *Danjūrō no shibai*, 184.

36. Ibid., 183.

37. Ichikawa Danjūrō V, "Tsurezure azuma kotoba," 67.

38. *Gose Ichikawa Danjūrō shū*, 597.

39. Ichikawa Danjūrō V, "Gigeiron," 183.

40. Ibid.

41. Ibid., 184.

42. Ibid., 187.

43. Ichikawa Danjūrō V, "Tsurezure azuma kotoba," 65.

44. Ibid.

45. Ibid., 67.

46. Nampo's anthology was *Ichikawa hiiki: Edo no hanaebi* (All for the Ichikawas: flowery lobster of Edo). It was a one-hundred-poem parody of the famous *Hyakunin isshu* (One hundred poems by one hundred poets), set in the fairy-tale palace of the dragon king of the sea.

47. Ōta Nampo (Yomo Akara), ed., "Kyōka saizo shū," in *Gose Ichikawa Danjūrō shū*, 610.

48. Utei Emba, "Oedo kazari ebi," in *Gose Ichikawa Danjūrō shū*, 612.

49. Ibid.

50. Furuido Hideo, "Kinsei engeki to chihō," *Kokugo to kokubun* (May 1987), 110.

51. *Gose Ichikawa Danjūrō shū*, 615.

52. Santō Kyōzan, "Kumo no ito maki," in *Gose Ichikawa Danjūrō shū*, 616.

53. *Gose Ichikawa Danjūrō shū*, 617.

54. Ibid.

55. The poem reads as follows: "I have given up the world and now have many friends, / the moon, snow, flowers, and the mountain cuckoo," in *Gose Ichikawa Danjūrō shū*, 619.

56. Ihara, *Ichikawa Danjūrō no daidai*, 59.

57. Ichikawa Danjūrō V, "Haiyu kei," in *Gose Ichikawa Danjūrō shū*, 625.

58. Utei Emba, "Ichikawa Hakuen tsuizen juzu no oyatama," in *Gose Ichikawa Danjūrō shū*, 628.

59. Ibid.

Mitate-e in the Art of the Ukiyo-e Artist Suzuki Harunobu

Tadashi Kobayashi

In Japan, the method of relying on past works of art to determine composition or subject matter in painting was a widely accepted practice.

In premodern Japan (for that matter, in the Orient in general, including China and Korea), artistic creation consisted of adding a cautious amount of personal expression to sample works chosen from the revered paintings of the classical past. New works of art were much like *honkadori* in poetry, which relied on allusive references to classical Japanese poems. In accordance with the *Analects* of Confucius ("I am a transmitter, not a creator"), it was considered a virtue to cultivate and propagate the seeds sown by the great masters and ancient sages. In contrast, the attempts by minor personalities of later generations to recultivate self-expression were despised as heretical behavior. In Japan's Middle Ages, ink paintings of the Muromachi Period (1336-1573) strove to imitate the "brush methods" of Song (960-1280) and Yuan Dynasty (1280-1368) Chinese artists, whose production was strictly governed by Confucian principles. For a brief moment, during the Sengoku (1467-1568) and Momoyama (1573-1615) periods, individual freedom like that of the artists Sesson and Kanō Eitoku was appreciated and praised. However, during the Edo Period (1615-1868), the concept of paintings as humble imitations of classical artwork once again prevailed. In particular, painters of both the Kanō and Tosa schools, which were patronized by the Tokugawa government, succumbed to artistic formalism. For the most part, they relied upon the "honka" of painting, namely *funpon*, or model books, comprising copies of ancient paintings.

Unlike the allusive variations of honkadori, *mitate* in *haikai* (linked haiku verse) was enjoyed for the startling and dramatic changes in meaning that later verses imparted to earlier ones. This same formula is used in *mitate-e*, a picture in which one anticipates a remarkable transfiguration of an old artwork and the witty transformation of classical aesthetics into contemporary vogue. Similarly, mitate-e allowed a lighter, almost iconoclastic approach to the classics by bringing them into the immediate reality of the present. They would be readily familiar to the viewer, and would occasionally be flavored with a gentle humor pervaded with a certain awareness of the art of love. It is thus not surprising that exquisite

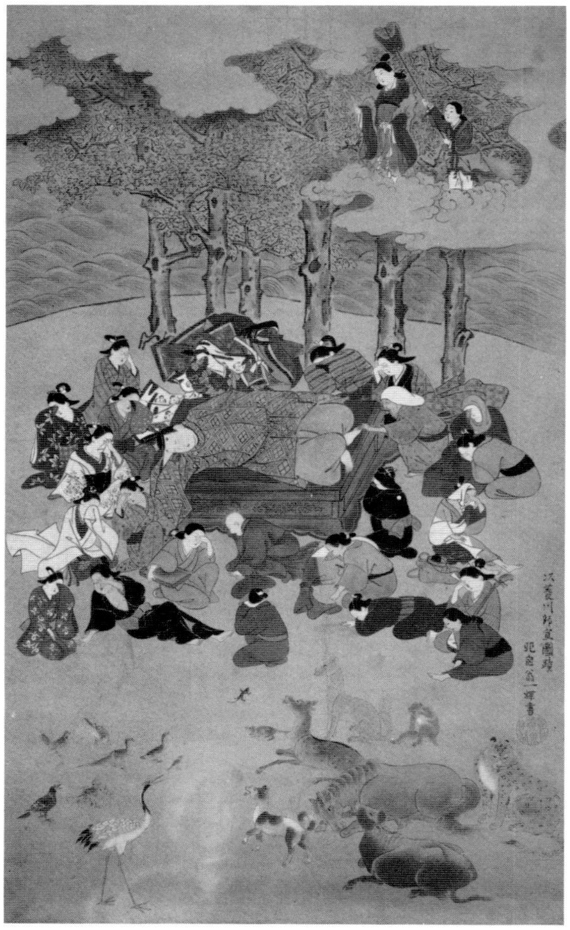

FIGURE 1
Courtesy of Tokyo National Museum

examples of mitate-e were produced by the genre painters of Edo and their counterparts, the ukiyo-e artists who designed paintings that were inseparable from popular customs and manners and yet were imbued with elegance and refinement.

A depiction of the parinirvana of Buddha is supposed to be replete with solemnity and represents one of the saddest spectacles for the Buddhist community. A painting with the signature of Hanabusa Itchō (Figure 1) transforms this somber image into a scene showing the death of the handsome Heian courtier Ariwara Narihira, surrounded by all sorts of women dressed in the popular styles of the Genroku era (1688-1703). A varied array of females (including birds and animals) mourn the young man's passing. Although the painting does not represent the standard work of Hanabusa Itchō, it bears an extremely interesting inscription by the artist: "Following a work by Hishikawa Moronobu." If we allow that the painting is an authentic work by Itchō and that it is based on an earlier model, then an established tradition of this mitate-e, namely the parinirvana of Narihira, existed in the work of the founder of ukiyo-e, Hishikawa Moronobu (1645-1715). It is tempting to attribute to the "father of ukiyo-e" the idea behind this straightforward and astonishing parody, which transforms a Buddhist meditative icon into a genre painting of females grieving over the death of a great romancer. Moronobu was the driving force behind the emergence of ukiyo-e, and it would be fitting indeed if we could confirm that he stood at the font of Edo history as the first artist of mitate-e.

The parinirvana of Narihira was also painted by the ukiyo-e artist Yamazaki Ryūjo, who was active during the Kyōhō era (1716-36) and who is documented in *Kinsei itsujin gashi* as "creating an unusual painting of Narihira's parinirvana." It is said that Yamazaki Ryūjo was a precocious artist who produced paintings when she was one, two, and three years old. However, her genre paintings of beauties cannot be deemed original or creative; they follow the styles of Miyagawa Chōshun and the artists of the Kaigetsudō and Hishikawa schools. It would be difficult to imagine that the eccentric concept of Narihira's parinirvana was Ryūjo's own invention; the assumption is, therefore, that her painting (formerly in the collection of Kishida Ryūsei) and the work attributed to Itchō both derive from, and contain, the essential elements of an earlier model.

The Two Types of Harunobu's Mitate-e

Parodies of the classics were specialties of Edo-period literature, and the issue of mitate-e was decidedly not limited to ukiyo-e. In particular, we should not overlook the artists who were considered somewhat outside the norm in the latter half of the period. These artists were characterized by the quirky little twists and turns they gave their subject matter and artistic expression (composition, techniques, design, and so on). Anyone can easily see and enjoy the generous spirit of humor in Itō Jakuchū's *Vegetable Nirvana* (Figure 2), in which

Sakyamuni is replaced by a giant radish, and in Nagasawa Rosetsu's *Seven Dogs of a Bamboo Grove*, which parodies the "Seven Sages of the Bamboo Grove," a subject drawn from Chinese painting. However, as the scholar Susumu Hayashi (Yamato Bunkakan) has been quietly explaining for years, many artworks, including the figure paintings of Soga Shōhaku, still await the unriddling of their mitate.

All this aside, ukiyo-e is probably *the* branch of painting in which the production of mitate-e is all-important. After all, ukiyo-e represents the essence of the Edo middle-class society, whose members shared the same aesthetics and knowledge, the same education and taste. Active among this society during the Meiwa era (1764-72) was the artist Suzuki Harunobu (1725?-1770). He was patronized both by the wealthy townsmen who had at last self-consciously arisen as the true "sons of Edo" (*Edokko*), and by the educated samurai who had fallen into the popular culture so much a part of the merchant class. Working during the onset of full-color print production, Harunobu is recognized as an artist who not only helped instill a love for mitate-e as a fixture in the ukiyo-e world but as one who demonstrated genius in its making.

There are, roughly, two types of mitate-e by Harunobu. In one, a modern interpretation is superimposed over the original subject; figures and animals familiar to everyone as characters from famous events, narratives, and paintings from the classical past are converted into stylish young men and women of the present. In the other, images are inscribed with well-known classical poetry (sometimes including *kanshi* and haiku). They attempt to amuse by abbreviating, inflecting, or adapting the tone and meaning of the classical poem to current customs and manners.

Let us consider several examples.

Figure 3 is a reproduction of Harunobu's masterpiece *Lovers Sharing an Umbrella*. A man and a woman snuggle together as they walk under an umbrella in the falling snow. Both wear hooded cowls and black lacquered *geta*, but the black and white of their garments clearly distinguishes them. A general painting category of black-and-white imagery includes such depictions as "The Crow and Heron" and Harunobu's print may be interpreted as a mitate-e of this theme, which may also be thought of as a mitate of "mandarin ducks in snow," a standard symbol of faithfulness in love. Among Harunobu's *nishiki-e* are several prints resembling this design and depicting a man and woman sharing an umbrella. One such print shows a couple gazing at a pair of courting mandarin ducks. Above them is inscribed the following poem:

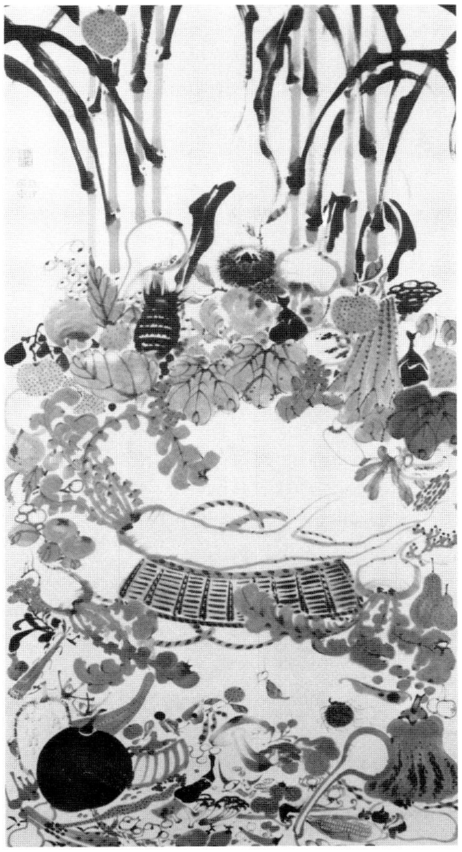

FIGURE 2
Courtesy of Tokyo National Museum

FIGURE 3
Courtesy of the British Museum

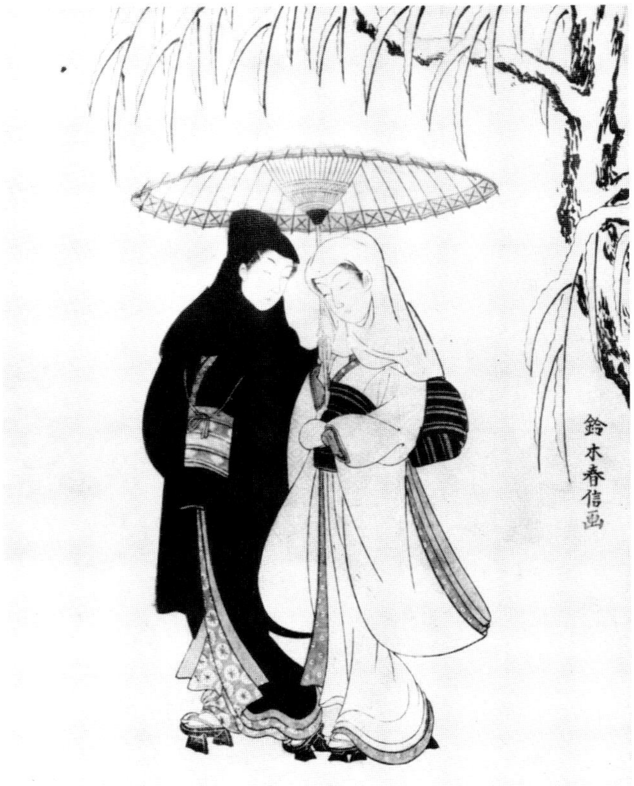

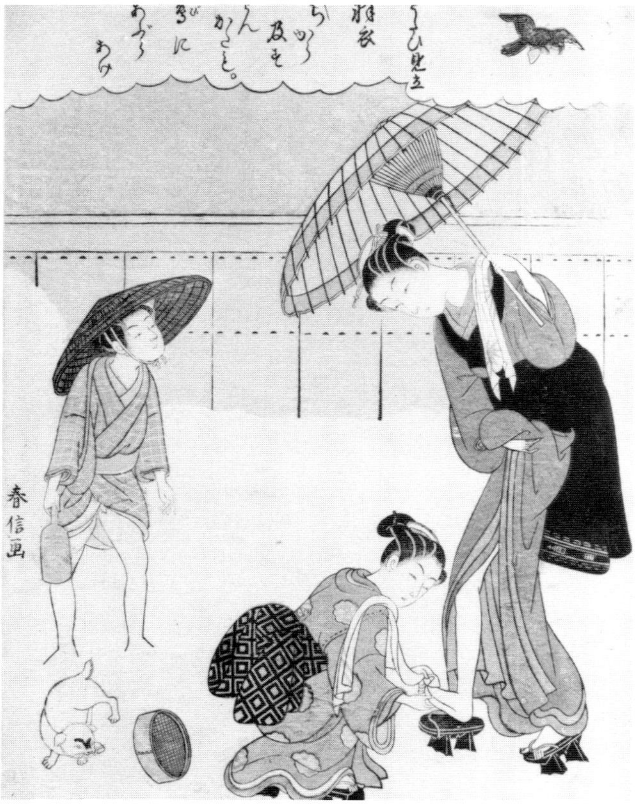

FIGURE 4
Courtesy of the British Museum

My heart aches
And is filled with jealousy.
If only we could promise ourselves
Such tender feelings.

In many instances in Chinese painting, a pair of birds displaying deep affection is shown beside a stream under a willow or in the snow. While *Lovers Sharing an Umbrella* was probably designed as a mitate of black-and-white imagery and "The Crow and Heron," it also sings the praises of young love following this Chinese tradition.

Another example comes from a set of Harunobu's *chūban nishiki-e*, and is called *Fūryū utai mitate: Hagoromo* (A fashionable recitation of *Hagoromo*, or "The Robe of Feathers," a famous No play) (Figure 4). At the top of the picture plane is a cloud within which is inscribed

A parody of No,
The Robe of Feathers:
Powerless and without recourse,
It was snatched from my hands.
The black hawk has my fried tofu.

In *Fūryū utai mitate: Hagoromo*, a major snowfall has covered the town to such a point that one could easily make a giant snowman. Along the road on her way home from the bath, a woman of the brothel district suddenly stops when her geta strap breaks, and her young attendant wipes her feet. In the instant before she can regain her footing, the woman drops the bucket she is holding, and the fried tofu she has just bought is snatched away by a black hawk. The bird flies overhead in a cloud, grasping the prize in his beak. On the ground below, a small white dog looks resentfully wistful, having missed its chance at a meal.

In a brief summary of the No chant *Hagoromo*, the fisherman Hakuryō (the secondary character, or foil) finds a heavenly robe of feathers; disregarding the pleas of its owner, a heavenly maiden (the protagonist), he at first refuses to return it.

Hakuryō, if you do not return my robe,
I am powerless and without recourse.
My bejewelled headdress and flower ornaments
Weep tears of sadness and wilt.
Before your very eyes I am dying,
O, so miserable am I!

This poem in Harunobu's print is drawn directly from the No text. However, Hakuryō takes pity on the sight of the forlorn and weeping maiden and promises to return the heavenly robe of feathers if she performs the "Heavenly Maiden's Dance." The joyous maiden plays a song and dances. In the end, she returns to the heavens.

Meanwhile as time goes by,
The Heavenly Robe of Feathers, in the sea breeze,
  trails over the pine grove at Miho.

Into the clouds, like floating islands.
Over Mount Ashitaka and the lofty peak of Mount Fuji,
Merging into the mists of the hazy heavenly sky,
she vanishes from sight.

In Harunobu's print, the woman holding the umbrella and wearing a green robe represents Hakuryō, while her young attendant is another fisherman. In this manner, the hawk flying high in the sky is the protagonist, the heavenly maiden.

In a visual parody of the play, the image transforms the setting to a common street scene. The rustic fishermen are audaciously changed into chic women, young and old, while the exquisitely charming maiden of heaven is boldly transfigured into a gruff black hawk. The extreme divergence itself is one of the delights of mitate-e.

Other prints that reportedly belong to the same set are *Kagekiyo, Tōboku*, and *Takasago*, all of which are the names of No plays and all of which bear the series title *Fūryū utai mitate*, each being prefixed with the two characters "fūryū" (i.e., fashionable or up-to-date). In addition to these works, there is another series of prints in the *hosoban* format, *Fūryū utai hakkei* (Songs of the eight views fashionably depicted). Harunobu (or, at least, the buyers of ukiyo-e) must have been deeply interested in No chants (*utai*).

Because the production of ukiyo-e prints was intended for broad distribution, the concepts behind the mitate were often either overtly rendered or clearly specified in the titles. In many cases, the allusion was readily understood. However, the viewer must always be on the lookout for prints whose mitate contain an even greater degree of allusive twist, such as Harunobu's *Shrine Visit in Evening Rain* (Figure 5) and *Boating Party* (Figure 6).

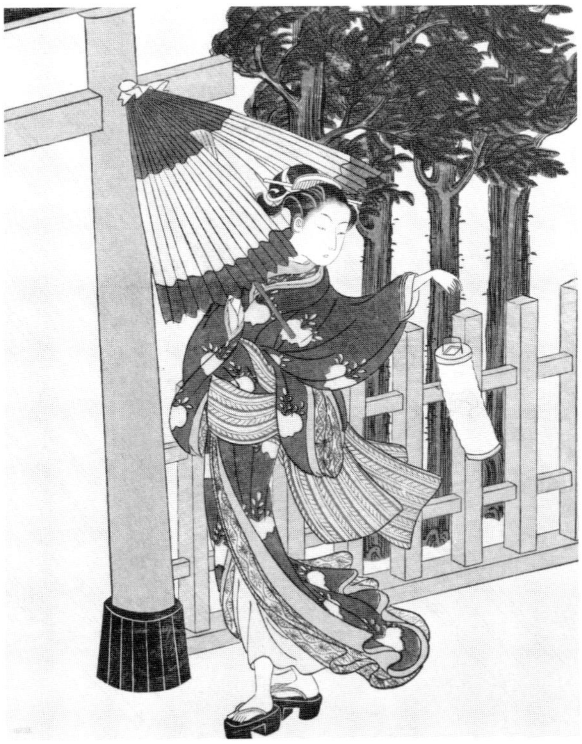

FIGURE 5
Courtesy of Tokyo National Museum

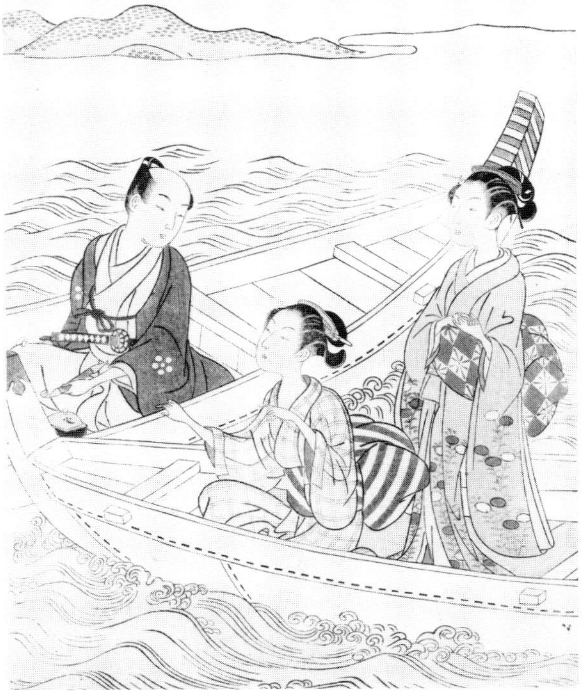

FIGURE 6
Courtesy of Tokyo National Museum

Both these works represent mitate of other No chants. The *Shrine Visit* seemingly transforms the Shinto deity Aridōshi Myōjin from the No chant *Aridōshi* into the waitress Osen of the Kagi-ya tea stall at the Kasamori Shrine. The *Boating Party* even suggests a parody of the shogun's councilor Tanuma Okitsugu as the Chinese poet Bai Juyi, from the No chant *Hakurakuten*.

Harunobu's Choice of Poetry

It is already evident that Harunobu loved to use mitate techniques like those discussed in the previous examples. He was well versed in the classical literature and painting of China and Japan, and by using them as references he created popular contemporary imagery. At the same time, much of his artistic output consisted of wonderfully perfected mitate-e, which were modern genre images intertwined with poetic meaning. Famous *waka* (the standard classical five-line poem, varying in syllables of 5, 7, 5, 7, 7) would be inscribed somewhere on the picture, such as in cloud-shaped areas, and the genre image would never be too closely related to, or too distantly removed from, the poetic text.

At one time, as part of my studies on Harunobu, I looked up all the classical poetry found on Harunobu's prints in the *Kokka Taikan* (Comprehensive collection of Japanese poetry). The result did not suggest broad referencing from all the collections of celebrated waka—the *Kokinshū, Shinkikinshū,* and so on. On the contrary, it became evident that rather than saying Harunobu selected waka directly from these various poetry anthologies, it is probably closer to the truth to say that he randomly chose waka that had become familiar because they were popular favorites in the basic learning of his contemporaries.

After making this conjecture, I saw a Harunobu print on satin (Figure 7), which parodied the traditional image of Murasaki Shikibu sitting at Ishiyamadera while working out the final details of her book *The Tale of Genji*, and any longstanding doubts about my conclusion began to fade. On the desk in Harunobu's print is spread writing paper on which the author is about to write a poem. Furthermore, there is a stack of books labeled with the title *Meidai waka zenshū* (The Meidai poetry anthology). I am convinced that Harunobu kept this same anthology by his side as a handy reference in which he could look up appropriate classical poems.

FIGURE 7
Courtesy of Tokyo National Museum

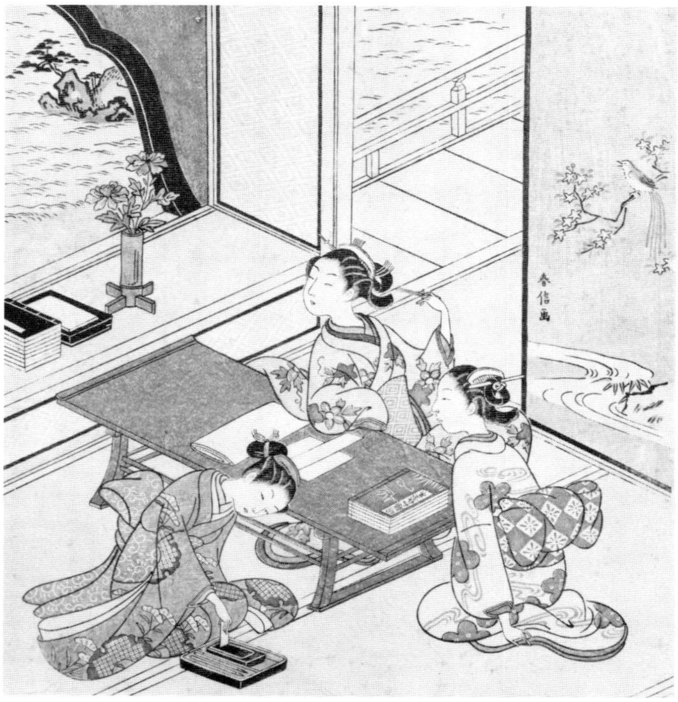

When an average person decided to take pleasure in the recitation of even a single poem, he wanted to have at his fingertips a one-volume compilation of famous poems from the ancient past on any subject. Convenient anthologies to meet this type of demand, such as the *Meidai waka zenshū* and the *Ruidai waka shū*, were widely published during the Edo Period. When Harunobu was basing an image on classical poetry, he would first go to the table of contents in his handy *Meidai waka zenshū*. Under the section on spring, for example, there are actually listed forty-four entries for plum, from *ume* (plum itself) to *baika niwaka ni chiri* (the sudden falling of plum blossoms). Turning to the entry *mizube no ume* (plum at the water's edge), one finds the poem by Taira no Tsuneaki from the *Goshūi-wakashū* (Later collection of gleanings from Japanese poetry).

Ure musubu
hito no te sae ya
niouran
Ume no shimo yuku
mizu no nagare wa

Even the hands
That bind new branches
Partake of the fragrance
Beside the stream
Flowing under a plum tree.

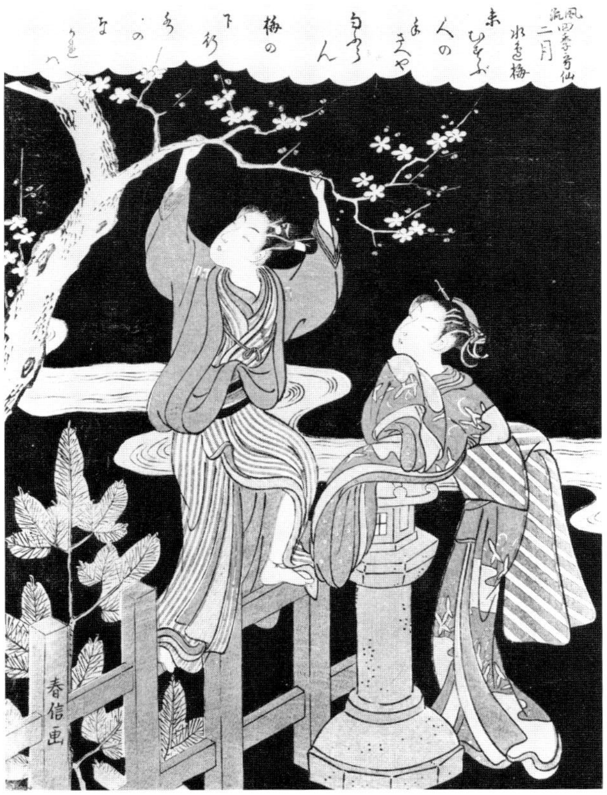

FIGURE 8
Courtesy of Keio University

This is what probably gave birth to Harunobu's romantic print in the series *Second Month—Plum at the Water's Edge, Poets of the Four Seasons* (Figure 8). A young couple meets for an evening date within a shrine precinct, where a branch of the white plum tree is broken and presented as a symbol of their love.

For someone who made a living by his wits—that is, by adding the appropriate imagery to subjects he dreamed up—Harunobu was a remarkably lazy artist. He would take a single verse from classical waka collected in works like *Hyakunin isshu* (Single poems by a hundred poets) or *Meidai waka zenshū,* then work out a rough pictorial design, either by using figural images from the prints of his predecessors such as Nishikawa Sukenobu or by grouping together one or two poses from his own repertoire of figure types. He would then fill in the final details and motifs and, giving full play to his genius as a colorist, determine the pigments for each color block. The final result was a solid pictorial world filled with deep lyricism, which, despite his frequent borrowings, clearly displayed Harunobu's distinctly personal style.

One could say that Harunobu was the first to prosper as an artist-producer whose methodology was one of constructive interpretation, much like that of a stage director or a music conductor. His career lasted a brief ten years, from 1760 to his death in 1770. Between 1765 and 1770—that is, in the space of only five years—we can postulate that he produced nearly a thousand prints. Moreover, from this large body of work, few pieces stand out as inferior or lifeless. The balance between Harunobu's evocation of classical poetry and his delicate sensibility is part of the reason for this stream of successful designs. When we admire one of his prints, we relish reading the waka inscribed on the work, and must then be prepared to seek out the two kinds of hidden meaning underlying the popular graphic representation.

In order to decipher mitate-e, it is necessary to pay attention to the illustration. The key to understanding the visual allusion is somewhere in the picture. Similarly, the fascinating body of work known as mitate-e serves as an important clue in helping us understand the characteristics not just of ukiyo-e but of Edo painting in general.

The Japanese Writing System

The Japanese had no written language before the introduction of Chinese characters (*kanji* in Japanese) in the sixth century. At first this newly introduced writing system was probably used solely for writing and reading Chinese, which the Japanese were eagerly learning at the time, but before long it was being used to record Japanese as well. This could be done because Chinese characters are semantic units—logographs—whose meaning is largely independent of sound (the character for "water," for instance, conveys the same basic meaning, whatever it is called in a particular spoken language). Using Chinese characters to represent spoken Japanese was not without its problems, however. One of the worst of these was caused by the fact that Chinese and Japanese are not only completely unrelated languages but differ from one another dramatically in grammar and word order. Moreover, many particles, prefixes, and verb endings essential to Japanese have no equivalents in Chinese and so had no characters to express them.

The Japanese overcame the latter difficulty by using certain Chinese characters for their sound rather than their meaning—something the Chinese themselves did in transcribing foreign words. The resulting combination of logographic and phonological elements has remained a feature of the Japanese writing system right up until today.

The use of Chinese characters to represent sounds was not limited solely to words or particles with no Chinese equivalents. There were other instances in which the Japanese must have found the logographic use of Chinese characters inadequate for their purposes. It was not, after all, a very effective way of transcribing the music of poetry or the pronunciation of unusual place names. One early way of overcoming these difficulties was provided by the *man'yōgana* system (already in existence by the early eighth century), in which Chinese characters were used to represent *every* sound in the Japanese language. This system had problems of its own, however. Unless a text was written exclusively in man'yōgana, it was impossible to tell—visually, at least—whether a given character was being used for its meaning or for its sound. This problem would eventually be overcome with the development of the *hiragana* syllabary, which came into widespread use in the tenth century. Hiragana, which are simplified characters used exclusively for representing sound, evolved from the cursive forms of man'yōgana characters. Unlike the latter, however, they are totally unintelligible to the Chinese.

Names, Dates, and Hours

Names

For those unfamiliar with Japanese customs, the handling of names, particularly those of artists, writers, actors, and other professional people, can be rather bewildering. Take the case of the writer we call Ōta Nampo. Nampo was actually only one of his names, a *gō*, or pen name; his "ordinary name" (his legal name, the name he used for everyday affairs) was Ōta Naojirō. As a *kyōka* poet, he took on another pen name, Yomo no Akara (a name that, incidentally, he later gave to someone else); and in some of his humorous writings in Chinese he went by the name of Neboke Sensei, "Master Sleepyhead." During the last two decades of his life, he generally called himself Shokusanjin. We will encounter him under all of these names—except Naojirō—later in this catalogue.

Nampo used a greater number of different names than most of his contemporaries, but, Japanese customs being what they were, this was what one would expect, given the length of his life and the many different literary genres in which he wrote. After all, a gō was normally related to the school or genre in which one was working. Under the same principle, the writer Santō Kyōden, for instance, went by the name of Kitao Masanobu when he was working as an artist. This name, which he had been given by his master, Kitao Shigemasa, not only made it clear that Kyōden belonged artistically to the Kitao family but acknowledged, through the character *masa*, his direct relationship with Shigemasa.

Just as the name "Masanobu" was *given* to Kyōden, many gō were acquired in the same way: they were earned by apprenticeship under a master, some of whose prestige inevitably attached to the names he awarded to his pupils. Other gō, however, were self-selected. Hokusai provides an interesting case in point. He began his career as Shunrō, the name he had received from his teacher, Katsukawa Shunshō, but as the influence of his master waned and he began to strike out in new directions artistically, he dropped that name for one of his own choosing, Sōri. It was not long, though, before he gave up that name, too, in favor of the one we now know him by. Even this was only one—albeit the most enduring—of the many names he used at one time or another during his long lifetime. Fortunately for the bedevilled student of Japanese art, Hokusai's is a relatively extreme case.

Actors' names can be just as confusing, if not more so. The actor featured in this exhibition, Ichikawa Danjūrō V, went by at least five different names at different times in his acting career (he had yet other names as a poet). Moreover, most of these names, like the name Danjūrō itself, had been borne previously by other members of his family. To make matters even worse, contemporary records usually referred to him simply as Danjūrō (or Ebizō, or whatever name he was then using), not as Danjūrō V.

As confusing as all this might sound to us, there was reason behind it. An individual actor, no matter how great a star in his own right, was seen as a representative of a proud family tradition, and these names embodied that tradition. They were precious family possessions, to be handed down to subsequent generations whose duty would be to add even further luster to them. Each name carried with it a certain status, represented a certain level of professional achievement. Ichikawa Danjūrō, for instance, was the most prestigious name within the gift of the Naritaya family to which Danjūrō V belonged. It was a name to conjure with, but it also had to be earned.

Considerable prestige was also attached to certain courtesans' names, and, like actors' names, these, too, were thought of as precious possessions to be handed down from generation to generation. In this case the names were the property of the house rather than of a family. The attitude, however, was essentially the same. Illustrious names like Hanaōgi of the Ōgiya or Segawa of the Matsubaya were jealously guarded by their respective houses, and the women who bore them had to live up to the highest expectations.

Kyōmei, the fanciful names writers took on in their personae as kyōka poets, were an entirely different matter. The first requirement for a kyōmei was that it be amusing; the second, that it sound as much as possible like the name of a classical court poet. This resulted in names like Hamabe no Kurohito, "Burnt on the Beach," or Moto no Mokuami, "All for Naught."[1] The resemblance of names like this to the high-sounding names of classical poets like Yamabe no Akahito or Mibu no Tadamine is obvious.

Dates

Before modern times, the Japanese used a lunar calendar in which the months (which were all either twenty-nine or thirty days long) were linked to the phases of the moon in such a way that the full moon always fell on the fifteenth day of the month. Years consisting of twelve lunar months are only 354 days long, however, which—barring adjustments of some sort—makes it impossible to keep them in alignment with the seasons. The Japanese overcame this difficulty by periodically adding a thirteenth month to keep New Year's Day from falling too long after the winter solstice, which would otherwise have happened about once every three years. In doing so, they followed a formula that almost always placed New Year's somewhere between the third week of January and the third week of February in the western calendar.

We are so used to the western way of numbering years consecutively from the birth of Christ, which allows us to see at a glance how events relate to one another in time, that it is hard for us to imagine any other kind of system. Yet until only recently in Japan, the standard way of recording dates was in terms of the *nengō*, or eras, in which they occurred. *Nengō*, which lasted on average about nine or ten years (some as long as twenty), were declared by government decree, usually with the intent of signalling some kind of new beginning. The declaration of a new nengō might be brought about by events as different as the promising accession of a new emperor or a disaster that the government wished to put behind it. In any case, the names chosen for them were invariably auspicious. The two nengō that coincide with the focus of this exhibition, for instance, are Temmei, "Heavenly Brilliance," and Kansei, "Magnanimous Regime."

The standard way of recording a date during the Edo Period, therefore, would be to give the year of the nengō or era, followed by the number of the month, followed in turn by the day of the month, thus: Temmei 4, first month, sixth day—which coincided, incidentally, with January 22, 1784. Nothing was ever simple in eighteenth-century Japan, however, and frequently this system was replaced or combined with another, involving the use of the Chinese sexagenary cycle. Under that system, a year's position in a sixty-year cycle would be indicated by combining the name of one of ten "stems" with that of one of twelve "branches," the latter being identical with the twelve animals of the zodiac. This explains the occurrence of dates such as *Temmei kinoe tatsu*, the Dragon year (or branch) of the Kinoe stem of Temmei, which was identical with the Temmei 4 date given above.

Months and days were usually referred to by number, though months also had poetic names, such as Shimotsuki, "The Month of Frost," and days could be designated by their place in the sexagenary cycle, as in "the first rat day of the second month." Instead of weeks, months were divided into ten-day periods called *jun*.

Hours

The day was divided into twelve rather than twenty-four hours. These "hours," however, were not identical in duration, as in the West. Six of them were daylight hours and six of them were nighttime hours, and therefore varied in length according to the time of year. During the winter, the nighttime hours were longer than the daylight hours, and in summer the opposite was the case. Only during the spring and fall equinoxes would every hour be exactly 120 minutes long. Later we will see how clockmakers dealt with the problems presented by such a complicated system of timekeeping.

A variety of bell towers at designated points throughout the city tolled the hours: nine strokes for midday (approximately 11 AM to 1 PM), eight for the next "hour," and so on consecutively down to four, at which time the count would return to nine strokes for midnight. The hours were referred to either by these numbers or by the names of the twelve animals of the zodiac.

NOTES

1. The translations of these names come from Haruko Iwasaki, "The World of *Gesaku*: Playful Writers of Late Eighteenth Century Japan" (Ph.D. diss., Harvard University, 1984), 62.

Catalogue of the Exhibition

All dimensions are given in centimeters, with height preceding width. Artists' signatures and seals, where decipherable, have been transliterated and form part of the entries. Inscriptions have been transliterated only when relevant and appear as part of the extended discussion of each work.

Catalogue Section I: The Setting

At the heart of eighteenth-century Edo, surrounded by massive stone ramparts and ringed by concentric moats, rose the castle of the shogun, its tall, whitewashed towers dominating the city fanning out below it toward the bay. Immediately in front of the castle, between the inner and outer moats, in an arrangement originally designed for defense, were the residences of the shogun's most loyal vassals. The higher land behind and to either side of the castle, known as Yamanote (literally, "the hilly or mountainous direction"), was also primarily inhabited by shogunal vassals or daimyo and their retainers. The part of the city that concerns us most in this exhibition, however, occupied the low-lying land closer to the bay and along the banks of the Sumida River. Criss-crossed by canals and waterways, the Shitamachi ("Low Town"), as it was aptly called, was the commercial and entertainment center of Edo and the most densely populated section of the city. Much of it had actually been reclaimed from the bay when the Tokugawas built their great castle in the early seventeenth century. It was populated primarily by commoners (*chōnin*).

Edo in the 1780s was a safe, clean, and relatively open city, with trees and greenery visible almost everywhere except in the most densely built-up parts of the Shitamachi. Contemporary views from hills overlooking the more crowded sections of the city show a sea of low tile roofs penetrated here and there by an occasional fireman's watchtower or the massive gables of a temple. In other directions, the expanse of rooftops was broken by groves and wooded hillocks. Almost all the buildings were of wood, the principal exceptions being the thick-walled masonry warehouses specifically designed to withstand the fires, the "flowers of Edo," that were an unavoidable part of life in the city. And there were bridges everywhere (as might be expected in a city much of which had been reclaimed from the sea)—upwards of six hundred of them. The largest were those crossing the Sumida, such as the Ryōgoku, which was over 170 meters long. Almost all of these were also of wood.

There were no parks as we understand them, but plaza-like areas at both ends of the Ryōgoku Bridge and the spacious grounds of some of the larger temples (such as Asakusa Kinryūzan) provided outdoor sites for a variety of festivals and carnival-like entertainments, while the sheltered precincts of neighborhood shrines and smaller temples were open to anyone who sought a moment of quiet. Moreover, nature was never far from the life of the Edokko. Birdsong and the sounds of autumn insects could be heard even in the center of town. The shell-strewn beaches of Edo Bay were virtually in the city's front yard, and the countryside was within easy reach for spring, summer, or fall outings. The Sumida River, closer at hand, was always available to provide refreshment and a sense of contact with the wider outdoors.

Though Edo did have its share of poverty, the squalor, drunkenness, and disease that afflicted the poorer classes of Europe at the time seem to have been less in evidence. As Henry D. Smith points out in his essay, standards of sanitation were almost certainly higher than in late-eighteenth-century London or Paris, and without question the city was cleaner and safer than its contemporary European counterparts. Thanks to an excellent public water system, safe drinking water was available everywhere, and night soil was collected regularly to be carted off to the countryside for fertilizer.

The basic unit into which the city was divided was the *chō*, or "block," which usually meant the area along both sides of a street from one intersection to the next. Many of the chō were set off from one another by wicket gates (*kido*) and guardhouses. Since streets rarely had names, locations were generally identified by their chō. To say that a kabuki theater was in Sakaichō, for instance, pinpointed its location to a specific block.

The fourteen works in this section offer a variety of different perspectives on Edo as it appeared in the late eighteenth and early nineteenth centuries. Only two (Catalogue nos. I-2 and I-4) provide overviews of the city; the rest focus on particular sites, especially its "famous places." These are not the only glimpses of Edo included in the exhibition (the crowded streets of the Yoshiwara and views out over the Sumida will appear again later), but the fourteen works shown here should at least help visitors to the exhibition gain some sense of the layout and general appearance of the city. They are like windows on another place and time, and afford us tantalizing views of the city.

I-1

Teisai Hokuba (1771-1844)

Beauties in Different Seasons

Circa 1815-20

Six-panel screen; colors on silk; 91.5 x 33.8 (each panel)

No signature

Los Angeles County Museum of Art, Joe and Etsuko Price Collection

Each panel of this screen seems to be devoted to a pastime or occurrence associated with a particular month, beginning with the seventh month at right and continuing through the year to the twelfth month at the far left. Since most Japanese screens were designed as pairs, it is generally assumed that this is the surviving member of a pair of screens depicting activities traditionally associated with each of the twelve

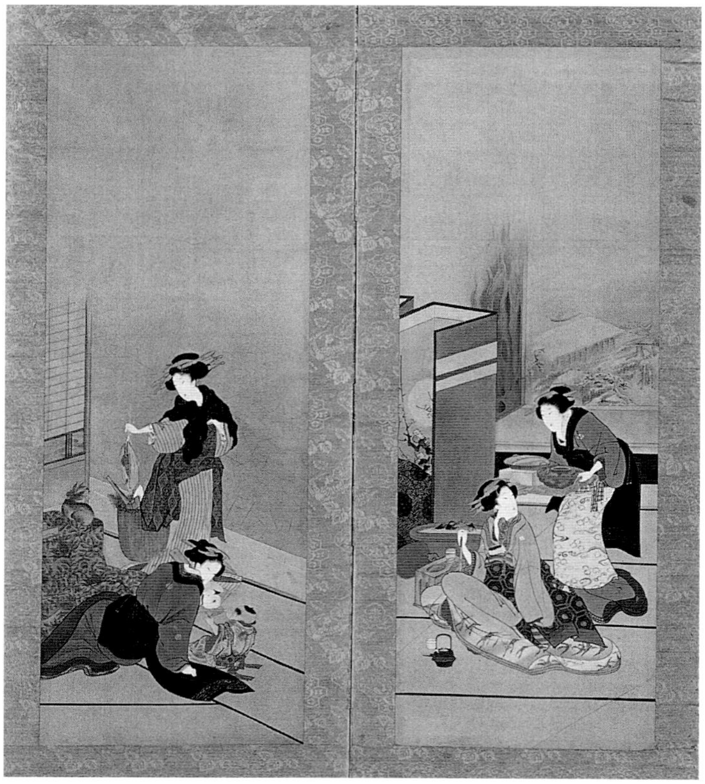

months. Incidentally, according to the lunar calendar in use in Japan during the Edo Period, New Year's Day fell anywhere from three to seven weeks later than it does in the Gregorian calendar, and the months were displaced accordingly. The seventh month would, thus, correspond more closely to August than to July.

Let us take the panels one by one, from right to left in Japanese fashion:

1. Two women and three children are getting ready for the Tanabata Festival, which took place on the seventh day of the seventh month. One of the women, with a little boy at her side, pauses in the midst of inscribing a *tanzaku* to turn toward her companion, who holds a cut bamboo tree already decorated with a number of poem slips. Behind the women, two older boys are busy tying additional poem slips to one of the bamboo's branches. Blank sheets of decorated paper, in both the narrow *tanzaku* and square *shikishi* formats, lie on the ground by the first woman's knees, ready to be inscribed with yet more poems.

2. A courtesan wearing her finest attire, her elaborate coiffure thickly set with combs and hairpins, passes a lamppost on her evening promenade as one of her *kamuro* points to a pair of geese descending from the early autumn sky above her. The Japanese seem to have been unusually sensitive to the change of seasons, and the sight and sound of migrating geese (*kaerigane*), one of the first signs of approaching autumn, was a frequent subject in traditional art and poetry.

3. Inside a temporary enclosure, a mixed crowd moves past the exhibits in a chrysanthemum show. Outside, three women, who appear to have been conversing, stare at something beyond the picture frame to the left. The chrysanthemum show is virtually identical to those still held today throughout Japan in October and November. Banked flowers outside the enclosure contrast with the meticulously tended plants, pinched back to only a few splendid blossoms, ranged in tiers inside.

4. Two women, one hastily trying to open her umbrella, the other wearing a rain hood, hurry home before the onset of a coming storm. A little boy trotting beside them gleefully thrusts his whirligig into the stiffening wind. Maple leaves fly through the sky, a sure sign that autumn is all but over.

5. A maid brings a tray of food to her mistress, who sits on the floor with her *tabako-bon*

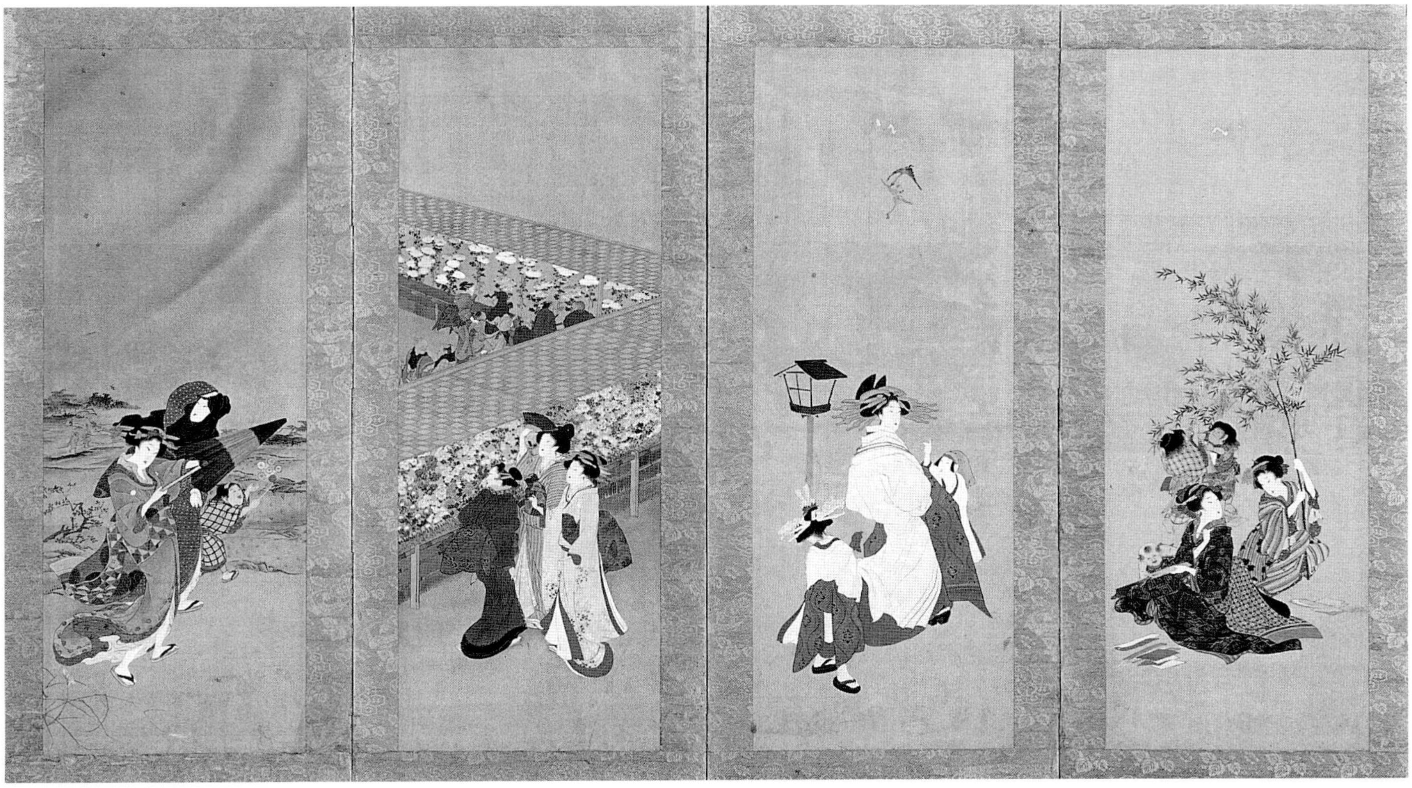

I-1

and tea kettle close at hand. Nearby is a large bronze hibachi, and just beyond that, partly closed off from the rest of the room by a folding screen, a pile of bedclothes. One can assume that it is morning, since the bedclothes have not yet been put away. At the back of the room, the shoji have been opened, showing a snow-muffled landscape with boats approaching the shore and an arched bridge crossing a little stream. Hokuba deftly contrasts the sense of warmth and coziness inside with the wintry monochrome outdoors. The view may well be of the boat landings on the Sanya Canal where it flows into the Sumida.

6. A young mother turns to look at her child, who is holding a toy with an O Kame mask. The room opens onto a veranda, beyond which all that can be seen is a body of water covered with cracked ice. It is cold, and the mother's legs are still partly covered by the quilted comforter of a *kotatsu*. A maid stands nearby, holding up a lobster, which she has just taken from a basket of toys and decorations for the New Year's holiday (the lobster was commonly used as a New Year's decoration).

Though not signed, this screen is so close in subject matter and style to other work by Hokuba that there can little doubt regarding its attribution. Hokuba, as one might guess from his name, was a pupil of Hokusai and, like his master, was active as both a print designer and a painter. The bulk of his print production was in the surimono genre, of which he was one of the foremost exponents during the first two decades of the nineteenth century. As a painter, too, he seems to have favored subjects with literary overtones, and a number of his paintings bear inscriptions by Ōta Nampo.

I-2

Kuwagata Shōshin Keisai (1764-1824)

Bird's-eye View of Edo

1809

Six-panel folding screen; ink and colors on silk; 176 x 352.8

Date (Bunka 6 tsuchinoto mi) and signature (Shōshin zu) and seal (Shōshin) of artist at lower-right corner of first panel at right

Tsuyama City Museum

When Keisai painted this extraordinary panoramic view of Edo in 1809, nothing like it had been attempted before. Keisai's achievement is all the more remarkable when one realizes that nothing remotely resembling this view could actually have been seen by anyone living in Edo at the time. The vantage is from high in the air somewhere east of the Sumida, yet the land in that direction was uniformly flat, with no hills or towers high enough to offer more than a glimpse of the other side of the river. The only hills of any substantial height from which even a part of this panorama could have been seen—Atago Yama, overlooking the bay, and Kanda Myōjin, at the northeast edge of the Shitamachi—were both on the west side of the river and were famous for their views to the east. This screen, therefore, in spite of all its vivid detail, had to be a mental construct rather than a scene actually drawn from nature. As such, it represents an impressive advance over earlier screen paintings of Edo, which had presented the city in a much more stylized, almost map-like fashion. For anything even approaching Keisai's concept in daring, one would have to go all the way back to the early sixteenth century and Sesshu's remarkable view of Amano-hashidate depicted from a vantage high out over the ocean. Sesshu's painting, however, was rooted in Chinese-derived traditions and was essentially a landscape. Keisai's vision is more embracive, not only taking in an entire teeming city but extending to Mt. Fuji, a hundred kilometers to the west, and even drawing in the hills of the Bōsō Peninsula and the rising sun to the southeast.*

The focus of the screen, however, is on the part of Edo that stretches out from the great castle toward the bay and along the lower reaches of the Sumida River—in other words, the Shitamachi (much of the Yamanote district is out of sight behind the castle and ridge of higher land to either side of it). Here, from a point just north of the Yoshiwara on the right to Shinagawa on the left, ten kilometers to the south,

* The hills are so identified in Keisai's woodblock version of this scene published around 1803. See Henry D. Smith II, in *Japan and the World: Essays on Japanese History and Politics in Honour of Ishida Takeshi*, ed. Gail Lee Bernstein and Haruhiro Fukui (London: Macmillan, in association with St. Antony's College, Oxford, 1988), 15.

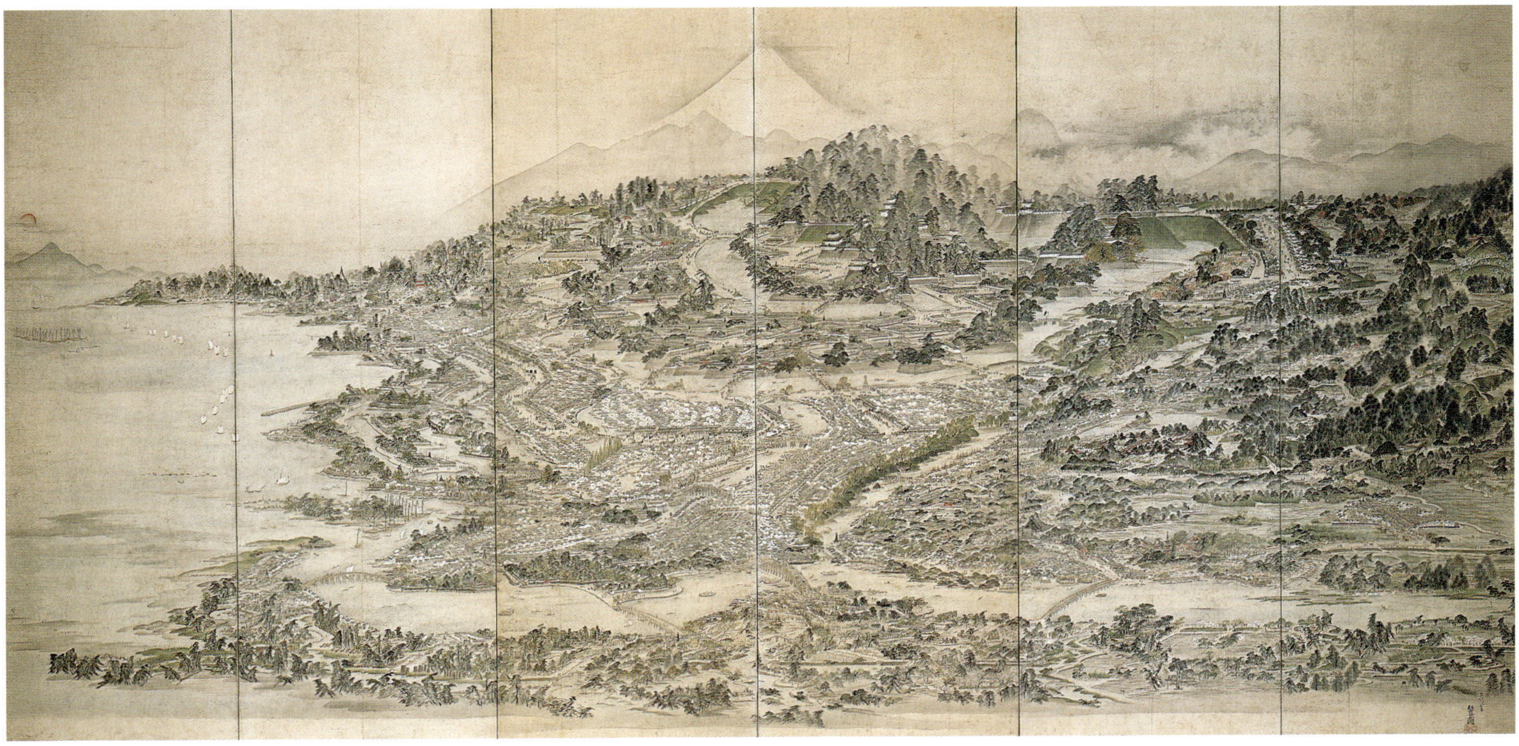

I-2

Keisai has depicted the streets and well-known landmarks of the city in astonishing detail and with an impressive degree of accuracy. This is not to say that the scene is laid out with map-like precision. A comparison with the *Great Survey Map of Edo* of 1798 (Catalogue no. I-4) shows that Keisai has given much more space proportionately to the area north of the Kanda River than to the area south of it. The distortion is most evident in the section of Shitamachi between the Kanda River and Nihombashi, which has been severely foreshortened. This distortion seems to tie in with another, perhaps related, way in which the scene is at variance with the map: everything to the north is splayed out somewhat toward the east (the dike leading to the Yoshiwara, for instance, seems to run straight north instead of northwest as it did in reality), while everything to the south is pushed in correspondingly to the west. One can only assume that Keisai's purpose in doing this was to allow him to bring in the hills of the Bōsō Peninsula, which would otherwise have remained out of view to the east.

It would be impossible to describe the screen in detail within the limits of this catalogue, so we will merely point out some of the more interesting landmarks depicted. The Sumida River runs across the bottom of five of the six panels, and Mt. Fuji rises in the background, in the top center of the composition. Just below Fuji to the right, rising like a mountain itself inside its moat, is the shogun's castle, with its towers, ramparts and forested precincts. Fanning out in front of the castle is the city, and to the left, stretching off into the distance, is the bay.

Looking at the screen more closely, beginning at the right, we come first to the Yoshiwara and, below it to the left, the Sanya Canal with its boat moorages. In the center lower part of the next panel are the red buildings of Asakusa Kinryūzan Temple with the Azuma Bridge to the left, and above these one can make out the various temples at Ueno with Shinobazu Pond and the Benzaiten Shrine above them. Farther up, looking like a covered bridge as it crosses the Kanda River, is the aqueduct at Ochanomizu. The next panel shows the crowded Ryōgoku Bridge at bottom left and above it, a bit less than halfway up toward the castle, Nihombashi and the busy fish market just northeast of it. Farther up yet, daimyo processions may be seen crossing several of the bridges leading to the castle.

The most prominent feature in the next panel (the fourth from the right) is the broad thoroughfare leading south from Nihombashi through the Ginza in the direction of Shinagawa and the start of the Tōkaidō. Keisai has exaggerated the width of the street in order to show the fence-like gates or barricades (*kido*) that crossed it at intervals. Such gates were to be found throughout the Edo, marking the boundaries between the blocks (*chō*) into which the city was divided. The next panel shows Eitai Bridge at bottom with Tsukudajima (Tsukuda Island) immediately above it, at the mouth of the river, and the red gate of Zojōji Temple near the top.

Keisai studied under Kitao Shigemasa, who gave him his first brush name, Kitao Masayoshi. In 1780, at age sixteen, he began illustrating kibyōshi, an activity that absorbed much of his time over the next ten years or so. He did, however, also illustrate other kinds of books and design perspective prints (*uki-e*), and in 1785 he produced a remarkable woodblock-printed scroll, *Edo meisho zue* (Catalogue no. I-13), which includes many of the landmarks depicted here.

In 1793 Keisai's career took an unusual turn for an artist from an ukiyo-e background, when he was appointed official painter to the daimyo of Tsuyama. It was in the service of his Tsuyama patron that he painted this screen. It is said that it was originally designed as a sliding screen (*fusuma*) for Tsuyama Castle and was only later mounted in its present form. The daimyo of Tsuyama were distant relatives of the Tokugawas, and their castle was destroyed during the brief civil war that ushered in the Meiji Restoration of 1868.

I-3

Chōbunsai Eishi (1756-1829)

Journey to the Yoshiwara

1801

Handscroll; ink and colors on silk; 30.8 x 1,123.4

Signature (Chōbunsai Eishi hitsu) and seals (Eishi) and (Shubun hōin) of artist on screen in last scene; date, late summer of Kyōwa 1 (Kyōwa kaigen ka no tori kika), and signature of author (Tōto tonsho O Bokuan) at end of preface

Idemitsu Museum of Arts

Eishi, who was the son of a high-ranking official in the *bakufu*, first studied art under a well-known painter of the Kanō School and mastered the Kanō style so well that he went on to serve for a while as artist-in-attendance to the shogun. At a relatively early age, however, he gave up this position in order to devote himself full-time to ukiyo-e. It seems, though, that he never wholly abandoned his upper-class contacts, and in 1800 he received a visit from a priest of one of the Imperial temples in Kyoto, who commissioned him to paint a handscroll of the Sumida River. The priest thought so highly of the work that he decided to give it to the retired emperor, who is also said to have admired it. Apparently word of this got out, because Eishi was soon pressed to paint additional versions of the scroll. Some ten of these, seemingly all authentic, still exist.

Most of these appear to have been commis-

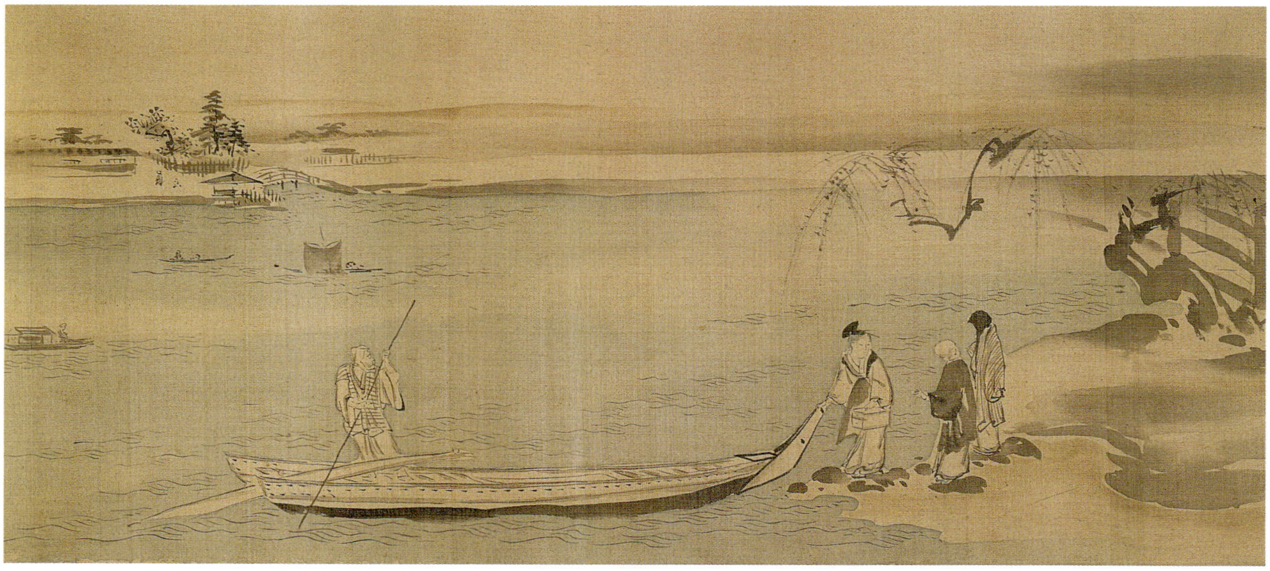

I-3

sioned by more worldly patrons, however, because nearly all of them (unlike the original) use the "visit to the Yoshiwara" theme that had long been associated in ukiyo-e with views of the Sumida River. In this respect, the Idemitsu scroll is similar to most of the other versions but it also differs from them in several key regards. For one thing, it has a final bedroom scene, which, combined with the attached preface, makes it longer than any of the others. Also unique is the contrast between the river scenes, which are rendered in ink monochrome, and the scenes in the Yoshiwara, which are painted in color.

As Masato Naitō, one of the curators at the Idemitsu Museum, has pointed out, the fact that the preface is dated only a year after the original scroll was commissioned points to the likelihood that this is the earliest of all the later versions. Certainly it is painted with a verve that suggests that Eishi still found the subject of interest.

The narrative thread tying the scroll together is announced at the outset, where two men, one with the shaven pate of a monk or an older man in retirement, the other with features shrouded from view with a hood, engage a boat to take them upstream. The boat, with its single oarsman, is a *chokibune*, a kind of water taxi particularly favored for trips to the Yoshiwara. The willow tree arching over the small rustic bridge to the men's right also suggests their destination, since Yanagibashi (literally, "Willow Bridge") was the usual starting point for such outings.

Eishi makes no effort to depict such well-known features of the cityscape in realistic detail, nor does he provide a complete panorama of the scenery along both banks of the river. The landmarks he does focus on are rendered in a kind of visual shorthand, and he offers mere impressionistic hints of the broad sweep of the river itself. It is a technique more often seen in paintings of the Kanō School than in ukiyo-e.

Though identifiable sites occasionally appear along the opposite shore, the landmarks along the nearer, western bank were more often associated with trips to the Yoshiwara, and it is these that attract Eishi's greatest interest. The first of them, the *Shubi no matsu*, "Pine of Fate," quickly comes into view as one unrolls the scroll.

Next come the roofs of the warehouses where the *bakufu* stored the rice that it handed out as stipends to its vassals. It would be impossible to underestimate the importance of these warehouses in the economic life of Edo. Since they were just upstream from the Ryōgoku Bridge, which was at the center of one of the liveliest entertainment districts in the city, they often appear in the background of the many prints that took that popular site as their subject.

Across the river, a crowded boat noses into the Oumayabashi ferry landing. Midway between the Ryōgoku and Azuma bridges, the Oumayabashi ferry crossing was one of the busiest such crossings on the river. As though to prove the point, Eishi introduces another crowded vessel approaching the nearer shore. The passengers would have had a good view of the distinctive roof of the Komagatadō, which is the next landmark depicted.

Unrolling the scroll further, we come to Azumabashi, "Bridge of the East," also known as Ōkawabashi. A motley crowd crosses the bridge and a log raft passes under it. The tree-studded hillock upstream, with the temple roof just visible at the top, is Matsuchiyama, and the break in the trees across the river indicates the approach to the Mimeguri Shrine. These last two sites had particular significance for those who were making the trip to the Yoshiwara, for the Sanya Canal, which marked the end of the river portion of the trip, lay just beyond them.

The remainder of the trip was by land, along a dike between paddy fields, and it is at

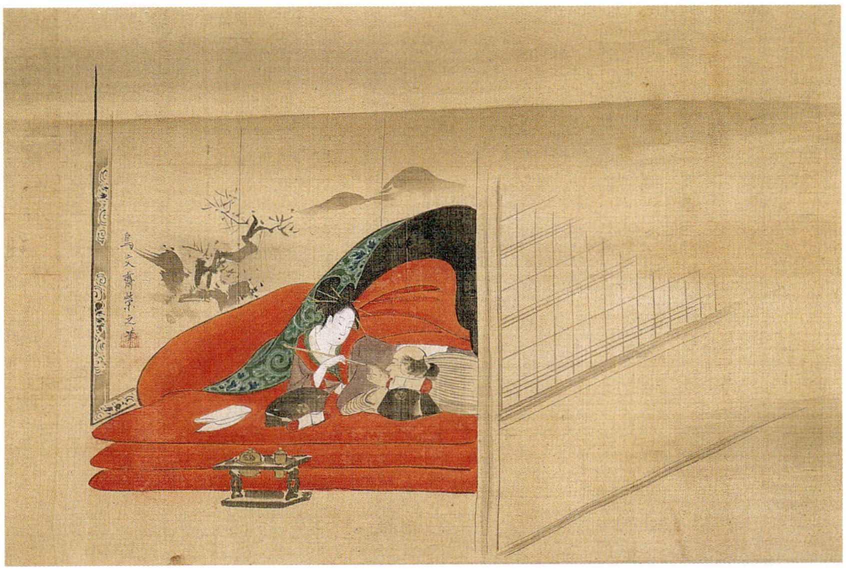

I-3

this point that we reencounter the two men we met at the beginning. They are shown standing on the dike, the older man pointing ahead to the slope leading down to the Yoshiwara's Great Gate. Now the tempo picks up, and the monochrome palette and sense of spaciousness of the first part of the scroll is replaced by the color and liveliness of the pleasure quarters. First the two men are shown seated on the porch of a teahouse, watching the spectacle of courtesans promenading on the Nakanochō; then, in a brief return of monochrome, they are shown outside the cage-like windows of a brothel, discussing the comparative merits of the courtesans on display inside. The final two scenes are again in color. In the first of these, a party is in full swing, and the two men, seated beside a bronze hibachi, an array of food on trays in front of them, look on as a group of geisha entertain them with *shamisen* music and a male entertainer proffers them a cup of sake. Two courtesans, with *tabako-bon* in front of them, sit decorously to one side, and a *tokonoma*, decorated with a basket of flowers and a scroll depicting Fukurokujū, opens off to the left.

The final, culminating scene shows the samurai quietly conversing with one of the courtesans in bed. The courtesan's lacquer pillow has been pushed over, and she lifts herself up on one elbow as she talks with her guest. Luxurious quilts cover the couple, and the bed itself is made up from a stack of three rich, red futon. These are the *mitsubuton* that were one of the status symbols of a high-ranking courtesan. The bed is closed off from the rest of the room by a monochrome landscape screen in Kanō style with Eishi's signature and seal.

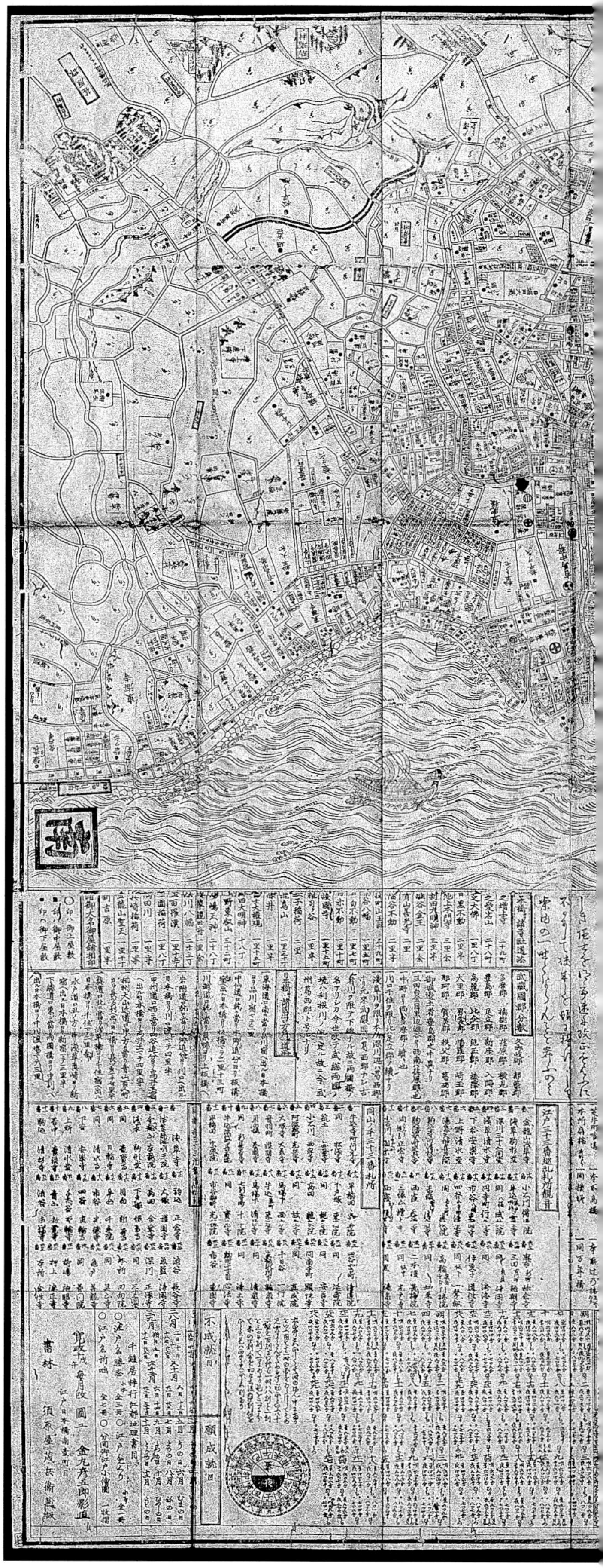

I-4

***Bunken Edo ōezu*, "Great Survey Map of Edo"**

1798

Woodblock-printed map, pieced and folded; 160 x 193

Name of draftsman (Kanemaru Hikogorō Kagenao) and name of publisher (Suwaraya Mohei) with date (Kansei 10 tsuchinoe uma) in panel at lower left

East Asian Library, University of California at Berkeley

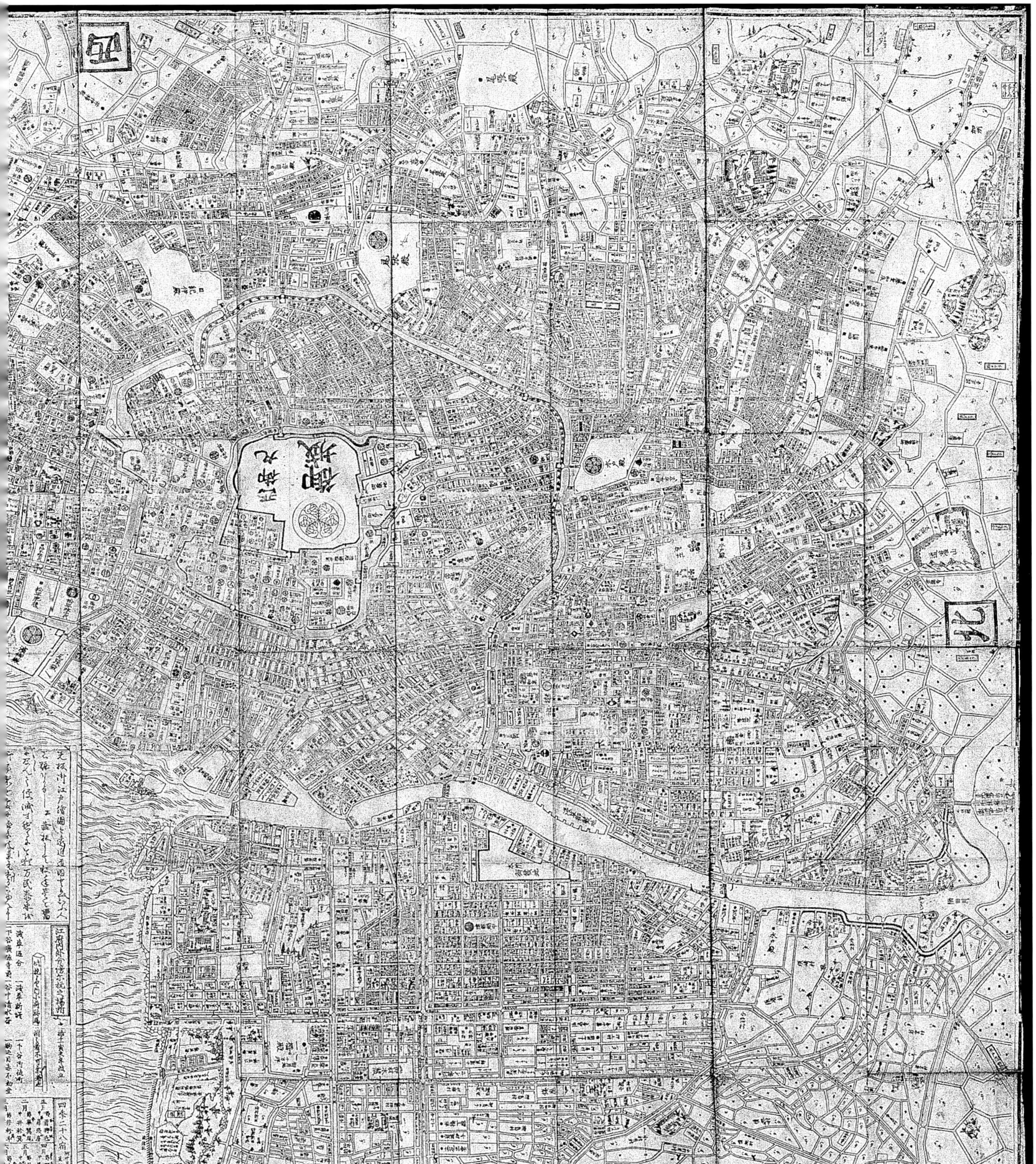

I-4

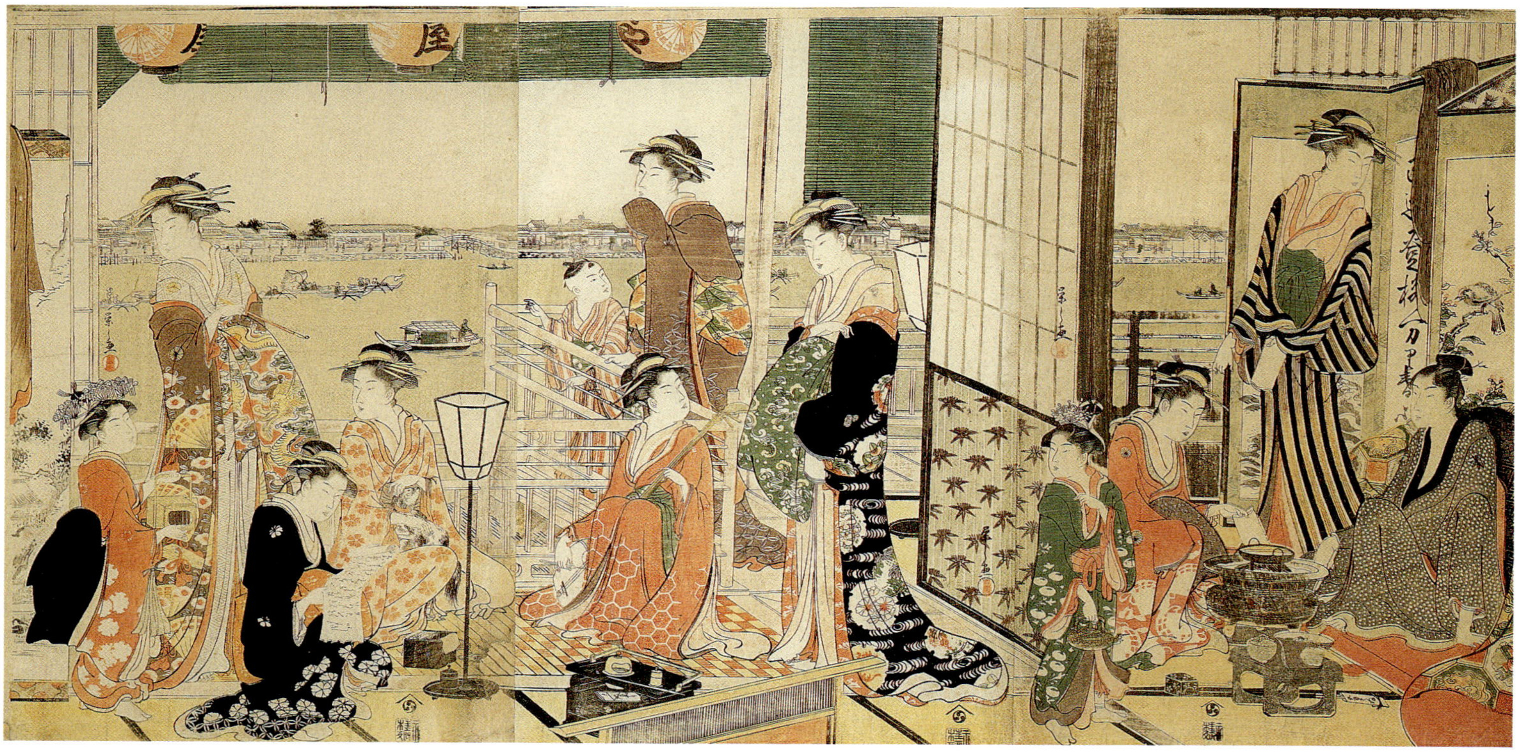

I-5

The most obvious feature setting this *Great Survey Map of Edo* apart from European and American maps seems to be its orientation to the west rather than the north. In actual fact, however, even though the symbol for "west" appears at what we must take as the top of the map in relation to the tables at the lower left, only some of the legends and place names are written with the same orientation in mind. The direction in which street names and place designations are written seems to follow no discernible system whatever. Descriptions of pieces of property lying side by side will sometimes be written upside down or at right angles in relation to one another. In order to "read" the map, in other words, one must constantly turn it around or approach it from a different direction.

Another interesting aspect of the map is the way little pictures are used to represent temples and shrines and certain natural or man-made features, such as the water in the bay and the rocky seawall bounding it. Daimyo estates are identified not only by family crest and name but also by a system of symbols indicating whether the estate in question is a primary, secondary, or alternate residence. The names of bridges and *chō* are sometimes given in *kanji* and sometimes only in *katakana*. Paddy fields are identified by the square character for field (*ta*).

The tables in the lower-left corner provide information about things like distances to various temples and shrines (including, oddly enough, the Yoshiwara!), the starting points of the leading highways, the names of popular pilgrimage sites in the Edo region, and tide charts.

This map appeared in numerous editions over the years and, given the number of surviving copies of different dates, seems to have been extremely popular. The publisher, Suwaraya Mohei, specialized in maps.

I-5

Chōbunsai Eishi (1756-1829)

Temporary Quarters at Nakasu

1788

Woodblock print; ōban triptych; 38 x 75.4

Signature of artist (Eishi ga) and trademark and seal of publisher, Nishimuraya Eijudō, on each print

Portland Art Museum, Mary Andrews Ladd Collection

The view is out over the Sumida River from the upstairs apartments of the Ōgiya's temporary quarters in Nakasu (a devastating fire in the fall of 1787 had levelled the Yoshiwara). A single guest sits in front of a folding screen in the far right corner of the room, watching a kneeling courtesan preparing some food on a hibachi, while other courtesans stand or lounge about elsewhere in the room. A young courtesan or *shinzō* has gone out on the veranda to look upstream at something that has been pointed out by a boy attendant. In the center of the room, a geisha plucks her *shamisen* as she turns to look up at a courtesan standing beside her, while to the right a *kamuro* stands holding a sake kettle as though not quite knowing what to do with it.

The open shoji, the bamboo blinds hanging from the eaves, and the number of boats on the water make it clear that it is summer. The courtesan reading a letter near the standing lamp at left also suggests that it is early evening. Nakasu was a thriving entertainment district in the 1780s and a favorite site for summer parties. More will be said about it later. Two other prints in the exhibition (Catalogue nos. I-6 and I-7) also depict riverfront establishments in the district.

This is one of Eishi's earliest works and, like much of the ukiyo-e at the time, still shows the strong influence of Kiyonaga.

I-6

Angyūsai Enshi (active 1785-1795)

View from the Balcony of the Yamashiro Teahouse

Circa 1789-90

Woodblock print; ōban triptych; 37.5 x 73.5

Signature of artist (Angyūsai Enshi ga or Enshi ga), trademark of publisher (Iwatoya Kisaburō), and kiwame seal on each print

The Art Institute of Chicago, Clarence Buckingham Collection

Two men, surrounded by courtesans and geisha, are enjoying a party on the balcony of the Yamashiro teahouse overlooking the Sumida River. To the left, more courtesans, helped by a maid, are stepping up onto the balcony from a large boat that has just moored below. Out on the river, another large vessel, a twin of the one that has just moored, seems to be making straight for the teahouse with additional guests. The two boatmen poling it from its roof appear to be too busy to pay much attention to the river traffic around them. A small roofed boat passes in close to the teahouse from the right, and open *chokibune*, or water taxis, move briskly along the water in all directions. The two larger boats are

I-6

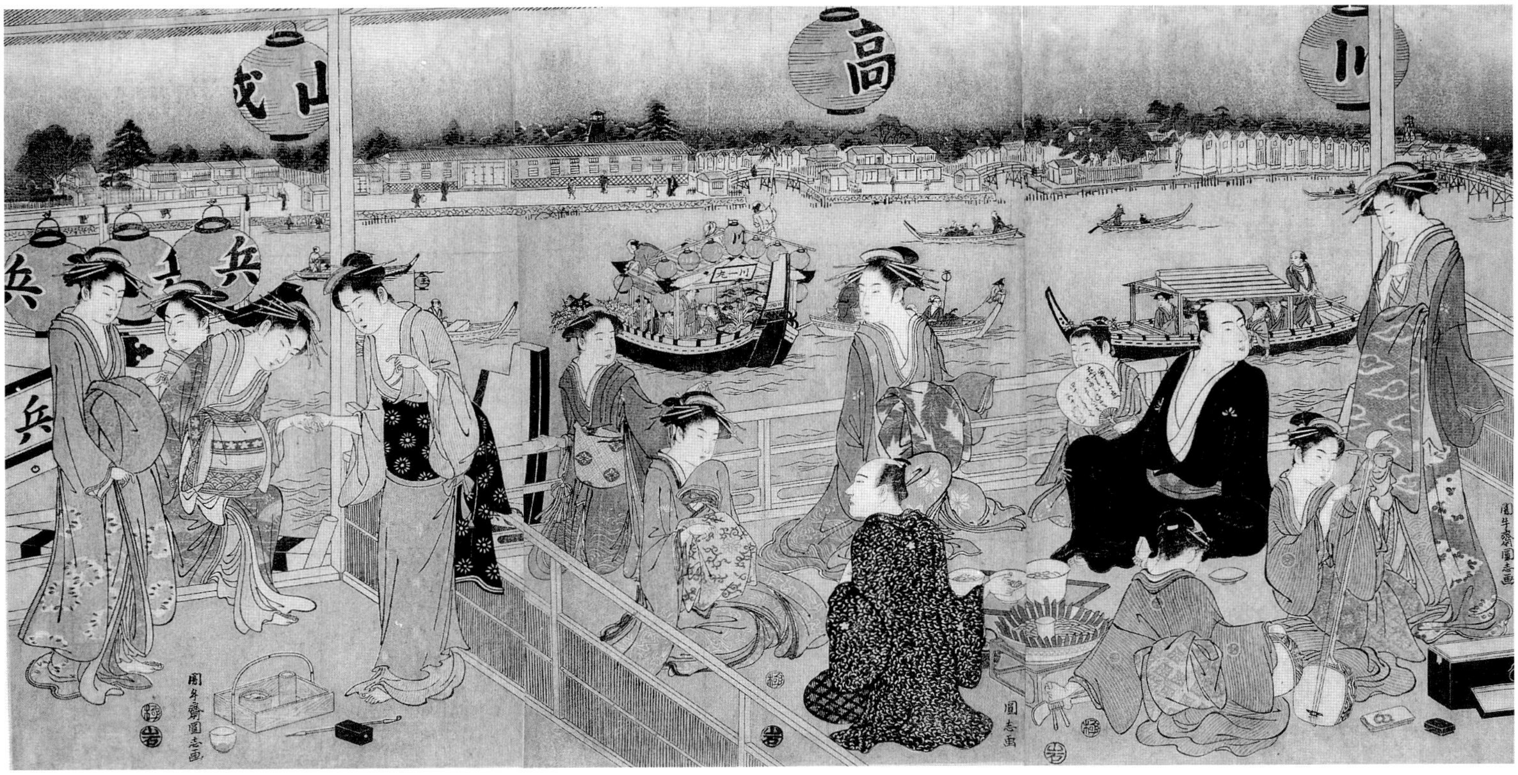

festooned with lanterns imprinted with the characters for their respective names. The name of the one still out on the river, *Kawaichi Maru*, is also written on a plaque hung from the gable of its roof, but only one of the characters for the name of the boat that is moored is visible, *Hyō*.* Large, roofed pleasure boats like these, which could accommodate sizable parties, were called *yagatabune*. They were a common sight on the river during the summer months.

It has always been assumed that the Yamashiro teahouse was in the Ryōgoku district, but in fact it must have been in Nakasu. A comparison with Catalogue no. I-7, Shumman's *Shikian Restaurant* (the Shikian was in Nakasu), will show that the opposite shoreline is nearly identical in both prints. If this is indeed the case, it might explain the presence of so many courtesans. Normally special permission was required for courtesans to be allowed out of the licensed quarters, but in 1787 a fire forced most of the Yoshiwara brothels to find temporary premises elsewhere, and several of them ended up in Nakasu, where they probably remained into the summer of 1788. It may also be the case that one or another of the two men partying here was a person of enough influence to secure the special permission required. Since the crests of both men are visible, it might be possible to identify them.

* A similar pleasure boat bearing the name *Hyōgo* is depicted in a pentaptych of a somewhat later date by Eishi. See Henry D. Smith II, *Ukiyo-e ni miru Edo meisho* (Tokyo: Iwanami Shoten, 1993).

I-7

Kubo Shumman (1757-1820)

The Shikian Restaurant

Circa 1787-88

Woodblock print; ōban diptych; 25.3 x 72.6

Signature (Kubo Shumman ga) and seal (Shumman) of artist and name of publisher (Shūeidō) on shōji at right; signature of artist (Shumman ga) and name of publisher on trunk of tree at left

The British Museum

A party is in progress in an open room overlooking the Sumida River at the famous Shikian Restaurant in Nakasu. Sake and a sea bream (which was considered a particularly auspicious delicacy) have already been served, and a maid brings in a tray with other treats. The room has

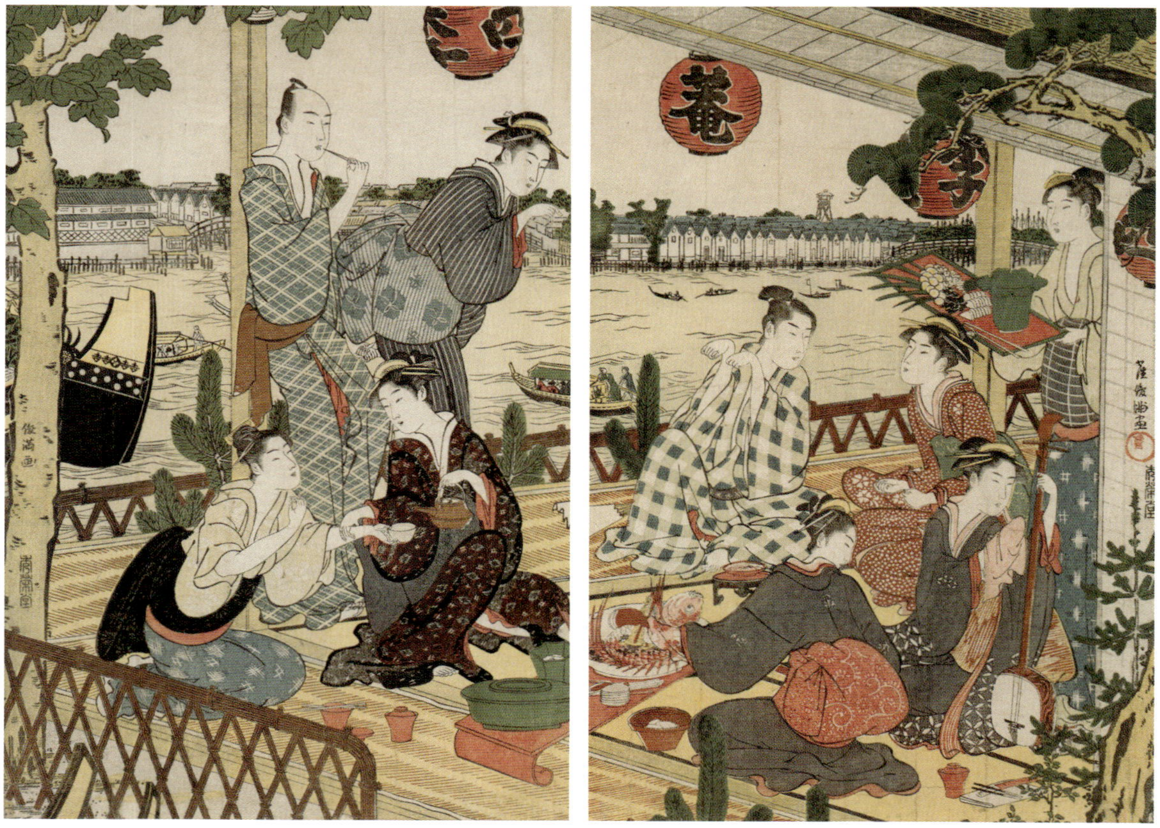

I-7

probably been engaged by the two young men in light summer robes, one of whom is busy playing a hand game with a young woman while the other lounges against a pillar, nonchalantly raising a toothpick to his mouth while holding the hand of the woman beside him. Elsewhere in the room, two young women, possibly geisha, get their *shamisen* ready to play some music, and a third young woman, dressed in a gauze summer kimono, grasps the arm of a kneeling waitress while she pours sake into her cup.

The characters *shi*, *ki*, and *an* are boldly emblazoned on the festive red lanterns hanging from the eaves, leaving no doubt as to the restaurant's identity. The Shikian (the "Pavilion of the Four Seasons"), though not the only restaurant on the riverfront at Nakasu, seems to have been especially popular with artists and poets. A well-known kyōka by Ōta Nampo published in 1785 is entitled "On hearing a Cuckoo (*hototogisu*) at the Shikian."

Though Nakasu means "low island" in Japanese, it was actually a stretch of filled-in land along the riverbank that had not even existed until the early 1770s. By the 1780s, however, it had become one of Edo's most thriving entertainment districts, perhaps in part because of its proximity to—and ease of access from—the heart of Shitamachi. But its days were numbered. A series of floods in the late 1780s gave rise to calls for widening the river (to relieve the pressure of the water on the adjoining land), and in 1790 Nakasu was abandoned.

The view out over the river is to the east, toward Fukagawa, with its many canals and rows of masonry warehouses. A variety of pleasure boats ply the water, and at the far right, downstream, one can just make out Eitaibashi, the last of the bridges to cross the river before it flows into the bay. The tall structure at right on the Fukugawa side is a fireman's watchtower.

Shumman, like his slightly younger contemporary Masanobu (Santō Kyōden), was a pupil of Kitao Shigemasa. His first known prints (his output was never large) date from the mid-1780s and are clearly influenced stylistically by Kiyonaga, who was the dominant ukiyo-e print designer of the time. Yet even in these earliest prints, there was something distinctive about Shumman's work. He seemed to prefer subject matter associated with poetry over the more conventional subjects—particularly those dealing with the pleasure quarters—favored by other ukiyo-e artists. And there was invariably a certain refinement to his work, which often incorporated landscape elements and atmospheric effects unusual for ukiyo-e in the 1780s. Shumman was also an accomplished kyōka poet, and from the early 1790s he turned almost exclusively to the new surimono genre.

I-8

Kitagawa Utamaro (1753-1806)

Colors and Scents of Flowers of the Four Seasons

Circa 1784

Woodblock print; ōban diptych; 37.5 x 25.5 (each)

Signature of artist (Utamaro ga) at left edge of each panel

The British Museum

A young dandy lounging against the cabin of a small pleasure boat languidly holds a fan in front of him as he swabs the sweat from his chest with a handkerchief. He is evidently feeling the effects of the heat, although he is wearing the lightest gauze attire, unlike the women in the picture, all of whom wear layered garments. A young woman already in the cabin peeks playfully through the gauze of the man's *haori* at another woman kneeling near the prow. On the shore, about to step onto the boat, is a courtesan, wearing a sedge hat, accompanied by an attendant and a child (who is probably a *kamuro*). The child wears a fan fastened to her head with a kerchief as a kind of makeshift sun visor, and the attendant has pinned a cloth over her forehead, presumably for the same purpose.

Utamaro's interest is chiefly in the figures in this composition, and everything else is subordinated to them. Waves disappearing into a haze in the background suffice to indicate the river; a few planks and pilings are all that is needed for the dock. Only when it comes to the boat is he somewhat more detailed; but even here all we are shown is the tall, curved prow, the planking of the deck, and the front of the little cabin with rolled-up bamboo blinds on one side. This is a relatively early work by Utamaro and, like his other prints of this period, is strongly influenced by Kiyonaga. Kiyonaga's influence is particularly apparent in the stately poses of the women and the relatively subdued treatment of their costumes, but even the rather curious sway-backed posture of the man was sometimes found in Kiyonaga's work at the time, as was the conceit of using seal characters for the title. The question of influence aside, however, this is a masterly composition and one that evokes the languor of a humid summer day with great effectiveness. The playful touch added by the woman peeking through the man's gauze *haori*, incidentally, is entirely Utamaro's own. He was fascinated by transparency, veiling, and other see-through effects and often exploited their possibilities ingeniously in his later work.

The verses by Yomo no Akara (Ōta Nampo) and Akera Kankō inscribed on the young man's fan show how popular kyōka had become in Edo's fashionable circles.

Though other copies of separate panels of this diptych are known, this seems to be the only copy of the complete diptych. The title, *Shiki asobi hana no iroka*, may also be translated "Amusements of the Four Seasons: The Allure of Flowers," a reading that gives more weight to the probable double-entendre intended.

I-9

Katsushika Hokusai (1760-1849)

***Ehon Azuma asobi*, "Picture Book of Amusements of the East"**

Circa 1801

Illustrated book in three volumes; 26.3 x 17.4

Signature of artist (Gakō Hokusai)

New York Public Library, Spencer Collection

In spite of the word *Azuma*, "East," in its title and the illustrations, all of which are of Edo scenes, this is actually a collection of kyōka from all over the country, like *Otoko dōka* (Catalogue no. IV-16). The collection was compiled by Asakusa-an (or Sensōan) Ichindō, who also wrote the preface. Asakusa-an was a well-known Edo kyōka poet whose verses often appear in surimono by Hokusai and Shumman. The first edition of this book, which was published as one volume in 1799, was in black and white only. The Spencer Collection copy is from one or another of the color editions that first came out around 1801.

Since the illustrations seem to be totally separate from the text, this book is included in the exhibition primarily for its many vivid depic-

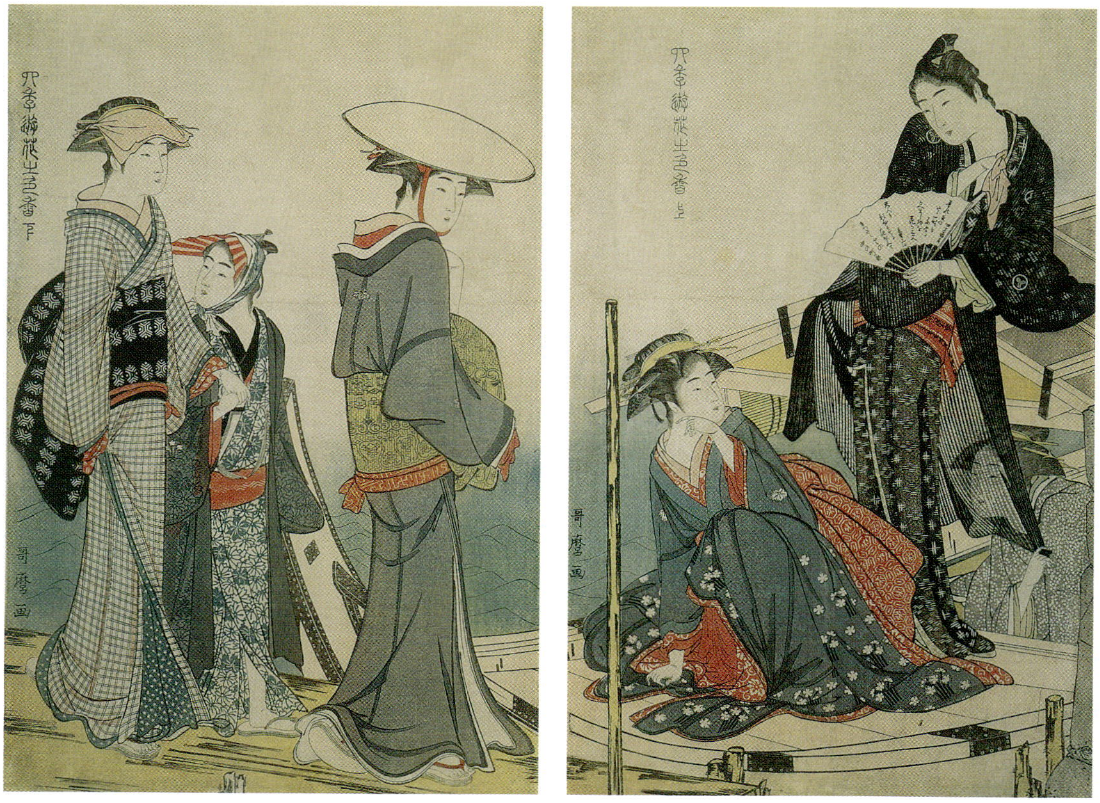

I-8

tions of well-known places in Edo. The subjects range from crowded scenes like Nihombashi and its adjoining fish market to intimate glimpses of craftsmen at work. Among the better-known illustrations are those depicting the Echigoya (the Mitsui dry-goods store at Surugachō), the year-end market at Asakusa Kinryūzan, and the Tsutaya print and book shop. The latter might be thought of as a "plug" for the book's publisher. By this time, however, the firm was no longer being run by its founder, Jūzaburō, since he had died in 1797.

The illustration we have chosen to reproduce here is the view of Nihombashi. Probably no other site so effectively symbolized Edo. The bridge was in the commercial heart of the city and was a key link in its major north-south transportation artery. It was also the point from which all distances in the nation were measured. No wonder, then, that it was a favorite subject for artists. Readers are invited to compare Hokusai's rendition of it with those by Kitao Masayoshi, or, as he later called himself, Keisai (Catalogue nos. I-2, I-13). Here Hokusai seems deliberately to be contrasting the aloofness of the political sphere, symbolized by the tower of the shogun's castle thrusting up through the picture frame at top right, with the bustling activity of commercial life. The bridge itself is thronged with pedestrians of all kinds and descriptions, but the real congestion occurs in the fish market in the adjoining side street.

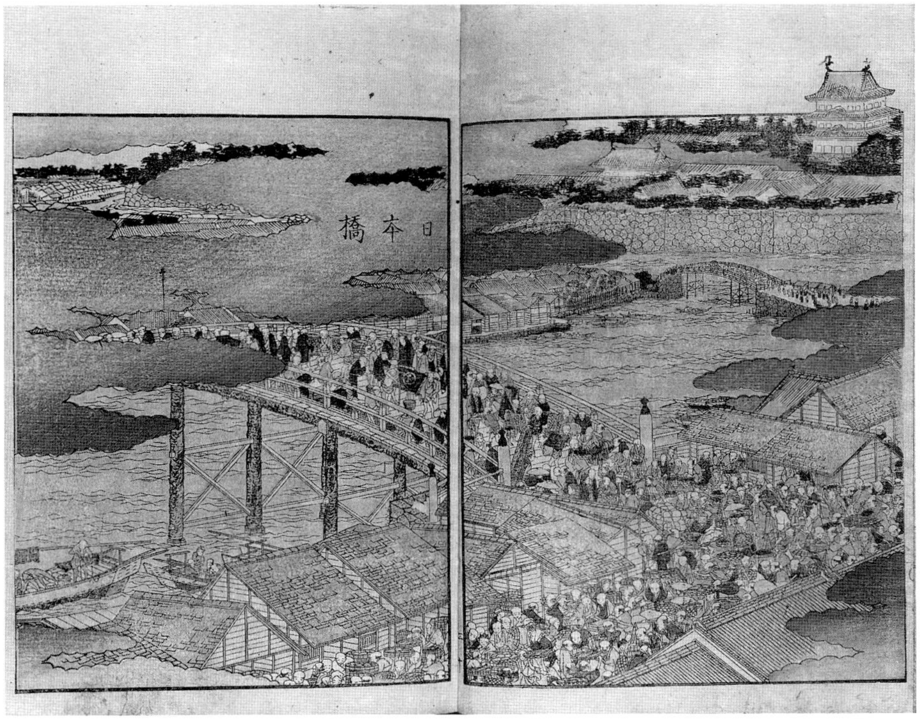

I-9

I-10

Katsushika Hokusai (1760-1849)

***Tōto meisho ichiran*, "Famous Views of the Eastern Capital at a Glance"**

1800

Illustrated book in two volumes; 25.7 x 17.8

Signature of artist (Hokusai Shinsei)

New York Public Library, Spencer Collection

Like *Ehon Azuma asobi* (Catalogue no. I-9), the first edition of which was published only one year earlier, in 1799, this book is a collection of kyōka compiled by Asakusa-an, with illustrations depicting famous places in Edo. In other respects, however, the two books could hardly be more different. In the former, the illustrations were completely separate from the text, with which, in fact, they had little or no relation, even thematically. Here, the poems are written along the top of each illustration and make specific reference to the sites depicted. Apart from the preface, there are no sections of solid text. Several of the illustrations could almost pass as surimono—which is hardly surprising, given the extent to which the poems and imagery are related.

This is not the only way in which the illustrations differ from those in the earlier book, however. Most of the sites depicted in *Ehon Azuma asobi* were viewed from above and at a distance, and the figures tended to be overwhelmed by their settings. Here the vantage has been brought closer to ground level, and the figures, which are usually larger, play a more central role in the designs. A perfect case in point is provided by the illustration reproduced here. A couple make their way through the snow to the Mimeguri Shrine, the torii gate of which is just visible below the dike at right. Icy club-like branches reach up in front of the smooth oval of the couple's huge, snow-covered umbrella. Across the river, the wooded hillock of Matsuchiyama, mirroring the shapes of the branches, overlooks the entrance to the Sanya Canal. The shrine, the hillock, and the canal were all land-

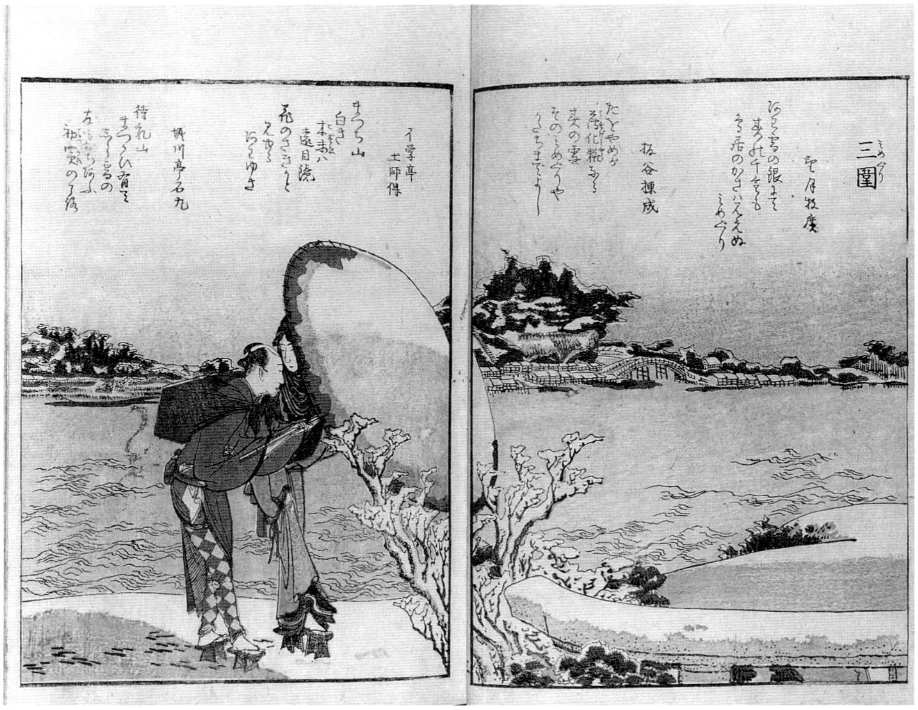

I-10

marks on the way to the Yoshiwara and, as such, figure in other works in this exhibition (Catalogue nos. I-3, II-5, and IV-2), but here these familiar sites have been transformed by the ice and snow into a kind of fantasy landscape. As fascinating as it is, however, the landscape itself would have seemed lifeless were it not for the two figures slowly making their way through it.

This seems to have been a popular book. A second edition was brought out the same year with a different title, *Tōto shokei ichiran.*

I-11

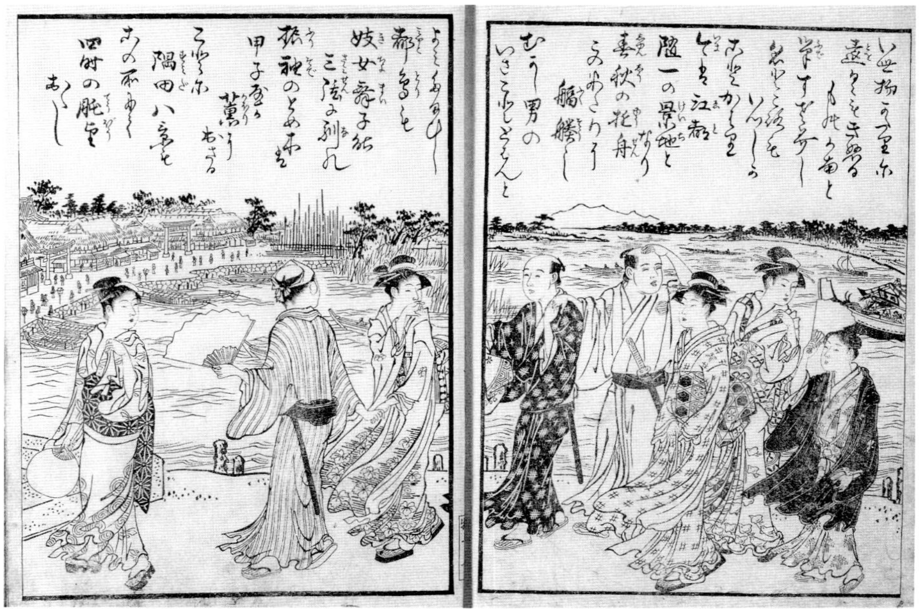

I-11

Torii Kiyonaga (1752-1815)

***Monomi ga oka*, "Picture Book of Hills for Sightseeing"**

1785

Illustrated book; 22.2 x 16.3

The British Museum

It is hard not to compare this modest little picture book by the leading ukiyo-e artist of the 1780s with Utamaro's *Ehon Edo suzume* (Catalogue no. I-14), published only one year later. Both books are printed in black and white only, and both depict well-known sites in Edo. But where Kiyonaga seemed to prefer designing single-sheet prints to books, Utamaro was quite active as a book designer and produced some of his most brilliant work in the book and album formats (e.g., Catalogue nos. II-34 and IV-15). Certainly the pictures in this work seem a little flat—a little unadventurous, even—compared with the illustrations Utamaro came up with the following year, while still a relative unknown. Too often, as in the scene reproduced here, Kiyonaga's figures seem to move across the foreground as though they had no real connection with the scenery behind them, which becomes little more than a backdrop. The effect is exacerbated by the curtain of calligraphy that fills the top third of each page and forces the eye back to the surface of the picture plane. In a few instances—in the illustration of a party taking place on the veranda of a brothel overlooking the bay at Shinagawa, for example—the figures do interact more dynamically with their environment, but even with them one has the sense that Kiyonaga felt cramped both by the format and the inclusion of the calligraphy. The calligraphy, by the way, consists of prose commentaries on the scenes depicted. The inscriptions in Utamaro's book are poems.

The two pages reproduced here show a party of samurai on a family outing to a Shinto shrine on the Sumida River. The site is well north of any of those (such as the Sanya Canal and the Mimeguri Shrine) depicted in other works in the exhibition.

I-12

Torii Kiyonaga (1752-1815)

***Saishiki mitsu no asa*, "The Three Mornings in Color"**

1787

Printed album; 28 x 18.7

Signature (gakō Torii Kiyonaga) and seal (Kiyonaga no in) of artist on last page, with name and seal of publisher (Nishimuraya Eijudō)

Pulverer Collection

In the previous entry, we spoke somewhat disparagingly of Kiyonaga's work in book design. None of his shortcomings as an *ehon* artist, however, are visible here. Kiyonaga clearly found the addition of color and the larger page size available to him in this instance more to his liking.

The "three mornings" of the title refer to the "three beginnings"—of a new day, a new month, and a new year—traditionally associated in Japan with the commencement of a new year, so it is no surprise to find that each of the seven double-page illustrations in this volume deal with New Year's observances. In the Edo Period, great importance was placed on proper beginnings. It was thought that if something was begun in the right way, its chances for ending satisfactorily would be much better. Such beliefs invested the New Year's holiday—which traditionally included the first several days of the new year—with special significance. It provided people with an opportunity to start their work afresh in a way that would guarantee them success in the months ahead. Activities such as the "first writing" (*kakizome*) or the "first business transaction" (*akinai-hajime*), therefore, were regarded as momentous occasions, not to be passed over lightly. Many of these "beginnings" came to be observed with almost ritual solemnity.

All seven illustrations in this book depict such auspicious beginnings. They are:

1. Noblewomen putting brush to paper or admiring flowering plums;

2. Courtesans of the Yoshiwara parading in their new clothes;

3. A nobleman drawing his bow in an archery contest;

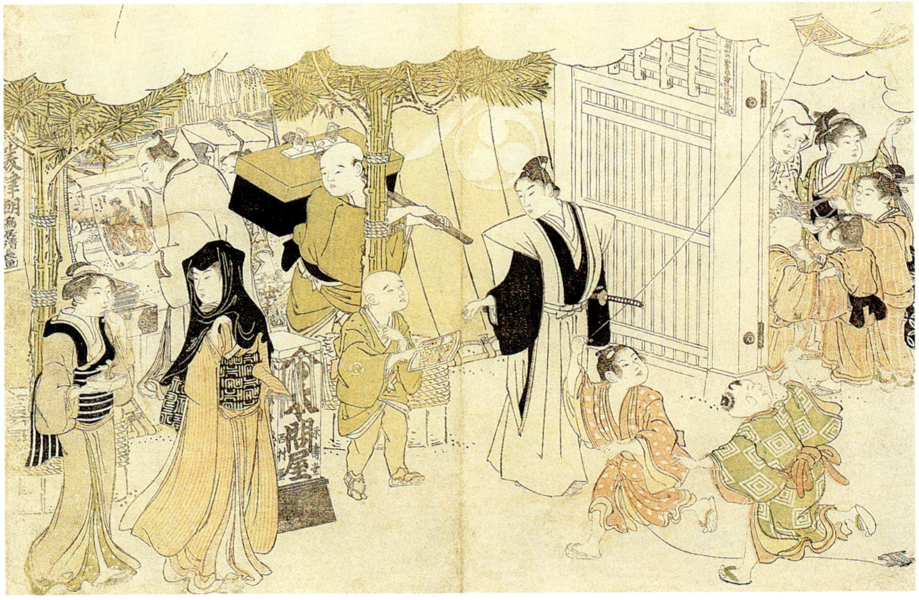

I-12

4. A merchant opening his storehouse and taking out a new account book;

5. A young man taking his first horse ride of the year;

6. Women washing and combing their hair;

7. The year's first day of business at the Nishimuraya print shop.

Several of the illustrations, especially those dealing with the more courtly observances, seem purely imaginary, but the last two convey a sense of having been based on direct observation, and it is because of them that the book is included in this section. The scene showing women grooming their hair or preparing to bathe in a steaming hot tub affords a glimpse of what must have been an important aspect of life in Edo. The rooms the women occupy are open on both sides to snowy courtyards, in one of which may be seen an ice-covered stone water basin. The scene reproduced here shows the street in front of the Nishimuraya print shop. (Nishimuraya Eijudō was Kiyonaga's publisher of preference, so we can assume that he would have been intimately familiar with this subject.) Pine and bamboo New Year's decorations have been set up outside the shop, which a samurai is just leaving, having apparently bought a print, which is being held out to him by his boy attendant. Another customer, still inside, is examining a print of a courtesan and her *kamuro* while two porters carrying boxes on their backs move past him in front of a *noren* with the Nishimuraya crest. Outside, two women walk by, conversing together, and two boys, one holding a kite decorated with Danjūrō's *mimasu* crest, run past a wooden *kido* gate. Just outside the gate, children gather around a man holding what looks like a skein of cords. On a pillar at the left side of the shop, Kiyonaga has inscribed his name and the title of the book.

I-13

Kitao Keisai Masayoshi (1764-1824)

Edo meisho zue

1785

Woodblock scroll remounted as a folding album; 19 x 25.4

Address, signature, and seals of artist (Tōto Horidomegai, Sugi Hokora . . . , Kitao Keisai Masayoshi zu) on final page, with address and name of block carver (Kanda Nakachō, Kobayashi Mohei) and name of proofreader (Kobuna Tora-akira); no publisher given

Robert Ravicz

This is a relatively early work by the artist who painted the *Bird's-eye View of Edo* screen of 1809 (Catalogue no. I-2). Masayoshi was the name given to him by Kitao Shigemasa, with whom he studied at about the same time as Masanobu (Santō Kyōden).

From the start of his career, Masayoshi seems to have struck out in a direction of his own. He produced only a few single-sheet prints, almost all in the *uki-e* ("perspective print") genre popularized by Toyoharu, and most of his work during the 1780s appears to have been in illustrating kibyōshi. Nothing in his training would seem to have prepared him to create a work like this, which is without precedent in ukiyo-e.

It is hard to imagine how Masayoshi got the idea for this work, which was originally designed as a handscroll. The notion of using the woodblock medium to create a handscroll was fairly unusual in itself. A woodblock-printed handscroll of scenes along the Yodo River between Kyoto and Osaka, designed by Itō Jakuchū (1716-1800), had been published eighteen years earlier in Kyoto,* but that scroll had sought to imitate the effects found in stone rubbings and seems an unlikely precedent for this one. Here Masayoshi seems, if anything, more intent on duplicating the effects found in the Chinese blue-green landscape style. The colors are lightly printed, and the palette consists almost exclusively of reds, pinks, yellows, and blue-greens. The scenes, which are often abbreviated or detached from their surroundings by intervening clouds or bands of mist, are all depicted from the same relatively high, somewhat distant vantage. There are fifty scenes in all, each preceded by a vertical panel identifying the site and enclosing one or more haiku related to it. Several of the more expansive scenes also bear inscriptions in the manner of a Chinese painting. Though none of the scenes leads directly into the next, the consistent vantage and the uniformity of the palette provide a sense of unity.

Among the sites given more expansive treatment are Ueno, Ryōgoku Bridge, Nippori, Nihombashi (illustrated here), the Temple of Kannon at Asakusa, and the approach to the shogun's castle. The impression one gets from this scroll is of a spacious, verdant, uncrowded city. Even the views of Nihombashi and Ryōgoku show little of the congestion seen in Hokusai's depicitions of the same locales.

Although this copy has a few scattered losses

I-13

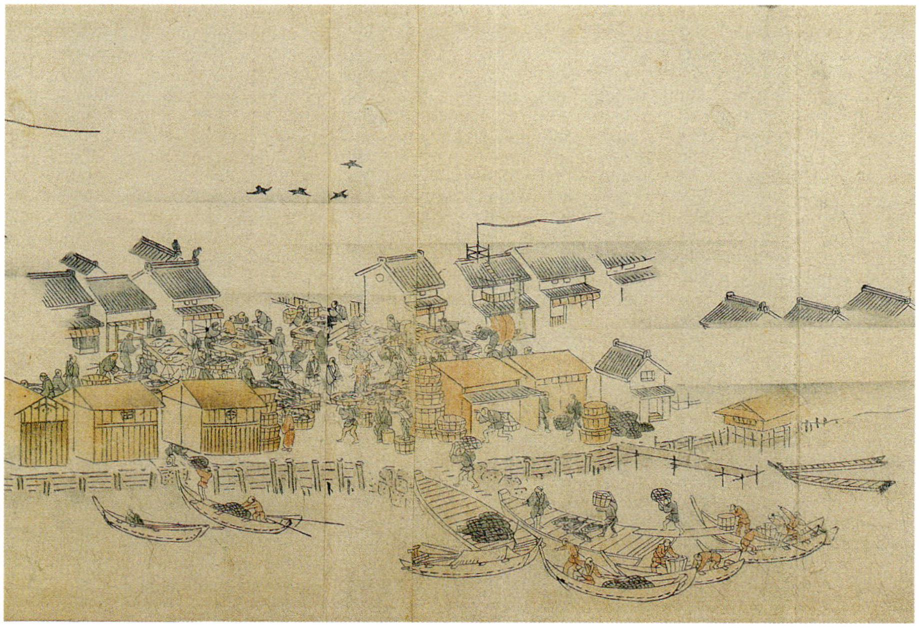

* See Miyeko Murase, *Tales of Japan, Scrolls and Prints from the New York Public Library* (New York and Oxford: Oxford University Press, 1986), 183-86.

(at the end of the Sumida River section, for instance), and there is some running of the reds, it is still in remarkably good condition. The faintness of the printing is intentional rather than the result of fading. The delicacy of the effects Masayoshi was seeking may be seen most clearly in the final passage, where the pale, white image of Mt. Fuji rises almost imperceptibly above the ramparts of the castle.

I-14

Kitagawa Utamaro (1753-1806)

***Ehon Edo suzume*, "The Sparrows of Edo Picture Book"**

1786

Illustrated book in three volumes; 21.5 x 15.5

Name of artist not given; preface by Akera Kankō; published by Tsutaya Jūzaburō

The Art Institute of Chicago, Ryerson Collection

At first glance the black-and-white illustrations in this unpretentious booklet would seem to have little in common with a superbly composed diptych like *Colors and Scents of Flowers of the Four Seasons* (Catalogue no. I-8) or the masterly designs in an album like *Momochidori kyōka awase* (Catalogue no. IV-15), yet all three works are not only by the same man but were produced within a few years of each other. The diptych was published two years earlier, and the album came out only four or five years later.

Undoubtedly, some of the differences are due to the relatively small scale of the *ehon* format. Many of the illustrations in the book seem almost forcibly confined within their borders, as though the artist had more information to convey than the pages could contain. This seems true even of a scene as open as the one reproduced here. Other differences probably have to do with the lack of color and the greater informality of the *ehon* genre in which studied effects of the kind found in albums and single-sheet prints would seem out of place.

Once allowances are made for the differences imposed by the format, the real qualities of this charming book become apparent. Like the sparrows of its title, Utamaro flits about the city at will, sometimes viewing its activity from a distance, sometimes moving in close to catch

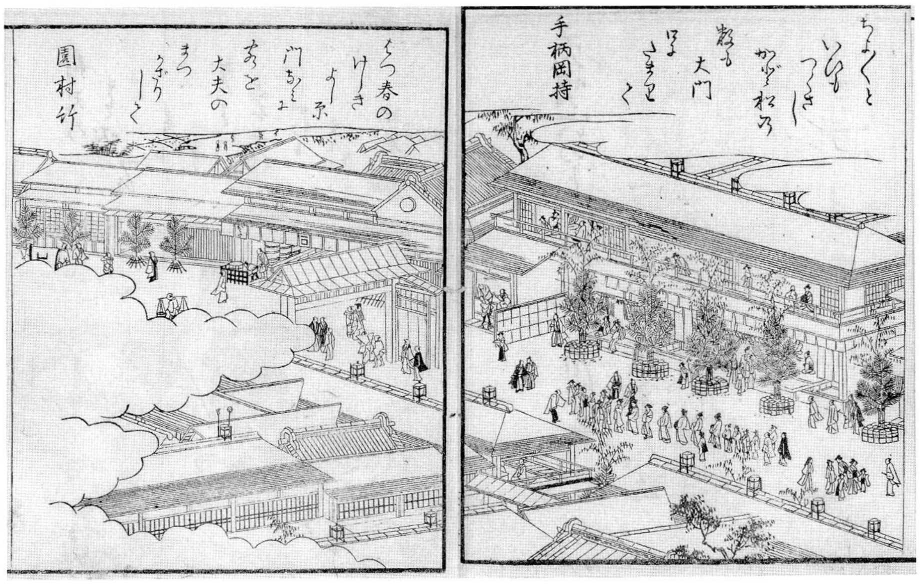

I-14

details at street level. The vantage is always from somewhat above—from a sparrow's eye view, one might say—and many of the scenes are drawn as though glimpsed through parted clouds.

Kyōka, probably chosen by Akera Kankō, who wrote the preface, appear at the top of each page. Kankō was part of the circle of kyōka poets associated with Ōta Nampo, and his involvement with this modest *ehon* is significant. As far as is known, this book is the first instance of Utamaro's active association with the kyōka movement, an association that would soon lead to some of the most memorable collaborative works of art in the history of ukiyo-e (e.g., Catalogue no. IV-15).

The illustration reproduced here shows a procession of courtesans moving along the Yoshiwara's broad central street, the Nakanochō, toward the Great Gate (*Ōmonguchi*). New Year's decorations of pine and bamboo have been set out in front of the teahouses along both sides of the Nakanochō, and smaller trees line the street outside the gate. At the top of the left-hand page, just visible under the cloud-like form enclosing the poem, is a glimpse of the Nihon Dike, which led from the mouth of the Sanya Canal to the Yoshiwara. Note the barrels of water (for dousing fires) placed on the ridges of the roofs. Also note the guardhouse attached to the building at one side of the Great Gate.

Catalogue Section II:
The Yoshiwara and the Courtesan Hanaōgi

The location of the Yoshiwara, the layout of its streets, and at least some of its unique customs have been described in the introduction. The works that follow will add substance and detail to that earlier discussion. They will take us behind the scenes into two or three of the more prosperous brothels and even afford us glimpses of the courtesans' private quarters during their leisure hours. They will also introduce us to several of the great *yobidashi*, and allow us to look on as they make their nightly appearances along the Nakanochō.

Images of courtesans, particularly of the great yobidashi, were central to ukiyo-e; and of all the glamorous courtesans of the late eighteenth century, probably none was more celebrated than Hanaōgi. (The name, incidentally, meant "Flower Fan," and was clearly related to the name of her brothel, the Ōgiya or "House of Fans.") Yet what was this fabled beauty really like? Do the various portraits of her in this exhibition reveal anything of her personality, or are they nothing more than idealized icons?

Actually, this exhibition coincides with the careers of two different Hanaōgis. The woman portrayed in Masanobu's *Yoshiwara keisei shin bijin awase jihitsu kagami* (Catalogue no. II-33) of 1784 was the third to bear the name. A year after being depicted by Masanobu, she was involved in a botched double-suicide attempt with a samurai lover, and by 1787 was already being succeeded by Hanaōgi IV. This latter is almost certainly the beauty depicted in portrayals of Hanaōgi in the exhibition. In 1794 she, too, became involved in a scandal when she eloped with a lover. She was soon caught, however, and forced to return to the brothel. Such a sensational event would have come under the censorship laws, and for a while thereafter no prints depicting her were published.

Almost any portrayal of Hanaōgi—whether of Hanaōgi III or IV—makes some reference to her knowledge of poetry and her skills as a calligrapher. Apparently such accomplishments were prerequisites for anyone aspiring to the name. More surprising is that both Hanaōgis seem to have been women of spirit, willing to take chances when their hearts so dictated. Whether any of the portraits convey this trait in their personalities, we leave to our viewers to decide.

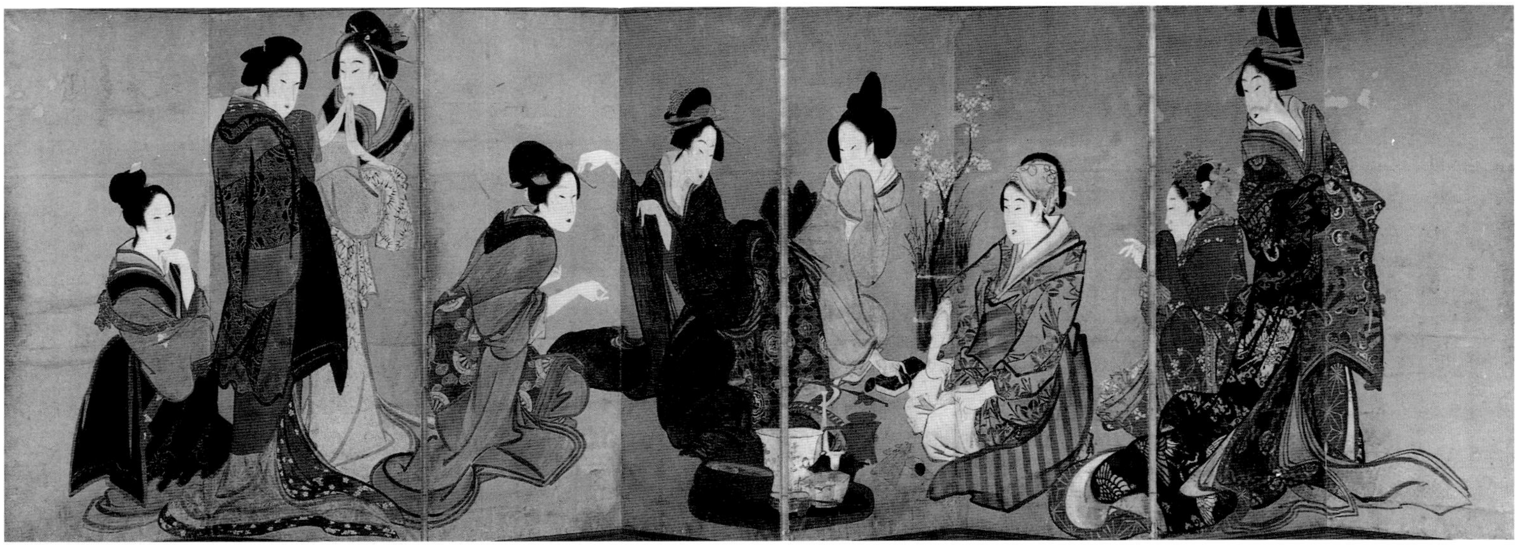

II-1

II-1

Attributed to Hokusai School

Nine Women Playing *Kitsune-ken*

Circa 1800-05

Eight-panel screen; colors on paper; 179.8 x 600

No signature

Musée Guimet

This unusually large screen portrays nine women from various walks of life, in almost full life-size. The background scenery has been eliminated, placing full attention on the women playing and watching a game of *kitsune-ken*. The figures are composed in a highly symmetrical fashion with the skill that indicates an accomplished painter.

Kitsune-ken, similar to "scissors-rock-paper," was a popular hand game that was frequently played at parties, and it appears in a number of prints depicting entertainment scenes. The game was played by two people; the artist's choice to depict it with three players gives us a clue that something more than a party game is being portrayed.

In the game, the fox (*kitsune*) succumbs to the hunter, who is outranked by the village chief, who wins the game. The woman in the fifth section from the right holds her hands in the fox position; the woman in the sixth section, who appears to be aiming a gun, would be the hunter; and the woman in the third section with her hands in her lap is the village chief. It is interesting to note that the painting shows the full spectrum of women in Edo society.

Viewing the game in the second section of the screen (reading from right to left) are an *oiran* and a *kamuro*, dressed in predictably lavish apparel. The woman in the "village chief" pose is the wife of either a farmer or a woodcutter, judging by the bundle of kindling lying nearby. The branches of blossoming cherry introduce an atmosphere of elegance.

In the fourth section, hiding her laughter behind her sleeve, is a lady-in-waiting in the service of a noble, as we infer by her hairdo (*kata hazushi*). Playing the fox in the fifth section is a townswoman (*chōjō*), and the hunter in the sixth section appears to be a merchant's wife. The woman holding a hand towel (*tenugui*) in her mouth is a "night-hawk" street walker, while the woman next to her seems to be a widow. Kneeling in the eighth section is a waitress or servant, since her sleeves are tucked up and her hair is worn in a shell topknot.

Although no artist is identified on the screen, Hokusai's influence is unmistakable even in the theme (see *The Six States of Woman*, Catalogue no. IV-9), and the painting style resembles Utamaro's. There is speculation that the screen is an early work by Fujimaro, and it certainly bears a resemblance to his hanging scroll entitled *Kyōka Poets Mimicking the Six Immortals of Poetry* (Catalogue no. IV-3).

II-2

Attributed to Utagawa Toyoharu (1735-1814)

Courtesans of the Tamaya

Circa 1781

Six-panel screen; ink, colors, and gold on paper; 144.1 x 314.6

No signature

The British Museum

Among the unique features of the Yoshiwara were the latticed rooms in which courtesans were put on display like mannequins in a shop window. These rooms were on the ground floor facing the street, so that prospective customers could examine the occupants at will. Such rooms appear in several other works in the exhibition. A passage in Eishi's *Journey to the Yoshiwara* (Catalogue no. I-3), for instance, shows two men actually "window shopping" in front of one, and Hokusai's *New Year's Day at the Ōgiya* (Catalogue no. II-24) offers a glimpse of what such a room would have looked like from inside the brothel. Here the courtesans are arrayed in semi-formal fashion in the center of the room with their *shinzō*, paired in matching kimono, seated along the wall at left.

Courtesans were put on public view twice a day, once during the afternoon and again during the evening. Each session (called *harimise*) lasted four hours. This is probably the afternoon session, since a certain air of ennui permeates the scene. Only one of the women (at the far left) turns to look outside. The rest seem completely absorbed in their own activities. One woman turns to light a pipe from a small brazier on her *tabako-bon*; the woman behind her fusses over a doll; and at the back of the room another woman languidly lifts up her hand to adjust a hairpin. Meanwhile, the row of *shinzō* presents some amusing contrasts. One of the young women busily folds a paper crane as her fellow *shinzō* looks on; but her neighbor to the right has nodded off to sleep, oblivious of the fact that her companion is preparing to strike up her *shamisen*.

Though this screen is not signed, its attribution to Toyoharu on stylistic grounds seems quite firm. The faces and figures are typical of his work of this period, and the competence with which the complex spatial relationships between the figures are handled is of the kind one would expect from an artist who had mastered, as Toyoharu had, the technicalities of the perspective print genre.

Large six-fold screens by ukiyo-e artists of

II-2

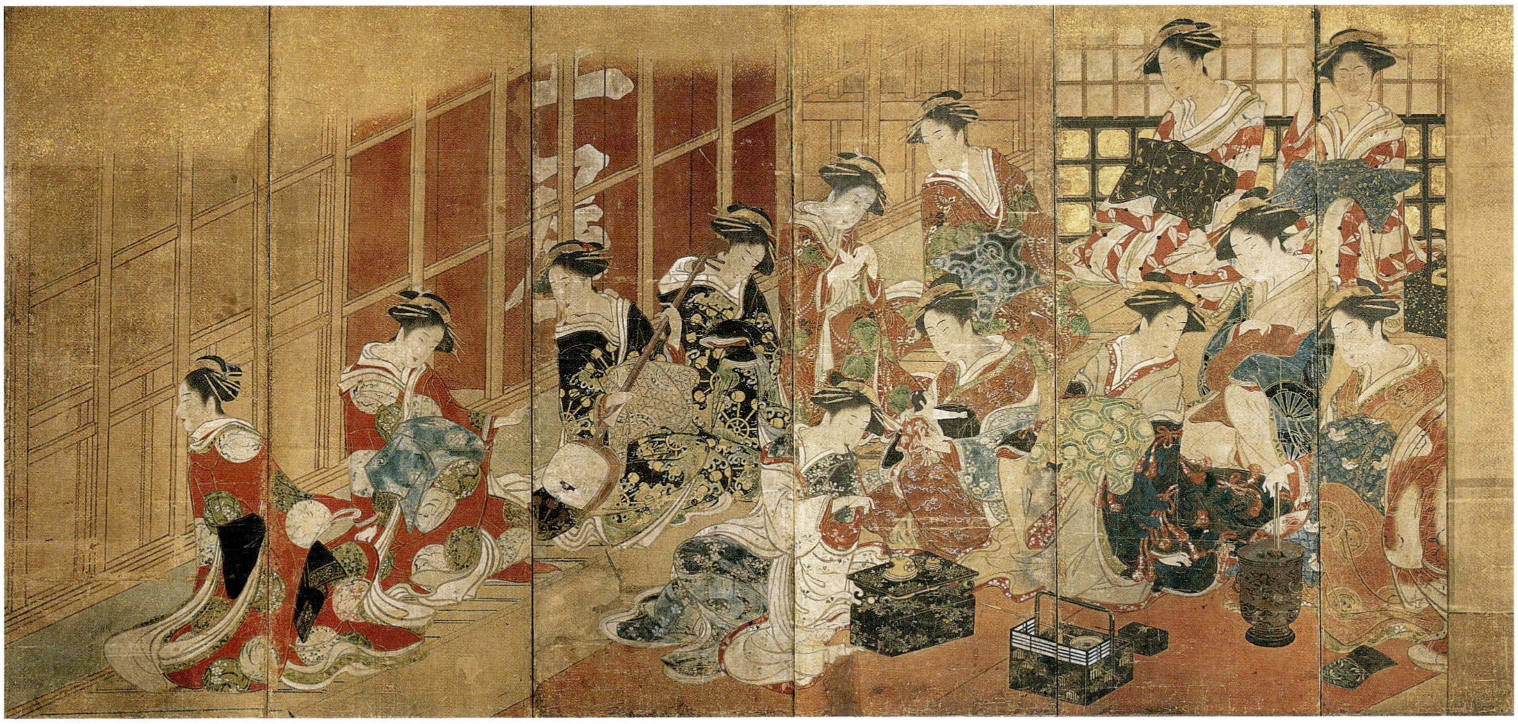

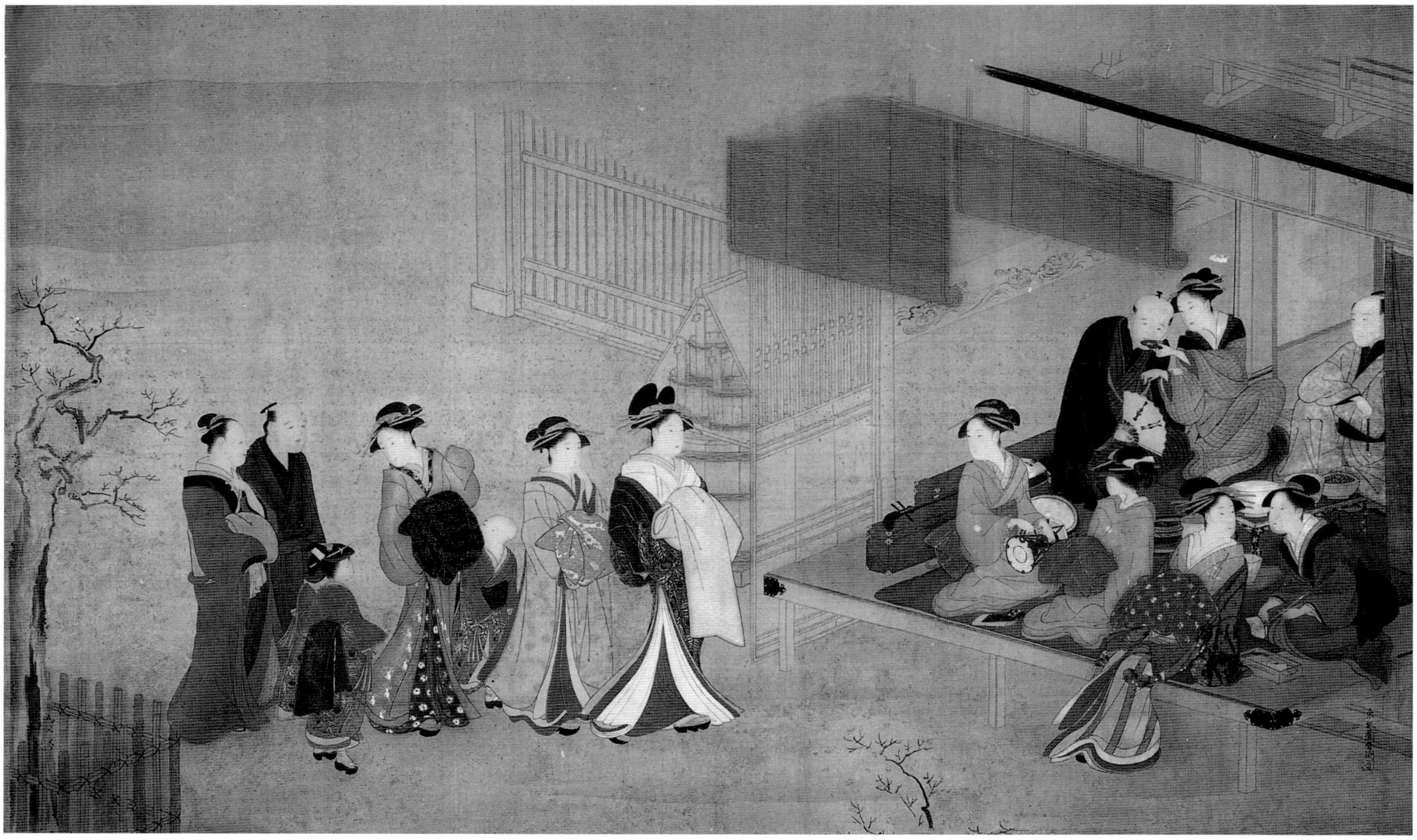

II-3

this period are quite rare, and this is the only one so far recorded by Toyoharu. The only other screens in this exhibition are all of the early nineteenth century.

Like a number of other ukiyo-e artists, Toyoharu gave up designing prints in later life. From the 1780s he concentrated almost exclusively on painting and became one of the most prolific ukiyo-e painters of the period. He was also an influential teacher and the founder, with his pupils Toyohiro and Toyokuni, of the Utagawa lineage that dominated nineteenth-century ukiyo-e.

Toyoharu continued working until well into old age. He was seventy-nine when he contributed the figure of Jurōjin to the scroll of *The Seven Gods of Good Fortune* (Catalogue no. III-6).

II-3

Katsukawa Shunchō (active 1785-1800)

Entering the Teahouse

Circa 1790

Hanging scroll mounted on panel; ink, colors, and gold on silk; 64.5 x 150.7

Signature of artist (Tōshien Shunchō zu) at lower right; seal damaged and illegible

The British Museum

A high-ranking courtesan and her entourage approach an open teahouse, where her client and a group of entertainers await her. The courtesan's party is made up of her two *shinzō*, a boy and girl attendant, and a middle-aged couple who may have been the brothel owner and his wife. The group moves forward in a stately procession, the formality of which is only slightly broken by the little girl attendant who stops to ask a question of one of the *shinzō*. The scene inside the teahouse is much more animated. Preparations for the evening's entertainment have already begun. Two geisha have taken out their hand drum and *shamisen*, and a professional jester leans forward to sip the sake offered to him by a waitress. Another waitress chats with a courtesan seated on the edge of the porch. The one still point in all this activity is provided by the figure of the patron, who sits quietly, holding his pipe, at the back of the room, gazing out at the approaching courtesan. The only other person who seems to notice the courtesan's approach is the geisha holding the hand drum.

Compositionally, with its strong horizontal emphasis, the painting has more in common with the handscroll format than with the hanging-scroll format for which it was presumably designed. It is highly unusual for hanging scrolls to be thus divided into two almost equal halves. Yet, as Timothy Clark points out in *Ukiyo-e Paintings in the British Museum*, Shunchō has drawn the two halves together by focusing "on the central figure of the courtesan, who mediates, as it were, between the formality of the procession and the convivial bustle of the teahouse scene."* For a hanging scroll, the painting is also unusual in scale and in complexity of subject matter. Clark considers it "the most ambitious composition by Shunchō yet discovered."

* Timothy Clark, *Ukiyo-e Paintings in the British Museum* (London: British Museum Press, 1992), 113.

II-4

Rekisentei Eiri (active 1790-1800)

Standing Courtesan

Circa 1795

Hanging scroll; ink and colors on paper; 121.6 x 26.3

Signature of artist (Rekisentei Eiri) and two undeciphered seals at upper right

Kimbell Art Museum

It is hard not to be startled by this striking picture, particularly when coming across it in the company of so many works depicting courtesans clad in richly colored robes. One cannot help wondering what quirk of taste or arcane ritual would have prompted this beauty to wear a costume so scrupulously limited to white-on-white. And what is the purpose of the long scarf attached to her headdress? Even many ukiyo-e

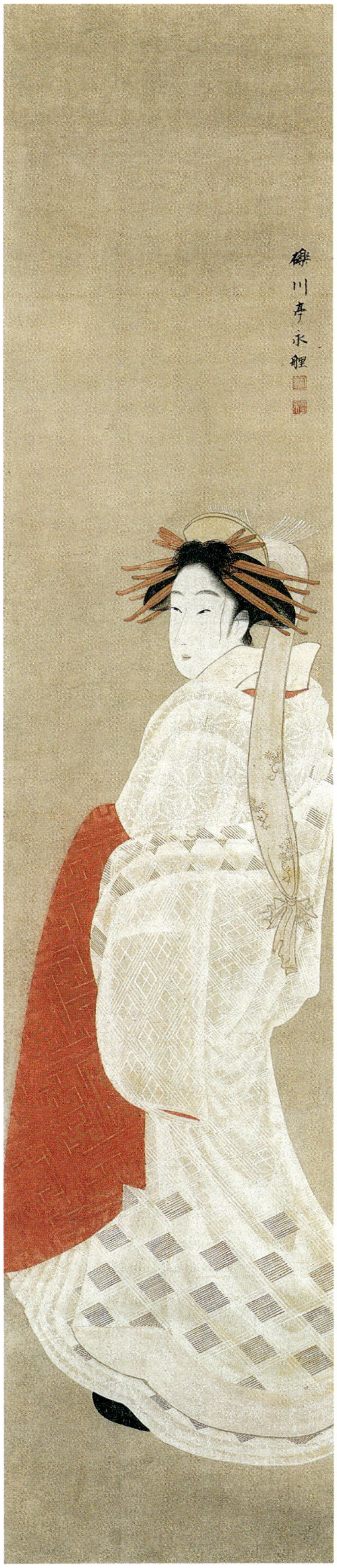

II-4

specialists might be hard-pressed to answer such questions, because figures wearing this kind of clothing were only rarely depicted in paintings and probably never in prints. Eighteenth-century *senryū*, however, often refer to the Yoshiwara custom behind this courtesan's unusual costume. It seems that every year, on the first day of the eighth lunar month (which was one of the principal *mombi*, or "festival days," of the Yoshiwara), all the higher-ranking courtesans were expected to put on immaculate white clothes and parade along the Nakanochō. The spectacle went by various names, such as "eighth-month snow" or "fall snow." There were several different explanations for the origin of the observance, which fell on the anniversary of Tokugawa Ieyasu's first entry into Edo in 1590. One of the more poetic of these was that it had been started in the Kambun era (1661-73) by a courtesan with the evocative name of Yūgiri, "Evening Mist."

As this painting shows, neither the obi nor the underclothes (glimpses of which may be seen at the courtesan's neck and the tip of her sleeve) had to be white, and the touches of red this allowed prevent the figure from appearing too ghostly, as it otherwise almost certainly would. The challenge lay in endowing the white costume itself with sufficient interest. Eiri met this challenge by introducing a subtle variety of geometric forms suggestive of snow crystals, creating an effect that almost seems like lace laid over gauze. In the end, the limited palette—white, ivory, pale gold, and red—becomes fascinating in itself.

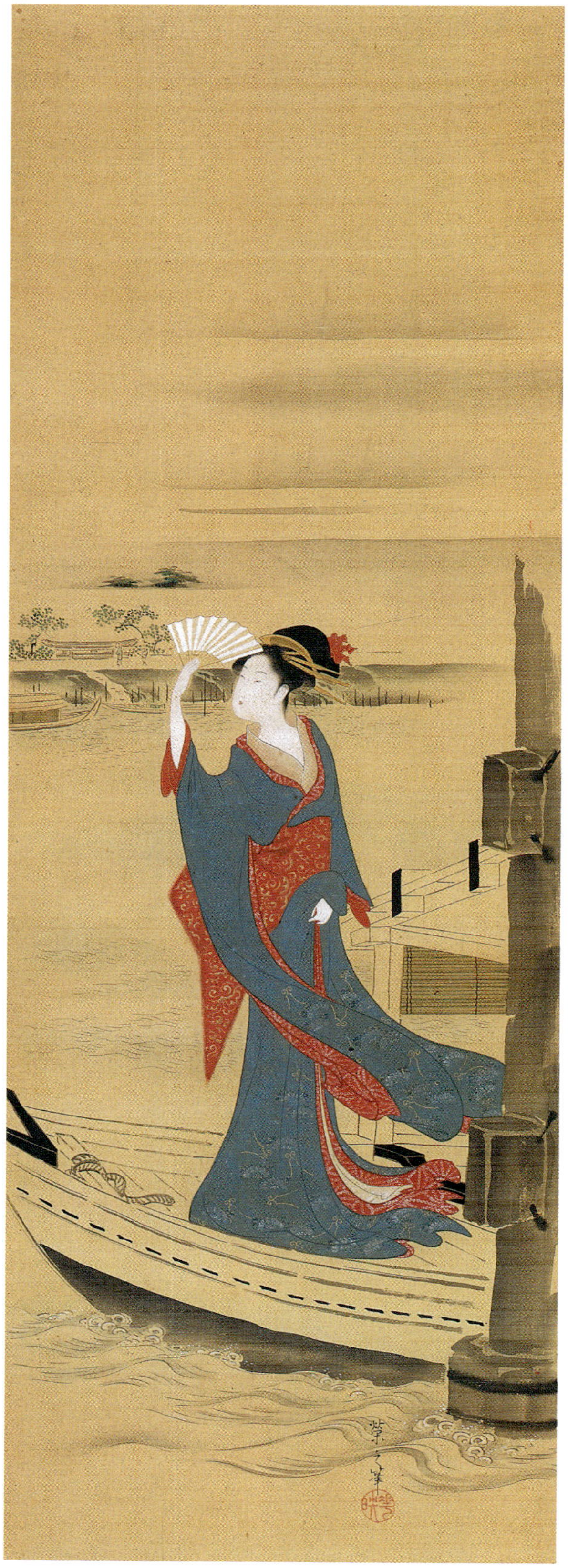

II-5

II-5

Chōbunsai Eishi (1756-1829)

Beauty in a Boat on the Sumida River

Circa 1795

Hanging scroll; ink and colors on silk; 95.3 x 33

Signature (Eishi hitsu) and seal (Kaei) of artist at bottom right

The Cleveland Museum of Art, The Kelvin Smith Collection, Gift of Mrs. Kelvin Smith

A tall woman, possibly a geisha, stands alone in the bow of a small boat moored to one of the pilings of the Azuma Bridge. It is summer, and she holds a fan to her head as though to shade her eyes from the glare of the sun as she turns to look upstream. A breeze pushes wavelets against the bow of the boat and lifts the long sleeves of the woman's *furisode* so that they flutter out in front of her. Across the river is a boat landing, and a pathway leading up to the top of a dike. The torii gate just visible beyond the dike marks the entrance to the Mimeguri Shrine.

As we have already seen, the Sumida River was a popular refuge from the heat and humidity of Edo during the summer months, yet the only other human being visible in this picture is a small figure walking along the dike on the opposite shore. The heavy foot traffic usual on the Azuma Bridge is either nonexistent or out of view overhead. The woman stands alone, her isolation underscored by the contrast between the cool blue of her robes and the virtual monochrome of everything else. What accounts for the curious emptiness of the scene and the sense of wistfulness to which it gives rise? The intensifying breeze and the bands of haze or mist above the river suggest that the summer season may already be coming to an end.

Though we have suggested that the woman may be a geisha, there is no way to know this for sure. She is clearly not a courtesan, and her presence on a pleasure boat would imply that she was an entertainer of some sort, but there is no sign of a *shamisen* or hand drum nearby. Her obi and kimono, though elegant, are relatively sober, of the sort one would normally associate with geisha or women of more mature years, yet her long sleeves indicate that she is quite young.

II-6

Chōbunsai Eishi (1756-1829)

Courtesan with Two Attendants under a Flowering Cherry Tree

Circa 1810

Hanging scroll; ink and colors on silk; 73.3 x 53.3

Signature (Chōbunsai Eishi no fude) and seal (Eishi) of artist at lower right

University of Michigan Museum of Art, Margaret Watson Parker Art Collection

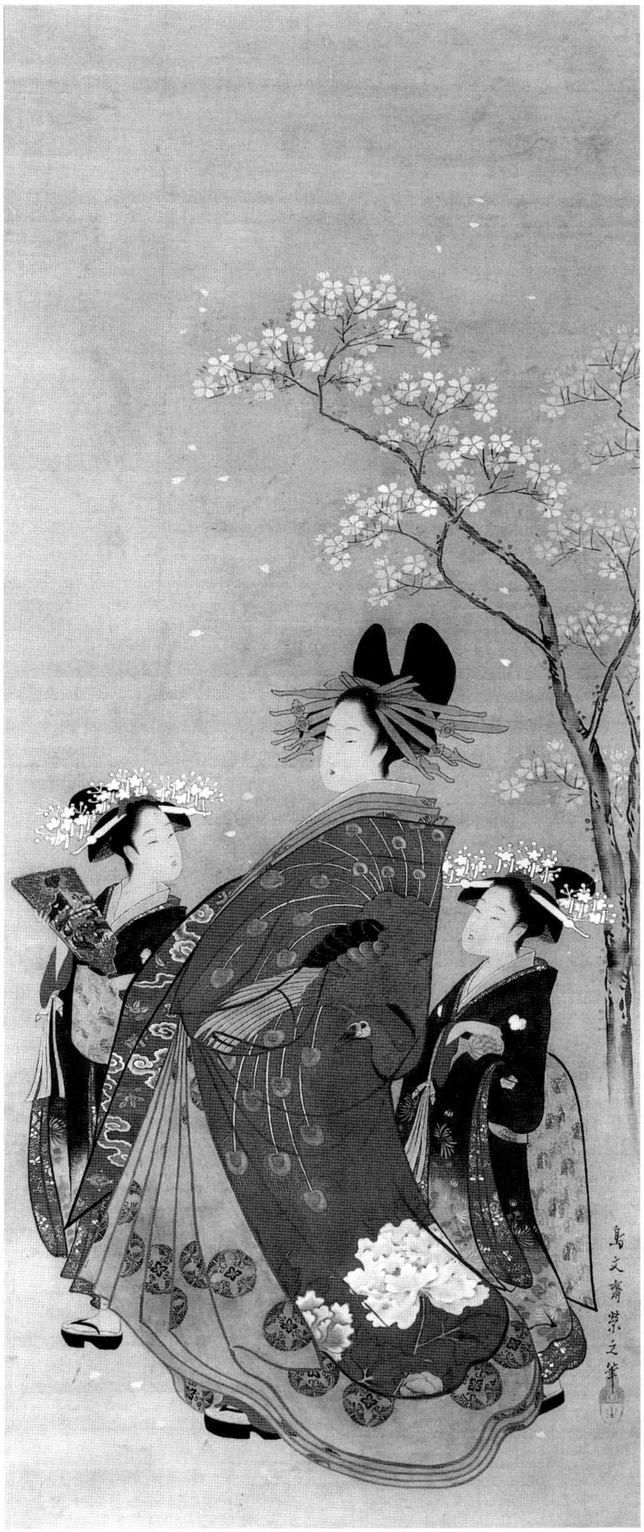

II-6

A gorgeously clad courtesan moves majestically past a flowering cherry tree from which a few petals are already falling. She is accompanied by her two attendants, one holding a battledore richly decorated in Tosa style, the other clutching a ball of colored thread known as a *temari.* Muffled in layers of kimono bound in front with a full, cascading obi, the courtesan's body seems curiously stubby in comparison with her frail neck and high butterfly coiffure. The impression is reinforced by the way Eishi has had her attendants walk so closely beside her that their kimono seem to merge with hers. The courtesan's hair is thickly set with long, stout hairpins, and she wears a red *uchikake* with a bold design of a phoenix (*hōō*) flying above a peony in full bloom. The attendants' more sober kimono are beautifully rendered in an ink wash that thins to make way for a delicate chrysanthemum pattern, and they wear the colorful, flower-like hair ornaments associated with their calling.

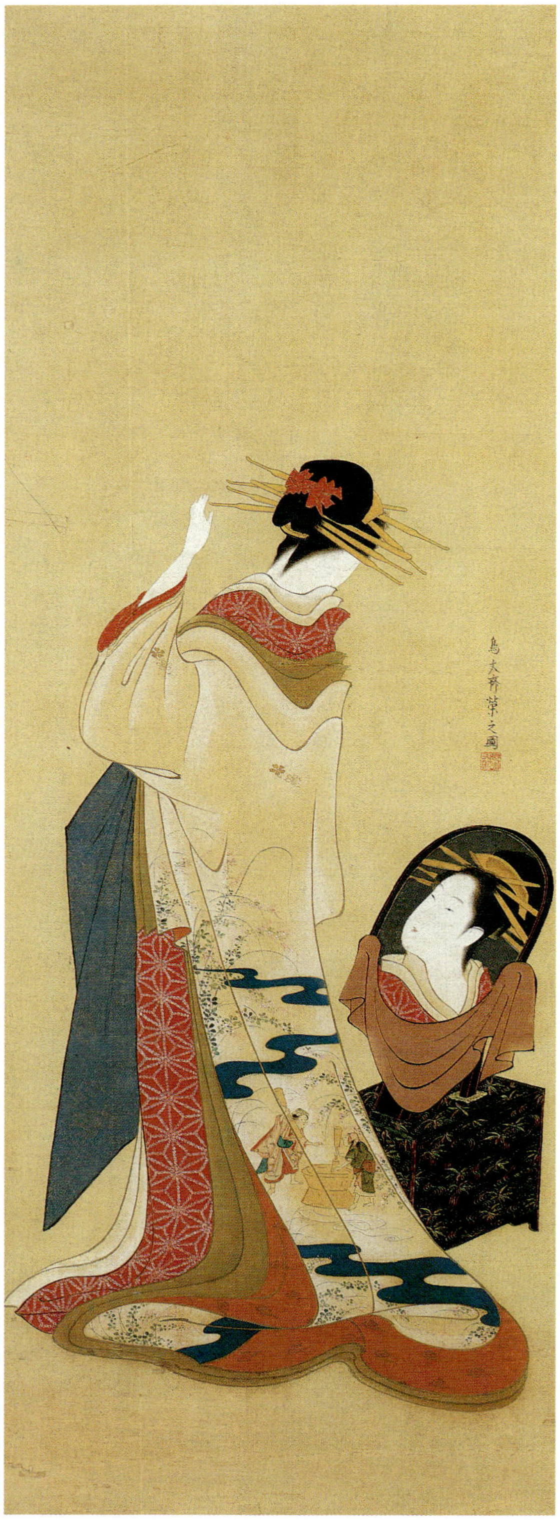

II-7

Every year during the cherry-blossom season, young cherry trees were planted along the Nakanochō, and while they remained in bloom, troops of courtesans from the various houses paraded past them nightly. It was in some respects the most festive of all the seasonal observances in the Yoshiwara. The Yoshiwara, after all, was often called the "flower and willow world," and the courtesans themselves were traditionally referred to as flowers, which for the Japanese invariably meant cherry flowers. The battledore and *temari* carried by the courtesan's attendants underscore the festiveness of the occasion, since these were playthings usually associated with the most festive of all Japanese holidays, New Year's. The falling petals, however, introduce a more sobering note, a reminder of the transience of everything that is beautiful.

There are some interesting resemblances between this painting and Eishi's print of Takihime and two attendants in the collection of the Cleveland Museum of Art (Catalogue no. II-20). However, while the print may be fairly firmly dated to 1795, the heavier hairpins and showier *uchikake* worn by the courtesan here, together with her stouter figure, suggest a date in this case closer to 1810.

A painting similar to this one in the collection of the Asian Art Museum of San Francisco is part of a triptych of beauties with the trees of different seasons—a cherry tree, a willow, and a maple.* Since Eishi is known to have painted triptychs on other occasions as well (his set of three paintings in the Burke Collection [Catalogue no. IV-2] is a case in point), it is quite possible that this work, too, was once part of such a grouping.

---

* Narasaki Muneshige, ed. *Nikuhitsu Ukiyo-e*, v. 6 (*Utamaro*), pl. 39. The San Francisco triptych was formerly in the Bigelow Collection.

II-7

Chōbunsai Eishi (1756-1829)

Standing Courtesan Gazing into a Mirror

Circa 1795

Hanging scroll; colors on silk; 95.8 x 34.3

Signature (Chōbunsai Eishi zu) and seal (Doku U) of artist at mid-right side of image

Tiger Collection

A courtesan, seen from behind, turns to gaze in a mirror as she reaches to adjust a hairpin. Her elegant *uchikake*, worn low on her shoulders, is decorated in the Rimpa manner with a man and woman pounding *mochi* against a background of blooming *hagi* (lespedeza, or bush clover) and a winding, highly stylized river. The inconspicuous crest that appears on the back and sleeves of the *uchikake*—a pair of cherry blossoms—suggests that this regal figure is intended to portray the celebrated Hanaōgi. The mirror, placed against a purple cloth, is supported by a rack attached to a lacquer cosmetic stand.

Eishi seemed to be fond of the mirror motif, and used it often in his prints and paintings, as seems to be borne out by the fact that this is one of three examples in this exhibition alone (see Catalogue nos. II-17 and II-21). In Japanese art, mirrors were traditionally associated with the moon as well as with feminine beauty, and both associations seem to be intended here. The motifs of pounding *mochi* and blooming *hagi* on the courtesan's *uchikake* were signs of fall inextricably linked in the Japanese mind with the full moon, which was thought to be at its most beautiful in that season. (The gold pattern of maple leaves and waves on the lacquer mirror stand also alludes to fall.) Eighteenth-century Japanese mirrors, which were of bronze rather than glass, gave darker, more flattering reflections, and it is easy to see how their round shape and dull sheen would remind one of the moon.

In Japan, the nape of the neck is generally considered one of the most alluring features of a woman's body. Here Eishi has come up with an ingenious way of drawing attention to this feature while still offering a tantalizing reflection of the courtesan's face in the mirror. The concept was simple, but the result was seductive.

There is a painting virtually identical to this one, except for the placement of the signature, in the collection of the Azabu Museum of Arts and Crafts in Tokyo.*

* It is reproduced in *Azabu Bijutsukan shozō, Nikuhitsu ukiyo-e meihinten* (Tokyo: Azabu Bijutsukan, 1988), no. 51, p. 73.

II-8

Takeshiba Genkei (dates unknown)

Courtesan Painting Fans

1795

Hanging scroll; ink, colors, and gold on silk; 33 x 50.5

Date and signature of artist (Kinoto u shuka motome [ni] ōji Takeshiba Genkei gisho, "Written for amusement by Takeshiba Genkei, at special request in the 4th month of Kansei 7") at lower left, preceded by artist's seals (Zuiko, Takeshiba [?] gihitsu and Hakkei no in)

The British Museum

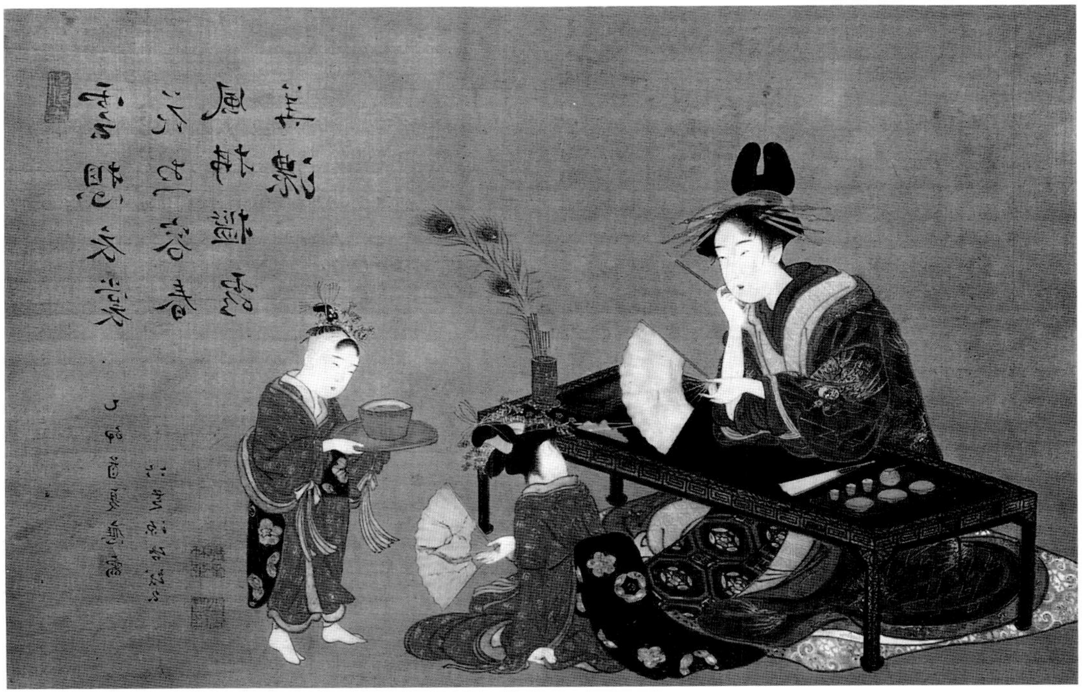

II-8

A courtesan seated at a black lacquer writing table holds a brush to her chin as she ponders what to paint on the blank folding fan she holds open in front of her. On the other side of the table, her *kamuro* turns her head inquiringly toward her mistress as she holds out another fan on which a flowering cherry branch has already been painted. Meanwhile, a little boy, wearing a kimono and obi matching the *kamuro*'s, carefully approaches the table carrying a bowl on a tray. The edges of the writing table are decorated in Chinese fashion with what looks like inlaid mother-of-pearl, and the traditional accessories of the scholar-painter are laid out on top: a large inkstone, a brush rest in the shape of a mountain range, a brush holder with peacock feathers, and a tray filled with containers of paint. A folded fan lies on the table by the courtesan's elbow.

Every facet of this intimate little painting bespeaks a taste for things Chinese. Even the courtesan's *uchikake*, of dark maroon silk decorated with golden dragons, seems to have more in common with Chinese court robes than with the flamboyant garments usually worn by women of her profession. A passage from a verse by the Tang Dynasty poet Li Bo, written backwards (or more probably on the back of the painting before it was mounted) in the upper-left corner of the work, fits perfectly with the sinified sensibility of the rest of the painting.

Nothing is known about the artist, though it is thought that he may have been primarily a calligrapher who only occasionally tried his hand at painting. A painting similar in style to this one, though with a different signature, has turned up in a Japanese collection.*

* Timothy Clark discusses this painting and Tadashi Kobayashi's comments on it in *Ukiyo-e Paintings in the British Museum* (London: British Museum Press, 1992), no. 90, p. 140.

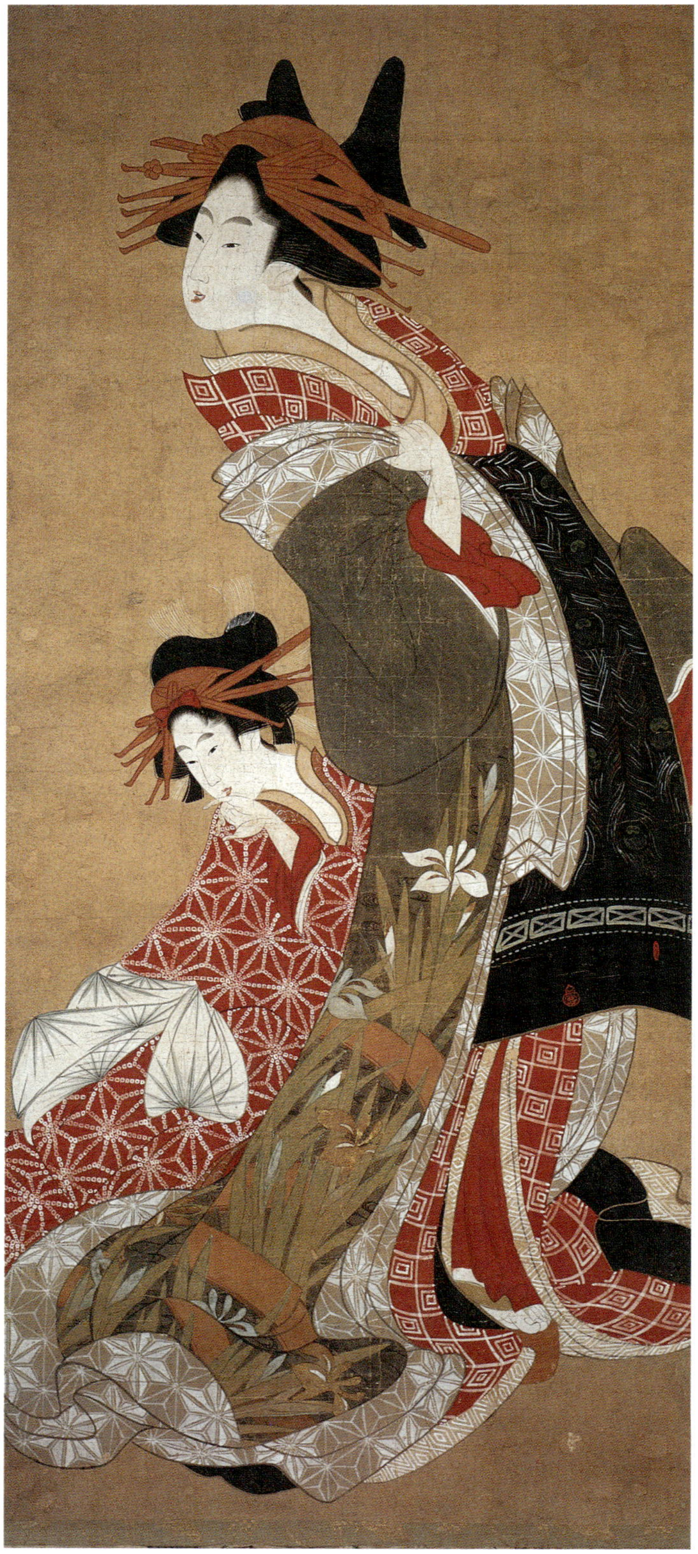

II-9

II-9

Kitagawa Kikumaro (died 1830)

Courtesan and Shinzō

Circa 1804

Hanging scroll; ink and colors on paper; 124.7 x 55.8

No signature

Los Angeles County Museum of Art, Joe and Etsuko Price Collection

A tall courtesan standing beside her seated *shinzō* strikes a dramatic pose as she arches back to stare at something beyond the picture frame. Everything about this extraordinary figure is pushed to a stylish extreme: her supple, sway-backed posture; her narrow shoulders; the curious twist to her head. There is enormous energy in the upward thrust and bend of the woman's body, and her white face seems to emerge from the clasping collars of her multi-layered kimono as forcefully as the iris flowers break from their sheaths in the design on her *uchikake*. Nothing in the courtesan's clothing or stance detracts from the powerful upward push that culminates in the outstretched twist of her head. Her right arm is pressed to her side as she clutches at the hems of her kimono, and the collars of her underkimono form sharp tips as they clasp her narrow shoulders. Even the iris design on her *uchikake*, with its massed, blade-like leaves at the bottom thinning to a few pointed shafts at the top, contributes to the effect.

The way the composition has been cropped may have been done deliberately in order to emphasize even further the vertical elongation of the courtesan's pose; but it seems likely that at least some of the painting surface has been lost through remounting. This might explain the puzzling absence of a signature. The attribution to Kikumaro is based on an inscription on the painting's box. If the attribution is correct—and there seems no reason to doubt it—Kikumaro seems to have been a more accomplished artist than his relatively obscure reputation would suggest. Little is known about him, other than that he was a pupil of Utamaro. His known oeuvre consists of only a handful of paintings and prints, most of which date from the first decade of the nineteenth century.

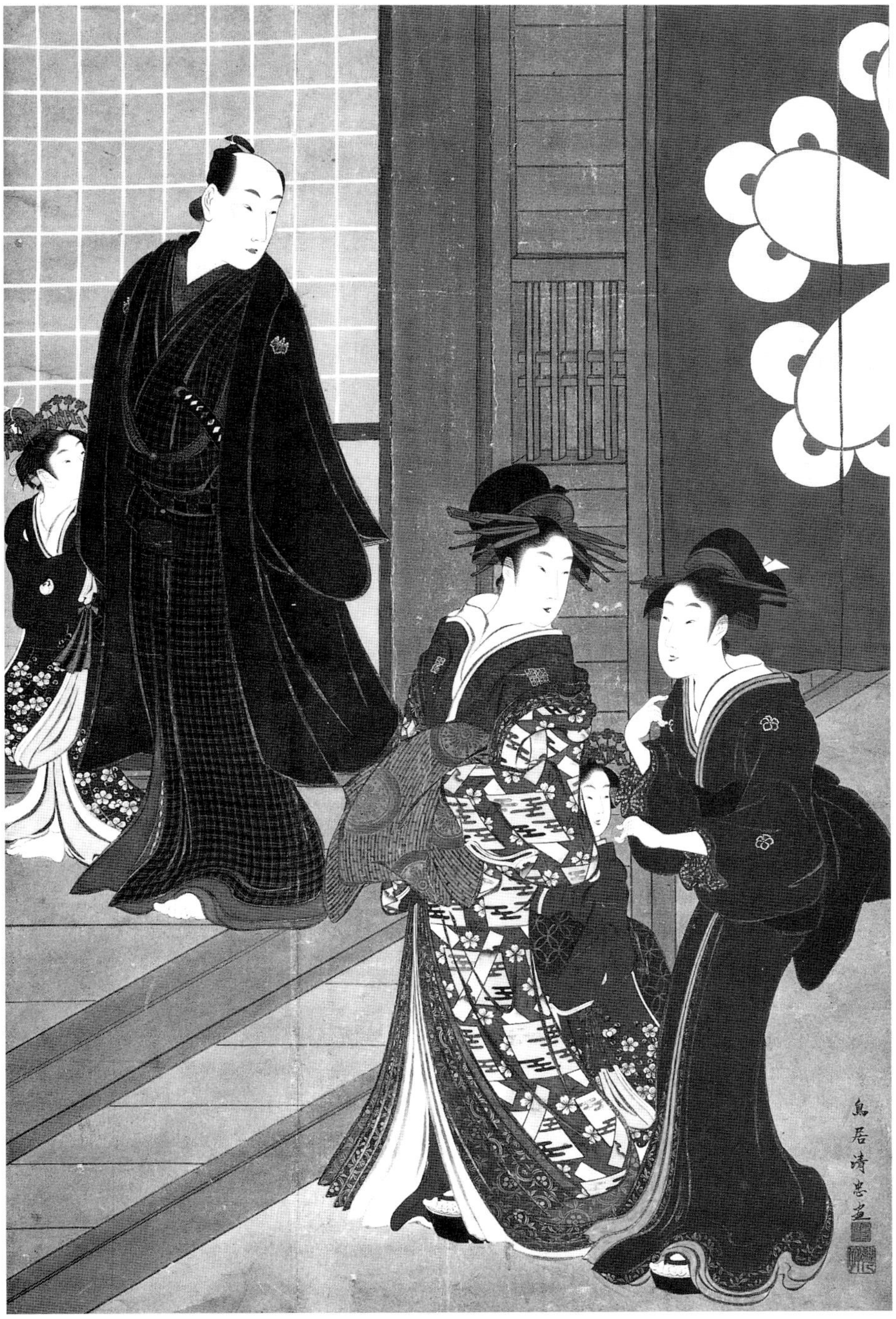

II-10

II-10

Torii Kiyotada II (active circa 1790-1818)

Courtesan Arriving to Meet Her Guest at a Teahouse

Circa 1792

Hanging scroll; ink and colors on paper; 128.3 x 83.8

Signature (Torii Kiyotada ga) and seals (Torii) and (Kiyotada) of artist at lower right

Azabu Museum of Arts and Crafts

Katsukawa Shunchō also depicts a courtesan and her retinue approaching a teahouse where her client awaits her (Catalogue no. II-3). Here Kiyotada offers another view of the first encounter between a courtesan and her client. In this case the two principals are closer, but even so a certain distance still separates them. The courtesan, who is still in the street, turns to listen to a maid or *yarite*, perhaps to get some last-minute instructions, while the client looks down on the proceedings from the porch of the teahouse. One of the courtesan's *kamuro* is already on the porch, standing beside the client, while her companion is still with her mistress, half-hidden behind her. The two *kamuro* wear bright

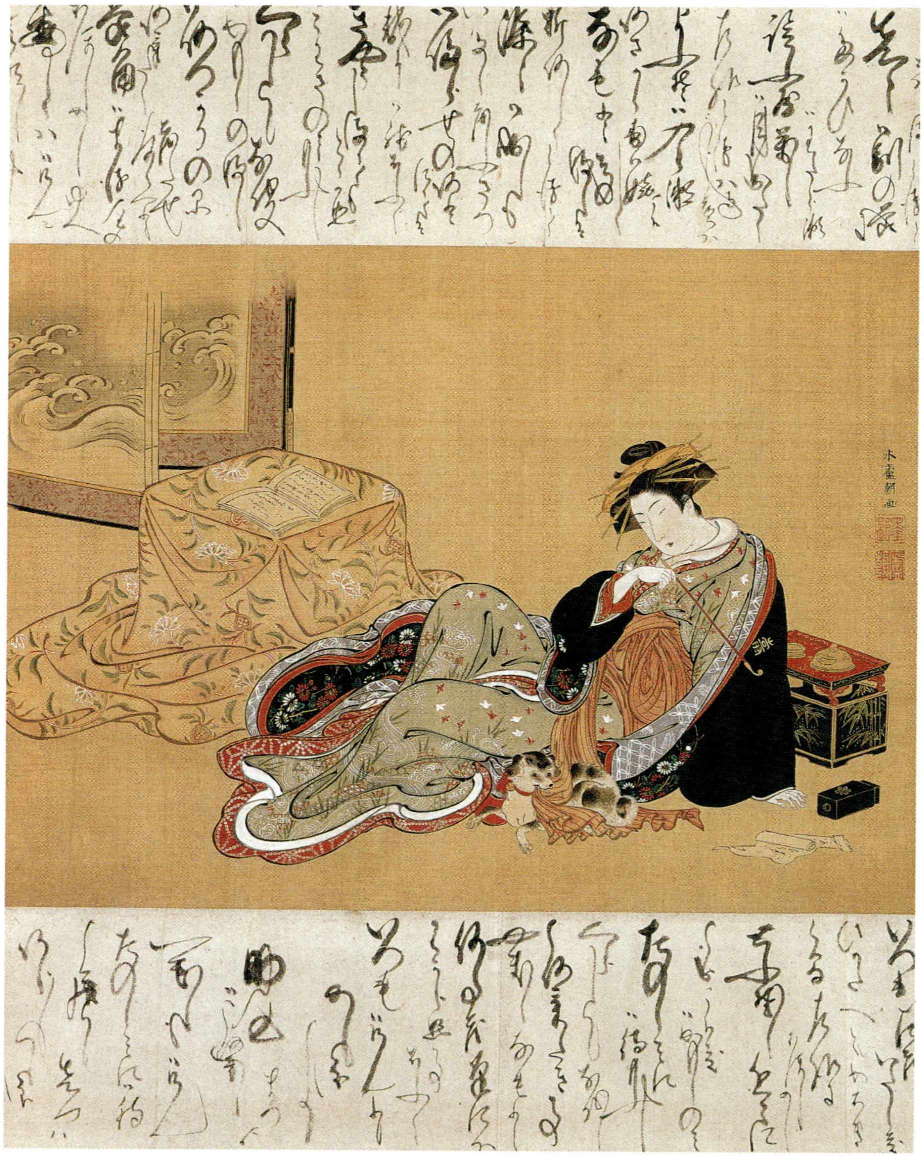

II-11

red *furisode* decorated with branches of blooming plum. The courtesan's elegant steel-blue *uchikake* is decorated with *tanzaku* (poem slips), *shikishi* (poem sheets), and scattered plum blossoms. The client cuts a handsome figure with his black *haori*, checked kimono, discreet obi, and red tobacco pouch. The upper-right corner of the painting is dominated by the bold white crest on the teahouse's blue *noren*.

Little is known of Kiyotada other than that he was a pupil of Torii Kiyonaga and probably worked primarily with theatrical subjects. Even with a nontheatrical subject like this, the boldness and lack of fussy detail, as well as the rather dramatic touch provided by the crest-emblazoned *noren*, suggests a style that would be at home in paintings of kabuki posters and *ema* of actors. A glance at two of Kiyonaga's works in this exhibition, the screen from the Tsubouchi Memorial Museum (Catalogue no. V-1) and the *ema* from the Takoyakushi Temple (Catalogue no. V-2), will show where the style comes from.

II-11

Mizuno Rochō (1748-1836)

Seated Courtesan with a Dog

Early 1780s

Hanging scroll; ink and colors on silk; 51.5 x 69.2

Signature of artist (Mizu Rochō ga) at right

Tiger Collection

A half-reclining courtesan props herself up with one arm as she gazes down at a little dog beside her. The dog is lying on the long, loose end of her obi, one edge of which it holds in its mouth. Two letters, one still unopened, lie on the floor nearby, next to a small, black scroll box. The courtesan languidly holds a long *kiseru* in her right hand, and there is an elegant red-and-black lacquer *tabako-bon* behind her. She is dressed in a pale gray-green kimono with a pattern of waves and plovers, over which she has thrown a black *uchikake*. The *uchikake* is plain at the top (except for the character *ju*, "longevity," in gold at the shoulder) and decorated discreetly with chrysanthemums at the bottom.

The courtesan's somewhat awkward pose suggests that the artist may have caught her just as she turned away from the *kotatsu* beside her to look at her dog. A book has been left open on top of the *kotatsu* as though someone had been interrupted in the process of reading it. (Until recently, Japanese houses were not heated, and one of the few ways people could get warm in winter was by putting their legs under a *kotatsu* —a quilt-covered frame or table placed over a sunken section of the floor containing a brazier.) The only other article of furniture in the room is a folding screen depicting breaking waves.

The sophisticated taste found in ukiyo-e paintings should also, ideally, be reflected in their mountings. Here an ingenious mounter has used passsages from a real courtesan's love letter to set off the painting at top and bottom. The loose, sensuous flow of the calligraphy is the perfect match for the elegant languor in the painting.

Mizuno Rochō was, like Kitao Masayoshi (Kuwagata Keisai) and Kitao Masanobu (Santō Kyōden), a pupil of Kitao Shigemasa. He was a samurai, and restricted his activity in ukiyo-e to painting.

II-12

Katsukawa Shun'ei (1762-1819)

Courtesan Reading a Letter

1790s

Hanging scroll; ink and colors on silk; 84 x 33

Signature of artist (Shun'ei ga) and hand-painted cypher (kao)

Art Gallery of New South Wales

The idealized courtesans usually depicted in ukiyo-e were figures of extraordinary allure. Clad in sumptuous garments, courted by admirers—those few who could afford their expensive company—they were indeed the imperious "castle breakers" of popular legend. Yet an occasional work hints at a darker side to these glamorous creatures' lives. Chōki's *Rain on the "Morning After"* (Catalogue no. II-16), for instance, reminds us of the hours of boredom to which their caged existence condemned them. But boredom is not despair, and despair is what Shun'ei confronts us with in this unusually frank painting of a distraught courtesan staring down at a letter unrolled in front of her. The courtesan's features are unmistakably distorted by emotion, and there is something strangely awkward in her rigid pose. If there were any doubt as to what the artist had in mind, that doubt would be dispelled by Shokusanjin's (Ōta Nampo's) inscription in dark calligraphy in the upper half of the scroll. It is written in Chinese, in four five-word lines, and reads: *Yūkun gochō kaku / kukai jūnen ryū / nijū shichi mei mu / Aa shin kirō* (Courtesans of the five streets of the quarter, ten years adrift on an ocean of troubles, released at twenty-seven with misguided dreams. Ah! This bitter mirage of the brothels.* [Twenty-seven or twenty-six was the usual age at which courtesans were released from their contracts.]) It is interesting that Nampo chose to

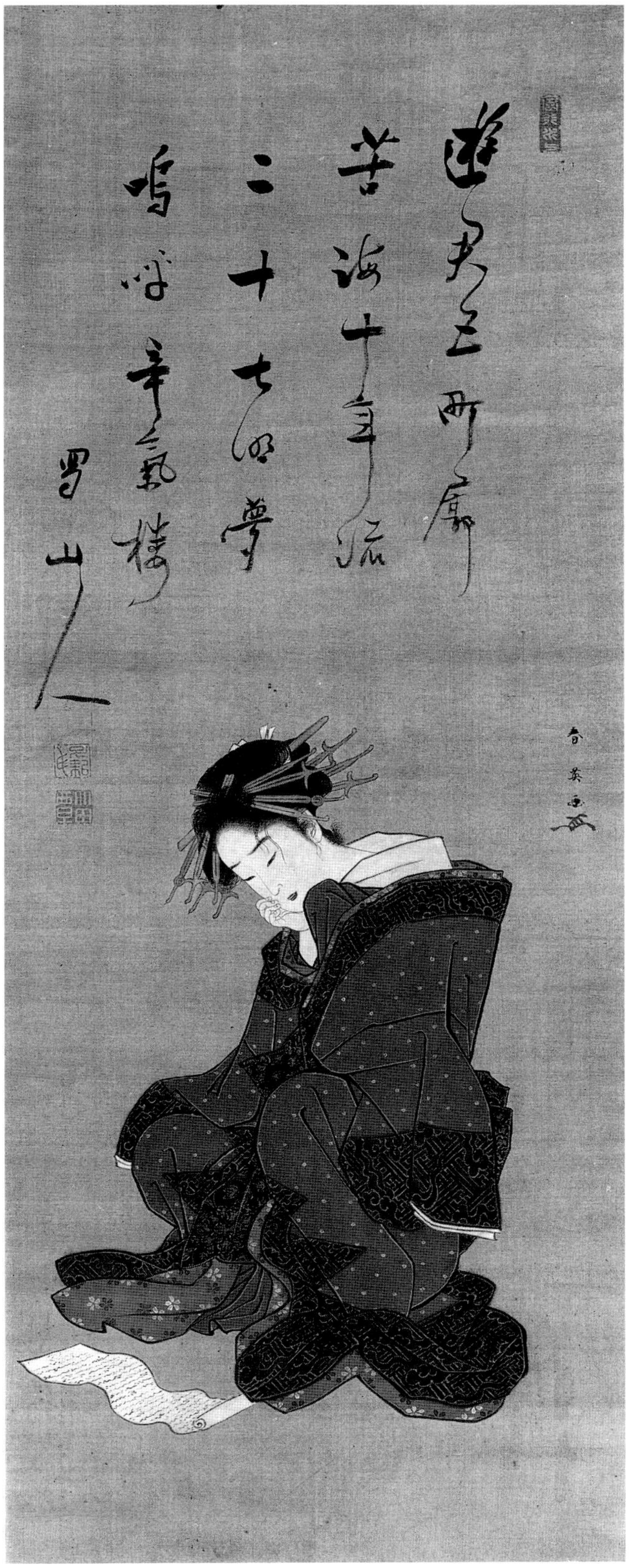

II-12

write the poem in Chinese. Some of his most personal and expressive poetry is in that language. His writing in Japanese was usually lighter in mood.

* The translation is by Timothy Clark, and is taken from his *Ukiyo-e Paintings in the British Museum* (London: British Museum Press, 1992).

Shun'ei, as his name suggests, studied under Shunshō. As a print designer, he specialized, like his master, in subjects connected with kabuki. There are four other prints by him in the exhibition (Catalogue nos. V-14 through V-17).

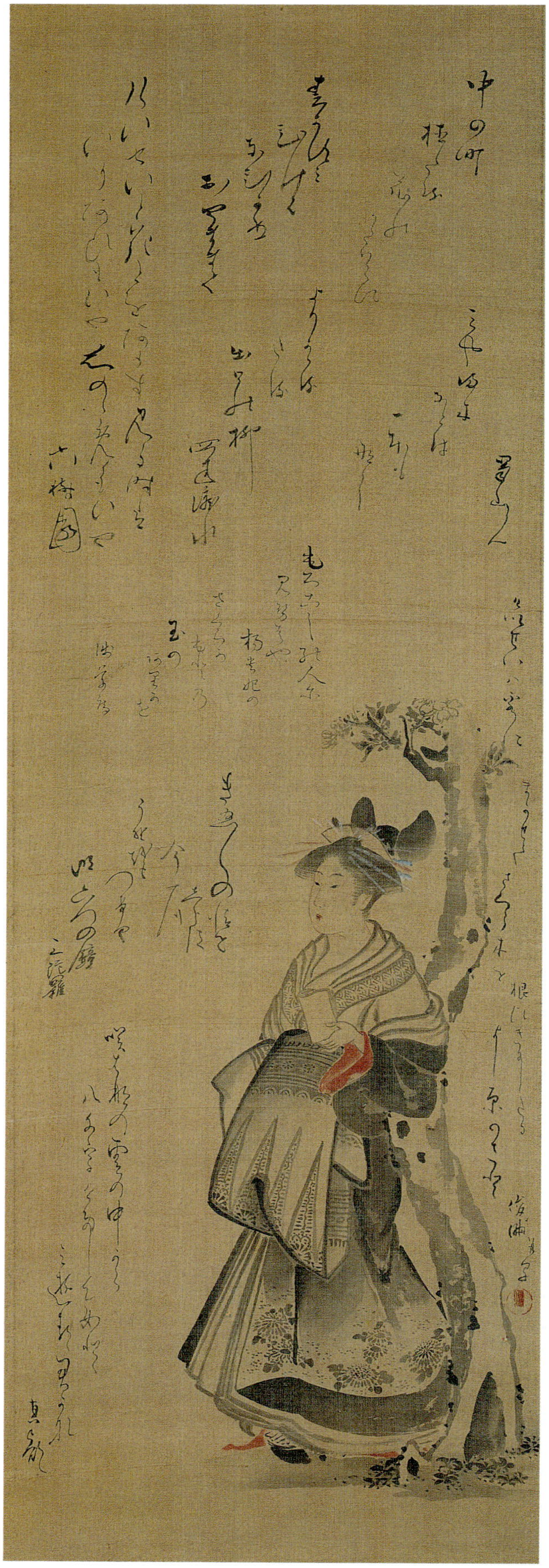

II-13

II-13

Kubo Shumman (1757-1820)

Courtesan beside a Tree, with Kyōka by Seven Poets

Circa 1802

Hanging scroll; ink and light touches of color on silk; 94.2 x 31.6

Signature (Shumman – [?] sha) and seal (Shumman) of artist at lower right

Art Gallery of New South Wales

This scroll has been included in Section II (The Yoshiwara) because of the courtesan depicted in the lower-right quarter of it. It could as easily have been included in Section III (Santō Kyōden) or Section IV (Ōta Nampo), however, as an example of the collaborative works so often created by artists and writers at poetry parties. The man who painted the courtesan on this scroll, Shumman, also contributed a poem to it (it is just to the right of the courtesan, above his signature), and frequently contributed poems and/or sketches to other *sekiga* (party paintings). Seven poets (including Shumman) contributed verses to this work. They are, from top to bottom and right to left: Shokusanjin (Ōta Nampo); Yomo Takimizu (Sakatsuki no Komehito); Rokujūen (Yadoya no Meshimori); Sensōan (Hajintei Ichindō); Sandarabōshi; Shumman; and Shikatsube Magao. Five of these—Shokusanjin, Rokujūen, Sandarabōshi, Shumman, and Magao—were among the fourteen contributors to another *sekiga* in the exhibition (Catalogue no. III-5). The likelihood that many of these artists and writers got together for poetry parties quite often is borne out by mentions in contemporary journals and memoirs. According to these, Shokusanjin began holding kyōka parties again (after having retired from the literary scene at the start of the Kansei Reforms) soon after 1800.* The contributors to this scroll

* See Kasuya Hiroki, *Ishikawa Gabō kenkyū* (Tokyo: Kadokawa Shoten, 1986), 133.

were among those reported to have attended these parties with some regularity.

Though quite often the poems inscribed on such a scroll would have been composed on the spot, this was not always the case. Poets like Shokusanjin, for instance, who received countless requests for poems, could hardly have been expected to come up with an original verse each time; in fact, the kyōka he contributed here is identical to one he inscribed on another scroll in this exhibition (Catalogue no. IV-2): *Nakanochō / uetaru hana no / katawara ni / fukayamagi nado / ippon mo nashi* (Beside the flowering cherry blossoms of the Nakanochō, not a single tree from the deep mountain valleys).

We will not take the time to translate any of the other verses. Suffice it to say that their imagery all relates to courtesans, the Yoshiwara, and trees.

Shumman's courtesan is not one of the haughty beauties so often depicted in ukiyo-e paintings and prints. There seems to be something touching, perhaps even vulnerable, about her as she peers anxiously off to the left, holding what looks like a love letter to her breast. The unassuming nature of the subject is reflected in the way Shumman has drawn her, as though taking care not to encroach on his friends' calligraphic inscriptions. Rendered almost entirely in ink and highlighted with only a few small touches of red and blue, the unassuming drawing remains resolutely within the lower-right quarter of the scroll.

II-14

Katsukawa Shunrin (active 1780-1795)

Three Beauties

Circa 1785

Hanging scroll; ink and colors on paper; 38.4 x 50.6

Signature (Katsukawa Shunrin ga) and handwritten cypher (kaō) of artist

Los Angeles County Museum of Art, Joe and Etsuko Price Collection

It is hard to believe that we know so little about the painter of this elegant and beautifully delineated work, yet nothing is known about Katsukawa Shunrin other than what can be inferred from his name or concluded from the few extant works bearing his signature. That he studied under Katsukawa Shunshō would be obvious from his name, even if it were not apparent

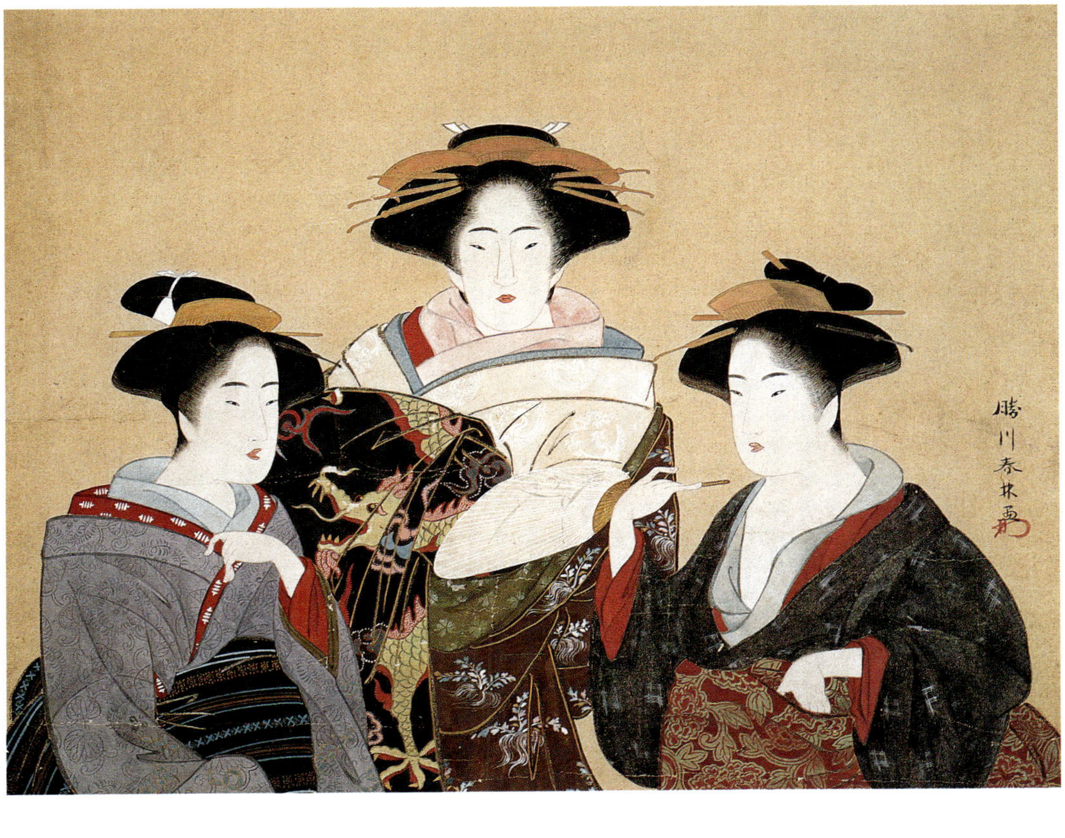

II-14

from his style. The women he portrays, with their squared-off faces and somewhat stocky bodies, closely resemble those found in Shunshō's paintings, and there is also something of his master's touch in the refinement of his brushwork. But beyond this, we know nothing. We have no idea of when he was born or when he died, and can only assume, based on his relationship with Shunshō, that he lived in Edo.

There is obviously something posed or studied about the way the three women in this work are placed together. They are definitely not conversing or interacting with one another. On the contrary, each of them stares fixedly in a different direction. It is almost as though they were taking part in a formal tableau. In a sense, perhaps this is what they were doing, because when we look closely, we see that each woman represents a different feminine type or profession. The woman in the center is certainly a courtesan; the one at right is probably a waitress at an outdoor tea stand; and the one at left appears to be a geisha. Such groupings of women from different professions are seldom encountered in ukiyo-e painting but were common for a while in prints. During the early 1790s, Utamaro designed a number of prints depicting trios of popular beauties of the day. Several of these included outdoor tea-stand waitresses similar to the woman shown here at right.*

None of Utamaro's beauties is depicted frontally like the courtesan in this painting, however; as is clear from the examples in this exhibition, straight-on portrayals of the human face are rare in ukiyo-e in general. They are most often found in paintings of the 1770s and 1780s by Shunshō; his contemporary, Koryūsai (fl. 1765-1788); and Toyoharu (1735-1814).

The details in this painting are rendered with a delicacy and restrained elegance that merit the closest scrutiny. The eye is first drawn to the courtesan's black silk obi with its pale-green-and-red dragon. The contrasting colors and the dragon's extended claws and open mouth add a sense of movement and drama to the composition, which might otherwise seem too placid. The obi seems all the more striking because of its placement against the courtesan's pale-white kimono with its discreet pattern of phoenix roundels. An elegant maroon *uchikake*

* Shunrin may also have had the somewhat blasphemous idea of comparing his three beauties to one of the Buddhist triads. The Bodhisattva Kannon was often depicted flanked by two lesser divinities.

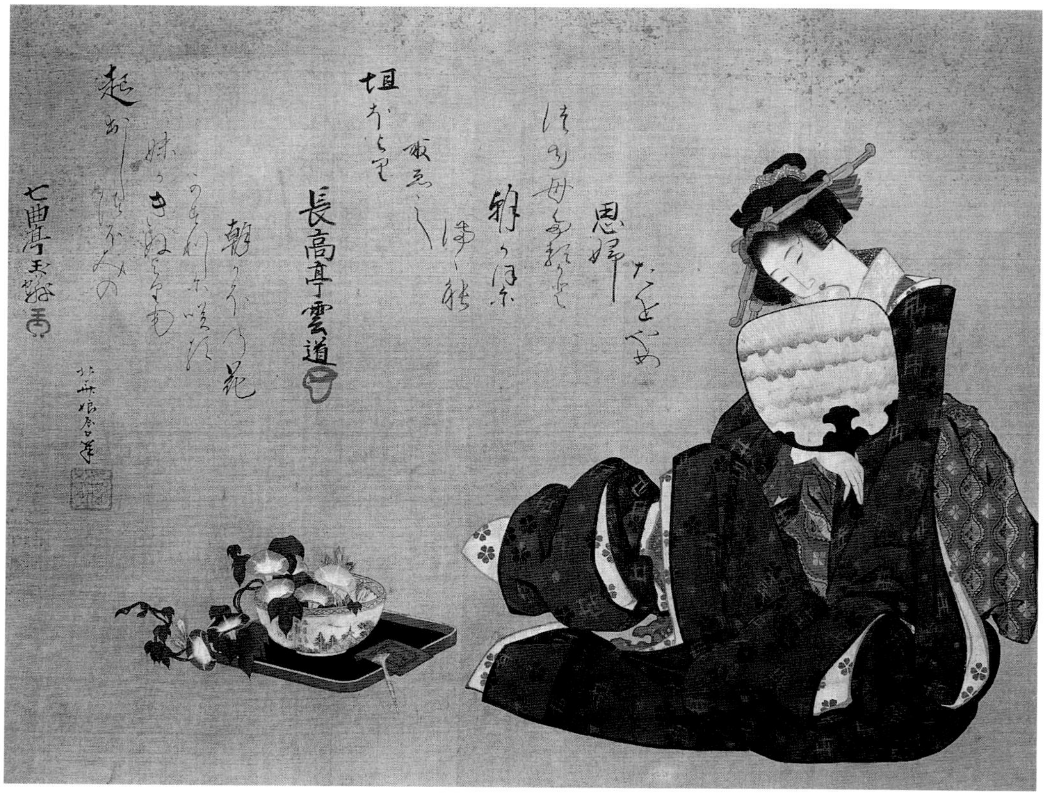

II-15

rides low on the courtesan's shoulders. (Note that the lines representing the folds in both the obi and the *uchikake* are rendered in gold.) The waitress, in contrast to the courtesan, wears a simple black *kasuri* kimono over her undergarments, which she has left open at the neck. The geisha is dressed conservatively, as was typical of her kind, in a purple kimono with a pattern of wild ginger.

II-15

Katsushika Tatsu (active 1810-1820)

Woman Viewing Morning Glories

Circa 1810

Hanging scroll; ink and colors on silk; 34 x 45

Signature of artist (Hokusai musume Tatsu jo)

Los Angeles County Museum of Art, Ernest Larsen Blanck Memorial Fund

The painter of this scroll was one of Katsushika Hokusai's daughters, O-tatsu, who died while still in her twenties. Clearly an accomplished artist who refined the style her father developed in about 1810, she introduced more than a hint of seductiveness into this delicate figure of a courtesan gazing at a bowl overflowing with summery morning glories. The crook of the courtesan's neck, the caress of her collar against her cheek, the twist of the fan to hide her smile, and the delicate grace of her fingers cast a spell strong enough to captivate even the casual viewer.

Innocent and fragile as she appears, the poems inscribed on the painting project a distinctly erotic mood. Contrary to convention, they appear to have been inscribed from left to right. Read in that fashion, the first poem unfolds as: *Tsubomi no / okidashi / imoto ga kinu yorimo / kasuri ni sakeru / asagao no hana* (For awakening the bud, little sister blooms more by a touch than by silks, Flower of the morning glory). The poet signs himself Nanamagaritei (Winding Path), and has painted a *kao* as part of his signature.

The next poet gives his name as Chōkōtei Undō (Long and High Cloud Road), and has also painted a *kao* cipher. The poem may be read as: *Kaki ni yori / tori eshi / mama no / asagaho ni / tsuyu mo shitataru / omofu / taoyame* (Freshly picked as it grew by the fence, the dew still trickles off the morning glory, the tender blossom deep in her thoughts).

Both poems are written in highly idiosyncratic cursive script, which may be read in various ways. Moreover, the poets, who have hidden their identities in fanciful pseudonyms, have played with the Japanese technique of *ateji*, in which *kanji* may be given unexpected interpretations. This playful attitude of the poets not only teases the reader into recognizing new connotations for the words, but prevents the sexual tenor of the verses from becoming overt and vulgar. Thus disguised, the scroll could be displayed and casually enjoyed for its pictorial charm.

II-16

Eishosai Chōki (active 1780-1800)

Rain on the "Morning After" in One of the Green Houses

Circa 1795

Woodblock print; ōban triptych; 38.1 x 76.2

Trademark of publisher, Tsutaya Jūzaburō, and kiwame seal in lower-left corner of each panel

The Art Institute of Chicago, Clarence Buckingham Collection

This particular "Green House"—the Matsubaya, or "pine-needle house"—is symbolized by the bonsai in the left panel foreground, which is also a seasonal reference to winter.

The scene portrays an elegant set of rooms and the courtesans in various states of fatigue and dishabille following a night of entertaining. The "morning after" in the title (*kinuginu* in Japanese) originally referred to lovers putting their clothes back on in the morning, in preface to parting, though it may be construed to mean simply the time when the revelers depart.

The three panels are a behind-the-scenes view of the courtesans' life, showing the cleaning up that lies ahead, the hard work of the entertainment that just ended, soon to begin again. The glorified chic of their lives is revealed as fatiguing and ultimately lonely. (The guests have left, the intimacy is over, the rain beats down.)

One figure stands out in each of this triptych's panels, the *yobidashi*, courtesan of the highest class. In each grouping she is attended

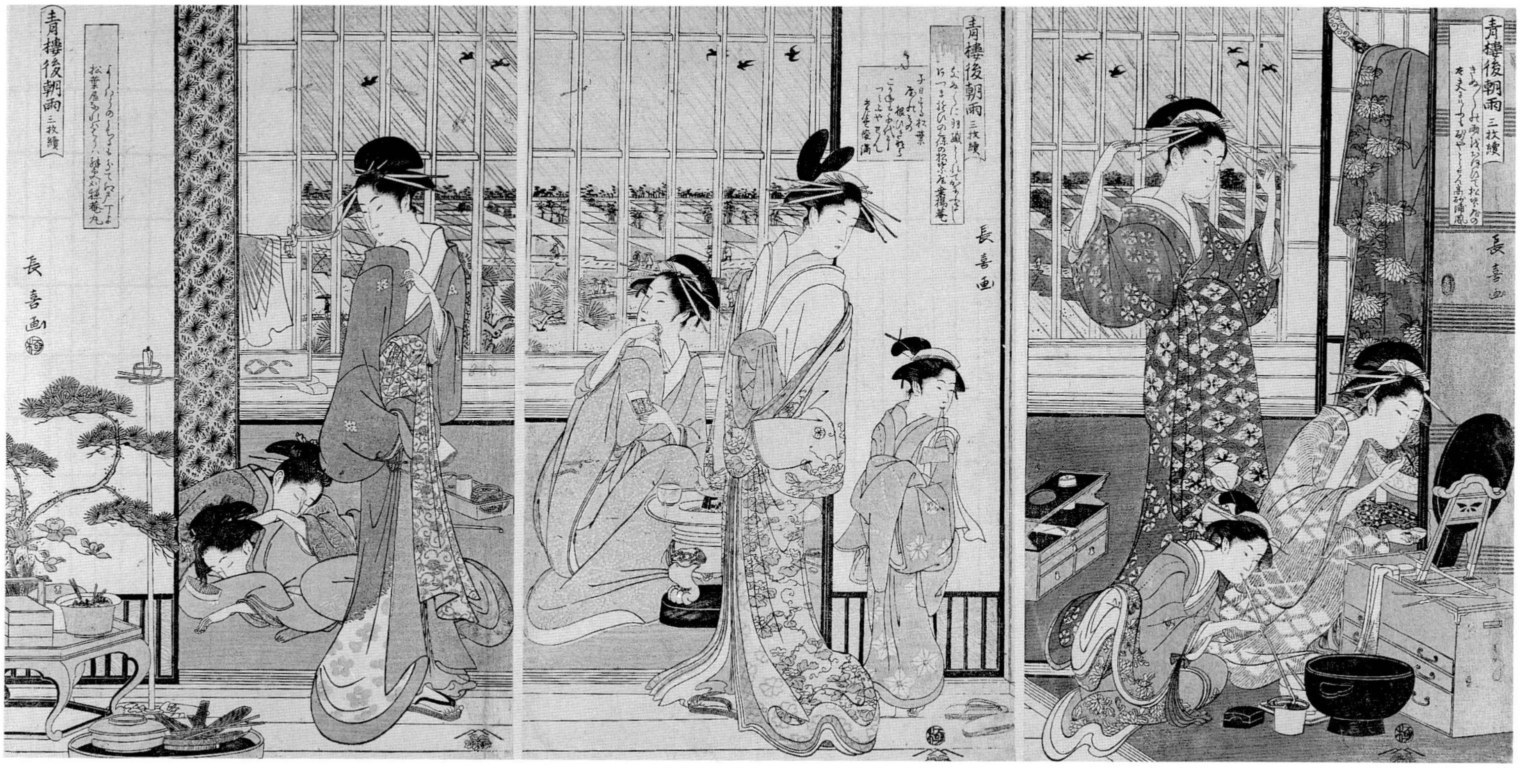

II-16

by *kamuro* and *shinzō*, junior courtesans who serve customers as well as the *yobidashi*.

Looking at the triptych frame by frame, we see on the far right a seated *shinzō* applying lip rouge at a mirror stand, while a *kamuro* stoops to clean a long pipe. There are, in fact, many awaiting her attention. Behind them stands a *yobidashi* adjusting her hair ornaments. We see the corner of a *tabako-bon* and a garment draped over a kimono rack. The rain slants over the rice paddies in the background, where birds fly free.

Beside the cartouche with the title for the piece is a kyōka: *Kinuginu no ame o ohohite / Matsubaya no tayu ni kefu mo / shaku ya torasen* (Wrapped in the rain of the morning after, the Matsubaya *tayu* must again today pour the sake for yet another party).

The poet Takasago Urakaze here sees through the carefully crafted mystique of these beauties and discerns that what for the guests is giddy pleasure is for the women another day's work. He refers to the highest class of courtesan as "*tayu*," though that classification no longer existed in the 1790s. Urakaze no doubt uses it as an honorific term.

In the center, we see another grouping of three, with the *yobidashi* in her butterfly hairdo sitting, casually enjoying a smoke by the Chinese-style hibachi. Her teacup rests on the rim—a rare moment of leisure. Two kyōka appear here, overflowing with nuance.

The first, by Raijo An, pivots on the famous locale Mio no Matsubara, which literally means "three treasures of the pine field." It is the site of the fable, immortalized in the No play *Hagoromo*, in which an angel danced to retrieve her cloak of feathers. "Matsubaya" is a parody of "Matsubara." *Kinuginu ni haori torarete kanau maji / Azuma asobi no Mio no Matsubaya* (Removing my cloak on the morning after is not the thing to do in the Edo-style revelry at the Mio no Matsubaya), or, assembling all the meanings in the images: "The morning after is the time to put clothes back on; remember the angel whose cloak was stolen until she danced for its return. Edo-style entertainment with the three jewels of the Matsubaya forbids me from now removing my jacket."

The second kyōka, written by the artist Kubo Shumman, cleverly refers to a New Year's festivity performed on *ne no hi*, day of the rat or seventh day of the new year, when young pines were pulled from the garden in a ritual called *nebiki*. *Nebiki* was also the word that meant buying out a courtesan's contract. *Ne no hi suru Matsuba / ya no sono / nebiki toru / kogane mo chiyo ni tsumiageyasen* (Not even in one thousand years would I be able to amass the fortune to pay the Matsubaya's ransom). Another way of translating the poem would be: "The seventh day of the new year celebrated by uprooting pine shoots from the garden of the House of Pines. Not in a thousand years could I get the money to uproot one myself."

In the left-most panel, where the courtesan stands in the hallway, a table is laden with a three-tiered lacquer box and a bowl of what seem to be noodles. A tray on the floor similarly holds the remnants of the party's feasting. Behind the *fusuma*, in the tatami interior, two *shinzō* are asleep, one with her hair combs in disarray. Their *tabako-bon* lies to the side, a *kiseru* strewn carelessly on the floor, and a kimono rack stands on the veranda just in front of the large bank of windows facing out to the fields.

Here the poem by Kariho Anmaru* reads: *Yoshiwara no uchi ni mo wakete Edocho yo / Matsubaya nareba hari wa kotosara* (If you are going to the Yoshiwara, Edocho is the place to be, and if you are at the Matsubaya, then their high-spiritedness is special). "High-spiritedness," of course, is not the image that comes to mind on viewing this scene, thus giving the kyōka its bite. The trait of *hari*—spunk, spirit, a mind of one's own—was greatly prized in Edo courtesans, and set them apart from courtesans of Kyoto or Osaka.

* Kariho Anmaru might have been a verse-name of Tsutaya, whose real name was Maruyama Kari (also pronounced Karamaru), and who is known to have used the name Tsuta no Karamaru.

II-17

Chōbunsai Eishi (1756-1829)

Courtesan before a Mirror Adjusting Her Hairpins, from a *Shin Rokkasen* series

Circa 1795

Woodblock print; ōban; 33.3 x 20.6

Signature of artist (Eishi zu), kiwame seal, and trademark and seal of publisher, Nishimuraya Eijudō

The Cleveland Museum of Art, Fanny Tewksbury King Collection

A courtesan, her obi loosely tied and wearing a light gauze *uchikake*, gazes at her reflection in a mirror as she adjusts her hairpins. The mirror, which seems unusually large, rests against a cloth-covered rack attached to a lacquer mirror stand. The courtesan's *shinzō* looks on from the side.

The portrait and name of the poet Kuronushi appear along with the series title in the round cartouche at upper left, and a poem attributed to Kuronushi is printed in the rectangular cartouche at the center top. The poem reads: *Kagamiyama / iza tachiyorite / mite yukamu / toshi henuru mi wa / oiyashinuru to* (If I were to go to Mirror Mountain, would I see in my reflection there how much I have aged?). Otomo no Kuronushi, who flourished in the ninth century, was one of the *rokkasen*, "Six Immortals of Poetry" or "Six Poetic Geniuses," whose names were mentioned in the preface to the famous tenth-century Imperial poetry anthology, the *Kokinshū*. The poem, which is not even firmly attributable to Kuronushi, was apparently chosen for its references to mirrors and reflections, not for its underlying sentiment, which, given that courtesans customarily "retired" by the age of twenty-six or twenty-seven,

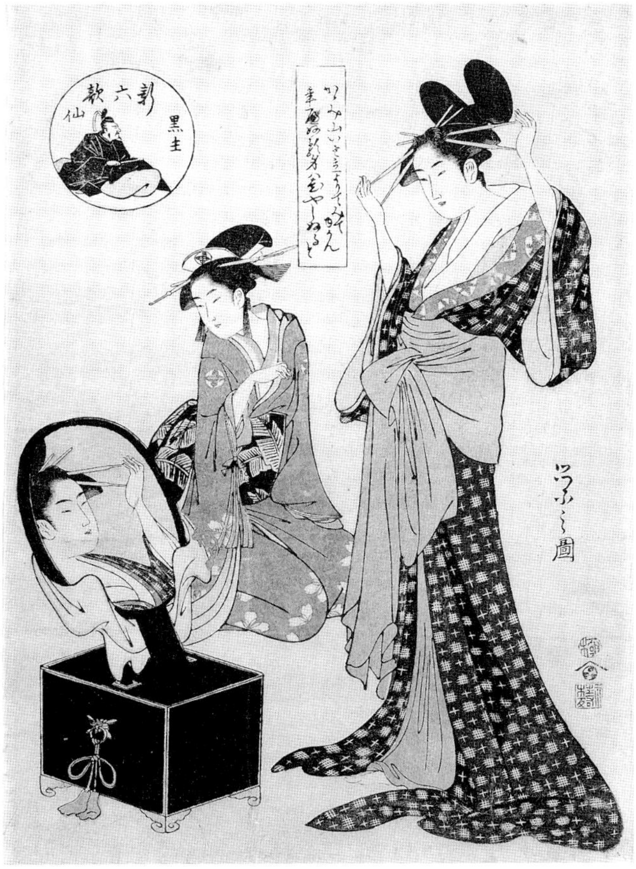

II-17

could only be interpreted ironically.

Mirrors, with their numerous associations with feminine beauty, were a popular motif in ukiyo-e, particularly during the 1790s. But none of the artists who made use of the motif at the time—not even Utamaro—seems to have been as fascinated by it as Eishi. It is no accident that mirrors appear in three of the twelve works by him in this exhibition.

That he was aware (as one might expect) of the expressive possibilities offered by the motif is certainly evident here. The large oval of the mirror, reflecting as it does the smaller ovals of the women's faces and the circle of the series cartouche, is a major formal element in the design. But far more important compositionally is the way the mirror anchors the lower-left corner of the print and becomes the receptacle, so to speak, of the gazes directed to it diagonally by both the courtesan and her *shinzō*. The confrontation between the courtesan's face in one corner and her image in the mirror in the other corner establishes a kind of polar field that draws the composition together and underscores the print's meaning. At the same time the motif loses none of its traditional associations with coquetry and feminine artifice. The human parallel is emphasized even more in this case by the cloth that wraps around the mirror like a collar.

II-18 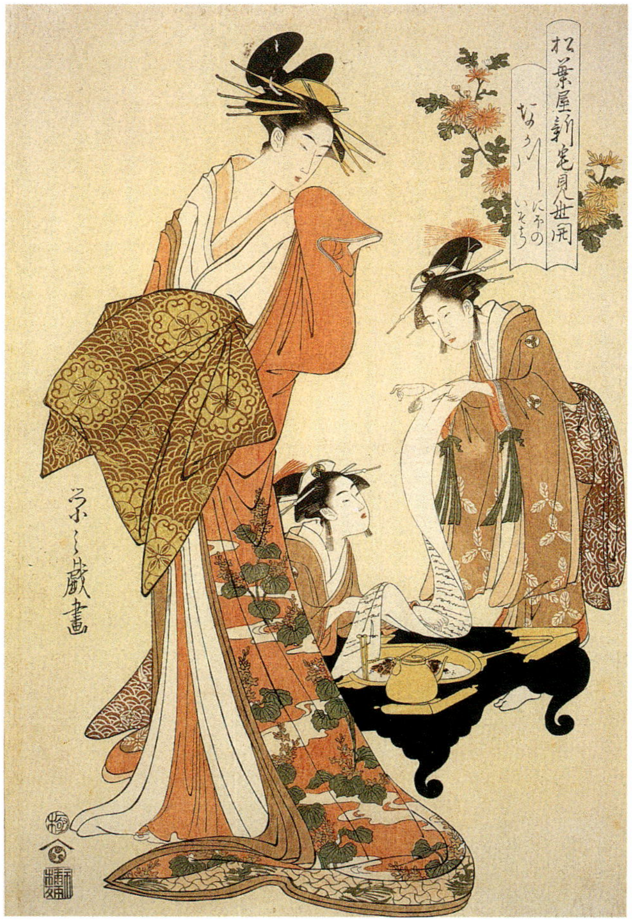

II-18

Chōbunsai Eishi (1756-1829)

The Courtesan Nakagawa of the Matsubaya with Two Apprentices

Late 1794

Woodblock print; ōban; 38.5 x 25.5

Signature of artist (Eishi giga ["playfully painted by Eishi"]), kiwame seal, and trademark and seal (Eijuhan) of publisher, Nishimuraya Eijudō

The British Museum

The tall, slender Nakagawa, her height emphasized by her top-heavy butterfly coiffure and her long, flowing robes, raises a sleeve pensively to her cheek as she listens to one of her *shinzō* reading a lengthy love letter. An elegant lacquer hibachi with fanciful cabriole legs sits on the floor between the courtesan and her two apprentices. In the upper-right corner, flowering chrysanthemum branches reach out from behind a double-panelled cartouche. The right-hand panel reads: *Matsubaya shintaku misebiraki* (Opening of the Matsubaya's new quarters), and the left-hand panel gives Nakagawa's name and those of her two *shinzō*, Nihono and Isochi.

An announcement like the one on the right-hand panel is rare. It suggests that the print may have been published late in 1794, when the Matsubaya, along with other famous brothels, reopened following the disastrous fire that had leveled the entire Yoshiwara earlier that year. The fire occurred in early May, which means that the brothels would have had to move to temporary quarters for most of the summer. The chrysanthemums behind the cartouche suggest that the opening took place in the fall. If the announced reopening is indeed connected with the 1794 fire, this print can be quite useful in helping date other works of the period. The only other major Yoshiwara fires anywhere close in date to the 1794 fire are those of Temmei 7 (1787) and Kansei 12 (1800); based on stylistic grounds, it seems unlikely, if not impossible, that the print would be related to either of those.

In its level of exaggeration and artifice, this print reminds one of Eishi's large double *ōban* print in the collection of the Portland Art Museum (Catalogue no. II-21). The same long, flowing lines and the same taste for elegance are apparent in both; and both works stop just short of going too far. Here it is not just Nakagawa's unusual height, or the affected way she bends back to listen to her *shinzō*, that contributes to this sense of excess, but even touches like the way the billowing of the improbably long letter is played off against the opposing curves of the *shinzō*'s hanging sleeves.

II-19

Chōbunsai Eishi (1756-1829)

The Courtesan Takigawa of the Ōgiya in a Picture of the "First Sale" Celebration in the Brothel's Parlor (*Hatsu-uri zashiki no zu*), from the series A Comparison of Selected Beauties of the Pleasure Quarters (*Seirō bisen awase*)

Circa 1795

Woodblock print; ōban with mica ground; 37.2 x 25.4

Signature of artist (Eishi giga ["painted in jest by Eishi"]) and trademark of publisher, Iwatoya, at left

The Metropolitan Museum of Art, Fletcher Fund, 1929

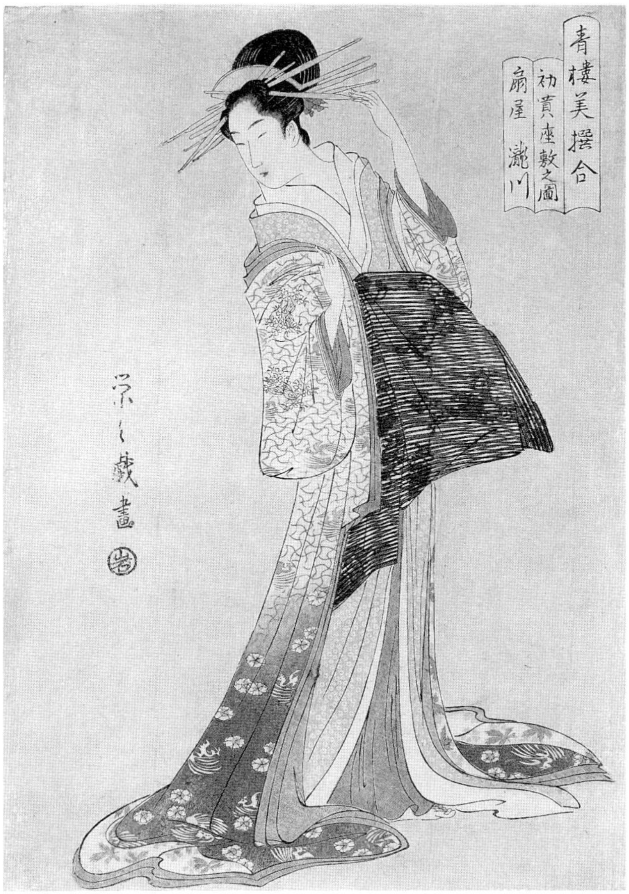

II-19

The beautiful Takigawa of the Ōgiya turns her head pensively to one side as she adjusts a hairpin with one hand and fingers the collar of her elegant *uchikake* with the other. She is indoors, as her bare toes peeking out from under her kimono make clear, but is already dressed for *hatsu-uri*, the celebration of the first sale of the year, which took place on the second day of the first month.

This and the other two known images Eishi designed for this series are among his most widely admired prints, and with good reason. His work is generally noted for the refinement of its draftsmanship and the elegance of its textile patterns; but in this series Eishi seems to have outdone himself in both regards. It is almost as though he was consciously striving to surpass his previous achievements in the medium. No distracting elements are allowed to intrude, and the figures are isolated against their brilliant mica backgrounds with a stunning sense of placement that makes them striking in themselves and enhances their interaction with the signatures and title panels.

This print occurs in four variations or states distinguished by differences in the treatment of the background, and experts have long been divided over which state is earliest or most desirable. A floor line appears in two of the states, and in one of these the portion of the print above the floor line is covered with mica so dark that it obscures the signature and title panels. In another variation, generally considered to be the latest in date, the artist's signature and the publisher's mark are missing, and the mica is sometimes omitted as well. Here much of the mica has been lost, but enough of its pale, silvery sheen remains to show how well it must have set off the delicate colors of the courtesan's robes. Eishi clearly gave great care to the harmonization of these colors, and his handling of the blues in the courtesan's *uchikake* surpasses even his own high standards of sensitivity and refinement.

II-20

Chōbunsai Eishi (1756-1829)

The Courtesan Takihime of the Ōgiya and Her Attendants, from the series *Wakana Hatsumoyō*

1795

Woodblock print; ōban; 38.8 x 26.1

Signature of artist (Eishi zu), kiwame seal, and trademark and seal of publisher, Nishimuraya Eijudō

The Cleveland Museum of Art, Gift of J. H. Wade

The courtesan Takihime, her brocade obi protruding in front of her like a huge muff, moves pensively ahead, oblivious of the two *kamuro* following behind her, one of whom turns as though to speak to the other. The series title indicates that it is New Year's, and the cartouche with its playful border of hares sporting in waves suggests that it is the Year of the Hare, i.e., 1795. The pattern on Takihime's *uchikake* consists of fragments of cloud-enveloped scenery—a bridge, a castle, wind-filled sails—of the kind that would have been associated with classical poetry or well-known views of famous places (*meisho-e*), while her *kamuro*'s long-sleeved outer robes are more conventionally decorated with scattered flowers. Long sleeves (*furisode*), sometimes adorned with tassels as here, were worn only by young girls. Along with elaborate flower-like hair ornaments, they were standard parts of a *kamuro*'s wardrobe. Here, however, Eishi has captured something childlike in the girls' behavior that needs no outer signs to convince us of their age. All three figures wear the triple-fan crest of the Ōgiya on the shoulders of their kimono.

The series title, "New Patterns for Young Greens," is identical, except for the omission of one word, to that of a long-lived series begun by Koryūsai in the 1770s. Prints in that series (which, like this one, was published by Eijudō in connection with the New Year's holiday) also depicted courtesans, often together with their *kamuro*. It is tempting to think that this print may have represented an attempt on Eijudō's part to recapture the popularity of the earlier series. It is hard to believe that the resemblances are purely accidental.

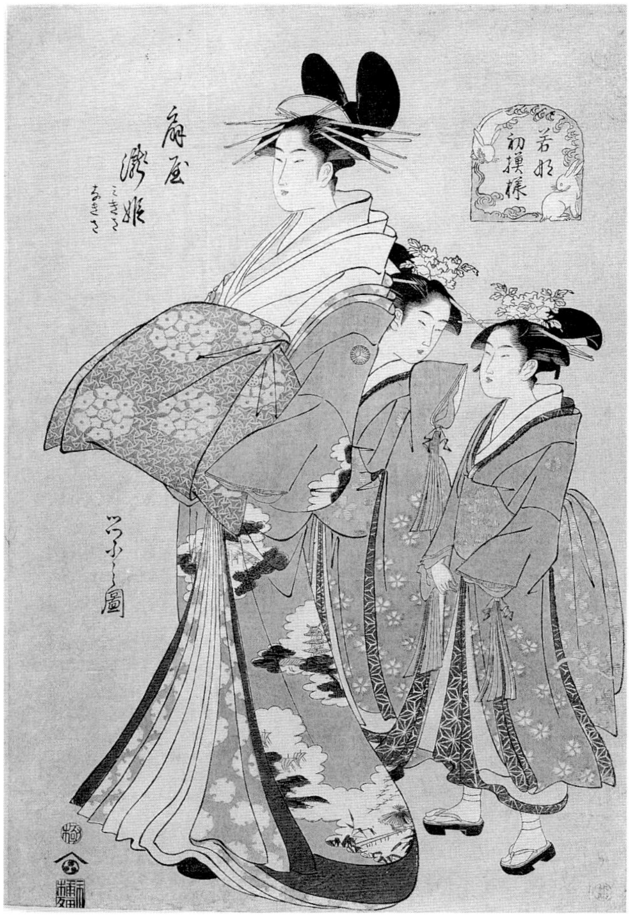

II-20

II-21

Chōbunsai Eishi (1756-1829)

The Courtesans Hanaōgi and Kasugano of the Gōmeiro with Their Attendant Kumegawa

Circa 1795

Woodblock print; double ōban; 37.5 x 50.7

Address, name, and trademark of publisher (Bakurōchō sanchōme, Yamaguchiya Chūsuke, hammoto) in lower-left margin

Portland Art Museum, Mary Andrews Ladd Collection

This rare work (these authors know of only one other impression) stands apart from Eishi's other prints not only in its unusual double *ōban* size but in the sheer sumptuousness of its design. The courtesans' lavish costumes and fashionable butterfly coiffures remind one of Utamaro's

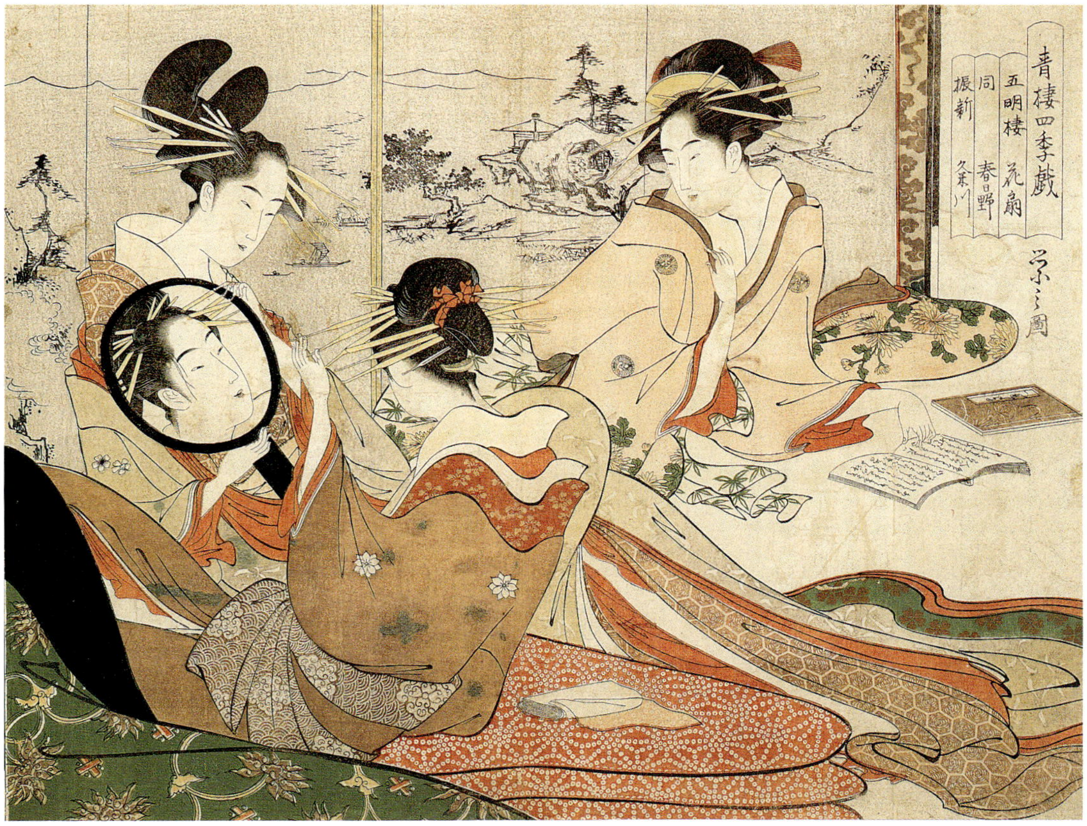

II-21

Twelve Hours of the Green Houses, but the lines are even more elongated and the forms more stylized, and there is none of Utamaro's restraint in the depiction of the room's interior. The effect is almost excessively rich and luxurious.

The use of a mirror to reveal the face of a woman whose back is turned to us was a coquettish device much favored by artists at the time. Here it adds a piquant touch of interest to a composition that might otherwise seem almost too uniformly gorgeous.

The woman at left holding the mirror is the celebrated Hanaōgi, as indicated by the double-cherry-blossom crest on her sleeve. She is seated directly on the floor with her legs extended, and her long, many-layered garments (which part seductively to offer a glimpse of her calves) flow like waves across the entire width of the print to end in the final curve created by the padded hem of her outer robe. The woman facing her and gazing into the mirror as she adjusts her hairpins is the other celebrated courtesan of the Ōgiya, Kasugano. She is seated on one of the three-layered cushions, known as *mitsubuton*, that were considered symbols of Yoshiwara luxury. A flattened roll of translucent paper lies on the cushion behind her. The woman sitting somewhat apart from the two courtesans, and dressed more sedately as befits her rank, is the *shinzō* Kumegawa, who glances up from her reading as though distracted by what Kasugano is doing. Closing off the room behind the three figures is a monochrome landscape screen in the style of the Kanō School. Whether or not screens of this kind were ever actually found in a courtesan's apartment, it is an interesting detail, and one that Eishi, who had once studied under a Kanō master, would have had no difficulty in depicting.

II-22

Chōkōsai Eishō (active 1793-1799)

***Ryaku Rokkasen*, "The Six Immortals of Poetry, Abbreviated"**

Circa 1795

Woodblock print; ōban triptych; 36.2 x 75.5

Signature of artist (Eishō ga) and trademark of publisher, Yamaguchiya Chūsuke, on each panel

The Art Institute of Chicago, Clarence Buckingham Collection

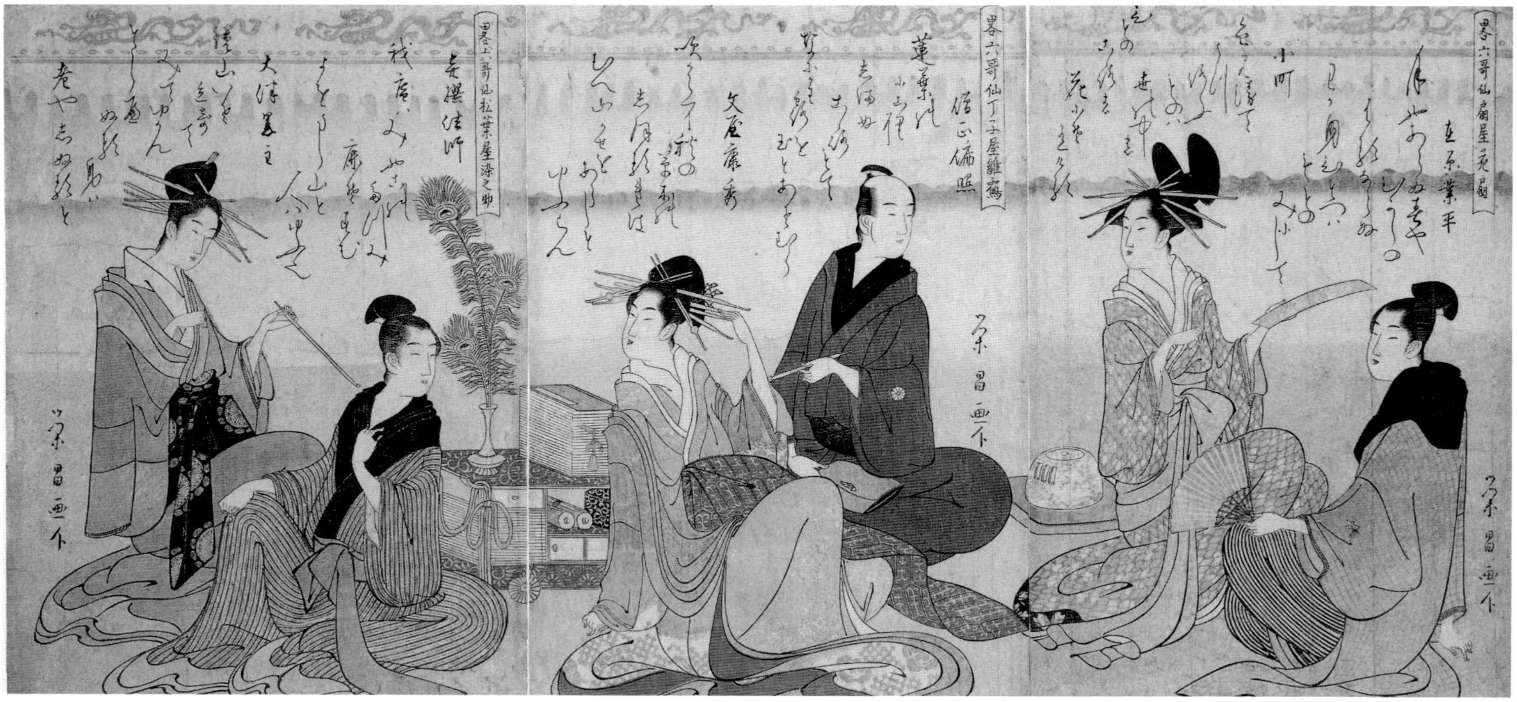

II-22

Each panel of this triptych depicts one of the celebrated courtesans of the Yoshiwara with a male companion. The courtesans are, from right to left, Hanaōgi of the Ōgiya, Hinatsuru of the Chōjiya, and Somenosuke of the Matsubaya. We have been unable to identify their male companions, though two of them—the young man at right and the somewhat older man in the center—have crests on their garments that might make eventual identification possible.

At the top of each panel, well-known verses by the Six Immortals of Poetry are written, two to each panel, in an elegant hand against a background of decorative patterns like those printed on *shikishi* (poem cards) or *tanzaku* (poem slips). The patterns consist of a band of archaic Chinese-style dragons at the top with rows of faint drips and waves or scallops below. The verses are linked with the figures in a way that implies some association with them, yet nothing in the figures' behavior suggests that a parody, or *mitate-e*, was intended. The linkage is at its closest between the two figures at right and the poems above them, which are both love poems. The poem at right is by Ariwara no Narihira, who was famous for his love affairs, and the one at left, above Hanaōgi, is by Ono no Komachi, the only woman poet among the Six Immortals. The two poems, which are among the most powerful and richly elliptical in the entire Japanese language, have been translated in many different ways. The following versions are by Brower and Miner:

What now is real?
This moon, this spring, are altered
From their former being—
While this alone, my mortal body, remains
As ever changed by love beyond all change.

Tsuki ya aranu
Haru ya mukashi no
Haru naranu
Wa ga mi hitotsu wa
Moto no mi ni shite
—Narihira

Find mutability
In that being which alters without fading
In its outward hue—
In the color, looks, and the deceptive flower
Of the heart of what this world calls man!

Iro miede
Utsurou mono wa
Yo no naka no
Hito no kokoro no
Hana ni zo arikeru
—Komachi*

---

* From Robert H. Brower and Earl Miner, *Japanese Court Poetry* (London: The Cresset Press, 1962), 193, 205.

The other verses are more in the nature of solitary musings and have nothing to do with love. They are (from right to left) by Sōjo Henjō, Bunya no Yasuhide, Kisen Hōshi, and Otomo no Kuronushi. Kuronushi's verse was used in another print in this exhibition (Catalogue no. II-17).

Though the six figures in this triptych clearly occupy a single room, there is so little contact between them and so little that otherwise ties the three panels together that it would be easy to imagine the panels' being sold separately. If this was the publisher's intention, it might explain the rather curious use of the word "abbreviated" in the title.

II-23

Chōkōsai Eishō (active 1793-1799)

Three Courtesans in front of a *Hōō* Bird (*Ōgiya mise ryaku*)

Circa 1798

Woodblock print; ōban triptych; 37.7 x 71.1

Signature of artist (Eishō ga) and trademark of publisher, Yamaguchiya Chūsuke, on each print

The Art Institute of Chicago, Clarence Buckingham Collection

Three courtesans of the Ōgiya are seated in front of a wall painting of a *hōō* bird. The bird's wings are outstretched as though it is about to alight, and its showy peacock-like tail feathers spread out in all directions behind it. The *hōō* bird, often called the Asian phoenix, was a mythological creature of Chinese origin. Like the dragon, with which it was often paired, it was associated with the heavens and was considered an auspicious symbol.

One of the illustrations in Utamaro's *Seirō ehon nenjū gyōji* (Catalogue no. II-34) shows the artist painting a similar *hōō* bird on the wall of a room, and illustrations in several other works indicate that a painting like this must have existed on the back wall of the *harimise* room of at least one of the major brothels. Unlike the scene depicted here, however, none of the other illustrations are identified by site.* They may well all have depicted the same room in the Ōgiya.

The three courtesans shown here are identified by name: Hashibata at right, Nana(?)-koshi in the middle, and Hanabito at left. Hashibata holds out a folded love letter to

* See Mitani Kazuma, *Edo Yoshiwara zushu* (Tokyo: 1977), 124, 159.

II-23

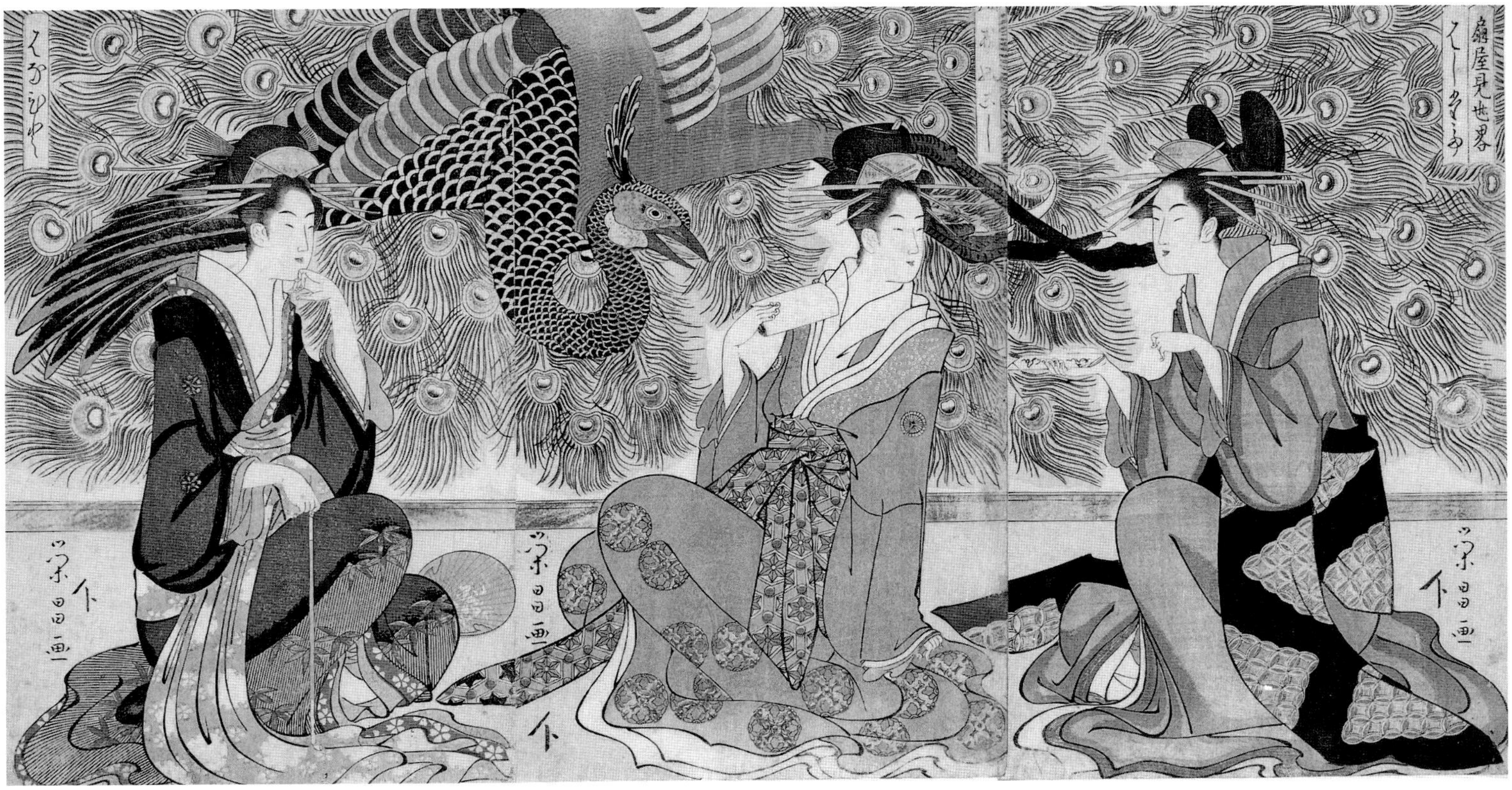

Nanakoshi, who leans back to look at it. Hanabito looks on, her left hand raised to her chin as though in wonder. Though more interaction takes place among these three figures than among the figures in the Eishō print just described (Catalogue no. II-22), each panel still seems more independent than is often the case in triptychs. Even the *hōō* bird's outstretched wings and fluttering tail feathers do not entirely succeed in drawing the three panels together.

In order to show the weight of the fabric, Eishō has shaded the outlines and folds of Hashibata's and Hanabito's kimono. This is the only instance in the exhibition of the use of such a technique.

II-24

Katsushika Hokusai (1760-1849)

New Year's Day at the Ōgiya

1811 or earlier

Woodblock print; ōban pentaptych; 36.8 x 123.2

Signature of artist (Katsushika) and trademark of publisher, Iseya Rihei, at lower right

The Metropolitan Museum of Art, Rogers Fund, 1914

Preparations for the holiday are in full swing at the Ōgiya, one of the principal houses in the Yoshiwara (the name, which was emblazoned on the *noren* hanging over the entrance door, is obscured by the huge pillar near the stoves at right). Parties of courtesans, already dressed in their New Year's finery, move in a steady stream across the tatami-covered *hiroma* while a group of maids prepare individual tables for a banquet and the brothel owner sits at his ease in the midst of the bustle surrounding him. The composition focuses on the *hiroma*, the largest room in the establishment, but also provides glimpses of other rooms and passageways off to the side. Since this is the only work in the exhibition to show what the interior of a brothel actually looked like, let us look at it more closely, panel by panel, starting, in Japanese fashion, from the right.

1. A party of courtesans and their attendants moves towards the *noren*-covered doorway at upper right while three men crouch in front of a row of earthen stoves in the foreground. One of the men blows air through a bamboo tube onto the coals in the open fire box in front of him; a placard with the characters *hi no yōjin*,

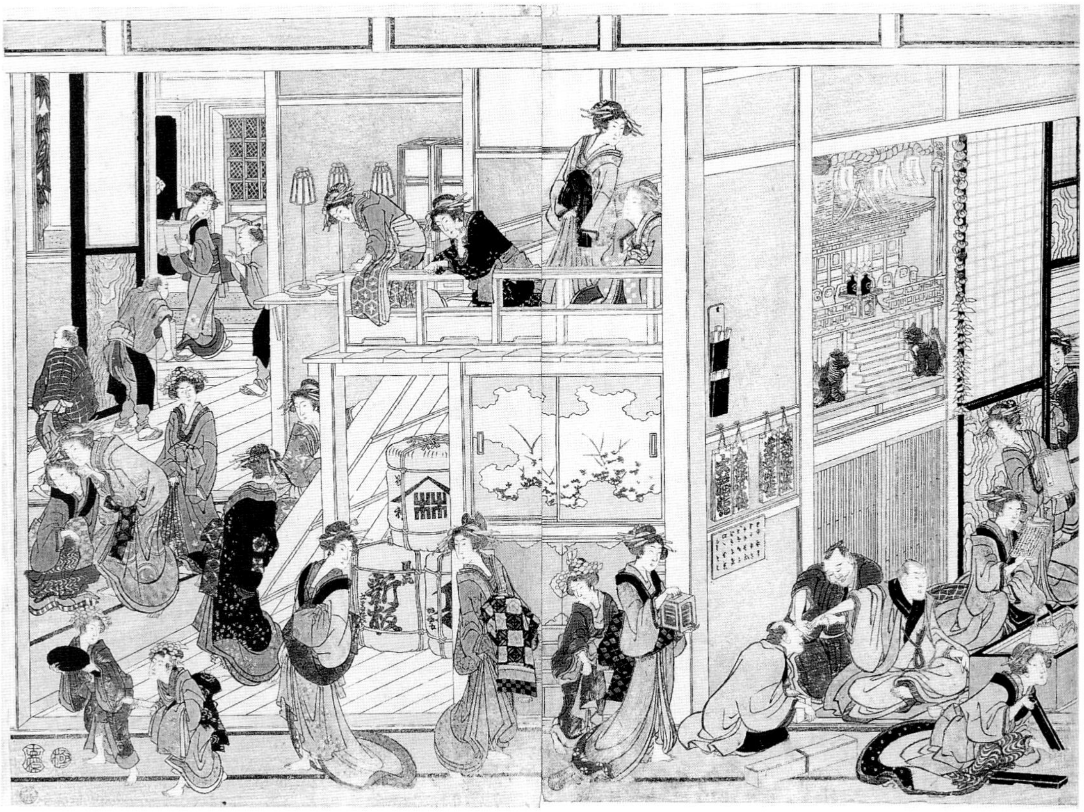

II-24

"Beware of fire," is appropriately attached to the large pillar to his left. At the other side of the passageway leading to the front entrance, a steep ladder-like stairway leads up to the second floor.

2. In the center of the room, four maids are busy unstacking and cleaning individual tables (*zen*) for a banquet while courtesans and their attendants move back and forth on both sides of them. In the background, parted screens *(fusuma)* afford a glimpse into the raised tatami-covered *harimise* room with its lattice-covered windows facing the street.

3. Much of this panel is taken up with a continuation of the previous scene, but in the upper-left corner the eye is drawn into an adjoining room with glimpses of yet other rooms beyond. These latter rooms open onto wooden-floored corridors or verandas surrounding a small sunken garden in which one can just make out some rocks, a low pine tree, and a stone lantern.

4. In the lower-right corner the owner and his wife sit in front of a rectangular hibachi. The wife seems to be engrossed in reading a book while a maid, standing beside her and holding what appears to be another volume of the same book, peers over her shoulder. The owner, seemingly oblivious of the man with a box kneeling at his right, who appears to be trying to engage his attention, stares vacantly ahead while holding out a hand to a manicurist working behind him. Set into the wall above the owner and his wife is a miniature shrine with a pair of *fu* dogs flanking its stairs, an offering of two sake bottles on a stand in front of its closed doors and a row of Daruma dolls on its tiny veranda. A chain of *kukurizaru* and origami cranes are hung as charms along one side of the shrine, and a row of account books and an abacus hang from pegs on the other side.

5. The final panel shows a passageway opening toward the back of the building and another flight of stairs leading up to the second floor. Three huge sake barrels are stored under the stairs next to some built-in cupboards. The passageway is filled with activity: workers bringing boxes to a storeroom; two *kamuro*, one grasping a mirror, hurrying off to the left; and a steady stream of courtesans coming and going. At the top of the stairs, two courtesans lean over the railing of an open landing to get a better view of what is going on below.

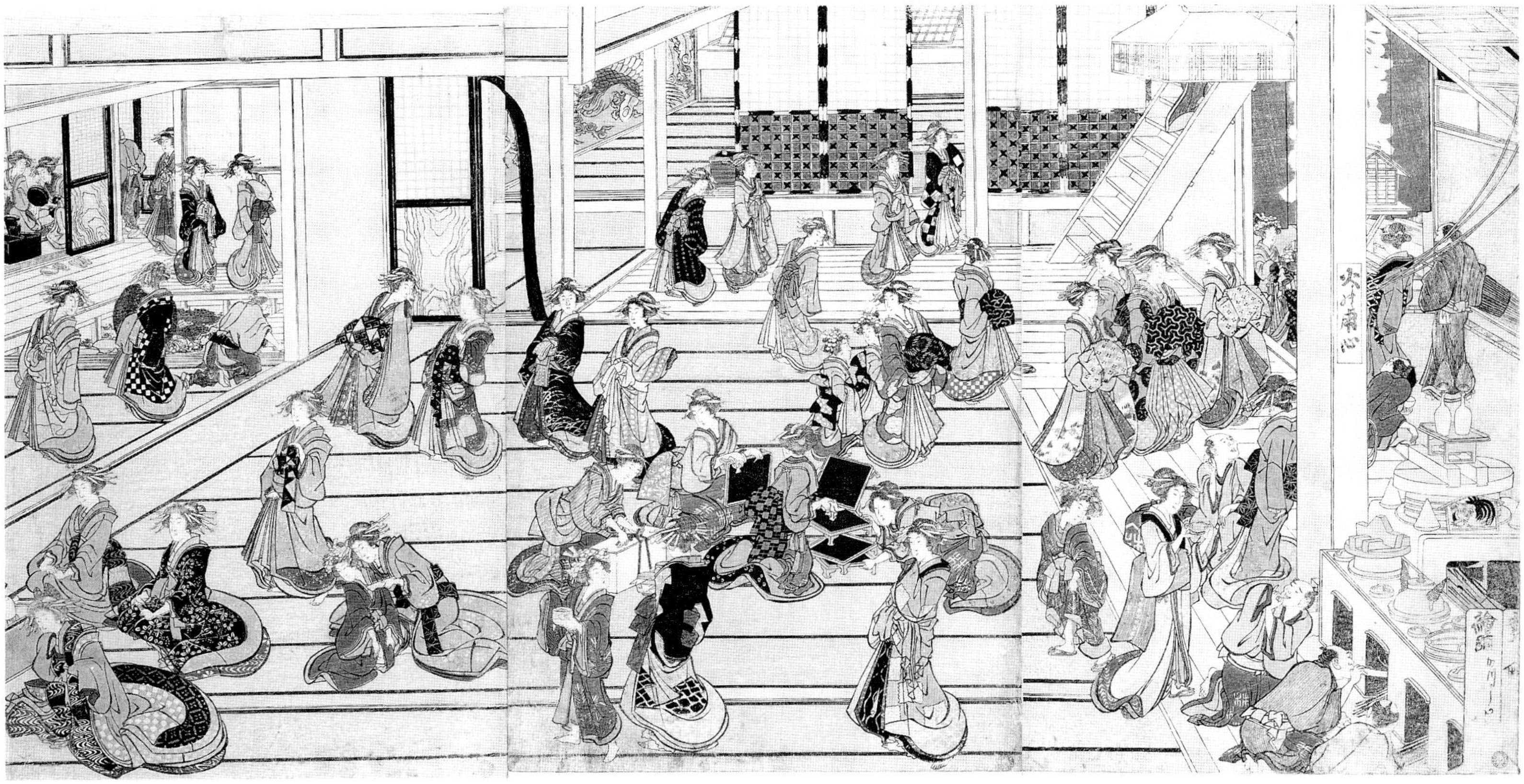

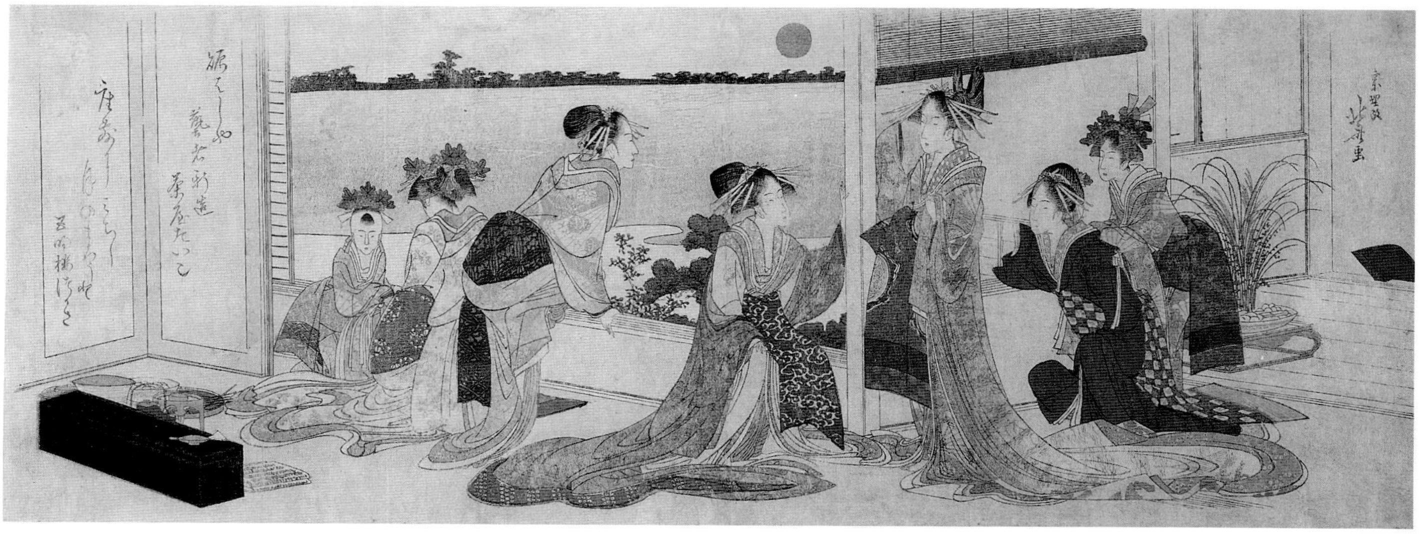

II-25

II-25

Katsushika Hokusai (1760-1849)

Viewing the Moon at the Gomeirō

Circa 1799

Surimono; 56.6 x 21.1

Signature of artist (Hokusai aratame Sōri ga) on fusuma at right

The Cleveland Museum of Art, Gift of Mrs. Ralph King

Two courtesans, each attended by a geisha and a *shinzō*, have gathered in one of the upstairs rooms of the Gomeirō brothel. A *kamuro*, speaking to the *shinzō* at left, is also present. It is autumn, and the shoji have been opened to afford an unobstructed view of the full moon just rising over the paddy fields that surrounded the Yoshiwara. A band of mist has gathered close to the building in the foreground, and a row of trees extends along the horizon line beyond the paddy fields in the distance. Indoors, the remains of a meal and a *shamisen* box with a sake cup on top of it lie on the floor in front of a folding screen at left, and a flower arrangement of miscanthus and reeds has been placed in the alcove at right. The two courtesans, their luxurious robes flowing onto the floor around them, stand on either side of a pillar where the outer walls of the room meet at right angles. The tranquillity of the evening, the brilliance of the moon, and the beauty and elegance of the women combine to create an atmosphere that is almost magical in its poetry.

It is interesting to compare this beautiful evocation of a moonlit evening with Shumman's rendition of a similar scene—but in a more urban setting—in the collection of the Chester Beatty Library (Catalogue no. IV-10). Shumman's print is equally poetic, though less elegant, and the format, with rows of verse filling up the lower half of the sheet, is quite different. The dimensions of this print correspond almost exactly to those of the upper half of the Shumman surimono. If the 1799 date is correct for this print, it may be one of the earliest examples of this long, horizontal format, which became first popular around 1800.

Gomeirō is another (somewhat sinified) name for the Ōgiya, the brothel to which Hanaōgi belonged. The poem inscribed on the screen at left is signed "Tsukasa." Tsukasa is recorded as being one of the courtesans of the Ōgiya at the time, and it is probable that one of the two courtesans portrayed here was intended to represent her. Her poem reads: *Nigiwashi ya geisha shinzō / chayataiko / zashiki ni michi shi / suki no maroudo* (What liveliness! Geisha, shinzō and jesters fill the room, all guests of the moon).

II-26

Katsukawa Shunchō (active 1785-1800)

Yoshiwara Street Scene (Edochō)

Circa 1791-92

Woodblock print; ōban triptych; 37.2 x 75

Signature of artist (Shunchō ga), kiwame seal, and seal of publisher (Tsuruya)

Musée Guimet

The artist has introduced the technique of perspective to get a wide-angle view of this bustling street, Edochō 2-chōme, in the evening. In the center background is the gate (*kido*) that leads into Nakanochō, where the teahouses stood. Edochō was lined with brothels, and the caged windows provide glimpses of prostitutes on display for the evening *harimise*.

Reading the scene from the right, we encounter first a little girl, possibly a servant at a teahouse, carrying an envelope in her hands. She has caught the attention of a courtesan manager (*yarite*). The young woman holding a lantern is from a teahouse; behind her is an apprentice courtesan (*furisode shinzō*), holding her sleeve up to cover her mouth. A manservant (*wakaimono*) holds a lantern with the crane insignia (*honda mon*) of the famous pleasure house Chōjiya. Beside him walks a high-ranking courtesan with her two small *kamuro* in her train. The cranes on her cloak identify her as Hinatsuru, who became the leading courtesan at the Chōjiya after Chōzan left the quarter, according to the roster of courtesans (*saiken*) published in the spring of Kansei 4 (1792). Thus it is fair to assume that this Shunchō triptych was made between late 1791 and 1792.

Behind Hinatsuru is a *furisode shinzō* exchanging a word with a woman who appears to be a maid or waitress. In the foreground is a large rain barrel with buckets on it—the Edo equivalent of a fire hydrant. The characters "EDO" are written on the shelter over the barrel, and a standing lantern obscures the numeral 2, which identifies the neighborhood.

To the left of the composition are two pairs of promenaders. In one of the pairs, a *shinzō* strolls with the *yarite* for yet another brothel. In front of them a playful *kamuro* tugs at the arm of a fashionable gentleman as she leads him to her waiting mistress.

II-27

Kubo Shumman (1757-1820)

Courtesan Reading by Lamplight

Circa 1800

Surimono; 13.7 x 18.4

Seal of artist (Shumman)

The Chester Beatty Library and Museum of Oriental Art

A courtesan, attended by her *shinzō*, kneels at a writing table reading a book, presumably one of the set of volumes stacked on the table. The

II-26

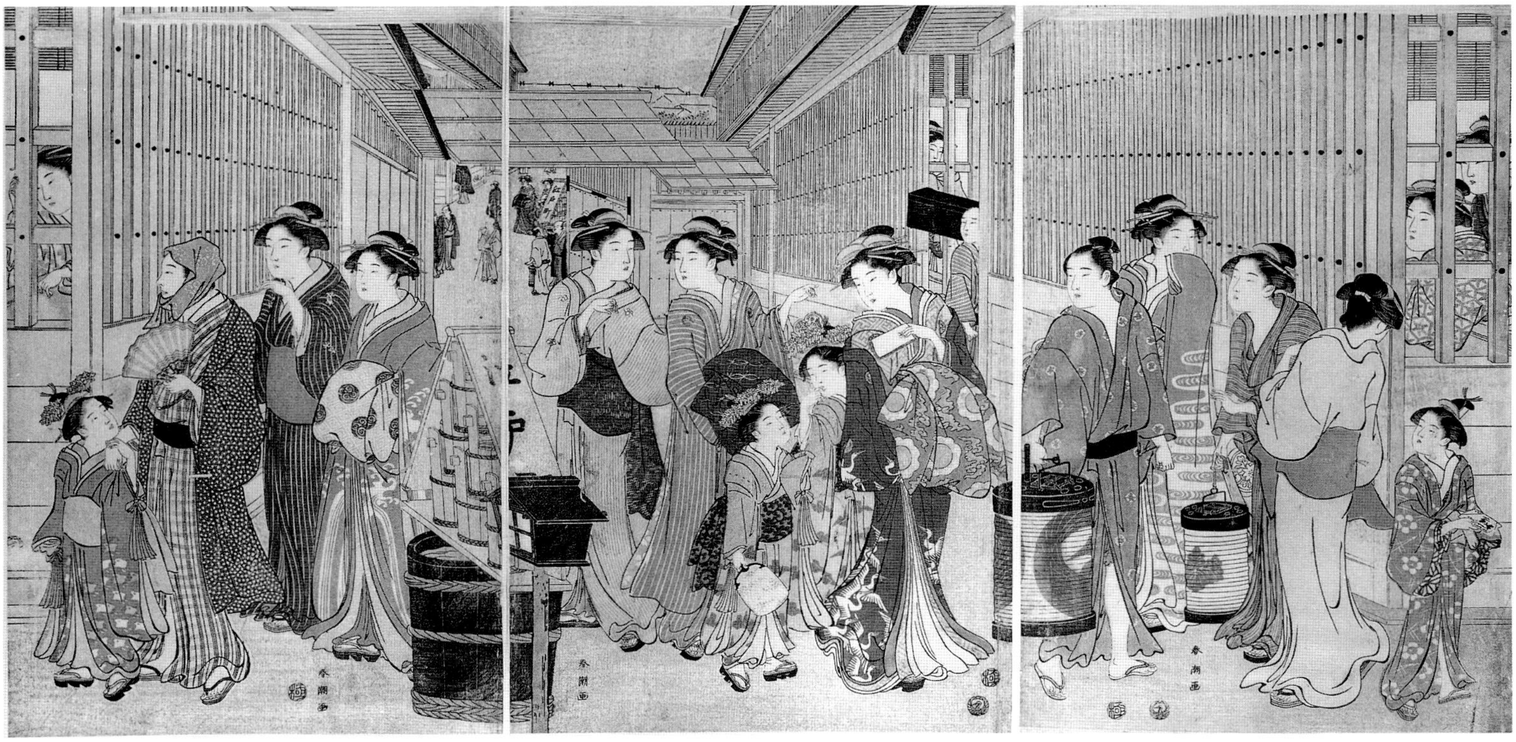

title slip of the top volume is legible and reads *Uguisu no koe* (The voice of the warbler). It is evening, and a wall lamp sheds light on the table. A lacquer *tabako-bon* sits on the floor at the courtesan's side.

Each of the two kyōka refers to the fragrance of plum blossoms, and the trunk and gnarled branches of a plum tree are depicted on the decorative panels at the bottom of the shoji at left. Adding yet another level of reference is the *uguisu* of the book's title. The *uguisu* is traditionally associated in Japanese art and poetry with the plum.

The kyōka at right, by Ikkantei Tegami Nagabumi, reads: *Ayashū mo / ideiru kaze ni / tomoshi kechi / makura ni kayou / neya no ume ga ka.* This has been translated by Roger Keyes as "Strangely, in the passing breeze, the lamp hardly burns, but the fragrance of the plum makes its way to the pillow in the bedroom."* The second kyōka, written by Shumman himself, using one of his alternative names, Shōsadō, reads: *Irosato no / ume o nekojite / uete miyo / mi o musubite mo / sui wa ukeai.* It is much more difficult to translate because of its use of puns. Essentially, it says that if you transplant a plum (that is, a courtesan) from the "village of love" (the Yoshiwara), the *mi* (fruit or body) will certainly be *sui* (excellent or sour).

Though other ukiyo-e artists—Utamaro and Hokusai, to name but two—tried their hands at kyōka, it remained nothing more than an occasional pastime for them, but for Shumman, kyōka seems to have been as important as painting or print design. No wonder, then, that he was one of the earliest designers of surimono.

* Roger Keyes, *The Art of Surimono, Privately Published Japanese Woodblock Prints and Books in the Chester Beatty Library*, Dublin (London: Philip Wilson, 1985), no. 306.

II-27

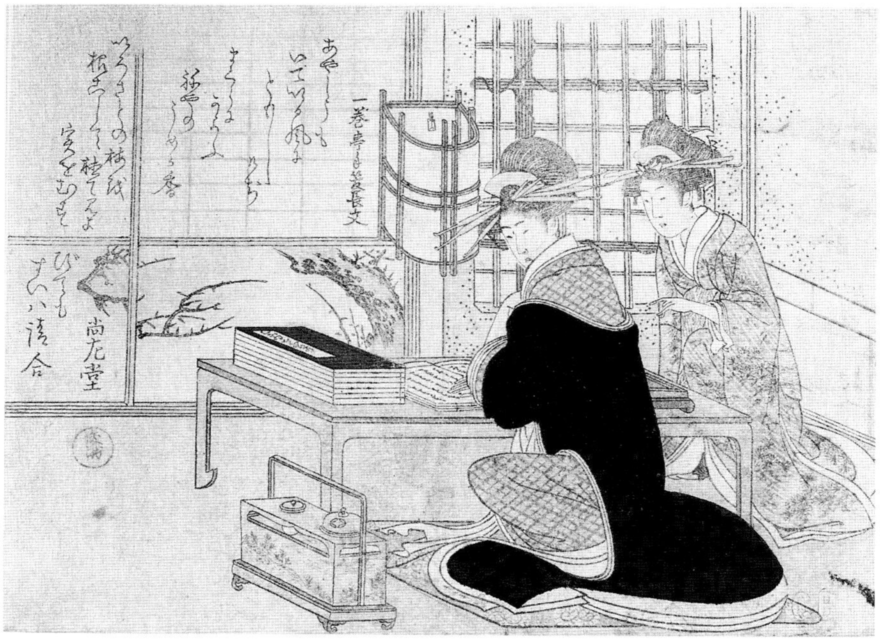

II-28

Utagawa Toyokuni (1769-1825)

Courtesans of the Ōgiya on a Spring Outing

Circa 1795

Woodblock print; ōban triptych; 36.6 x 23.8 (each)

Signature of artist (Toyokuni ga) and seal of publisher (Senichi-han) on each panel

The Cleveland Museum of Art, Gift of J. H. Wade

Two courtesans of the Ōgiya approach an open pavilion where four of their companions are gathered around a bronze hibachi and another courtesan kneels at a writing desk. The blossoms on the plum tree outside the pavilion indicate that it is early spring.

The courtesan at the writing desk is Hanaōgi. An open book with blank pages, a *suzuribako*, and a metal water dropper *(suiteki)* in the form of a rooster are laid out on the desk top in front of her, and she holds a brush poised in her hand as she gazes pensively to one side, as though gathering her thoughts before putting the brush to paper. She sits somewhat apart from her companions, and her loosened hair, falling in disarray over her shoulders and contrasting so oddly with the elaborate coiffures worn by the others, separates her from them even more.

Though depicting Hanaōgi in this way was an effective means of calling attention to the most celebrated courtesan of the Ōgiya, Toyokuni probably had something else in mind as well. The loose hair was almost certainly a reference to the long, flowing hair worn by court ladies during the Heian Period, and by placing Hanaōgi at a writing desk with an open veranda behind her, Toyokuni was deliberately comparing her with Murasaki Shikibu, the author

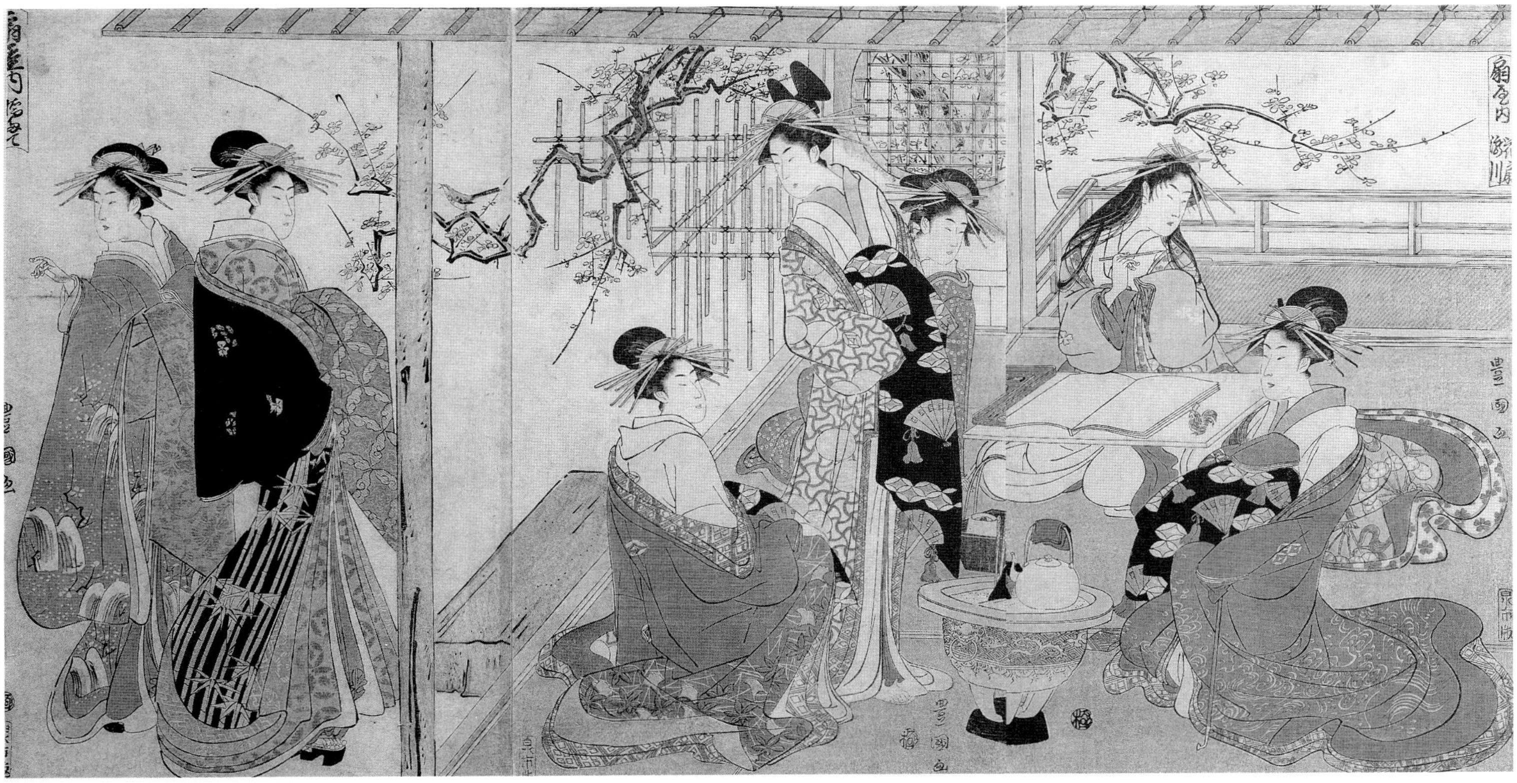

II-28

of *The Tale of Genji*, whose depiction in similar circumstances had become a standard part of Edo-period iconography. This is yet another, if more subtle, instance of the ukiyo-e penchant for investing the present with some of the aura of the classical past.

II-29

Utagawa Toyokuni (1769-1825)

Courtesans Promenading on the Nakanochō

Circa 1795

Woodblock print; ōban triptych; 37.5 x 25.4 (each)

Signature of artist (Toyokuni ga) and seal of publisher (Senichi han) on each panel; seal of collector, Hayashi (Hayashi Chū), stamped on each panel below artist's signature

The Cleveland Museum of Art, Bequest of Mr. Whittemore

The view is of the crowded Nakanochō during the early evening (toward the end of the hour of the monkey), when the leading courtesans emerged in full finery to promenade in public, accompanied by their *shinzō*, *kamuro*, and a male attendant carrying a paper lantern emblazoned with the house crest. Two such parties are shown in the foreground, the one at right attracting the scrutiny of two men, one of whom, presumably a samurai, wears a hooded cloak and hides his face behind a fan. On the other side of the street, an unaccompanied courtesan, holding a long, slender tobacco pipe, lounges on a porch while conversing with another courtesan standing beside her. In the background, at the end of the street, one can just make out the Great Gate of the Yoshiwara (Ōmon) and the curving, shop-lined road outside that led up to it. The open buildings on both sides of the Nakanochō, with round paper lanterns and *noren* hanging from their eaves, are the teahouses (*hikitejaya*) that specialized in providing introductions to the higher-ranking courtesans. Most of them are screened off from the street with bamboo blinds, which, however, must have afforded only a modicum of privacy. The names of the first few teahouses in the foreground are printed on their *noren* and can readily be made out. They are the Tamaya and Omiya at left and the Owariya at right.

Toyokuni seems to have been somewhat at a loss as to how to handle the middle distance in this triptych, and the transition from the size of the figures in the foreground to the size of those behind them is extremely abrupt. Among the varied groups of people in the background is a monk engaged in conversation with a middle-aged man. Monks were apparently not infrequent visitors to the Yoshiwara.

II-30

Kitagawa Utamaro (1753-1806)

***Seirō jūni toki tsuzuki*, "The Twelve Hours of the Green Houses"**

Circa 1794

The Art Institute of Chicago, Clarence Buckingham Collection

This series, in which the following four prints appear, includes some of Utamaro's most elegant and strikingly original compositions. It is also notable for the exaggerated height of its figures, which seem even taller because of their willowy proportions and high butterfly coiffures. Their height is remarkable even for Utamaro's oeuvre, in which tall women are the norm, and it may well be that these prints represent the most extreme expression of that fascination with height that had first begun to appear in ukiyo-e in Kiyonaga's prints of the late 1780s.

The figures are set off against pale yellow or ivory backgrounds lightly sprinkled with gold dust. Nothing about these noncommittal backgrounds gives any explicit indication of the settings or surroundings in which the figures appear, yet in every case we come away with an almost palpable sense of the place and time intended. A look, a gesture, the skillful placement of a single piece of furniture, seems to be all that is necessary. Indeed, the lack of descriptive detail itself becomes a powerful stimulus to the imagination. This is most apparent in prints like Catalogue nos. II-30 (a) and II-30 (d), in which the implied setting extends beyond the borders of the actual composition.

The stamp of Utamaro's originality is apparent even in the most mundane details in these prints. Rather than being content with a rectangular cartouche of the kind that had become standard for series of this sort, he came up with the charming—and thoroughly appropriate—conceit of using a lantern clock similar to the one in Catalogue no. II-35, placing the series title between the two hanging weights and the title of the specific print on the bell.

II-30 (a)

***U no koku*, "The Hour of the Hare"**

Woodblock print; ōban; 37.7 x 24

II-29

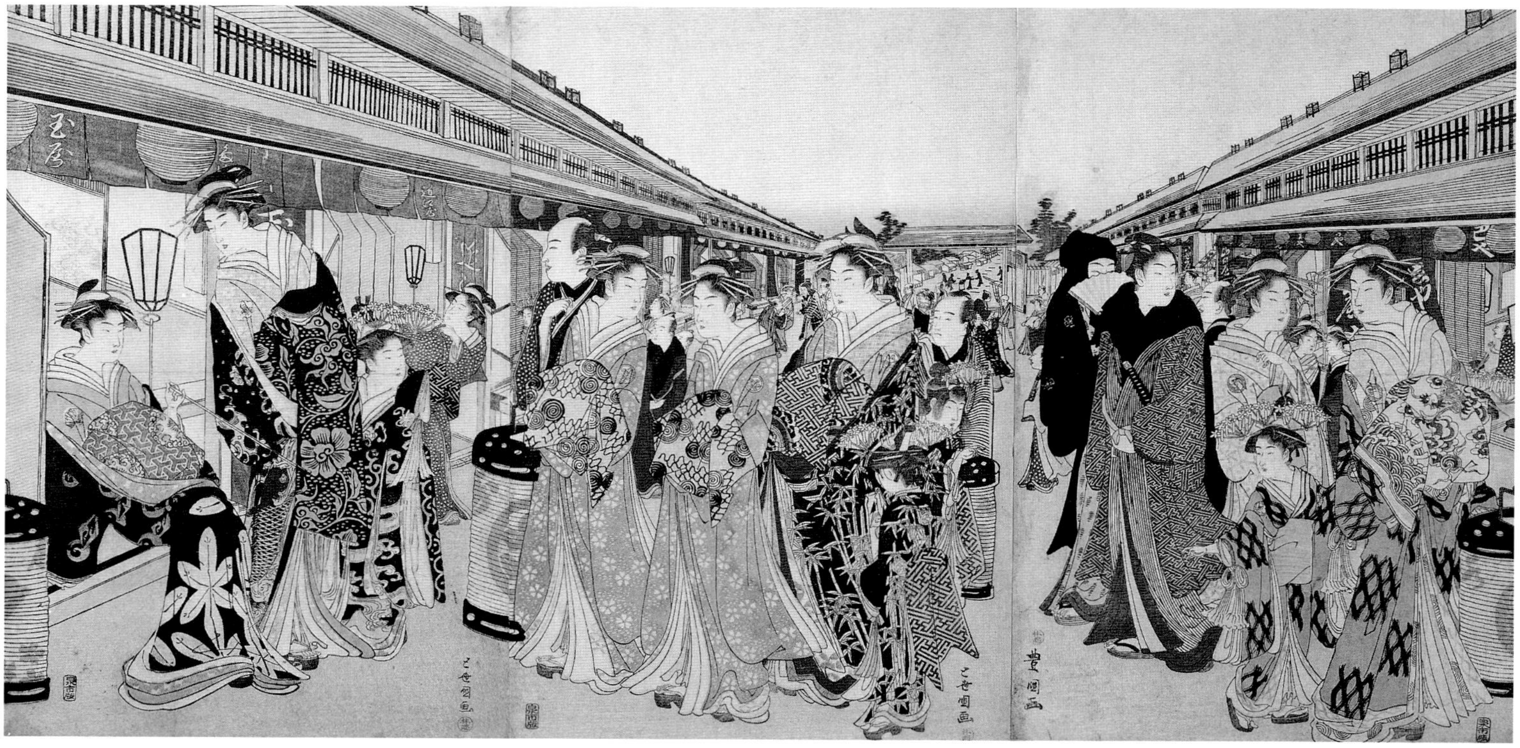

The hour of the hare, which extended more or less from 5 to 7 AM, was the time when a favored guest who had spent the night would be preparing to leave. Though Utamaro does not show us the guest in this case, we can imagine that he is standing just outside the picture frame at the right, about to be helped on with the elegant *haori* that the courtesan holds up to him. Interestingly, the most striking feature of the *haori*, the face of Daruma painted on its lining, could not be seen when the garment was worn. The design was much too flamboyant for the sumptuary laws of the time and could be displayed only in private. Daruma, who is always depicted, as here, with round, staring eyes, scowling features, bushy eyebrows, and a beard, was the founding patriarch of Zen Buddhism. To the uninitiated, the use of his image on a fashionable article of clothing must seem strange. In late-eighteenth-century Edo slang, however, the word *daruma* had two additional meanings: "prostitute" and "*haori*." The use of the image in this setting thus became a visual double pun.

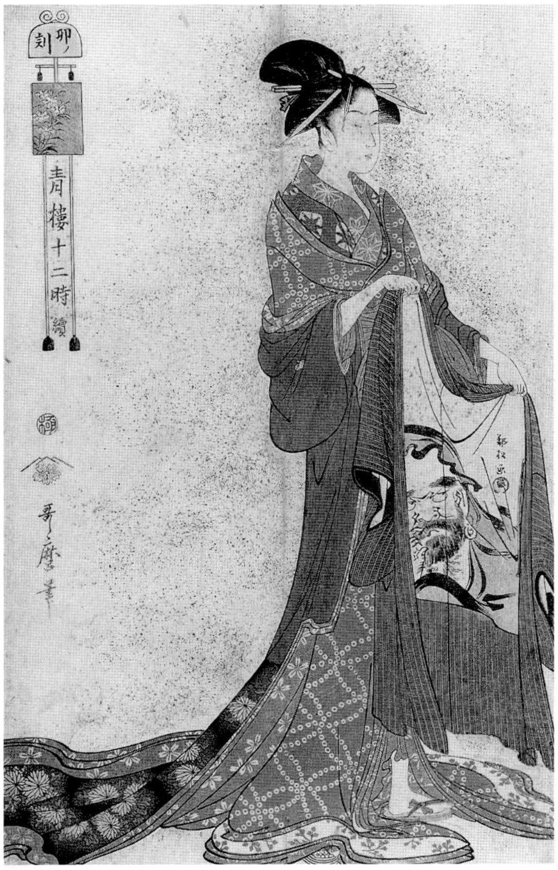

II-30 (a)

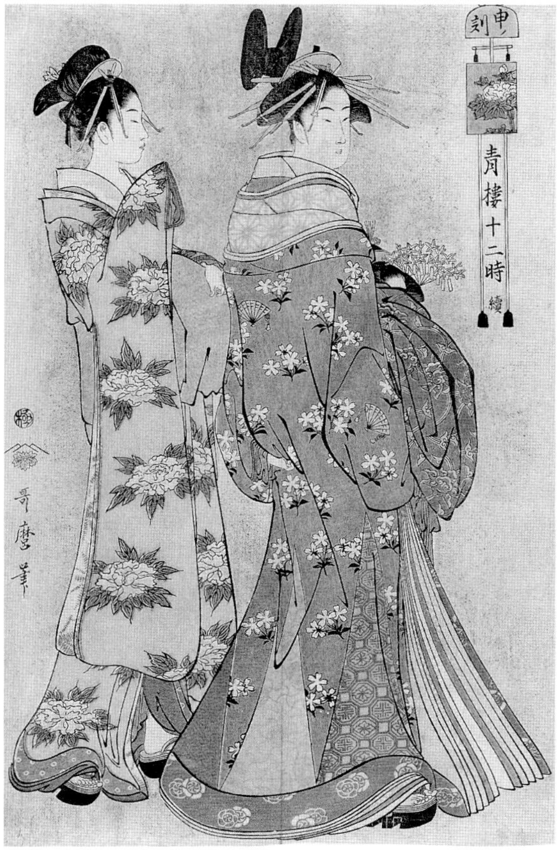

II-30 (b)

II-30 (b)

***Saru no koku*, "The Hour of the Monkey"**

Woodblock print; ōban; 37.4 x 24.2

The hour of the monkey, approximately 3 to 5 PM, was a period of relative quiet between the midday and the evening *harimise*, when the courtesans were put on public display (Catalogue no. II-2). Toward the end of the hour, the first lamps would be lit, and the higher-ranking courtesans would emerge in full regalia for their evening promenade (*dōchū*). This is the moment we are shown here. A tall *oiran*, her *uchikake* allowed to slip with seeming nonchalance from her shoulders, begins her stately progress toward the Nakanochō, accompanied by her youthful *shinzō* and a *kamuro* who is all but invisible behind her. The courtesan is clad (one might almost say swathed) in many layers of kimono and holds her hands as though in a muff under her fashionably protruding obi. Both the courtesan and her *shinzō* wear lacquered geta. The pattern of paired cherry blossoms on the padded hem of the courtesan's outermost kimono and the fans and sprigs of

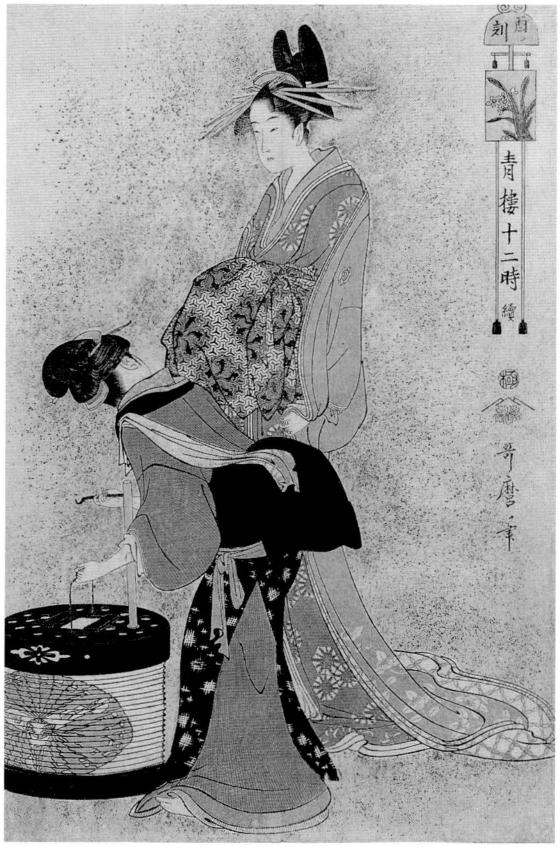

II-30 (c)

cherry blossoms on her *uchikake* suggest that this tall beauty is none other than the celebrated Hanaōgi. Notice the long, hanging sleeves (*furisode*) of the *shinzō*'s kimono. The fact that all one can see of the *kamuro* is a patch of forehead and her elaborate hair ornaments adds a delightful touch of whimsy to the print.

II-30 (c)

***Tori no koku*, "The Hour of the Cock"**

Woodblock print; ōban; 38 x 24.3

It is the hour of the cock (approximately 5 to 7 PM), and a tall, willowy courtesan, her slenderness emphasized by the swelling bulk of her obi, watches as a maid prepares a collapsible paper lantern so that she can go out. Many pictures of the period show big paper lanterns of this sort (which were called *chōchin*) being carried by the male attendants who accompanied courtesans to the teahouses where they met their clients. The crest printed on the lantern—three open fans in a circle—was that of the Ōgiya, and the courtesan herself may once again be Hanaōgi.

II-30 (d)

***I no koku*, "The Hour of the Boar"**

Woodblock print; ōban; 38 x 24.8

The hour of the boar, from 9 to 11 PM, when the courtesans and their guests returned from the teahouses along the Nakanochō, was usually the liveliest time of the day in the brothels. The partying, which had begun already in the teahouses, continued, though usually less boisterously, in the courtesans' rooms. This is what we are shown here. A courtesan, leaning back elegantly on her knees, proffers a lacquer sake cup to her unseen guest, who must be seated just outside the frame of the picture to the right. Her *shinzō*, kneeling beside her, carefully sets down a metal sake ewer from which, presumably, she has just filled the cup.

The presence of the unseen guest is reminiscent of *The Hour of the Hare*. Significantly, that is the only other print in the series in which the cartouche is placed on the left rather than the right. In both cases, the purpose seems to be to open the composition to the right, to remove any compositional barriers to the flow of our imagination in that direction.

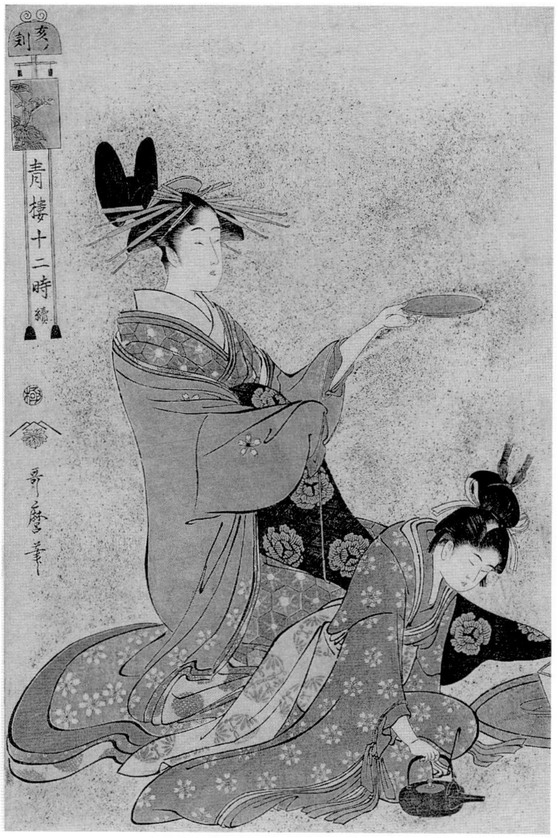

II-30 (d)

II-31

Kitagawa Utamaro (1753-1806)

Hanaōgi Holding a *Tanzaku* and a Writing Brush

Circa 1794

Woodblock print; ōban; 36.8 x 23.5

Signature of artist (Utamaro hitsu), kiwame seal, and trademark of publisher (Tsutaya Jūzaburō) at right

Minneapolis Institute of Arts, Bequest of Richard P. Gale

Hanaōgi, holding a *tanzaku* in one hand and a long brush in the other, gazes introspectively off to the right. The *tanzaku* and brush are reminders of her skill as a calligrapher and poet. Similar reminders occur in many of her portraits.

As one would expect of a print that had once been in the Ledoux Collection, this is an exceptionally fine impression of this exquisite image. The colors—the purple of Hanaōgi's *uchikake*, the pinks and whites of her layered kimono, and the curious brownish-green of her brocade obi—are relatively unfaded, and create a fresh, flower-like impression against the light-mica background. Compared with many of the other portraits of Hanaōgi in this exhibition, however, this one seems more crisp and stylized—almost icon-like. The effect is similar to that seen in other close up mica-ground portraits of the period, and is perhaps inevitable in a genre that excludes virtually any indication of action or setting.

The square cartouche gives the names of Hanaōgi (of the Ōgiya) and her two *shinzō*, Yoshino and Tatsuta. The names of the *shinzō* were clearly meant to remind one of the cherry blossoms of Yoshino and the maple leaves of the Tatsuta River—both frequent subjects in classical poetry. In the narrow cartouche at the right is a poem signed mysteriously by "one from the other side of Yanagiwara [a suburb of Edo]." It reads: *Noserarete / miru yūgao no / hanaōgi / hito no kokoro ni / aki no kizareba.* Since several key words in the poem (including Hanaōgi, which literally means "Flower Fan") may be interpreted in different ways, it is difficult to translate effectively, but one reading might be: "How can autumn enter my heart when I glimpse the night-blooming flower on the fan?"

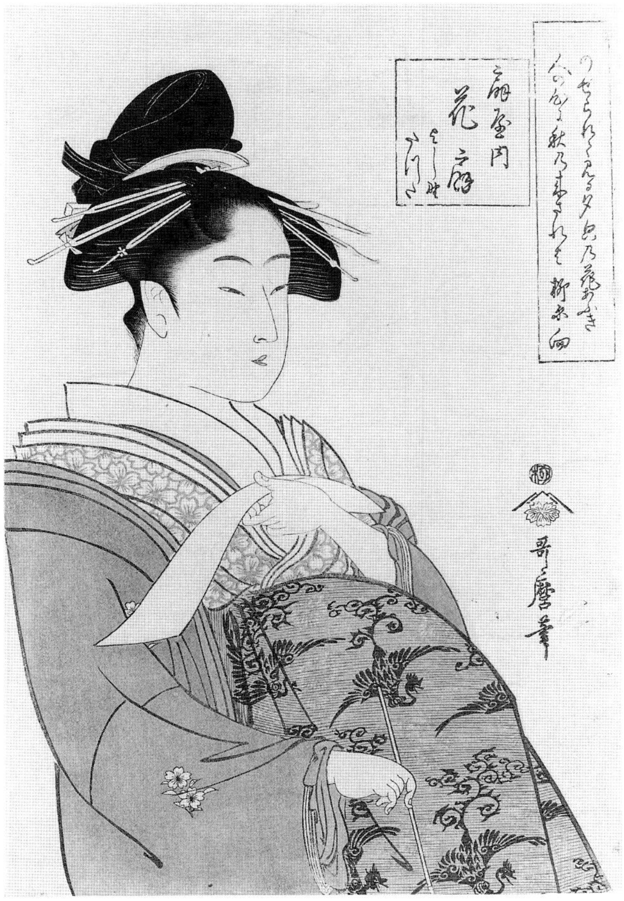

II-31

II-32

Santō Kyōden (1761-1816)

The Fox Dance, from *Yomo no Haru*, "Spring in the Four Directions"

1795

Woodblock print; page from an illustrated book of kyōka; 16.3 x 30.2

Signature of artist (Santō Kyōden sha)

The Art Institute of Chicago

The subject of this print is the Fox Dance, a New Year's Eve custom in the Yoshiwara in which a male dancer wearing a fox mask would appear in the courtesans' quarters. Carrying bells and a large staff with rope and paper streamers (*gohei*) used in Shinto ceremonies, and accompanied by a drum, he would emerge in the private rooms, and chase women. Superstition had it that any hapless young woman struck by the fox's staff would suffer a pregnancy in the new year. The chase was, therefore, lively, with the possible victims doing their best to keep clear.

II-32

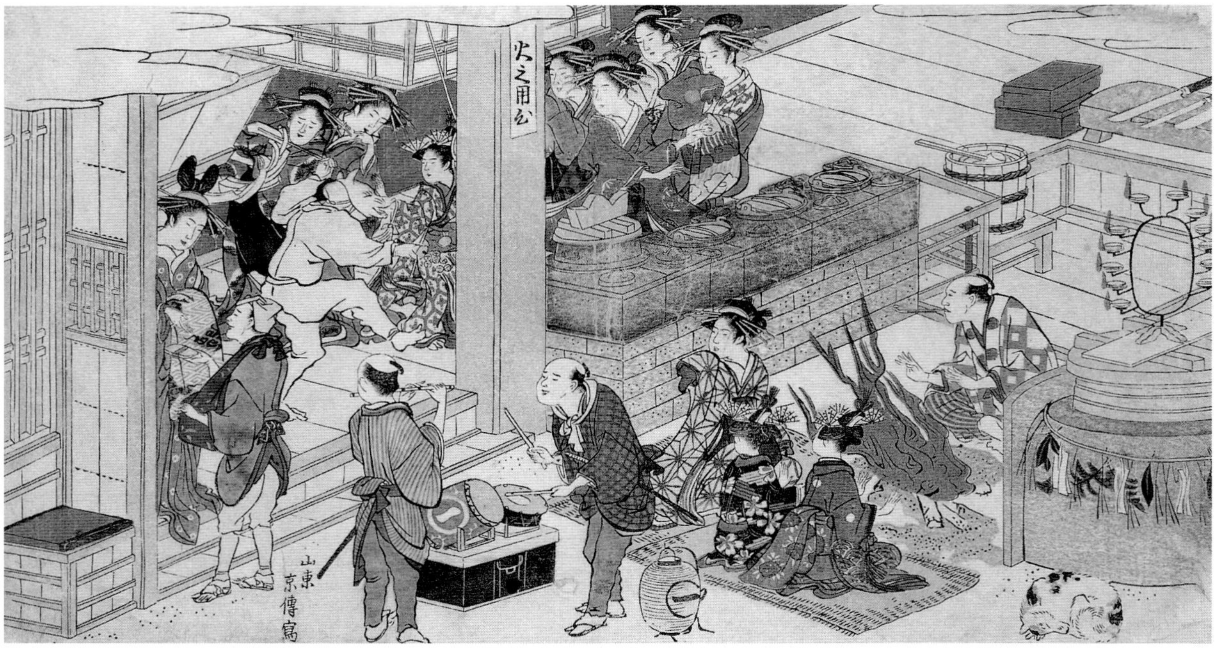

In this print by Kyōden, the dance is being performed in the kitchen of a pleasure house. The pillar in the center displays the ubiquitous warning "Beware of fire" (*hi no yōjin*), which was to be found anywhere flames were used. Being New Year's, and therefore the end of winter, a large fire is lit on the earthen floor, where a *wakaimono*, smoking nonchalantly, two *kamuro*, and a *shinzō* sit warming themselves. The dance and the chase are taking place on the raised floor, where six *shinzō* seem intent on keeping the leering fox at bay. In their midst, the young *kamuro* is probably enjoying the excitement of the chase more than fearing the consequences of being struck by the fox. At the left, quite unperturbed by the fracas, a courtesan with a butterfly-style coiffure is receiving a note from a messenger, perhaps summoning her to a customer. Meanwhile, the high notes of the flute and the lively beat of the drum raise the tempo in this extremely vivacious scene.

II-33

Kitao Masanobu (1761-1816)

***Yoshiwara keisei shin bijin awase jihitsu kagami*, "A Competition among the New Beauties of the Yoshiwara, Mirrored in Their Writing"**

Spring of 1784

Folding album (gajō); 37 x 25

Signature (Kitao Rissai Masanobu) and seal (Soseki) of artist with name and address of publisher (Kōshōdō Tsutaya Jūzaburō) on last page following afterword

Portland Art Museum, Mary Andrews Ladd Collection

Though Santō Kyōden, here using the brush name Kitao Masanobu, was only twenty-three when he put this remarkable album together, it is without doubt his greatest achievement in the field of print design. The phenomenal success of his kibyōshi, *Edo umare uwaki no kabayaki*, which came out the following year, seems to have encouraged him to give up printmaking in favor of writing. Though he continued to illustrate books and paint pictures thereafter, such activities would never again be the central focus of his life.

The album consists of seven double-page prints depicting fourteen of the most celebrated courtesans of the day in lavish settings with poems in their own handwriting inscribed above them. With one exception, the courtesans are shown, indoors, surrounded by their attendants and engaged in a variety of cultivated pursuits, including, in one instance, actually preparing to pen a poem. Seasonal references in the poems indicate that they were almost certainly written expressly for the New Year's holiday, probably as examples of *kakizome*, "the first writing of the new year." This supposition is borne out by the inclusion of motifs related to spring or New Year's in several of the prints.

The pairing of the courtesans on opposite pages, usually facing one another, with their poems inscribed above them, closely parallels—almost certainly intentionally so—the conventions used in illustrated scrolls of poetry competitions. The parallel is further underscored by the use of the term *awase* (as in *uta awase*, "poetry competition") in the album's title. The album has a preface by Yomo Sanjin (Yomo no Akara; i.e., Ōta Nampo) and an afterword or colophon by Akerakan Shujin (Akera Kankō, the compiler of *Shioi no tsuto*, another work modeled after classical poetry competitions). That two such pillars of the Edo kyōka movement should have been asked to lend their names to the undertaking suggests the extent to which the publisher, Tsutaya Jūzaburō, thought of the project in literary terms. The two poets did not let him down in this regard; the preface, in particular, with its lyrical description of the "brocade pictures of the East" (*Azuma nishiki-e*), is a minor literary masterpiece in its own right.

In his afterword, Kankō compares Masanobu's designs in flattering terms to those by Shunshō and Shigemasa (Masanobu's teacher) in *Seirō bijin awase sugata kagami* (A mirror comparing the forms of beautiful women of the green houses), a much larger publication that had come out eight years earlier. It, too, had shown women of the licensed quarters engaged in various leisure activities (though in this case the activities spanned all four seasons), and some of the illustrations had also incorporated poems by the women depicted. The three-volume work, which Tsutaya had published in collaboration with Yamazaki Kimbei, had been an extremely ambitious undertaking for him at a relatively early point in his career.

It seems that at least some of Masanobu's designs for this album had been brought out a year earlier, because two of them have Tsutaya's imprint with his earlier address (he moved in early fall 1783) and have a different title (*Seirō meikun jihitsu shū* [A collection of the handwriting of famous courtesans of the green houses]).

Taking the double-page illustrations in order, the courtesans are:

1 & 2: Azumaya and Kokonoe;

3 & 4: Hinazuru and Chōzan of the Chōjiya;

5 & 6: Hitomoto and Tagasode of the Daimonjiya;

7 & 8: Utagawa and Nanasato of the Yotsubaya;

9 & 10: Segawa and Matsundo of the Matsubaya;

11 & 12: Koi Murasaki and Hana Murasaki of the Kado Tamaya;

13 & 14: Hanaōgi and Takigawa of the Ōgiya.

Since space does not permit us to describe every diptych in detail, we will concentrate on only three of them (of which two are reproduced here), Hinazuru and Chōzan (3 & 4), Utagawa and Nanasato (7 & 8), and Hanaōgi and Takigawa (13 & 14).

Hinazuru and Chōzan. Chōzan, her obi puffed out on her lap like a cushion and her

II-33 (3 & 4)

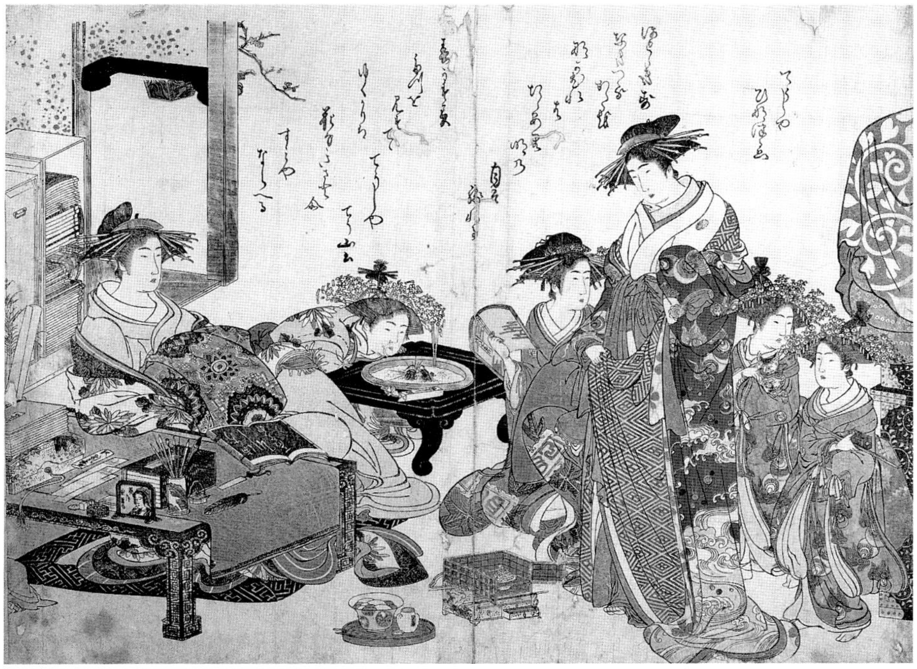

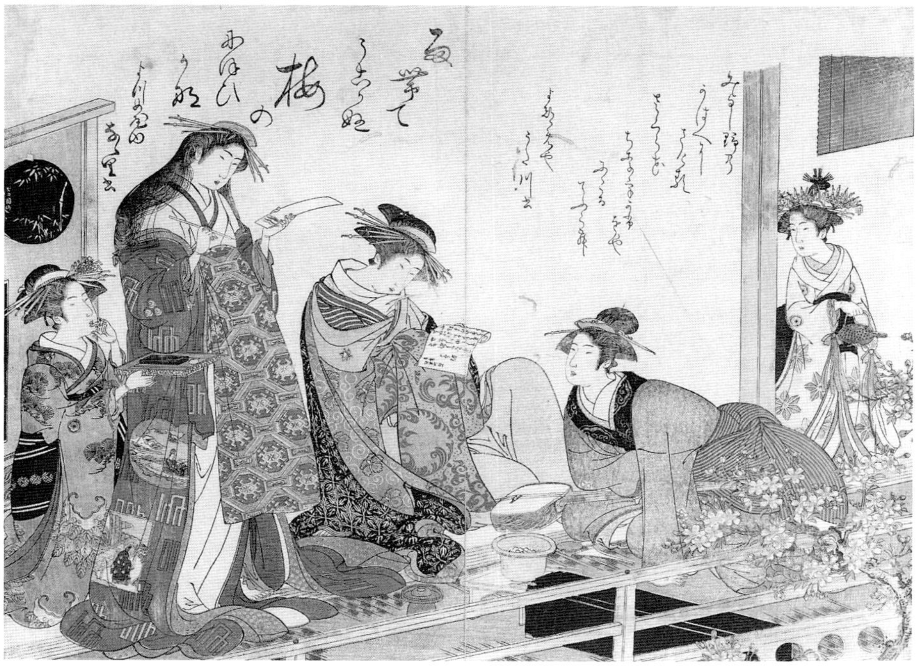

II-33 (7 & 8)

many-layered robes spread out on the floor around her, leans back beside her writing table, a shelf stacked with books behind her. A flowering plum branch projects into the room from a container hung on a partition to the right of the bookshelf. The table, of lacquer inlaid with mother-of-pearl, is covered with a cloth, on top of which are laid out the kinds of articles typically associated with a scholar-calligrapher—brushes in a porcelain holder, a water dropper, a lacquer writing box, seals and books. One of the books, apparently a collection of calligraphic rubbings, lies open on the table. Presumably Chōzan has been consulting it to prepare for making her own contribution to the album, an anonymous poem from the *Kokin wakashū*, which reads: *Harugasumi / tatsu o misutete / yuku kari wa / Hananaki sato ni / sumi ya naraeru* (Wild geese flying over the mists of spring, are you indifferent to the sight, used as you are to a flowerless land?). The *kamuro* shown next to Chōzan, blowing at the coals of a hibachi, introduces a down-to-earth touch into the courtesan's otherwise formidably bookish surroundings.

Opposite Chōzan stands Hinazuru, her head bowed in thought, drawing her robes round her. A *shinzō* holding a book is seated at her side and two *kamuro* (one clasping a kitten) stand behind her. Hinazuru's contribution is also a famous poem from one of the imperial anthologies. By Fujiwara Sanesada, it reads: *Hototogisu / nakitsuru kata o / nagamureba / tada ariake no / tsuki zo nokoreru* (When I turned to catch the source of the cuckoo's call, all I saw was the moon in the early dawn sky).

Utagawa and Nanasato. These two pages are dominated by the tall figure of Nanasato holding a *tanzaku* (decorated poem slip) in one hand and a brush poised in the other, as though caught in the very act of composing the poem that appears in such bold, highly individualistic handwriting above her. Kneeling beside her, a *shinzō* holds up an inkstone in readiness. Nanasato wears her long hair down over her shoulders, and her loosely tied obi hangs in front of her like an apron. The long, loose hair was almost certainly intended to remind viewers of the even longer hair worn by Heian court ladies (see Catalogue no. II-28), and the rather unusual motifs on her *uchikake*—Genji *kōmon* (emblems linked with the different chapters of *The Tale of Genji*) and album sheets of scenes from the *Tale*—were also included for their associations with the courtly past. Nanasato's poem, a haiku, reads: *Ame mutte / ugokanu ume no / nioi kana* (Though the raindrops gather, the scent of the plum lingers on).

Compositionally, Nanasato's head is at the apex of a triangle, the longest side of which extends diagonally past Utagawa's head and along the back of the kneeling geisha at Utagawa's feet to the lower-right corner of the design. Utagawa, with her back to Nanasato and bowing her head to read the half unfurled sheet of paper she holds in front of her, seems content to play a supportive role. Even her relatively restrained handwriting, so at odds with Nanasato's more flamboyant calligraphy, contributes to the same impression. Her poem (which we will not transcribe here) compares the falling cherry blossoms of Yoshino to fluttering butterflies.

Hanaōgi and Takigawa (*not reproduced*). In this, the only outdoor scene among the seven diptychs, the two courtesans, each accompanied by a *shinzō* and two *kamuro*, move in formal procession (*dōchū*) past a lamppost and stacked water buckets covered with a sandwich board inscribed with the name of their house. (The water buckets were for use in the event of fire.) Pine and bamboo set out in honor of the new year are visible at the left, and other symbols of the holiday—a cluster of rice stalks, ferns, and herbs—hang from the pillar at right. Two of the *kamuro* (one of Hanaōgi's and one of Takigawa's) carry battledores, the paddles used for the *hanetsuki* game traditionally played at New Year's, and an abandoned shuttlecock lies on the ground in the lower left corner of the picture. The robes of the courtesans, *shinzō*, and *kamuro* are all adorned with a variety of auspicious symbols such as cranes, pine, and plum.

The calligraphy in Hanaōgi's hand is in two parts. The first, in larger characters, consists of two stanzas from a poem taken from an anthology of Chinese poetry of the Tang Dynasty. The other is a *waka* of her own. It reads: *Ka ni zo shire / sato no hatsu hana / sakisomete / sode ni tamoto ni / niou ume zo mo* (Infatuated by the scent, one smells the fragrance of the first flowering plums of the Yoshiwara even in one's pockets and one's sleeves). Takigawa's contribution also begins with lines from a Tang Dynasty poem, but these are followed by a *waka* by the tenth-century Japanese poet Mibu no Tadamine, rather than with a verse of Takigawa's own. Curiously, Takigawa's inscription is written from left to right, the only calligraphy in the album to be so written.

II-34

Kitagawa Utamaro (1753-1806)

***Seirō ehon nenjū gyōji*, "Picture Book of Annual Observances at the Green Houses"**

1804

Illustrated book in two volumes

The British Museum

The Japanese term *nenjū gyōji* means "the round of annual observances" or "a calendar of annual events," and, as one might expect from the title, many of the illustrations in this two-volume book are of seasonal festivals or celebrations such as the Niwaka Carnival (which took place every year during the eighth month) or the Fox Dance (see Catalogue no. II-32). Other illustrations, however, offer glimpses of a less public side of the Yoshiwara. One, for instance, shows a courtesan and her attendants crowded together in a doorway, looking on as Utamaro paints a *hōō* bird on the wall of their *harimise* room. Another provides an even more intimate view of life in the pleasure quarters. It shows a courtesan and her attendants busily going about their morning chores—starting a fire in a hibachi, bringing in fresh water, tidying the apartment—while a male guest who has stayed overnight sits apart, gazing through an open window at the snowy scene outdoors.

The text was written by Jippensha Ikku (1765-1831), who had attracted considerable attention two years earlier with the publication of the first installment of his popular *Tōkaidō*

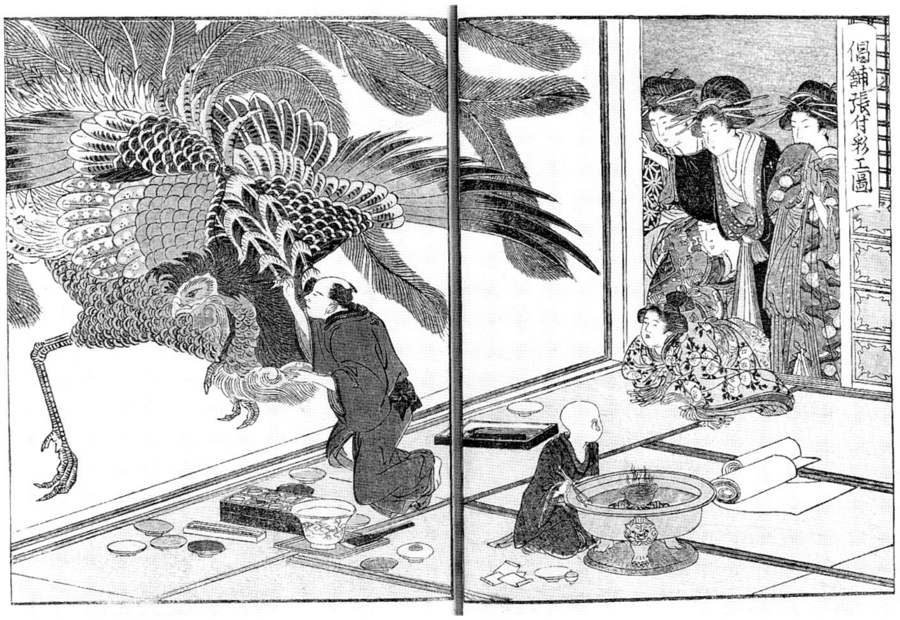

II-34

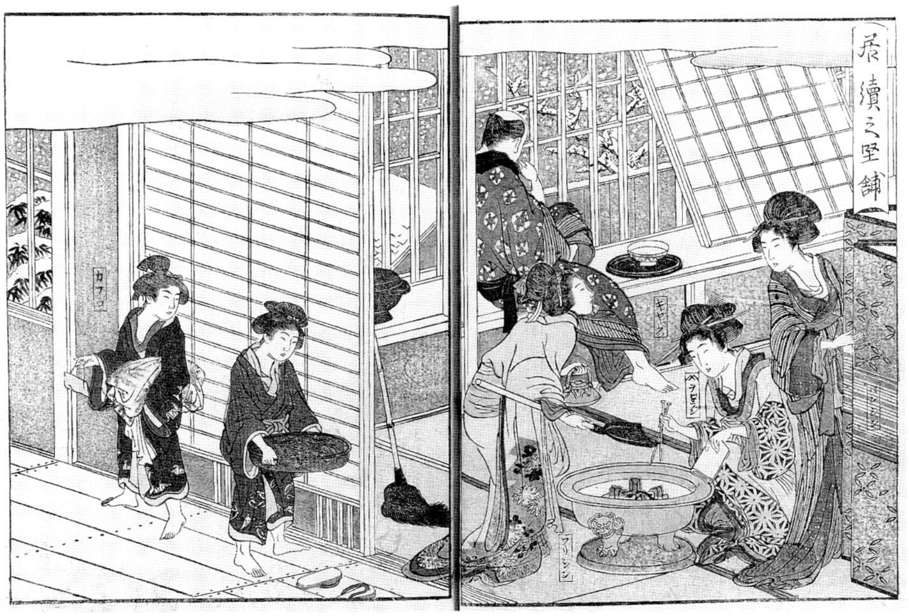

II-34

Hizakurige (The Tokaido on shank's mare).

Published only two years before his death in 1806, this is the last dated book illustrated by Utamaro.

II-35

Suspended Lantern Clock (*kakedokei*)

Circa 1790-1800

Shitan wood case, double foliate with single bell, scroll-like flowers in brass openwork; 68.3 (from top of clock to bottom of weight) x 10.8

Kazue and Mearl Snell

This type of clock is depicted in Utamaro's series *Seirō jūni toki tsuzuki* (Catalogue no. II-30). It is entirely possible that Utamaro had seen such a clock in a rich merchant's home. Clocks were generally owned by the nobility or by important temples, and would be displayed only in the safety of an inner chamber. Utamaro may also have seen clocks in illustrations, and would thus have been unfamiliar with their correct forms and mechanisms. The novelty of such a scientific object no doubt stirred great interest when his *Hours* series reached the stalls.

Lantern clocks (*yagura-dokei*, or *kakedokei*) are driven by weights supported on a stand, and were placed in an alcove (*tokonoma*) or suspended on a wall.* Originally they were controlled by a single balance, or foliate, with small weights on either end. These had to be adjusted throughout the year to correspond to the length of the day and night "hours." With the introduction of the double foliate, the adjustment became a little more advanced, since the arm (between the bell and the movement) would drop into place at the beginning of the day or night hours.

Later lantern clocks featured revolving hour dials with adjustable hour and half-hour plates. Like most clocks of the period, this one required adjustment when the seasons, and therefore the length of the day and the night, changed. The daytime "hour" plates would be spaced farther apart as the days lengthened, and the night "hour" plates moved closer together.†

* Ruji Yamaguchi, "Japanese Clocks and their History," *American Horologist and Jeweler* (April 1949), 71-86.

† The writer gratefully acknowledges the assistance of Mearl Snell in this discussion of Japanese clocks.

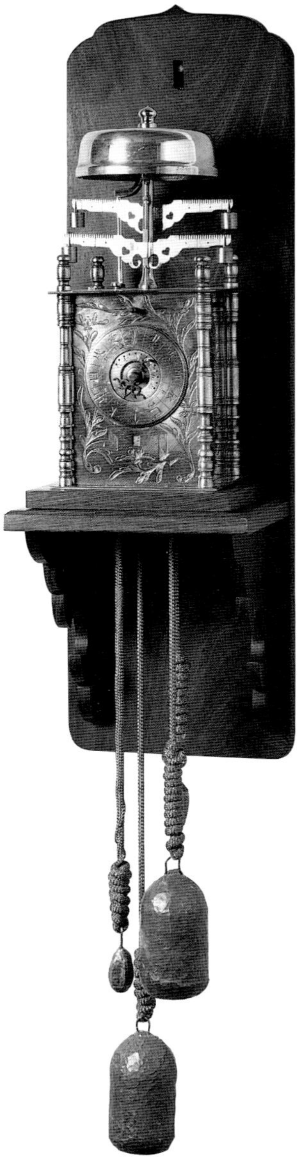

II-35

II-36

Footed Tray Table (*o-zen*)

Late Edo Period

Black lacquer with gold maki-e; 22 (h) x 36.5 (w)

Peabody Essex Museum

One example of a tray table used at restaurants in the late 1780s is shown in Shumman's print of the Shikian (Catalogue no. I-7). The tray before us here, with its elegantly curved and scalloped legs, is similar to the table laden with bowls of food in Chōki's triptych (Catalogue no. II-16).

The gold *maki-e* design depicts a flower crest of four triple-lobed petals, graced in the center with a delicate starburst. It is likely that this table was part of a set, and that the crest belonged to a family or a prosperous establishment.

The mirror-like black surface is a testament to the care with which artisans applied the toxic and sticky lacquer resin to prevent dust from settling on the surface before it had dried completely. Japan's humid climate has always been beneficial to the development of lacquer making; nevertheless, there are stories of craftsmen who would wait for the moment after a rainstorm to load their prized pieces onto boats and glide out to the middle of a lake, where, in the pure, damp air, they would apply the final coats to obtain a glistening finish free from impurities.*

* F. Bailey Vanderhoef, Jr., *Oriental Lacquer* (Santa Barbara: Santa Barbara Museum of Art, 1976), 7.

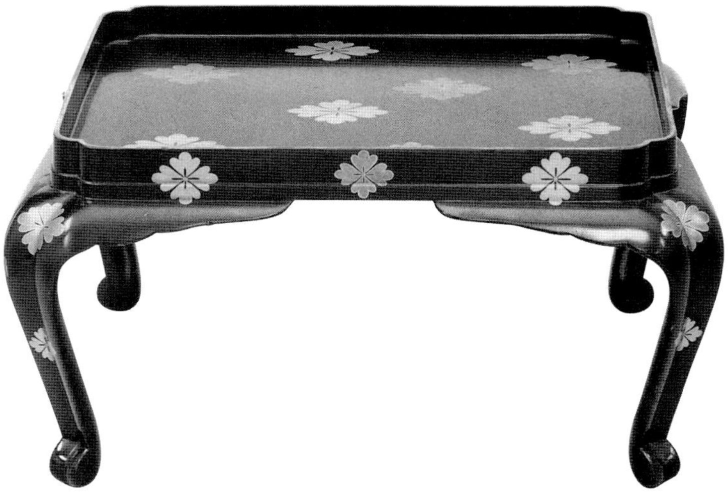

II-36

Tray tables and the containers placed on them added to the decoration of the room where guests were served. A harmonious composition of artfully displayed foods further enhanced the scene; however, once the meal was completed, the tray and everything on it would be whisked away (or put outside the door, as in the Chōki triptych) to clear the room for the next entertainment.

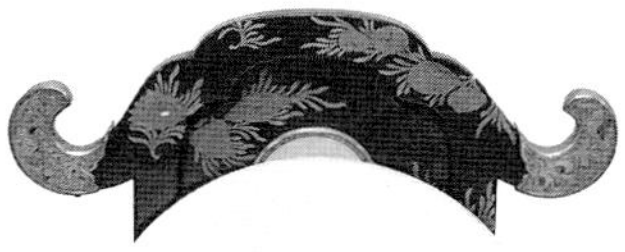

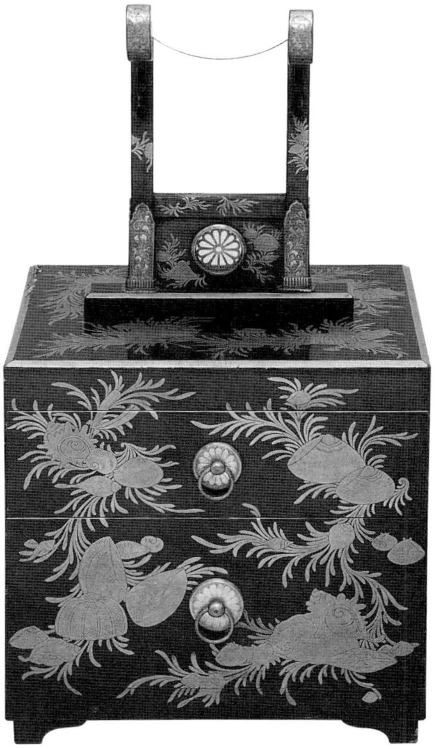

II-37

II-37
Mirror Stand ***(kyōdai)***

Mid-eighteenth century

Drawer cabinet of black lacquer on wood with gold shell and seaweed design, gilt copper alloy drawer pulls, bronze mirror; 27 (h) x 27.8 (w) x 27.8 (d)

Peabody Essex Museum

This small dressing table, with support for a hand mirror, is typical of such objects used by women. Its drawers would store combs, hair ornaments, powders, and oils. Placed on the tatami solely for toiletry purposes, it would then be returned to a cabinet for storage. Thus it was designed for portability, and, elegant as its decorations were, it was never on display for long, though it would be a cherished object of daily use for many years—possibly all of a woman's life.

The glamour surrounding courtesans helps explain the fascination their personal lives held for the general public, hence the many paintings and prints in this exhibition depicting the women in their private quarters and during their non-working hours. In scenes such as these, mirror stands are prominently displayed, symbolizing the intimacy and elegance of the setting. Eishi's *Standing Courtesan* and *Courtesan before a Mirror Adjusting Her Hairpins*, Chōki's *Rain on the "Morning After,"* and Masanobu's *A Competition among the New Beauties* (Catalogue nos. II-7, II-17, II-16, and II-33) are just a few examples of these glimpses.

The toiletry set exhibited here has an ocean motif, with gold *maki-e* shells and seaweed strewn on a black-lacquer background. Openwork brass chrysanthemums crown the stand for the bronze mirror, which would have reflected a clear image when new. The drawer pulls, repeating the chrysanthemum pattern, are made of a gilt-copper alloy.

II-38
Writing Box (*suzuribako*)

Nineteenth century (?)

Black lacquer with gold maki-e design; interior of box contains water dropper, inkstone, and ink stick in a holder; 23.3 (h) x 21.2 (w) x 3.8 (d)

Portland Art Museum, Gift of Mrs. Robert Sabin

The elegant writing box shown here is similar to those seen in Catalogue nos. II-28 and II-33, adorning the writing tables of courtesans. Their highly ornamented covers could themselves set a literary mood, inspiring sentiments suitable to the composition of poetry or letters. This one combines delicate plum blossoms with graceful stalks of bamboo (an early spring motif), which might be expected to imbue the writer's thoughts with the promise of a fragrant new beginning even while winter lingers. The interior of the box is decorated with young pine trees (a winter motif) on a rocky shore.

The box holds utensils essential to writing. The inner tray has a frame for a double-spouted silver water dropper engraved with three carnations, and a heavy slate inkstone rimmed with gold. An ink stick is inserted in the gold-spotted ink-stick holder, which would spare the writer from smudging her fingertips with ink.

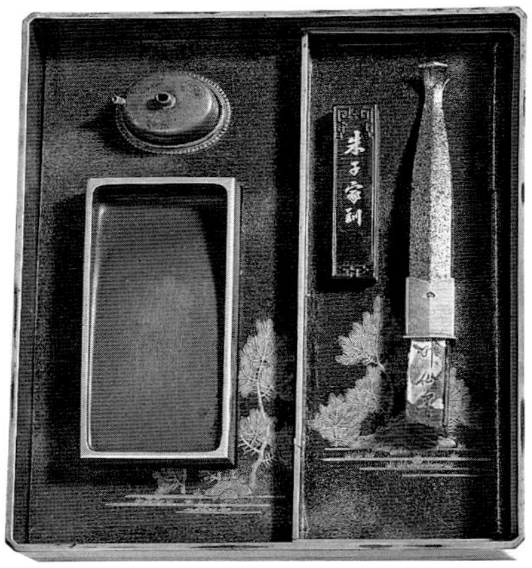

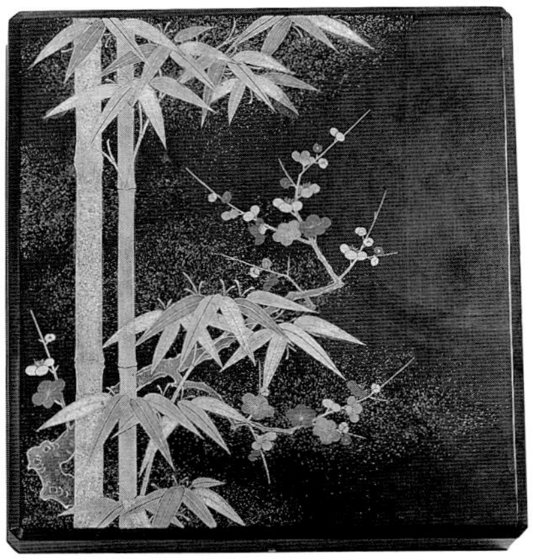

II-38

II-39
Smoking Sets (*tabako-bon*)

Edo Period

Tobacco & Salt Museum

Literally "tobacco trays," these sets were made up of the utensils required for smoking, conveniently arranged in enclosed, unlidded wooden boxes. Since tobacco smoking was a popular pastime throughout Edo society, it became a matter of etiquette to offer guests an opportunity to enjoy a pipe. *Tabako-bon* were, therefore, ubiquitous.

The main components of *tabako-bon* included a receptacle (*hi-ire*) for holding hot charcoal from which the tobacco was lit, and a hollow bamboo cylinder (*hi-otoshi*), occasionally with a small lacquered lid, which served both as ashtray and hand-held cuspidor. *Tabako-bon* sometimes had small lidded compartments or drawers for storing pipes and loose tobacco.

Tabako-bon appear in many of the works in this exhibition, particularly those dealing with entertainment (Catalogue nos. II-11, II-27, and IV-14). The wide range of style and decoration is represented by the examples of *tabako-bon* shown here.

remaining were Kyōden and his following. Kyōden's fine that year did not stop publishers from continuing to clamor for more best-sellers from him. His new works, however, leaned toward moralism and their humor was broader and less sarcastic.

In the second month of 1790, Kyōden married the twenty-seven-year-old Okiku (Little Chrysanthemum), upon her retirement as the courtesan Kikuzono at the Ōgiya. The master of the Ōgiya was a friend and kyōka cohort of Kyōden; he stepped in as matchmaker, saving the bride from an uncertain future and the groom from the expense of her ransom. Okiku became a hard-working, devoted wife, and appears in many Kyōden stories, in characters bearing such names as Kikuken, or Master Kiku.

That fall, Kyōkutei (Takizawa) Bakin burst into Kyōden's life when they met at Tsutaya's publishing house. Bakin appeared on Kyōden's doorstep one day, armed with a cask of sake, begging Kyōden to take him on as a student. Kyōden supported Bakin in a variety of ways until his writing was able to stand on its own. Bakin later became a successful author and was recognized as a key figure in the modernization of the Japanese novel. The Kyōden-Bakin relationship ended in a rift, though while Bakin was still struggling to make his name it was Kyōden who took him under his wing—literally so when Bakin's house was flooded and Kyōden opened his doors to him.

In the third month of 1791, Kyōden was again embroiled in a scandal over his writing. He had written three sharebon that Tsutaya published. They all looked closely at the worlds of Fukagawa and Yoshiwara, and derived from plots of plays or *jōruri.*

The authorities objected because, although all the stories were set in the ancient past, they too clearly depicted the cavorting and pleasure-seeking for which Yoshiwara and Fukagawa were famous, and described illicit relations between the sexes. Moreover, there was a ban against picture books dealing with licentious behavior, and the leaders of the writers' guild had instructions to inspect all works before publication to ensure that they complied with all edicts and regulations. In this case, the author, the publisher, and two guild leaders were found guilty of violations. Their sentences were harsh. The books were banned, Kyōden was ordered to remain in manacles for fifty days, Tsutaya was divested of half his estate, and the guild leaders were barred from the industry.

It is not that Kyōden or Tsutaya had ignored the edict. They had purposely set their stories in antiquity and reworked the text to avoid direct conflict with the publishing ban. "Educational material" was plainly printed on the cover as a camouflage, which infuriated the magistrates all the more after the contents were exposed.

The good-natured Kyōden took this setback hard. Disheartened and demoralized, he gave up writing and drawing sharebon when his sentence was over. Kyōden in handcuffs had been a sensation. Publishers counted eagerly on his new notoriety to boost sales. Tsutaya and Tsuruya pressured him for new manuscripts. It was Bakin who came to Kyōden's rescue, ghostwriting two or three of the four Kyōden kibyōshi that came out the next year.

After his punishment, in 1792 Kyōden got the cooperation of his trusted allies Tsutaya and Tsuruya to help him produce a show of calligraphy and painting (*shogakai*), using the revenue from it as capital to rent a space in Kyōbashi Ginza 1-chōme. In the fall of 1793, he opened Kyōya Denzō's Shop, his own tobacco store, where he sold paper tobacco cases. The shop was a success, as his devoted readers were curious to see the real man in action.

Kyōden designed the tobacco cases, wrote copy for his advertisements, and let his father handle the practical side of the business.

That winter, after only three years of marriage, Kyōden's wife, Okiku, became ill and died. Next year, for the first time, Kyōden had no new books on the market. Meanwhile, business continued to prosper. The shop next to the gate at Kyōbashi Bridge was running out of space, and, only three years after opening, the business moved to a larger building, still within the compound that Kyōden's father managed. His "favorite merchandise" expanded to include toothpick cases, pipes, "reading pills," and other tonics—even cosmetics. He sold his calligraphic works and drawings, and seals engraved by his brother.

Kyōden remarried in 1799. His new wife was Tamanoi, a twenty-three-year-old courtesan from the Yoshiwara. As she had not yet fulfilled the term of her service, he paid her ransom. She took the name "Yuri" when she became his wife, and after their marriage Kyōden no longer spent time in the pleasure quarters.

In 1799 Kyōden published his *yomihon*, or historical drama, *Chūshinsui koden*. He brought a new style to the form by integrating Japanese and Chinese and incorporating new ideas. The work stimulated fresh interest in the genre, both in Edo and in the Kyoto region where it had originated.

When Kyōden had stopped writing gesaku, the kibyōshi genre had changed into *gōkan*, which still combined text and pictures but included less humor. Kyōden maintained his popularity in the new genre, producing gōkan right up to his death. He also continued to write and draw *kokkeibon*, or comic books, in which the humor was broader but his style was still evident. He diversified into other areas as well, becoming fond of old calligraphic works, paintings, and antiques, and developing skills for researching and appraising them. This shift in taste reflected a change in the Edo climate as a whole. Intellectuals took their cue from late Ming Chinese literati and became interested in classical learning. Kyōden switched his focus to history, and in later years looked back on his work in gesaku as pointless, regarding research as his true calling. His last work, the *Kottōshū* (Collection of antiques), which took him more than ten years, was a piece of historical research, with a preface by Ōta Nampo. These pursuits led him to form connections with other scholars and patrons.

In 1816 Kyōden collapsed with chest pains on his way home from a party celebrating his brother's new library, and died the next day.

III-1

Santō Kyōden (1761-1816)

Courtesan with Lantern

1790s

Hanging scroll; ink and light colors on paper; 89.2 x 26.3

Signature (Santō Kyōden daisu awase utsusu) and seals (Hasanjin and Kyōden) of artist at center left

Portland Art Museum, Purchase of the Smith Fund

This sketch shows a courtesan, a wry smile on her face, her obi billowing in front of her, standing or walking by a large portable lantern (*chōchin*). She is drawn in rapid calligraphic strokes, in a stance that may be compared with the majestic silhouette of a courtesan by Eishi in *Snow, Moon, and Flowers* (Catalogue no. IV-2).

Above her, Kyōden has balanced a four-line poem that offsets the apparent simplicity and innocence of the painting. The poem reads: *Tsuisuke tabako no kumo to nari / itsuzuke hiyori no ame to naru / yogi no uchi futon no ue / ishhō no kankai kore ippan* (The lighted pipe transforms into a cloud spending the night as the rain comes. Lying upon her futon in nightclothes, all the festivities of a lifetime seem ordinary compared with this). "The lighted pipe" refers to the pipe the courtesan would prepare for her guest, who is then symbolized by the cloud. The full significance of the metaphor can only be appreciated when one realizes that "clouds and rain" allude to activities of an amorous nature.

A statement written on a separate piece of paper by Kyokutei (Takizawa) Bakin has been mounted on the top of the scroll.

III-2

Kitao Masanobu (1761-1816)

Geisha on Her Way

Circa 1775

Hanging scroll; colors on silk; 92.7 x 41.9

Signature of artist (Kitao Masanobu) with kakihan in red at upper right

Minneapolis Institute of Arts, Bequest of Richard P. Gale

In this early painting by Kitao Masanobu (Santō Kyōden), there is a sense of incongruity as the formally attired geisha and her retinue emerge from the rural thatched hut. No insignia on the *noren* indicates what type of establishment it may be, and its location—seemingly isolated in the serene mountains—is a far cry from the crowded urban scene with which the artist was most familiar.

The winged hairstyle of the geisha sets the probable date for this painting in the An'ei Period (1772-81). Masanobu had begun studying with Shigemasa in 1774, and by the end of An'ei he was already a popular kibyōshi writer with an extensive portfolio of illustrations for other authors' books. This carefully composed painting no doubt came early in his career, when he was aspiring to be a serious artist.

Geisha on Her Way shows Masanobu's eye for detail, which became one of his trademarks. He depicts every nail in the alcove of the humble structure accurately, and presents a delicate

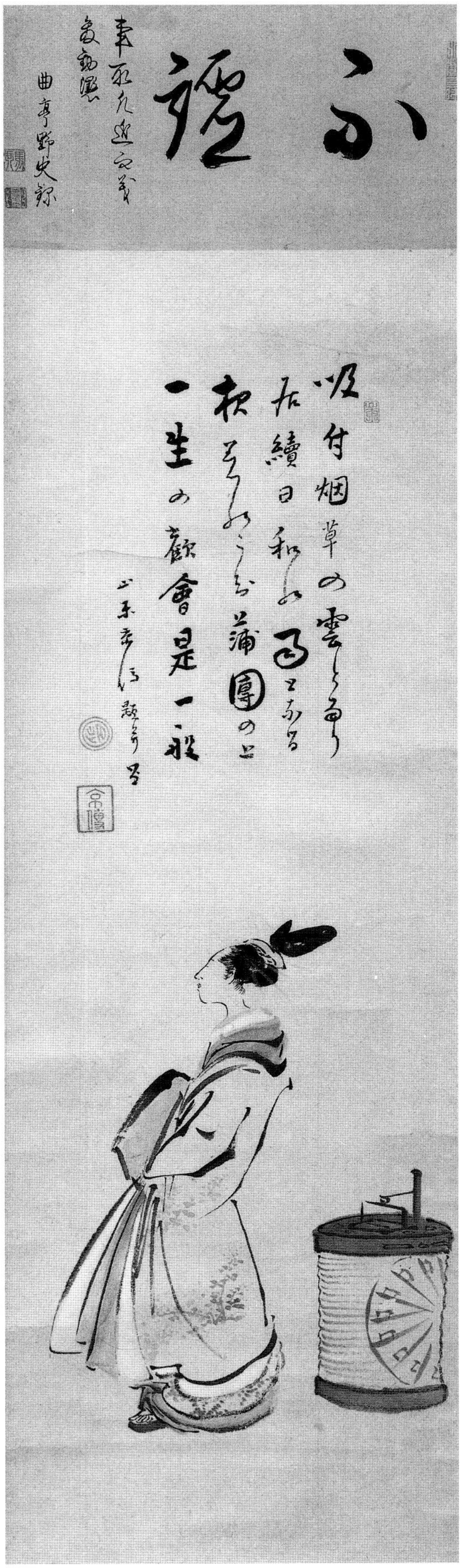

III-1

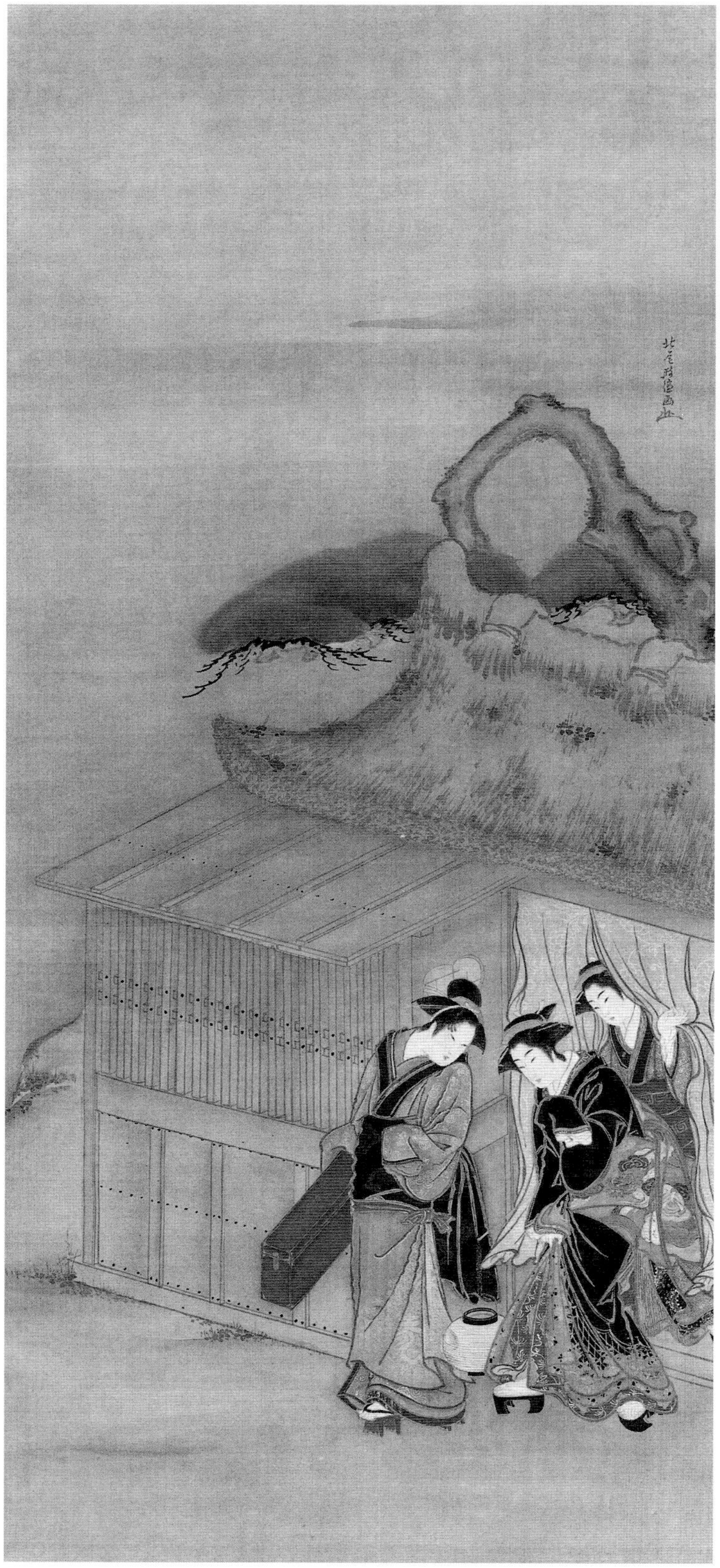

III-2

landscape in the distance, a style he abandoned in his later work. One of the geisha's attendants carries the *shamisen* box, while the geisha lights the way with her collapsible lantern, on which the expected identifying trademark is obscured. Yet another attendant is just on her way out, pulling the *noren* aside and creating a flow of drapery that contrasts with the rigid board-work of the alcove. As was typical of geisha, no crests appear on their kimono.

The institution of "geisha" differed from that of the courtesan: geisha were entertainers, called to parties to perform music and sing. They were employed by the pleasure houses in the early 1760s, but over the years they increasingly free-lanced, working at teahouses or being hired directly by customers to add music to their parties. After 1779 the geisha became a regulated industry under the *kenban-sho*, a registry office that imposed strict rules on their activities and movement in and out of the Yoshiwara.

III-3

Unchō (active late eighteenth century)

Courtesan and Attendants under a Willow Tree

1796

Hanging scroll; colors on silk; 92.7 x 34

Signature (Unchō) and hand-painted cypher (kao) of artist at lower right

The Mary and Jackson Burke Collection

A high-ranking courtesan with butterfly coiffure promenades beneath a willow tree, accompanied by her *furisode shinzō* and two *kamuro*. Her *komageta* are glimpsed as the many layers of her elaborate clothing are kicked open just slightly with each step she takes. Familiar as we are by now with Edo iconography, we can be sure that the willow tree refers to the Yoshiwara, with its famous "Looking Back Willow" (*mikaeri yanagi*), the Willow Bridge (Yanagibashi) where one would embark on the trip to Yoshiwara, as well as to the connotations of feminine allure that "willow" has in Japanese.

No other works with this artist's signature are known. The fine detail shown in the kimono patterns suggest that the painter had considerable skill, and the fact that Kyōden and Bakin inscribed the work with their poetry tells us that Unchō must have had some standing among the luminaries of Edo's literary world. The short stature of Unchō's figures is also of interest, for it goes against the contemporary fashion for elongated, "willowy" beauty.

Let us turn now to the inscriptions, which take up the entire upper half of the painting. On the right is a Chinese-style couplet, written as one line of bold-stroked characters: "Anyone can break a willow by the road or a flower inside the fence." Referring to low-class prostitutes, available to anyone, this contrasts with the kyōka that immediately follows: *Saigyō mo mada minu hana no kuruwa kana* (Not even Saigyō has seen anything like the flowers of the licensed quarters). The inference here is that the charms of the top-ranked courtesans can be enjoyed by only a few (not even Saigyō).

Saigyō (1118-1190) was favored by the former emperor Toba for his skills at both archery and poetry, but in his twenties he renounced all worldly duties to become a wandering priest—and one of Japan's greatest poets. His lyrical correspondence with a courtesan (Eguchi no Kimi) became the basis for a No play (*Eguchi*), expounding the theme of the sacred in the profane. Kyōden apparently found the poet-priest a pithy symbol for a truth-seeking lover of beauty who would nevertheless be awestruck by the opulence of the Yoshiwara of the 1790s. The poem is signed Santō Kyōden *san* (inscription) and affixed with his seal. This poem, incidentally, is virtually the same as the one in Catalogue nos. III-4 and III-7, indicating Kyōden's enjoyment of the ideas it expresses, as well as his business-like attitude of getting full measure out of his products.

The next poem picks up on the contrast of spiritual heights and depraved depths by referring to the Yoshiwara's proximity to the Kinryūzan Asakusa Temple. The lengthy stanza may be roughly translated as: Her house is near Kinryūzan to the north, so her thoughts fall on the Thousand-armed Kannon as she lies on her three-layered futon, touching the bodies of a myriad customers. Nevertheless, the prostitute's temperament is such that she wonders about the rich man: "Surely there are no fleas on his collar."* The poem is signed Kyokutei (Takizawa) Bakin *gisho* (a romp). Bakin had been a student of Kyōden, and later became a novelist who further defined the character of the Edokko.

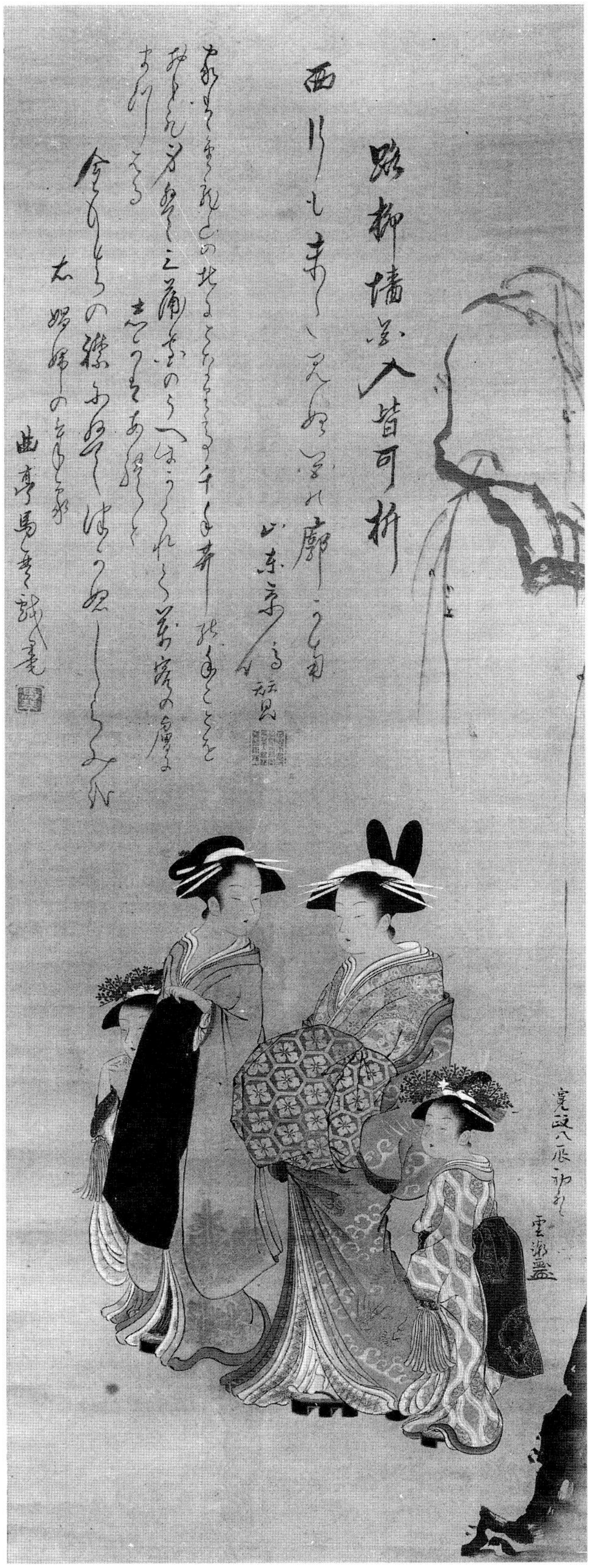

III-3

* Translations of these poems appear in Miyeko Murase's *Japanese Art, Selections from the Mary and Jackson Burke Collection* (New York:The Metropolitan Museum of Art, 1975).

III-4

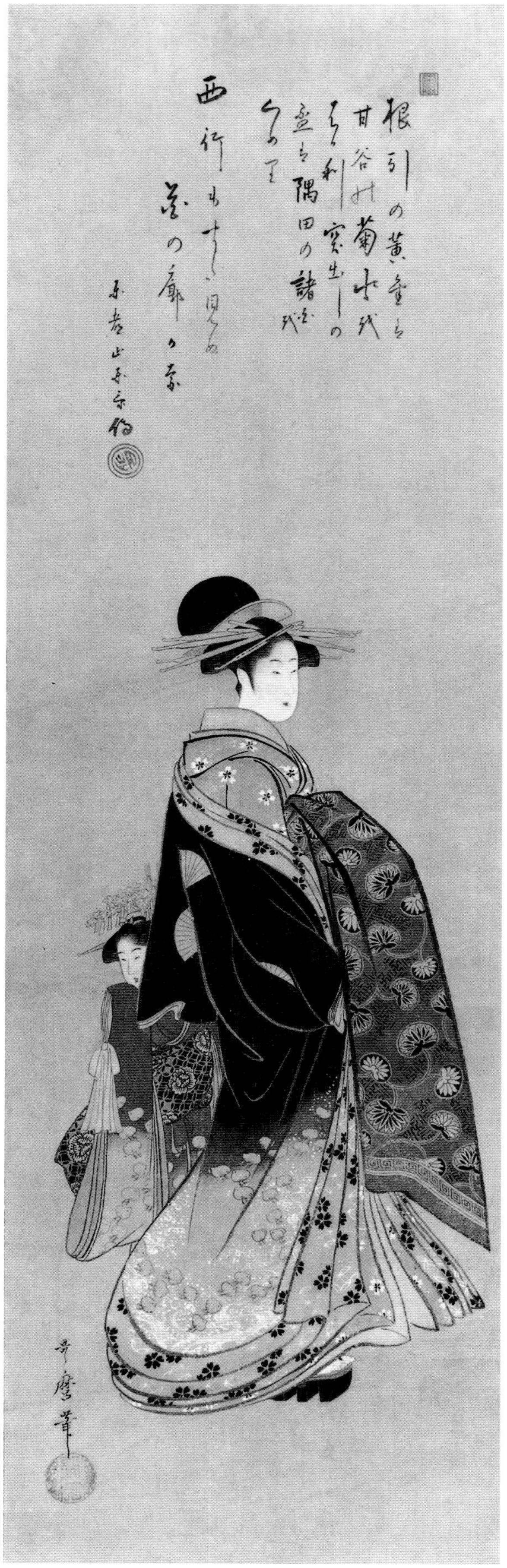

III-4

Kitagawa Utamaro (1753-1806)

Courtesan and Attendant

Circa 1795

Hanging scroll; ink, light colors, and gofun on paper; 85.7 x 26.8

Signature (Utamaro hitsu) and seal (Utamaro) of artist at lower left

University of Michigan Museum of Art, Margaret Watson Parker Art Collection

A tall, slender courtesan, her *uchikake* worn with studied nonchalance half off one shoulder, moves forward in the stylized, mannequin-like gait of the *dōchū*. Her long obi falls in a cascade in front of her, and the hems of her many-layered kimono undulate with her movement. She turns her head to the right but does not pause in her forward advance. A *kamuro*, her sleeve raised to her lips, peeks out timidly from behind the commanding figure of her mistress. As was usually the case with such paintings, no inscription identifies the courtesan, but the fans on her *uchikake* and the paired cherry blossoms on some of her other garments suggest that she is the celebrated Hanaōgi, the subject of so many of the prints and paintings in this exhibition.

Utamaro seems to have concentrated most of his energies on print design and book illustration, and only a few paintings by him are known. Among those few, this is the only one to use ink and ink washes to the virtual exclusion of color. As such, it is something of a tour de force. A gorgeously clad courtesan was colorful by definition. To attempt to depict such a figure using ink alone was a major challenge. Yet this is precisely what Utamaro has done. He alternates dense, lacquer-like blacks with graduated grays and the palest of ink washes, then sets these off with touches of white *gofun* and hints of pale blue to create an effect of such tonal complexity that one hardly notices the virtual absence of color. Though the palette may be limited, "monochromatic" is the last word one would think of applying to it.

During the mid-1790s, prints using a similarly restrained palette enjoyed a brief vogue. Curiously, Utamaro himself seems never to have designed any of these so-called *benigirai* (red avoiding) prints, most of which were designed by his leading rivals at the time, Eishi and Shumman. Is it possible that Utamaro tried to do his rivals "one better" by creating a *benigirai* painting?

Whatever his intentions, the end result was a painting of the utmost elegance and chic. It is also one that leaves no doubts as to Utamaro's skill as a painter. Every brush stroke is wielded with authority, with obvious awareness of its expressive purpose, from the broad, decisive outlines of the obi to the more delicate, almost fluttering, lines of the kimono skirts.

The inscription at the top of the painting is by Santō Kyōden, who was a close friend of Utamaro. It is in two parts. The first, which is preceded by a seal that reads *Kikuken*, "House of Kiku (or Chrysanthemum)," goes as follows: *Nebiki no kogane wa / kanya no kikusui o / hakari tsukidashi no / sakazuki wa Sumida no morohaku o / kumeri** (The gold for her ransom is measured out in the chrysanthemum nectar from the valley. The cup used for her coming-out ceremony pours the best sake of the Sumida). The poem seems to express a courtesan's thoughts when she realizes that the money spent on a coming-out party could have purchased her freedom. The Kikuken seal may have belonged to Kyōden's first wife, Okiku, whom he married in 1790. She was a retired courtesan who would certainly have recognized the sentiments expressed in the poem, which may well have been hers. The second part of the inscription is a haiku: *Saigyō mo / mata minu hana no / kuruwa kana* (Not even Saigyō has seen anything as beautiful as the licensed quarters in flower). Saigyō (d. 1190), a Buddhist priest and one of Japan's most famous poets, was known for his extensive travels. Many legends grew up around him, including one that linked him with a famous courtesan. The haiku must have been one for which Kyōden was well known. Another version of it is written on the fan in Eiri's famous portrait of him (Catalogue no. III-7).

* The transliteration of this poem is taken from Kobayashi Tadashi, "Kitagawa Utamaro hitsu yūjo to kamuro zu," *Kokka* 996, pp. 43-44.

III-5

Collaborative work

***Sekiga* (Impromptu Party Scroll)**

Circa 1801-06

Hanging scroll; ink and light colors on paper; 90.1 x 30.5

The Metropolitan Museum of Art, The Harry G. C. Packard Collection of Asian Art, Gift of Harry G. C. Packard, and Purchase, Fletcher, Rogers, Harris Brisbane Dick and Louis V. Bell Funds, Joseph Pulitzer Bequest, and The Annenberg Fund, Inc., Gift, 1975

This scroll commemorates a gathering of artists and poets that took place somewhere in Edo or its environs in the tenth month of an unspecified year between 1800 and 1806. We do not know what occasion, if any, the party was held to celebrate, nor do we know whether anyone attended besides the fourteen people who contributed these poems and sketches. The answers to these questions may emerge when all of the poems and inscriptions are deciphered and translated, a task the authors of this catalogue have not been able to complete. So far they have not been able to determine much more than that the poems almost all contain imagery related to late fall or early winter. At least five of the poems refer to snow and/or ice, and two mention ponds. Utamaro's sketch at the lower right depicts maple leaves against cracked ice (is the ice on the surface of the pond referred to in the poems?), and Sandarabōshi's kyōka also alludes to maple leaves. The white camellia depicted near the middle-right margin of the scroll fits with the same seasonal motif, since it is a flower that often blooms in Japan in late fall or early winter.

Ten of the fourteen contributors have been identified. All are represented in other works in this exhibition. Reading the scroll from right to left and top to bottom:

1. Shokusanjin (Ōta Nampo);
2. Shikatsube no Magao;
3. Santō Kyōden;
4. Kubo Shumman;
5. Tatekawa Emba;
6. Kyokutei Bakin;
7. Sensōan (Hajintei Ichindō);

8. Sandarabōshi;
9. Kitagawa Utamaro;
10. Rokujūen (Yadoya no Meshimori).

The presence of Rokujūen and Magao in the same party is significant, since the two were subsequently regarded as leaders of opposing schools of kyōka. The relations between Bakin and Kyōden would also be severely strained in later years. The unifying spirit behind the party may well have been Nampo, who was famous for his ability to bring people together.

Utamaro's death, which occurred in 1806, provides a terminus ad quem for the scroll, and since Yadoya no Meshimori did not use the Rokujūen signature before 1800, that year is the earliest at which it can be dated.

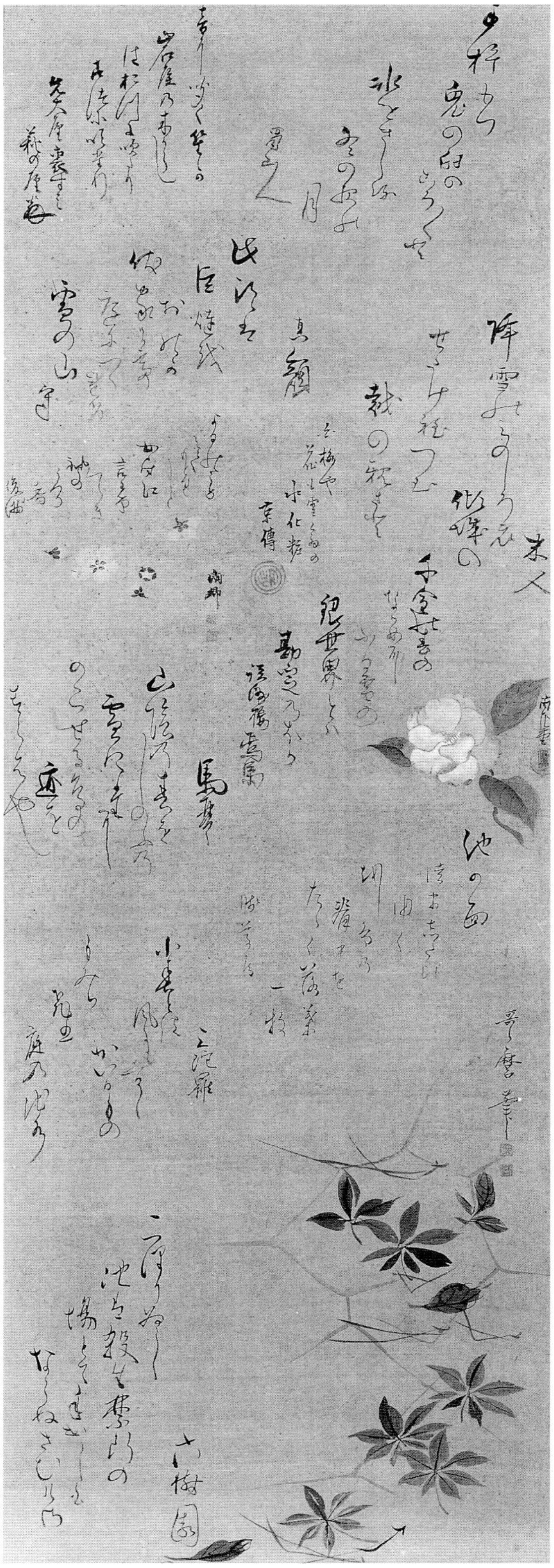

III-5

III-6

Collaborative work

The Seven Gods of Good Fortune

The "first rat day" of 1810 (Bunka kanoe uma, kinoe ne yoru)

Hanging scroll; ink and colors on silk; 67.5 x 82.5

City of Genoa, Museo d'Arte Orientale Edoardo Chiossone

The seven gods of good fortune are shown seated in a group. Each god is painted by a different well-known ukiyo-e artist, and an inscription signed by Santō Kyōden and his brother, Kyōzan, explains that the work was created at the request of the print publisher Eijudō (Nishimuraya Yohachi II). Since the work is dated not only to the year but to "the evening of the first rat day," one can conclude that it was painted at a party, perhaps a New Year's party given by Eijudō himself. It is so carefully composed, however, and the separate figures fit together so well, that it is hard to think of this as a typical spontaneous party painting—or *sekiga*—of the kind represented by Catalogue nos. III-5 and IV-8.

The seven gods of good fortune (*shichifukujin*) were relatively late imports into Japan and became really popular only during the Edo Period, when they began to be taken up as patron deities by the urban merchant classes. Two of the gods, Ebisu and Daikoku, were particular favorites, and their paired images would often be found in small shrines or on little "god shelves" in shops, restaurants, and other places of business.

From a modern western point of view, it is somewhat misleading to think of the *shichi-*

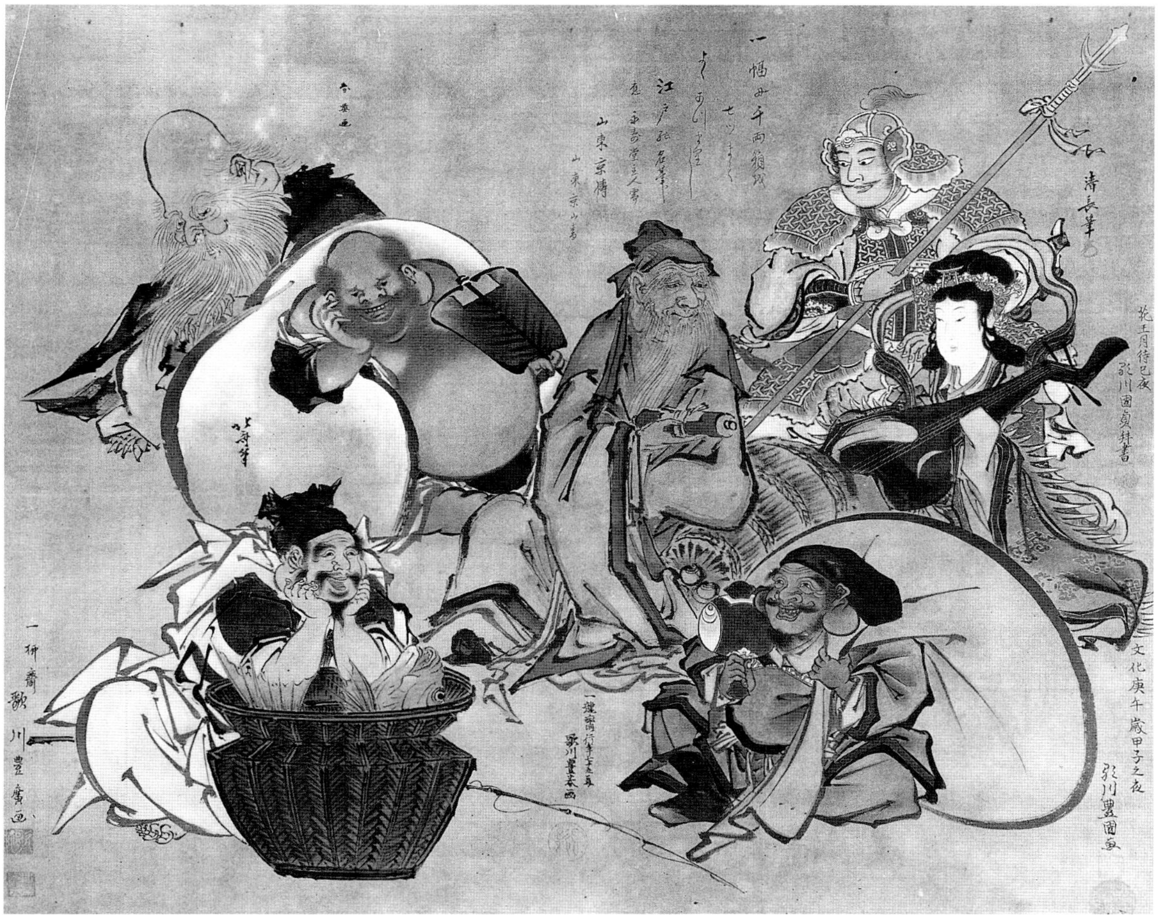

III-6

fukujin as gods. They might more appropriately be thought of as sprites or semi-divine beings who fulfilled a role analogous to that of a medieval patron saint. Though the seven gods are clearly based on Chinese prototypes, there is some doubt as to whether they ever appeared in that country as a group. It seems unlikely, since two of them, Fukurokuju and Jurōjin, are unmistakably of Daoist origin, while Hotei, Bishamonten, and Benzaiten are unquestionably Buddhist. The Chinese models for the more successfully domesticated Daikoku and Ebisu are harder to identify.

One wonders how it was that Eijudō decided to choose these particular seven artists to paint this picture. To be sure, the inscription characterizes them all as *meihitsu* (literally, "famous brushes"), but there were other ukiyo-e painters of the time who could have been so described with equal justice. Eishi is one who immediately comes to mind. We can also assume that all of them had had business dealings with Eijudō at one time or another. (Almost all of Kiyonaga's great *bijin* prints of the 1780s, for example, were published by Eijudō's father, Nishimuraya Yohachi I). But in other respects they seem rather oddly matched. Toyoharu, who proudly signed himself "the seventy-nine-year-old Ichiryūsai Toyoharu," was clearly the patriarch of the group.* Next in age, but some twenty years younger (born 1752), was Kiyonaga. Four of the artists—Hokusai, Shun'ei, Toyohiro, and Toyokuni—were all born in the 1760s. In such company, the seventh artist, the twenty-four-year-old Kunisada, must have seemed a mere youngster. His inclusion in the group must have been due to the fact that he belonged to the Utagawa School, which Toyoharu founded. It is probably no accident that four of the seven artists belonged to the Utagawa lineage.

* Toyoharu's birth date is usually given as 1735. The basis for this is probably a passage in *Ukiyo-e ruikō*, which states that he was eighty (seventy-nine by western reckoning) when he died in Bunka 11 (1814). But the passage in question is from a relatively late version of *Ukiyo-e ruikō* and could well have been erroneous.

Now let us look at the painting in greater detail. Proceeding clockwise, beginning in the lower right, we have:

1. Daikoku, with his great bag of treasure and his magic mallet. Signed *Utagawa Toyokuni ga, Bunka kanoe uma, kinoe ne yoru* (The evening of the first rat day of the horse year Bunka 7).

2. Ebisu, happily resting his elbows on a basket containing an auspicious sea bream (*tai*). Signed *Ichiryūsai Toyohiro ga.*

3. The pot-bellied Hotei, holding a fan, his huge bag behind him. Signed *Hokusai hitsu.*

4. Fukurokuju, half hidden behind Hotei's bag, his tall, domed head bent pensively. Signed *Shun'ei ga.*

5. Jurōjin, seated in the center, with one arm resting against Daikoku's rice bale and holding out a scroll in his right hand. Signed *Ichiryūsai gyōnen shichijūkyū sai Utagawa Toyoharu ga.*

6. Bishamonten, wearing Chinese armor and holding a lance, glaring intently ahead of him. Signed *Kiyonaga hitsu.*

7. Benzaiten, holding her lute, her scarves fluttering around her. Signed *Utagawa Kunisada haiga* (respectfully painted by Utagawa Kunisada) *Kaōgetsu machimi yoru* (Waiting-for-the-snake evening of the "King of Flowers" month).*

Interestingly, only Hokusai among the seven artists has treated his subject in a manner that reminds us of his prints. The others have all chosen to work in styles that the Edo public would have considered Chinese—vaguely Tang-derived in the case of Kiyonaga and Kunisada, more Song in inspiration in the case of Toyoharu and Shun'ei. In a composition in which most of the renderings show considerable detail, Shun'ei's contribution is remarkable for its shorthand use of splashes of ink and wispy lines. Regardless of the style chosen, however, each figure is painted with the kind of verve and authority one would expect of one of the "famous brushes" of Edo. Kyōden and his brother pick up on this idea in their inscription, which reads: *Ippuku ni / senryōbako o / nanatsu made / yoku atsumarishi / Edo no meihitsu* (The famous brushes of Edo have gotten together nicely, all seven of them, to paint all the treasures on one scroll). (The Japanese word *ippuku*, "one scroll," sounds exactly the same as the word for "one smoke." Given that Kyōden's shop specialized in tobacco pouches, the pun was almost certainly intended.) The inscription also provides the information that the scroll was painted at the request of "Master Eijudō."

* The meaning of this particular inscription is rather obscure. The "King of Flowers" usually refers to the peony, which is not a flower normally associated with New Year's, and the "waiting-for-the-snake evening" would be five days later than the first rat day. It seems unlikely, however, that Kunisada would have painted his picture after the others.

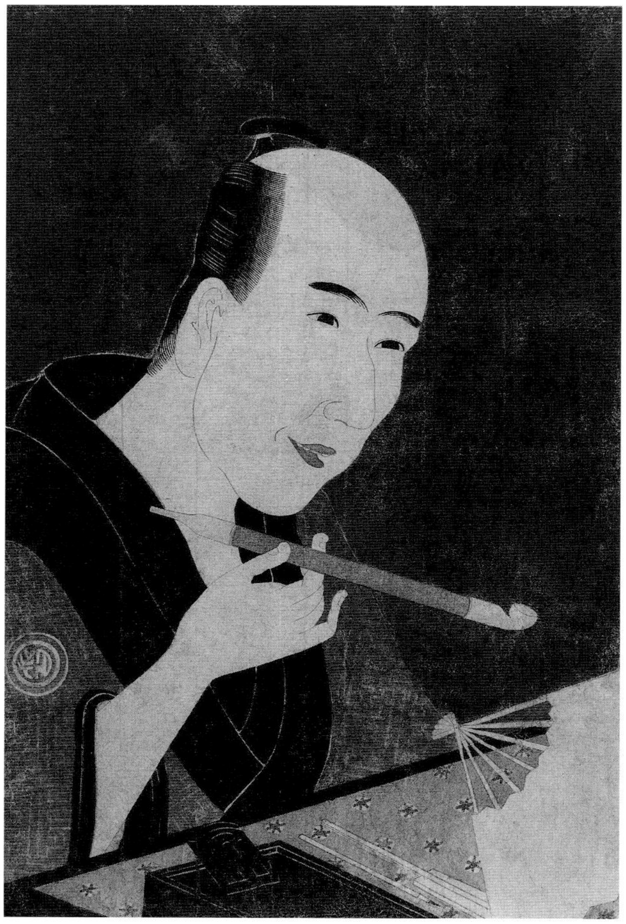

III-7

III-7

Chōkyōsai Eiri (active 1790s)

Portrait of Kyōden, or *Edo hana Kyōbashi natori*, "The Flowers of Edo—The Master of Kyōbashi"

Circa 1795

Woodblock print; ōban; 38.2 x 25.9

Signature of artist (Eiri ga) at upper right, at left of title

The Art Institute of Chicago, Clarence Buckingham Collection, and the Metropolitan Museum of Art, Fletcher Fund

Delicate lines describe the handsome demeanor of Kyōden in this companion piece to the portrait of Tomimoto Buzendayū II (Catalogue no. V-8). The elegance captured in the hand, the warm sparkle in the eyes, and the simple refinement of the garments and objects seem to convey Kyōden's style with precision. He sits at a writing table, with ink stick, inkstone, and brush arranged neatly before him, the ink perhaps still wet on the open fan.

Kyōden appears just to have finished writing a verse on the fan. It is a variation of the poem he inscribed on the paintings by Unchō (Catalogue no. III-3) and Utamaro (Catalogue no. III-4): *Saigyō mo mai minu kuruwa no iro wa ka na* (Not even Saigyō had seen such dazzling color as in the licensed quarters). Still another fan remains for him to inscribe, lying unopened beside his brush.

It is significant that Eiri shows Kyōden dressed in a kimono with this particular crest emblazoned on the sleeve. This was his *hasanjin* seal, nicknamed "*botamochi*," or sweet dumpling, presumably because of its heavy round lines. Kyōden affixed this seal to paintings and books, and used it as the trademark for his tobacco shop, where it appeared on the *noren*. The seal came into his possession when he was only eight or nine. Having been given permission by his father to choose any item from the pawnshop, it was for this chunky, foreign-style seal that he reached. Its copper knob had a hole in it, through which he looped a string so that he could hang it around his neck. He even used it as a counterweight for his kite.

III-8

Kitagawa Utamaro (1753-1806)

Utamaro's Self-Portrait in a Parody of the Chūshingura, from the series *Kōmei bijin mitate Chūshingura*

Circa 1792

Woodblock print; ōban diptych; 39.3 x 26.4 (each print)

Signature of artist (Utamaro hitsu) and name (Ōmiya) and trademark of publisher

The Art Institute of Chicago, Clarence Buckingham Collection

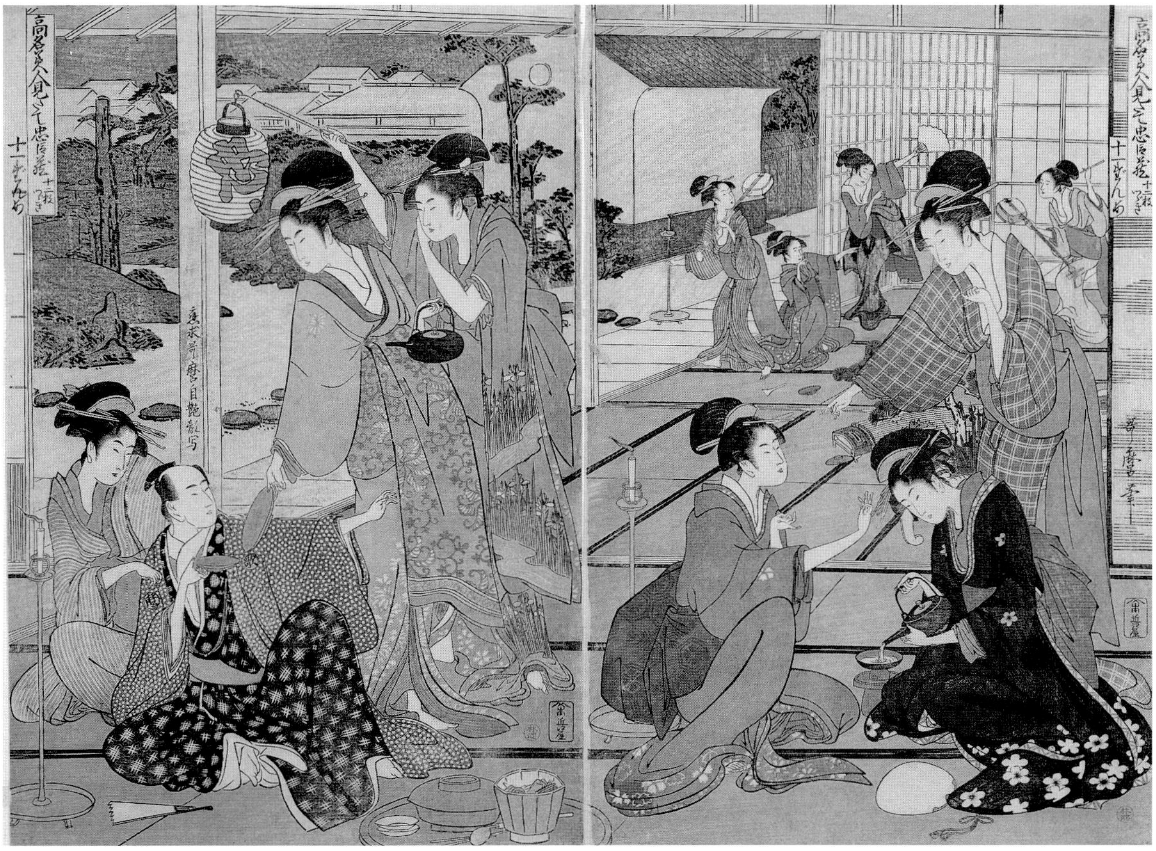

III-8

III-9

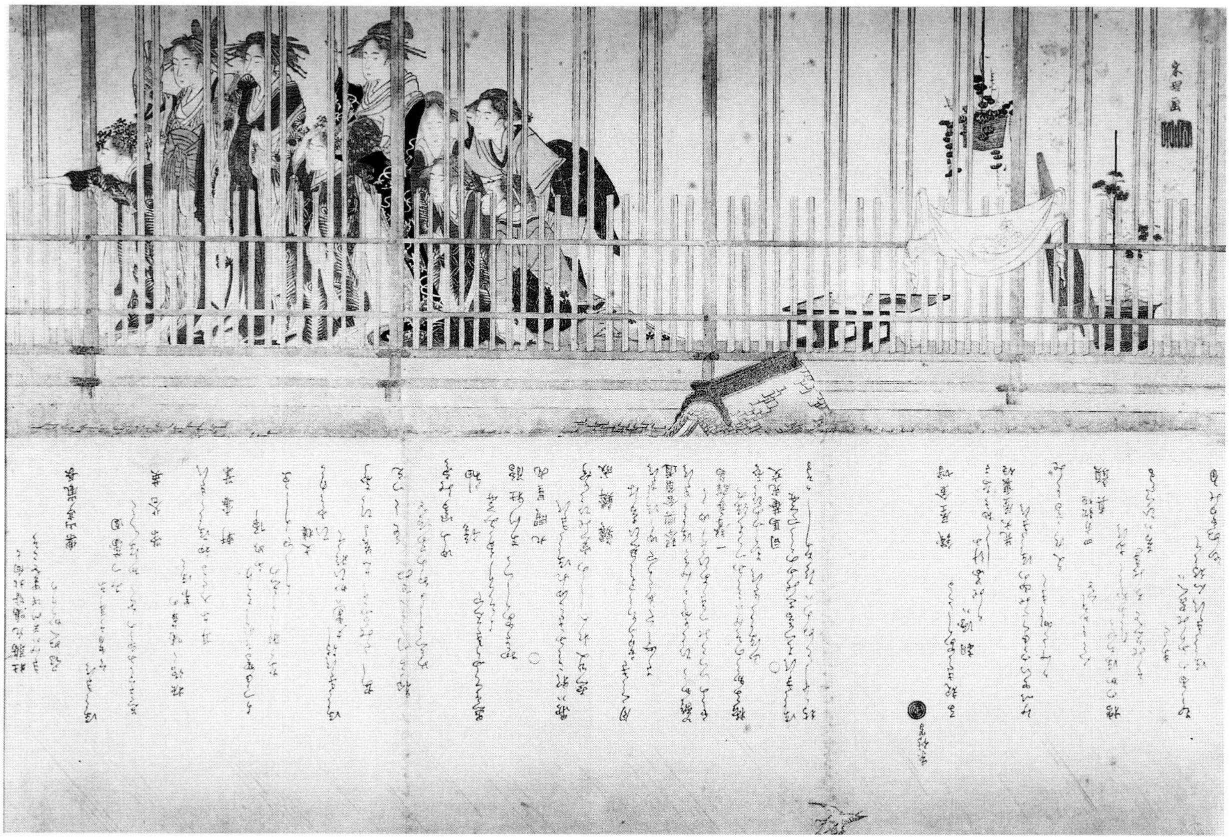

This diptych is part of a series of twelve prints in which celebrated beauties parody scenes from the eleven acts of *Kanadehon Chūshingura*, "The Storehouse of Loyal Retainers," one of the most perennially popular revenge plays of the kabuki repertory. The diptych is included here because of the portrait of himself Utamaro has worked into it. We know the portrait represents Utamaro because of the words inscribed on the pillar behind him, which say that he portrayed his features here "by request."

Utamaro is the only man visible in a large, open room filled with partying women. A courtesan standing beside him pours sake from her own cup into his while another woman sits close beside him on the floor. It is night; candles burn on tall stands in several different places in the room, and a young woman, probably a *shinzō*, holds a paper lantern over the courtesan's head as though to help her see as she ministers to her guest. (The character on the lantern is the word *chū*, "loyalty," from the title of the play.) Farther back in the room, two women perform a dance, seemingly unperturbed by the two geisha moving past them carrying *shamisen*. In the foreground, two other women play a hand game while a third pours sake into a cup on a stand.

It is hard to understand how this print is supposed to be a parody of the eleventh and final act of the *Chūshingura*. In the play, this is when the forty-seven loyal *ronin* finally break into their enemy's well-protected residence and exact their revenge. Most of the act consists of fight scenes in which the various *ronin* display their prowess as they struggle to gain possession of the house.

III-9

Katsushika Hokusai (1760-1849) and Santō Kyōden (1761-1816)

Courtesans and Attendants Watching a Cuckoo

Late 1790s

Surimono; 39.6 x 55.9

Signature of artist (Sōri ga) at upper right followed by undeciphered seal; signature (Kyōden sha) and seal (Denzō) of artist below and left of cuckoo

The Chester Beatty Library

Three courtesans and their attendants press against the enclosing latticework of their upstairs quarters, trying to catch a glimpse of the cuckoo that the little *kamuro* at left points at so eagerly. Another *kamuro*, standing farther back, holds a hand over her eyes to get a better view, while the courtesan to her left raises her sleeve to her mouth as though astonished by what she sees. Her two companions show less excitement as they stare out more stolidly, holding on to the vertical bars of the latticework for support. Four teenaged *shinzō*, huddled behind their mistresses, also attempt to have a look.

The viewer seeing the print as it is reproduced here, unfolded, may find the composition rather odd, with the women clustered together looking off to the left while the cuckoo is totally separate—and upside down—at the bottom. However, the print was designed to be folded in six parts in such a way that, when the first fold was lifted, the cuckoo would appear to the left and just beyond the group of women. The lower half of the print (with the poems) was first folded under the top so that only the picture showed; the left third of the picture was then folded under the middle third, which was folded, in turn, under the right-hand third. When the print was first distributed, therefore, all the viewer would see was this right-hand part of the picture with the artist's signature. Thus presented, the picture would appear to be nothing more than a pleasant, rather domestic, still life with a potted plant, a folded umbrella, a towel hung out to dry, and a hanging flower holder with trailing ivy.

Three of the kyōka at the bottom are signed by courtesans known to have belonged to the Daimonjiya, one of the largest brothels in the Yoshiwara, the owner of which, Kabocha no Motonari, was himself a well-known kyōka poet. The three courtesans—Hitomoto, Hitotsue, and Tagasode—are presumably the three depicted here. The poems all refer to autumn, and it seems likely that this surimono was commissioned to commemorate an autumn poetry party held at the brothel. Two of the verses are by Yomo Utagaki (Shikatsube) Magao, whose poetry appears in other works in this exhibition (e.g., Catalogue nos. II-13 and III-5).

The scene at the top of this surimono was drawn by Hokusai, who at the time was still going by the name of Sōri. The cuckoo, however, was drawn by Santō Kyōden. By the late 1790s, when this surimono was issued, Kyōden had long since given up print designing, but people still frequently asked him to dash off poems or sketches as souvenirs. The drawing of the cuckoo may have been in response to the same kind of request. Certainly it has the witty, extemporaneous quality one associates with sketches produced in that fashion.

III-10

Kitao Masanobu (1761-1816)

***Temmei shinsen gojūnin isshu: Azumaburi kyōka bunko*, "Newly Engraved in Temmei, One Poem Each by Fifty Poets: A Bookcase of Edo-style Kyōka"**

Published 1786 by Tsutaya Jūzaburō

Illustrated book; 26.5 x 18

Signature of artist (Kitao Denzō Masanobu) and engraver (Seki Jiemon) on last page

Pulverer Collection

By the eighteenth century, highly conventionalized imaginary portraits of the better-known classical poets were apt to appear in all kinds of contexts—as illustrations in scrolls or books of poetry; as decoration on objects associated with the literati; and, most widely, as part of the designs on the cards used in the game of *utagaruta*.* As a result, every literate Japanese of the period could be counted on to recognize them. Given the spirit of the age, this made it inevitable that the portraits would be parodied.

The notion of using living kyōka poets to parody these images, as is done here, seems particularly inspired. After all, almost everything kyōka poets did was some kind of takeoff of classical poetry. The names they chose for themselves mimicked the names of classical poets; the titles of their books were made to sound as much as possible like the titles of classical anthologies; and their verses were often parodies

* A popular card game based on the *Ogura hyakunin isshu* (The Ogura anthology of one poem each by one hundred poets). Each poem was divided into two parts, with one part written on one card and the other part on a second card. The object of the game was to match the cards with passages from the same poem.

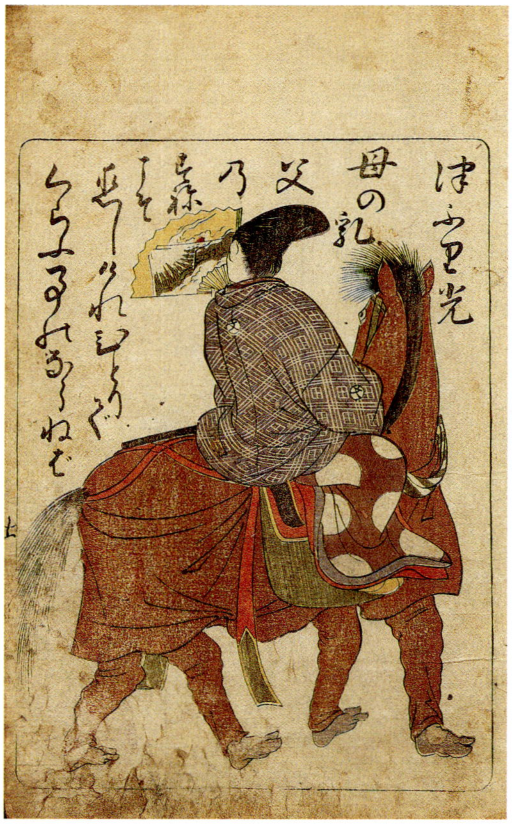

III-10

of classical poems. Yet, as far as this writer is aware, this book is the first example of the form of parody we see here.

Curiously, we cannot be sure who came up with the idea for the book. Though the poems were compiled by Yadoya no Meshimori (who wrote the preface), the project may well have been initiated by Ōta Nampo. Given his wide circle of acquaintance, Nampo was much likelier than Meshimori to have known the contributors beforehand; and it is significant that the poems are written in Nampo's hand. The artist, Kitao Masanobu (Santō Kyōden), and the publisher, Tsutaya Jūzaburō, may also have played a part in the book's conception. In the end, though, it may be best to think of the book as yet another example of the kind of collaborative creation that was so characteristic of the Floating World.

The book clearly struck a chord with the Edo public, and many later kyōka collections followed the same formula in parodying classical anthologies. Several examples are included in this exhibition (such as Catalogue nos. IV-13 and IV-14), including the sequel to this one, *Temmei shinsen hyakunin isshu: Kokon kyōka bukuro* (Catalogue no. III-11).

Some of the parodies in this pioneeering work are particularly creative. One of the more inventive is also among the most amusing. It depicts Tsuburi no Hikaru ("Shiny Head") riding on the back of a make-believe horse (actually two men in horse costumes), gazing at a fan with a drawing of Mt. Fuji. The picture is a takeoff of a famous scene from *The Tales of Ise*, in which the hero, riding on horseback, catches his first glimpse of the mountain. Some of the other "portraits" are almost as clever. Hezutsu Tōsaku, a pair of glasses dangling from one ear and a cat nestling against his chest, stares at a silken cord leading toward the opposite page, where the woman poet, Tamago no Kagume (She Who Smells Eggs), dressed in court robes, looks down at her own leashed cat. Her portrait parodies an incident in *The Tale of Genji*, in which a noblewoman running after her pet cat attracts the attention of a courtier, who promptly falls headlong in love with her.

Kagume is thought to have been a fictitious person, but most of the other poets depicted in this book were well-known kyōka poets of the day. One interesting aspect is that the book gave samurai and *chōnin* equal billing. To cite only a few examples, Tōsaku (mentioned above) was a tobacconist from Shinjuku, and the compiler, Yadoya no Meshimori, was an innkeeper, while Yomo no Akara (Nampo) was a samurai, and Shiriyaki Saruhito (Sakai Hōitsu) was the son of a minor daimyo. In his preface, Meshimori makes special mention of this feature of the anthology, which he likens to the mingling of high and low found in the pleasure quarters ("*seirō no majiwari no kisen naki ga gotoshi*").

III-11

Kitao Masanobu (1761-1816)

***Temmei shinsen hyakunin isshu: Kokon kyōka bukuro*, "Newly Engraved in Temmei, One Poem Each by One Hundred Poets: A Sackful of Kyōka, Old and New"**

Published 1787 by Tsutaya Jūzaburō

Illustrated book; 26.6 x 18

Signature of artist (gakō Kitao Denzō Masanobu) on last page

Pulverer Collection

Though the date of publication is not given in the colophon, the closing note by Hezutsu Tōsaku mentions that this book was published after *Azumaburi kyōka bunko* (Catalogue no. III-10), and, since the same team was involved in its production, it almost certainly appeared in 1787 as a follow-up to the success of the earlier work. Once again, Yadoya no Meshimori was the compiler (*sensha*), Kitao Masanobu drew the portraits, and Yomo no Akara (Nampo) provided the calligraphy. In other respects, however, this was a decidedly more ambitious undertaking—and not simply because it included twice as many poets. A somewhat bombastic preface by Akara was followed by five smaller forewords, and Tōsaku (as mentioned above) provided closing notes. Akara's preface is framed with a border of flowering cherries, and the five prefaces are accompanied by pictures depicting scenes relating to the *go sekku*, "five sacred festivals," namely, New Year's (the first day of the first month), the Peach Festival or Girls' Day (the third day of the third month), Boys' Day (the fifth day of the fifth month), the Star Festival or Tanabata (the seventh day of the seventh month), and the Chrysanthemum Festival (the ninth day of the ninth month). The authors of the prefaces were all major figures in the Edo kyōka movement: Akera Kankō (who will appear again in connection with Catalogue no. IV-14), Tegara no Okamochi, Karagoromo Kisshū, Manzōtei, and (once again) Yomo no Akara.

Though a few of the poets included were from earlier periods, thus justifying the use of the word *kokon* (old and new) in the title, most of them were contemporary, making the book a virtual Who's Who of the Temmei kyōka world. Thirty of the poets had been included in *Azumaburi kyōka bunko*, and it is interesting to see the similarities and differences in the way they are portrayed in the two publications. Baba no Kinrachi, for example, whose features were completely hidden by a snow-covered umbrella in the earlier book, is depicted here as a handsome young man playing a flute. Some of the others, however, are immediately recognizable from their earlier portraits: Hezutsu Tōsaku, with his totally bald head and glasses, is one, and the more solid, dignified figure of Akera Kankō is another. In general, the portraits in this book seem more straightforward, less whimsical, than those in the earlier one. Nothing in this book, for instance, matches the near-slapstick humor of the previous year's portrayal of Tsuburi no Hikaru mounted on a make-believe horse.

This is not to imply that humor is absent. It simply takes a milder form. Some of the portraits—those in which the sitter holds some outlandish object to his head to represent a hat, for example—were obviously intended as direct parodies of one or another of the stock portraits of famous poets of the past. The same kind of mimickry will be found in other works in the exhibition (such as Catalogue nos. IV-3 and IV-11). Other illustrations, however, poke well-intentioned fun at the poets themselves. One of these is the portrait of Tōsaku, which shows him on his knees, squinting through his glasses (which seem to have been inseparable from him) at a *tanzaku*. Another is the portrait of Yomo no Akara (Nampo) that concludes the volume. The great man, seated on the floor with fans still to be inscribed spread in front of him, has nodded off to sleep. Is the portrait a commentary on

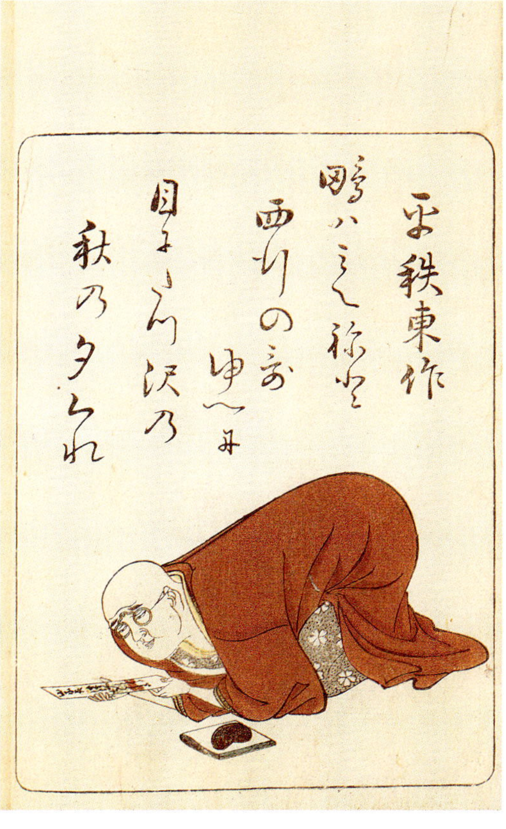

III-11

all the calligraphy he was called on to execute for this book, or did he take one sip too many from the sake cup beside him?

III-12

Santō Kyōden (1761-1816)

Ikkoku atae manryō kaishun

Published 1798 by Tsutaya Jūzaburō

Kibyōshi

Illustrations attributed to Kitao Masayoshi

Tobacco & Salt Museum

By 1798, Kyōden's interests had grown far beyond the fame and fashion days of Temmei. He was by now an established writer, artist, and businessman, and had become accustomed to mingling these interests, as this kibyōshi demonstrates. The only page of the book not sectioned into story squares shows two men displaying a list of merchandise. The text informs the reader that Kyōya Denzō's shop now carries an even larger range of goods for sale. We will not dwell on the plots of this story or the following one (Catalogue no. III-13), but offer these kibyōshi as examples of the genre.

By the mid-1790s, this type of novel was in its maturity, an established form of literary entertainment. For contemporary readers, the language of kibyōshi was easy to read. The lighthearted, sophisticated tone made for a pleasant pastime, fulfilling the Edo demand for stylish humor. Kyōden, who is reputed to have been Japan's first professional author, exercised his imagination in concocting outrageous plots and poking fun at the government. We gain a sense of the times when we realize that his humorous social commentary was quite in the mainstream.

The *bunjin* (literati) tradition in Japan assumed that a man of letters would also be adept at painting. Kyōden was unique, however, in the degree of excellence he brought to both forms of expression. The realistic details of his illustrations gave readers many clues about the characters through dress and setting, so that the texts could safely leave out a lot of description in favor of dialogue and jokes.

Kibyōshi provided an ideal format for Kyōden's considerable talent, whereas *sharebon*—an equally popular genre of *gesaku* literature—concentrated more on anecdotes and tales of the pleasure quarters.

As a designation of a literary genre, "kibyōshi" was first used in 1775, when Koikawa Harumachi wrote *Kinkin sensei eiga no yume* (The dreams of glory of Master Glitter). Books of this type had previously been called *aobon* (blue books, because of their blue covers), which told contemporary, fairly sophisticated stories. These, in turn, had evolved from the *karakami-byōshi* (Chinese paper-covered) books of the late seventeenth century, which were illustrated libretti of *jōruri* plays. The color of the covers changed to indicate the type of story the book contained, with *kurobon* (black books) and *akabon* (red books) providing folk tales, play summaries, and children's stories.

Edo was becoming the center for fictional works as the Kamigata area (Kyoto) declined in vigor. The new literary works were increasingly set in contemporary times and involved political or social topics. Takizawa Bakin, the popular author of the early nineteenth century who was at one time Kyōden's pupil, remarked that kibyōshi were "published in sets of two or three volumes in the new year season, and always sold ten thousand copies per set, while some made a

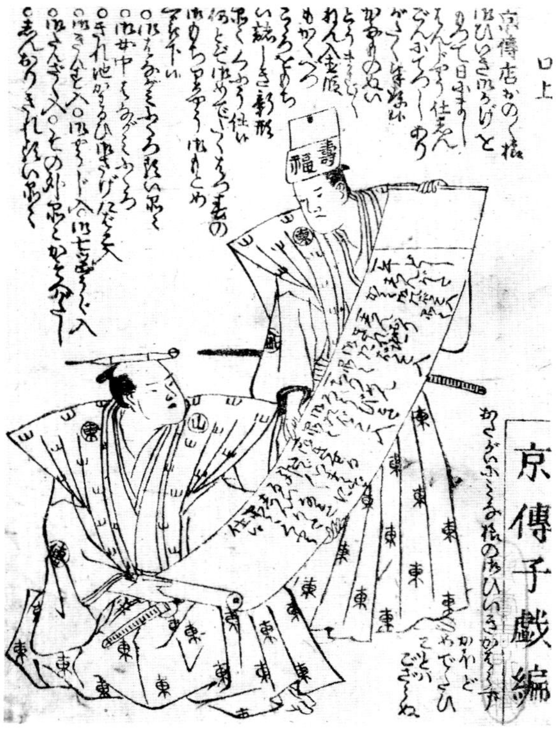

III-12

hit and sold twelve or thirteen thousand. Especially popular ones were sold in separate bags in three or four thousand additional copies." Topical and all the rage, they reflected and gave form to the values of the Floating World. More than two thousand titles were published.

Most importantly, though, kibyōshi entertained. Their language was funny, not preachy. The stories made clever use of puns, allegory, and *mitate*, as elaborate and extended as the author could achieve. At this, Kyōden was unexcelled. He devised entire plots that held together with multiple layers of meaning, challenging readers' awareness of current events and rewarding them with new twists and parodies.

III-13

Santō Kyōden (1761-1816)

Mikenjaku sannin nama'ei

Published 1794 by Tsuruya Kiemon

Kibyōshi

Tobacco & Salt Museum

Having just opened his tobacco shop in the fall of 1793, Santō Kyōden used all his kibyōshi of the following year to publicize his new business. The *Mikenjaku sannin nama'ei*, with its curious cover encircled in roman letters, gives us an example of the way he incorporated advertisements in his fabulously complex stories:

> Let me tell you a little about this place. Santō Kyōden has opened a new store that sells a new type of paper tobacco pouch, which is used the same as a fabric tobacco pouch, and hereby humbly seeks your patronage and honored esteem.
>
> Kyōbashi Ginza Chō
> Kyōya Denzō

Also of special interest in this kibyōshi (which was probably illustrated by Kitao Masayoshi) is the last page: here are eight crests, which are equivalent to name tags and are printed on a variety of textiles (kimono, wrapping cloths, towels, banners) even to this day. Kyōden uses them as a device for carrying layers of meaning: puns on family names, cross-identifications, character associations.

Moreover, Kyōden was a master at creating new crests, and for about ten years (1788-98) kept readers enthralled with innovative patterns.

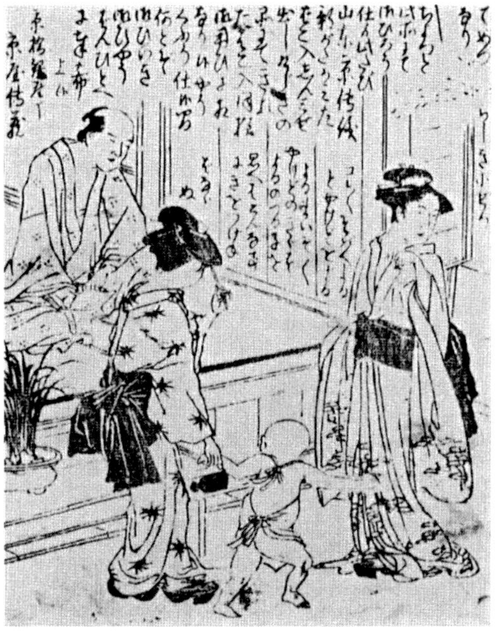

III-13

These often represented entirely new ways of looking at objects, through the use of closeups, unexpected angles, and other techniques of graphic design. His perceptions may have been influenced by the microscopes that had been introduced by the Dutch. Haruko Iwasaki has found that the first Japanese to own a microscope was the writer Hiraga Gennai, who was the teacher of Kyōden's literary patron, Shinra Banshō.* Access to a microscope would have magnified Kyōden's already pronounced penchant for detail, and provided him with a new source for patterns and shapes.

* Haruko Iwasaki, "The World of *Gesaku*" (Ph.D. diss., Harvard University, 1984), 302-7.

III-14

Santō Kyōden (1761-1816)

Kijimo nakazu-wa

Published 1789 by Tsutaya Jūzaburō

Kibyōshi; 17 x 12.7

Illustrations attributed to Kitao Masayoshi

East Asian Library, University of California at Berkeley

Kyōden tells the story of Tsuchiyama Sōjiro, the only man put to death under the Neoconfucianist administration of Sadanobu Matsudaira, and the courtesan Tagasode (Whose Sleeves?), whom he ransomed out of her contract to the Daimonjiya, and with whom he fled Edo when the new administration under Sadanobu sought his arrest for financial mishandling of the rice trade.

During the administration of Okitsugu Tanuma, Tsuchiyama was a high-ranking accountant in the financial ministry, which oversaw the development of pleasure quarters on reclaimed land (namely, Nakasu) and the development of the Hokaido frontier. Tsuchiyama pursued literary interests in the pleasure quarter and may have used his contacts there to help entertain and lure investments from wealthy merchants. Sadanobu perhaps singled him out as a symbol of Temmei corruption and excess.

For Kyōden to have told the story outright would not only have transgressed the edicts against portraying contemporary figures and events in literature, but would have been too obvious for his readers, who preferred camouflaged meanings and humorous resonances.

The Tsuchiyama story, therefore, is veiled in subplots. Kyōden likened it to the Chikamatsu play *Meido no hikyaku* (Messenger from hell), and on the surface seems to retell that story in *Kijimo nakazu-wa*. In the play, Chūbei, a messenger for a loan agency, loves Umegawa, a courtesan at a teahouse. Chūbei's rival, Hachiemon, has threatened to buy out Umegawa's contract, whereupon Chūbei feels honor-bound to embezzle money from his employer in order

III-14

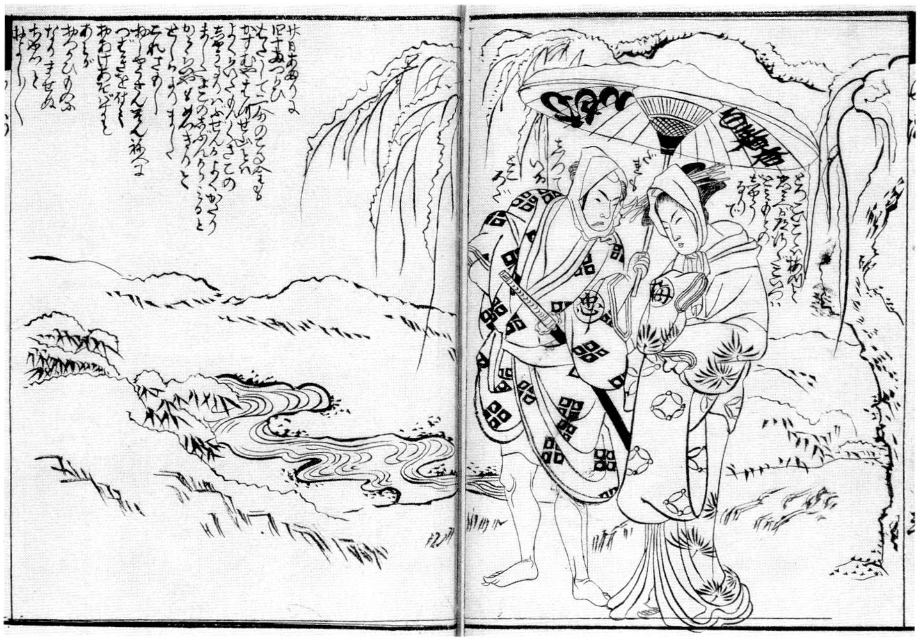

to pay the ransom himself. Hachiemon discovers the crime, which forces the couple to flee and ultimately to commit double suicide. In real life, Tsuchiyama and Tagasode left Edo together to escape the authorities. The subtlety to which readers were accustomed is evident in the minute clues: Kyōden must have intended people to make the connection between the name of Umegawa's master, Tsuchiya, and the real-life Tsuchiyama.

Two other characters in the novel are the famous Yoshiwara courtesan of the Miura-ya, Takao, and the kabuki actor Ogino Yaegiri, both of whom perished at Mitsumata (Three Forks), the site of the landfill named Nakasu. The story is set in 1787, when a fire in the Yoshiwara forced its evacuation to temporary quarters on Nakasu, for thirty years a haven for pleasure seekers.

Because this is a kibyōshi, the story is revealed as much by the pictures as by the words. The story opens with a picture of Chūbei and Umegawa behind a screen. The text, meanwhile, is a dialogue between two female readers who are trying to identify the figures in the pictures by their various insignia, and who are giving background information on the characters. A *mitate* is devised, with Chūbei wearing a kimono with the pattern worn by Matsumoto Kōshiro IV, a Kyoto-born kabuki actor, and Umegawa wearing the chrysanthemum pattern of Segawa Kikunojō III, an actor who impersonated women. They performed the roles of Chūbei and Umegawa onstage.

Each double page overflows with puns and jokes. In brief, the story carries the reader to the King of the Underworld, who has taken the deceased Takao as his concubine. However, she and the dead Yaegiri have become a couple, and decide to run away from hell. Returning to Nakasu as ghosts, they make a livelihood as a teahouse owner (Takao) and a male geisha (Yaegiri). Outside her teahouse, Takao meets Chūbei, while Yaegiri comes to know Umegawa at the pleasure house where she is working under the new name of Hanasode. Hachiemon, standing outside Takao's teahouse, thinks he hears the voices of Chūbei and Umegawa, and orders his henchman to drag them out and tie them up. Instead, the two are Takao and Yaegiri, who are accused of having stolen the ransom money and given the death sentence. The mistaken identity is discovered, Hachiemon's villainy is exposed, Umegawa and Chūbei, filling in for the two spirits who found it timely to depart from the world of the living, are questioned, but pardoned. Full of glee, they open a restaurant at Ryōgoku Yanagibashi and live happily ever after.

Along the way, the reader is challenged to guess the identity of a man on horseback who doesn't reveal his face, and is led to suppose that this was the real Tsuchiyama. Later, the real-life face of Ichikawa Danjūrō V appears in the guise of a shaman, hinting at a play about Takao in which Danjūrō performed in 1782 at the Nakamura-za. The playwright Sakura Naobe had consulted with Kyōden about the play, since Kyōden was himself fascinated by Takao's story and spent much time investigating the real circumstances of her death. In the Nakamura-za performance, Takao's ghost was played by Kikunojō.

The title of this novel is taken from a popular proverb, "*kijimo nakazuba utaremai*" (the pheasant who doesn't cry out doesn't get shot). By using different *kanji*, Kyōden forms a pun that means "The strange tales of Nakasu."

III-15
Tobacco pipes (*kiseru*)
Edo Period
Tobacco & Salt Museum

The first records of tobacco cultivation in Japan are dated 1605, and the first mention of *kiseru* appears two years later in the *Chronicle of Words and Actions between Lord and Vassal* (Kunshin genkō roku), in which the act of smoking is noted as being useless and forbidden. Tobacco was subject to further bans, yet was nevertheless enjoyed by many, regardless of class or gender, as a medicinal herb. Introduced by the Portuguese through the port city of Nagasaki, it travelled swifty to Kyoto, where it became the rage. No pipes from that time have been identified, though it is known that they were portable and carried about outside, for in 1610 the pipes were banned after incidents in Kyoto when they had reportedly been used as weapons in street fights.

The popularity of smoking and the pipes involved was irrepressible, and the activity became extremely fashionable. It was an affordable luxury, within reach of commoners. The pipes used initially were made from silver and copper, though by 1615 bamboo had come into use as the elongated pipestem joining a metal mouthpiece and bowl. Reflecting myriad styles, price ranges, and preferences, the pipe, more than any other utensil in daily use, displayed great diversity of shape and decoration. Perhaps because of the private pleasure derived from the activity of smoking, the objects associated with it are extremely individualized.

Kiseru were naturally embraced by the upsurge in production of finely crafted, highly decorated articles during the Temmei Period (1781-88), and became the chief item through which people projected their tastes and personalities. In the Yoshiwara, a man's *kiseru* indicated what kind of customer he would be, and determined the treatment he would receive. "Replacing the bamboo pipestem" became synonymous with parsimony, and anyone daring to exhibit such a pipe (or such an attitude) would be subject to aspersion.

As the Kansei Reforms (1789) evolved, *kiseru* were again the subject of sumptuary repression. As in the past, the effort was not altogether successful. Smoking had become a common pastime, and the social implications of smoking paraphernalia were not easily dispelled.

Nevertheless, tastes and attitudes changed. Where the image-conscious *tsū* sophisticate characterized the Temmei Period, the more internalized attitude of *iki* became prevalent during the Kansei Period (1789-1801). One attribute of *tsū* had been to show one's status and glamour materially, but the refinement of *iki* found greater satisfaction in an attitude of proud self-worth and in keeping one's elegant tastes under wraps, offering only glimpses of them. *Kiseru*, as symbols of pleasure and luxury, reflected whatever fashion dictated and, through a variety of forms and decorations, projected the images their bearers demanded.

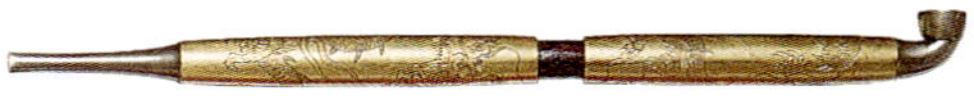

III-15 (a)

27.3

Late Edo. Silver "snow-viewing" style, *hotei* bamboo stem.*

* The *hotei* style is representative of Kansei-period pipestems.

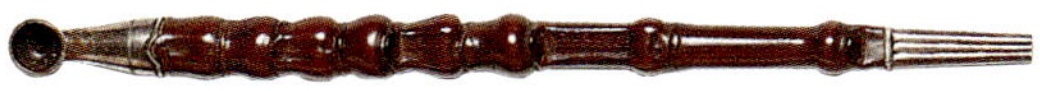

III-15(b)

25.7

Silver-plated; silver bowl and tip. Nagoya style (popular among courtesans), with finely engraved twin-dragon design. Wood stem.

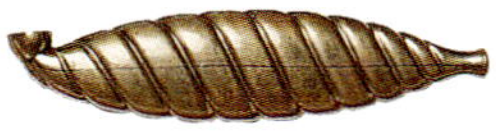

III-15(c)

12.6

Gold-plated copper, horse-bridle style.

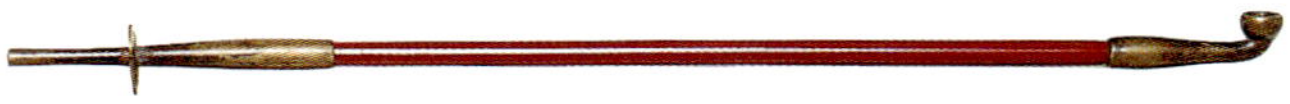

III-15(d)

31.8

Brass, narcissus style, with flange at mouthpiece. Red-lacquer pipestem. The mouthpiece is engraved "Sumiyoshi," the name of the craftsman.

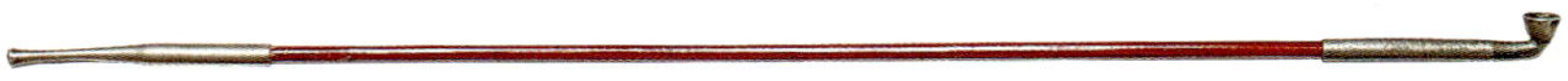

III-15(e)

41.7

Early Edo. Red-lacquer pipestem, brass bowl and mouthpiece.

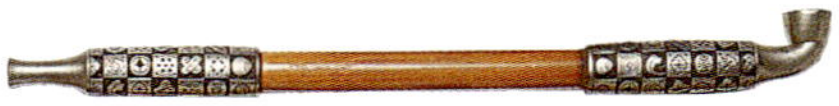

III-15(f)

23.5

Silver Tamagawa style, with finely engraved symbols of health, comfort, and prosperity in a checkered pattern.

III-16
Tobacco pouches (*tabako-ire*)

Tobacco & Salt Museum

More than just cases for carrying loose tobacco, *tabako-ire* were carefully selected accessories, personal statements of style in an age when rules dictated almost every aspect of life. In these pouches, form and decoration were every bit as important as function.

Not that *tabako-ire* were exempt from the sumptuary laws of the shogun's government. For instance, the use of gold or silver clasps was occasionally forbidden as being too luxurious. However, these restraints only encouraged people to resort to clever ploys: they took to wearing their fancy objects on the inside, exposing only the plainest of materials and surfaces to public scrutiny. This particular trait was favored by the people of Edo, who relished private extravagance.

During the Meiji Period (1868-1912), when the shogun's restrictions were lifted, *tabako-ire* became even more widespread as expressions of individual liberty. Moreover, because the samurai class was disbanded with the Meiji Reforms, the artisans who had produced their swords and the embellishments for arms found themselves out of work, and turned their skills to creating such accessories as *tabako-ire*, with their netsuke toggle beads and ornate buckles. It was the refined eye of the late-eighteenth-century Edo resident, though, that really got the trend moving. Exquisite materials such as imported leathers and printed fabrics were combined with exotic beads and fine carvings to create objects of individual charm and craftsmanship.

One of the elements of a *tabako-ire* was the pouch itself, in which the tobacco was carried. A flap kept the contents secure inside, and a clasp or buckle on the outside was linked to another piece of hardware inside to keep the pouch closed. It usually dangled from a cord or chain suspended from a netsuke, which the wearer attached to the cord beneath his or her obi. A case for the pipe was also strung onto the cord, and a drawstring *ojime* bead held the elements in place.

Women's *tabako-ire* were often tucked inside the folds of the kimono rather than dangled from the waist. These were called *kaichū* (pocket) pouches, and were typically made out of fabric. The rectangular Rikyū style was considered particularly refined, being the essence of simplicity favored by the sixteenth-century tea master Sen Rikyū.

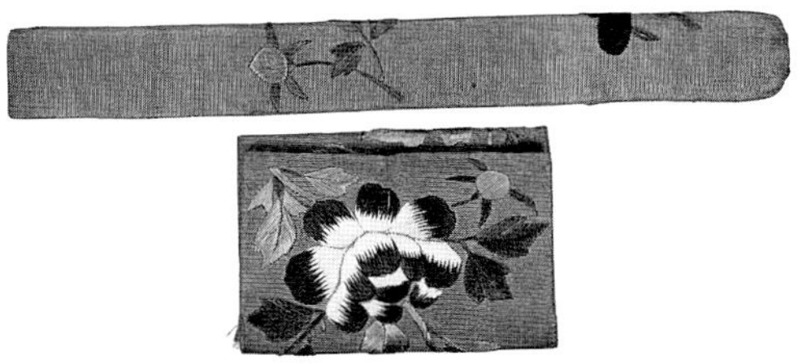

III-16(a)
Pouch; 7.3 (h) x 10.3 (w)

Embroidered silk pocket-style (*kaichū*) *tabako-ire* for women. Rikyū style with tortoiseshell clasp. A peony pattern is embroidered onto red woven silk for both the tobacco pouch and pipe holder.

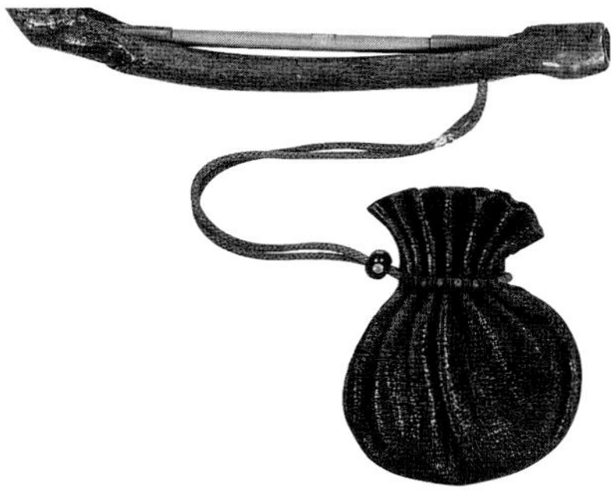

III-16 (b)
Pouch; 11.6 (h) x 9 (w)

Crinkled leather, pleated pouch with wooden pipe case on which a Chinese poem is carved. This style of *tabako-ire* (*dōsashi*) was hung from the belt by the pipe case instead of by a netsuke. An imported glass bead resembling a dragonfly's eye keeps the pouch closed.

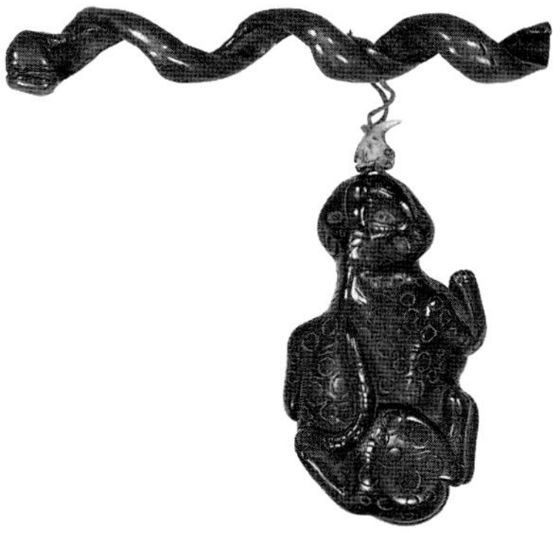

III-16 (c)
Pouch; 8.5 (h) x 15 (w)

Carved wood, lidded box in the shape of a tiger is suspended by a cord from the wooden pipe holder in the shape of a snake. The pipe holder would be hung from the belt (*dōsashi*).

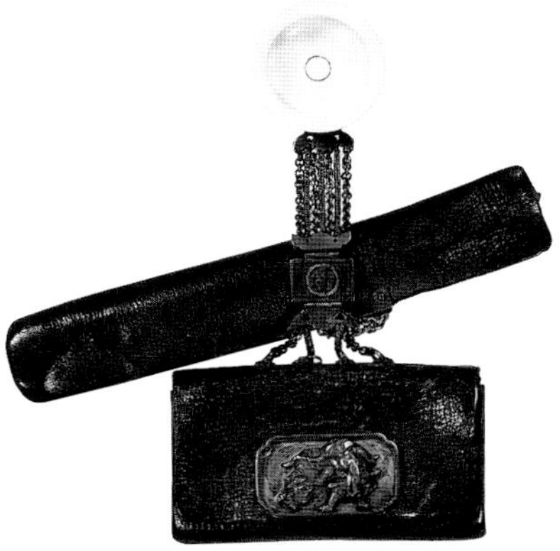

III-16 (d)
Pouch; 8 (h) x 14.3 (w)

Black chamois-leather pouch with carrying case for *kiseru*. Silver buckle engraved with scene of tiger hunt by Katō Kiyomasa. Besides anchoring the *tabako-ire* to the belt, the ivory netsuke served as a portable ashtray, holding the red-hot spent tobacco to light the next bowlful. Chains and clasp are silver.

Catalogue Section IV: Ōta Nampo

Ōta Nampo (b. 1749) was the son of an impoverished samurai family living in Ushigome, in the Yamanote district. His father was an *okachi*, a low-ranking guard whose primary duty was to be part of the retinue accompanying the shogun on special outings and hawking parties. Like others of his rank, he received a stipend that was barely sufficient to make ends meet.

Nampo's scholarly inclinations seem to have been apparent quite early, and were encouraged by his mother. We do not know where he first went to school, but, given the pronounced Confucian emphasis in education at the time, we may be certain that he received a thorough grounding in Chinese and the Chinese classics. His first recorded teacher was the *waka* poet Uchiyama Gatei (1723-1788), with whom he began studying in 1763, when he was fourteen. He seems to have found the atmosphere at Gatei's quite congenial and he quickly made friends with some of the brightest and most unconventional of his fellow students. One of these new friends, Hezutsu Tōsaku, though a *chōnin* and twenty-three years Nampo's senior, was destined to play an important role in Nampo's subsequent literary and intellectual development. It was through Tōsaku that Nampo met Suharaya Ichibei, whose publication of Nampo's *Neboke sensei bunshū* in 1767 gave the young author his first taste of literary success. Tōsaku also seems to have been responsible for introducing Nampo to the ill-fated Hiraga Gennai, whose brilliance as a *gesaku* writer, combined with his extraordinary knowledge of western science, had begun to attract the attention of some of Edo's brightest young intellectuals.

Already one of Nampo's most consistent personality traits had become evident—his ability to make friends with all kinds of people. He seems to have had an open, engaging manner that, combined with his ready sense of humor, made it easy for him to move in the most widely divergent circles.

Nampo's first book, *Minshi Tekizai*, published in 1766, was a dictionary of terms used in Ming Dynasty poetry. Though not a particularly original work, it was still an impressive accomplishment for a man only eighteen years old. Nampo's second book, published a year later, revealed his true literary gifts and set the stage for his subsequent career as a writer. Written in a kind of mock learned Chinese that allowed him to apply his enormous erudition to humorous rather than scholarly ends, the book, *Neboke sensei bunshū* (The collected writings of Master Sleepyhead), became something of an overnight bestseller. Nampo followed up on this success two years later (1769) with another book written in mock Chinese.

Meanwhile, he had begun taking part in some of the first *kyōka* parties held in Edo. Traditionally, kyōka had been thought of as an amusing form of verse to be tossed off on the spur of the moment, in the manner of a bon mot or a throw-away witticism. The notion of getting together to compose kyōka on a set theme, along the lines of a traditional poetry competition, would have been considered contrary to the very nature of the genre. At the start, Nampo seems to have shared this attitude. Nonetheless, he began attending some of the parties, and within a year or so became one of their most active participants. As interest in kyōka grew over the next few years, he became even more active, and before long his kyōka name, Yomo no Akara (taken from a widely used brand of miso, Yomo no Aka) had become firmly identified with the increasingly popular form.

Though Nampo had achieved his first literary success writing in Chinese, he soon proved himself equally gifted in writing in Japanese. In 1775 he turned his hand to the relatively new but already popular *sharebon* genre, which focused on the life and manners of the pleasure quarters. Since they were written almost entirely in dialogue, to be successful in sharebon required not only an intimate knowledge of the customs and usages of the pleasure quarters but a familiarity with the latest "in" language and a sensitive ear for conversational nuances. Most sharebon followed a fairly set formula revolving around the contrasted fortunes of the true sophisticate (*tsū*) and those who merely aspired to sophistication (*hankatsū*). Nampo's contributions (he wrote six of these witty novelettes in the course of four years) broke new ground by extending the limits of the standard formula in several crucial ways.

Nampo soon turned his attention to a yet newer genre of gesaku, the *kibyōshi*. In 1782, three years after completing his last sharebon, he published a kibyōshi critique, and soon began to write kibyōshi of his own. None of these were as successful as his other writings, however, probably because they failed to provide sufficient action for the illustrations that were such an essential element in the genre. But kibyōshi were hardly Nampo's only literary interest at the time.

If any one person may be thought of as being at the center of the kyōka movement during the Temmei Period, it was Ōta Nampo—or, as he should more appropriately be called in the context—Yomo no Akara. If there had been any doubts about his occupying this position, those doubts would have been dispelled with the publication of the kyōka anthology *Manzai kyōka shū* in Temmei 3 (1783). This innovative publication was more ambitious by far than any previous collection of kyōka; Nampo was its editor and clearly the guiding spirit behind it. The title, "A Collection of Kyōka of Ten Thousand Generations," parodied the title of the twelfth-century Imperial anthology, *Senzai waka shū*, "A Collection of Waka of One Thousand Generations," and the work mimicked the Imperial anthology in other respects—for instance, in the number and arrangement of categories into which it was divided.

Manzai kyōka shū was an instant success. Its popularity, which no one seems to have anticipated, must have opened publishers' eyes to the sales possibilities for this relatively new genre. The next year saw a marked increase in the number of anthologies published, and such books soon became a staple of the bookseller's trade (a status they would retain through the first few decades of the nineteenth century). One of the first publishers to take advantage of this new market was the always-enterprising Tsutaya Jūzaburō (Tsutajū). Some of the most popular—as well as some of the most sumptuous—anthologies brought out over the next few years bore his imprint.

At first, even Nampo himself maintained that it was inappropriate to be too earnest about kyōka, that it was a kind of verse meant to be composed on the spot, in a spirit of fun—the same spirit in which, today, one might come up with a spontaneous joke or bon mot. From that point of view, the idea of publishing a kyōka anthology must have seemed antithetical to the nature of the form.

In the years that followed, kyōka anthologies and illustrated kyōka albums began to be published in greater numbers. Most kyōka, however, continued to be composed at parties or special contests, and no one could organize such events better than Nampo. Indeed, his enormous influence in kyōka circles probably owed as much to his talent in this direction as to his undoubted brilliance as a poet.

Nampo's wit and companionability made him a sought-after guest at parties. He attracted friends readily and, despite the rigid class distinctions of the time, moved with relative ease among people of the most diverse backgrounds. By the early 1780s he was even associating with high-ranking government officials.

His relationship with one such person, Tsuchiyama Sōjiro, a highly placed bureaucrat in the Finance Department, would ultimately prove to be a source of embarrassment to him. Tsuchiyama seems to have profited greatly at the public's expense during the Tanuma years and was one of a number of corrupt officials to come under investigation at the start of the Kansei Reforms. Most of the offenders were merely dismissed; Tsuchiyama, however, was executed.

Tsuchiyama's fate seems to have cut too close to home for Nampo's comfort, and in 1787, even before most of the Kansei Reforms were enacted, he abruptly gave up writing kyōka and took steps to disassociate himself, at least publicly, from the gesaku community. For the next few years he busied himself with activities, such as translating from Chinese, considered more appropriate for a samurai, and in the 1790s began studying for the newly instituted civil service examinations. These he passed with honors in 1794, winning a cash award in the process. For the next decade he worked as a civil servant, chiefly in Edo but also for short periods in Osaka and Nagasaki.

During these later years Nampo continued to write, though now under a new name—Shokusanjin—and more for himself and his friends than for publication. Meanwhile, his large circle of friends grew even larger as as a result of his trips to Osaka and Nagasaki. Judging from the many inscriptions he left on paintings, his period of closest association with ukiyo-e artists also seems to date from these later years. This is not to say that he had hitherto ignored ukiyo-e. He is thought by many Japanese scholars to be the anonymous author of the first historical listing of ukiyo-e artists, *ukiyo-e ruikō*, the earliest version of which may go back as far as 1790.

Nampo's stature as a writer is hard to assess, in great measure because of the extraordinary variety and sheer volume of his oeuvre. He was astonishingly prolific, and not only in the gesaku genres already mentioned. Indeed, quantitatively the largest part of his oeuvre is probably made up of *zuihitsu*, a hybrid genre with no precise western equivalent, part diary and part miscellaneous jottings, some of which may even include extracts from the writings of others. His work does not translate well, either, perhaps because so much of its quality resides in the author's verbal dexterity and wit—precisely those qualities that are hardest to render in another language.

IV-1

Chōbunsai Eishi (1756-1829)

Portrait of Shokusanjin (Ōta Nampo)

1814

Hanging scroll; ink and colors on silk; 87.5 x 27.3

Signature (Chōbunsai Eishi hitsu) and seal (Eishi) of artist above image at right

Tokyo National Museum

We do not know when Eishi and Ōta Nampo first met, but by the time this portrait was painted in 1814 the two men had long since become fast friends. Many of Eishi's surviving paintings have inscriptions by Nampo, and entries in Nampo's diaries indicate that he wrote inscriptions on other paintings that have been lost. As far as we know, however, Eishi was not active in the literary scene of Temmei and early Kansei, and there is no evidence that the two men knew one another before the early 1800s.

This is one of the few known portraits of Nampo. It is also without doubt the best. A picture in the Tokyo National Museum portraying him at about the same age in a book of hand-painted portraits, attributed to Tani Bunchō (1763-1840), captures some of his personality.* However, pictures of him in both *Temmei shinsen gojūnin isshu: Azumaburi kyōka bunko* and *Temmei shinsen hyakunin isshu: Kokon kyōka bukuro* (Catalogue nos. III-10 and III-11) were intended to be parodies of stock images of classical poets, so they are not as revealing as one might wish.

Here Eishi has caught his friend at a characteristic moment, pausing to take a sip of sake as he prepares to inscribe a poem or epigram on one of the fans lying in front of him. His inkstone is in readiness on the floor beside him, and brushes of different sizes lean against a brush rest within easy reach. The poet looks leaner than he appeared in his Temmei portraits, there are deep lines on his brow, and his back is hunched; but he seems to have lost none of the wit and geniality for which he was famous earlier. There is no mistaking the intelligent glint in his eyes.

The portrait occupies only the lower third of the scroll, leaving room at the top for Nampo's inscription. Nampo was sixty-six at the time, so the inscription, as one might expect, is retrospective in mood. It reads: *Temmei no Yomo Akara, Bunka no Shokusanjin. Kagami ni mishirikoshi naru kono shimpu o me ni kakaru mo hisashiburi nari. Toshi mo haya sute ni, Nihon no kuni no kazoena o bankoku no su o ya hirakamu* (In Temmei, Yomo no Akara; in Bunka, Shokusanjin. It has been some time already since I have seen this old man when I look in the mirror. How fast the years have gone! My life spreads out in front of me with as many years as there are provinces in the map of Japan). The number of provinces in Japan was traditionally counted as "sixty-some," so the comparison is apt, all the more so given Nampo's extensive travels, which took him all the way to Nagasaki.

* Reproduced in *Nikuhitsu Ukiyoe*, vol. 6, *Utamaro*, ed. Narasaki Muneshige (Tokyo: Shūeisha, 1981).

IV-2

Chōbunsai Eishi (1756-1829)

Snow, Moon, and Flowers

Circa 1805

Triptych of hanging scrolls; ink and colors on silk; 82.4 x 30.2 (each)

Signature (Chōbunsai Eishi hitsu) and seal (Eishi) of artist on each scroll

The Mary and Jackson Burke Collection

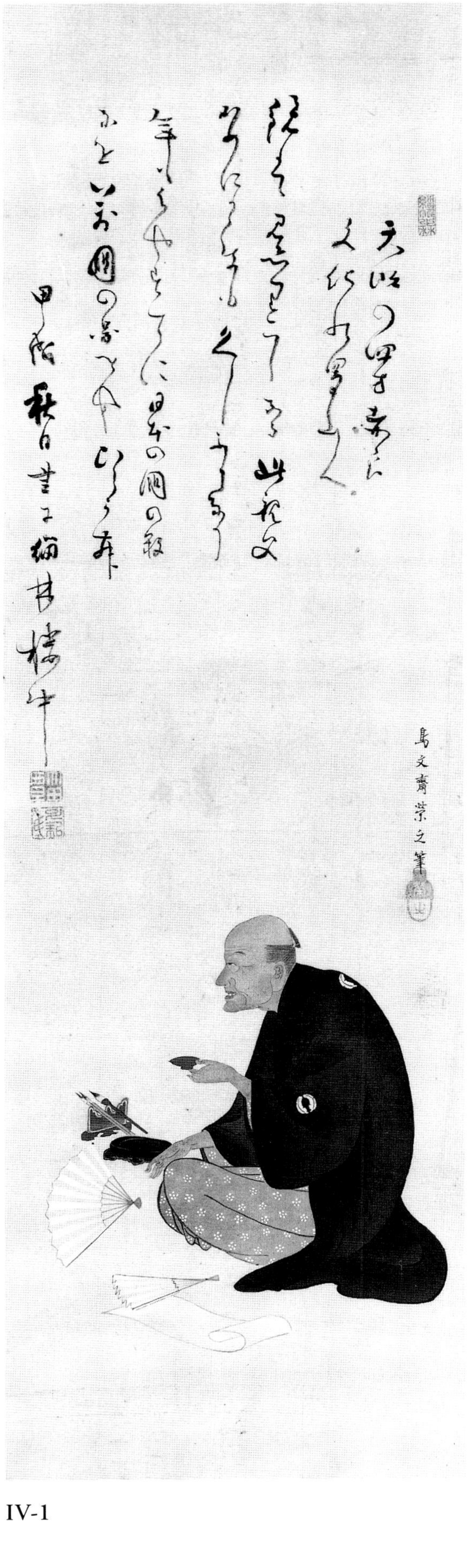

IV-1

Snow, the moon, and flowers—i.e, the snow of winter, the moon of autumn, and the flowers of spring—were each considered one of the most beautiful sights of their respective seasons. Grouped together, they became one of the standard subjects of classical painting. Here, in typical ukiyo-e fashion, this traditional subject matter has been deftly joined to scenes in or related to the Yoshiwara. On each painting, poems by Shokusanjin (Ōta Nampo) make additional references to the famous pleasure quarters. The subdued palette and summary treatment of detail is reminiscent of Eishi's treatment of the same or similar scenes in his *Journey to the Yoshiwara* of 1801 (Catalogue no. I-3), and it seems likely that the two works are relatively close in date.

The central scroll depicts a courtesan strolling past one of the flowering cherry trees that were planted along the Nakanochō during the blossom-viewing season. The seeming stoutness of the courtesan's figure, an illusion created by her many layers of kimono, contrasts oddly with the daintiness of her head and the exaggerated elegance of her butterfly hairdo. A similar effect may be seen in another courtesan in this exhibition painted by Eishi, *Courtesan with Two Attendants under a Flowering Cherry Tree* (Catalogue no. II-6), belonging to the University of Michigan Museum of Art. In other respects, however, the two works could hardly be more different. In the Michigan painting, the courtesan's flamboyant *uchikake* is richly colored, and her two attendants add a lighthearted, festive air to the composition. Here, the courtesan strolls alone, absorbed in her own thoughts, and the palette is more subdued. Her red obi and the gold carp deftly painted on her black *uchikake* speak more of restraint than of ostentation.

The verse at the top of the scroll, written in Shokusanjin's characteristic and somewhat ungainly hand, reads: *Nakanochō / uetaru hana no / katawara ni / fukayamagi nado / ippon mo nashi* (Beside the flowering cherry blossoms of the Nakanochō, not a single tree from the deep mountain valleys).

The right-hand scroll shows two boats moored side by side at the foot of a snow-covered dike near the Mimeguri Shrine. A path climbs up the dike toward the shrine, whose torii can just be made out between two trees on the other side. Beyond the dike, paddy fields stretch off into the distance. At the top of the scroll, Shokusanjin has written: *Yuki no Yoshiwara / tōki chikakute / omokereba / kasagi urumi no / Mimeguri (no) kado* (Heavy snow is piled on the lintel of the gate to Mimeguri Shrine. Yoshiwara is actually near, but it seems very far in this snow).

The left-hand scroll depicts a boat going upstream (toward the Yoshiwara) past the *Shubi no matsu*, "Pine of Fate." The tree's branches, supported by posts, extend out over the water. There is no sign of the rice warehouse that, in reality, would have been just behind the tree. A flight of geese descends toward the river as a full moon rises above banks of mist on the other side. Only one other boat is visible, and the two small figures walking along the far shore add to the sense of stillness permeating the scene. The poem reads: *Yūshio no / Tsuki no katsura no / kaji sashite / sate yoi shubi no / matsu o miru kana* (On the evening tide, rowing a boat with oars of the katsura growing on the moon, now

IV-2

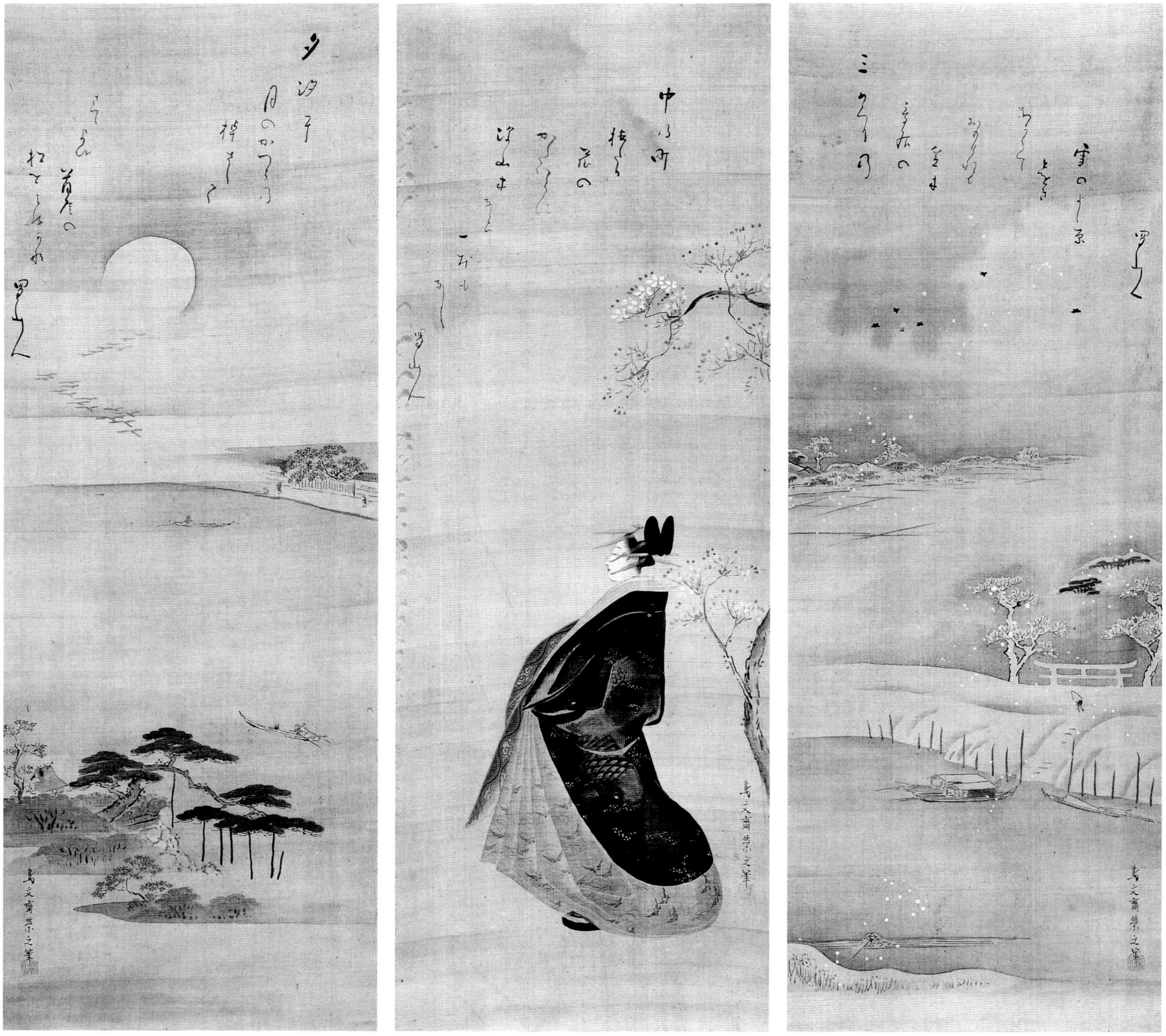

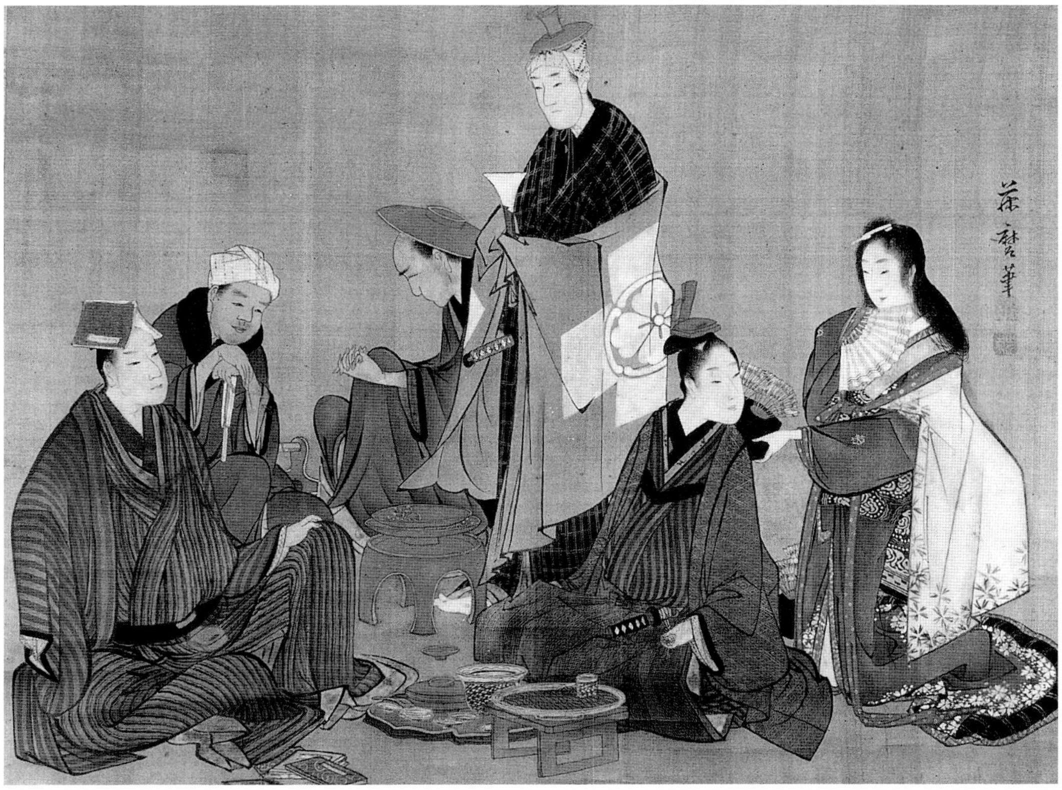

IV-3

I look at the Pine of Fate, wishing for luck).*

* The translations of Shokusanjin's poems, as well as other pertinent information, are taken from Miyeko Murase, *Japanese Art, Selections from the Mary and Jackson Burke Collection* (New York: The Metropolitan Museum of Art, 1975), 300-03.

IV-3

Kitagawa Fujimaro (active 1800-1820)

Kyōka Poets Mimicking the Six Immortals of Poetry

Circa 1800

Hanging scroll; ink and colors on silk; 40.7 x 51.5

Signature of artist (Fujimaro hitsu) and seals (Hōshū [top] and unread [bottom])

Tobacco & Salt Museum

Five men and a woman are shown at a party where they are playing a game similar to charades, in which they mimic the *rokkasen* (six immortals of poetry). A *zen* (small dining table), a serving tray laden with dishes, and a sake cup on the floor in front of the group suggest that the party has been in progress for some time.

By the Edo Period, anthologies of classsical poetry with stylized portraits of the poets represented had become an established literary-artistic genre. In the portraits, particular costumes, hairstyles, and badges of office or personal accoutrements were associated with each poet. Thus Ariwara no Narihira was almost invariably shown with a bow and quiver and wearing a military headdress known as an *oikake*, while Ono no Komachi was portrayed with a fan and the long, flowing hair of a Heian-period court lady. Such conventions made it relatively easy to play a game like the one pictured here. The challenge lay in thinking of the necessary accoutrements.

In this case, the players have shown themselves to be quite ingenious. The woman at right, portraying Ono no Komachi, holds a box of partially opened fans behind the shoulders of the man beside her in a way that suggests Narihira's quiver and arrows, and the man completes the pantomime by using a tobacco pouch to represent the poet's *oikake.* The standing figure beside him has placed an inverted lacquer cup stand on top of his head to suggest the tall, formal headgear worn by court nobles, and holds a *shamisen* plectrum in front of him like a *shaku*, the scepter carried by court officials of high rank. The player seated to his right uses a large inverted sake cup as though it were a brimmed hat; the next man rests his hands on top of a folded fan, which probably represents a staff; and the man at left has laid an open book on his head to indicate yet another kind of headgear. In every case the players have used articles that lay readily at hand to suggest the attributes associated with the poets they were mimicking. The six poets represented here are, from right to left, Ono no Komachi, Ariwara no Narihira, Bunya Yasuhide, Sōjo (Bishop) Henjō, Priest Kisen, and Ōtomo no Kuronushi.

One of the most remarkable features of this painting is the way in which each participant emerges as a distinct individual with sharply differentiated characteristics. Each looks like a real person, unlike the stylized representations typical of traditional depictions of the *rokkasen*, which, as we have said, relied on external symbols to distinguish one poet from another. This tends to support the possibility that the painting portrays an actual party. Kyōka poets almost certainly held parties of this sort. A scene in a kibyōshi by Koikawa Harumachi (1744-1789), *Yoshiwara Daitsū-e*, depicts a gathering in which the participants mimic twelve classical poets. Though the scene is part of a work of fiction and supposedly imaginary, most of the participants are named; among them are Ōta Nampo, Tsutaya Jūzaburō, and the owner of the Daimonjiya brothel, Kabocha no Motonari.

It should be remembered that even the *kyōmei*, the noms de plume under which kyōka poets wrote, were often humorous parodies of the names of well-known classical poets of the past; the same spirit of parody pervaded contemporary anthologies of kyōka verse, such as Masanobu's *Kokon kyōka bukuro* (Catalogue no. III-11), which was a direct spoof of the *Ogura hyakuni isshu*. Prints with *mitate-e* of the *rokkasen*—many of them with inscribed kyōka—were also quite popular during the last decade of the eighteenth century (e.g., Catalogue nos. IV-9 and IV-11). The close connection of this subject with kyōka is beyond dispute.

Virtually nothing is known about Kitagawa Fujimaro beyond what can be deduced from his work. That he was a pupil of Utamaro is obvious from his name, and is supported by the fact that many of his paintings are clearly influenced, both in style and subject matter, by the earlier master. The known dates of his activity—the paintings dated by inscription all fall between 1813 and 1820, but he almost certainly began working as early as 1800—also fit with such a master-pupil relationship. Unlike Utamaro, however, Fujimaro concentrated on painting and, as far as is known, never designed a single print.

Fujimaro seemed to have a penchant for subject matter with literary associations. This cataloguer has found nearly thirty works by Fujimaro in European, American, and Japanese collections, four of which are inscribed with kyōka. Two of the inscriptions are by the same poet, Sensōan, which suggests that he and Fujimaro may have been friends. Sensōan (1755-1820), also known as Hajintei Ichindō, was the head of the Tsubokawa *ren* (poetry club) and a leading figure in the Edo kyōka world of the first two decades of the nineteenth century. His kyōka appear on surimono designed by Hokusai, Toyokuni I, and Shumman, and he moved in the same circles as Ōta Nampo, Yomo no Magao, and Santō Kyōden. Inscriptions by him appear on several works in this exhibition (e.g., Catalogue nos. II-13 and III-5).

IV-4

Kitagawa Fujimaro (active 1800-1820)

Man Strolling with a Boy Carrying Flowering Branches

Circa 1810

Hanging scroll; ink and colors on silk; 94 x 31

Signature (Fujimaro hitsu) and seals (Kōkasai [top] and Fujimaro [bottom]) of artist at center right

The Cleveland Museum of Art, The Kelvin Smith Collection, Gift of Mrs. Kelvin Smith

The freshness with which Fujimaro approaches his subject matter and his lively use of color are again apparent in this very different painting of a young man returning from a stroll followed by his child attendant carrying flowering plum branches. Here the artist has used occasional touches of red to emphasize the relatively sober colors of the man's padded winter clothing while employing much brighter hues in the child's light-blue leggings, red undergarments, and smock-like coat of yellow-and-black plaid. By so doing, he calls attention to the child and—more importantly—the plum branches, despite their position behind the principal figure and at the edge of the composition. This focus away from the young man at the center of the painting introduces both an element of surprise and a sense of movement into a work that might otherwise seem too stable and straightforward.

As has been pointed out elsewhere in this catalogue, the flowering plum, which bloomed in late winter, was rich in poetic associations. It symbolized the new year (which in the Japanese lunar calendar usually began in February), and was a favorite with gentleman scholars, who admired its ability to bloom from leafless branches in the coldest weather.

Plum blossoms are the subject of the kyōka by Hinshin (dates unknown) that fills the top of the scroll. It reads: *Taoyakeru / sakura o nomi ya / hana to iwan / wakaki no ume no / iro moenaranu.* Translated literally, this would be, "The full blooming cherry is not the only flower worth mentioning. The color of the young plum tree blooms as well." As with most kyōka, however, the verse is full of words with double meanings. Two that are especially important here are *sakura*, "cherry blossom," and *iro*, "color." As we have seen, the beauties of the Yoshiwara were often referred to as cherry blossoms; and the Japanese word *iro* can also mean "love" or "sex." Knowing this, we can give the poem an entirely different, more risqué, reading: "The flowers of the Yoshiwara are not the only ones worth loving. The blossoms of the young plum [i.e., the young man] are attractive too."

The homoerotic implications of the verse are clear. Does this shed a different light on the painting? Perhaps so. Certainly the way in which the boy peeks out from behind his master's cloak is reminiscent of the way in which *kamuro* were often shown. Fujimaro's teacher, Utamaro, seemed to be particularly fond of placing *kamuro* so that they were almost hidden behind their mistress's robes (see Catalogue no. II-30). The similarity appears too close to be entirely accidental. Homosexuality, by the way, seems to have been regarded with considerable tolerance during the Edo Period (see Hokusai's depiction of a young man in Catalogue no. IV-17).

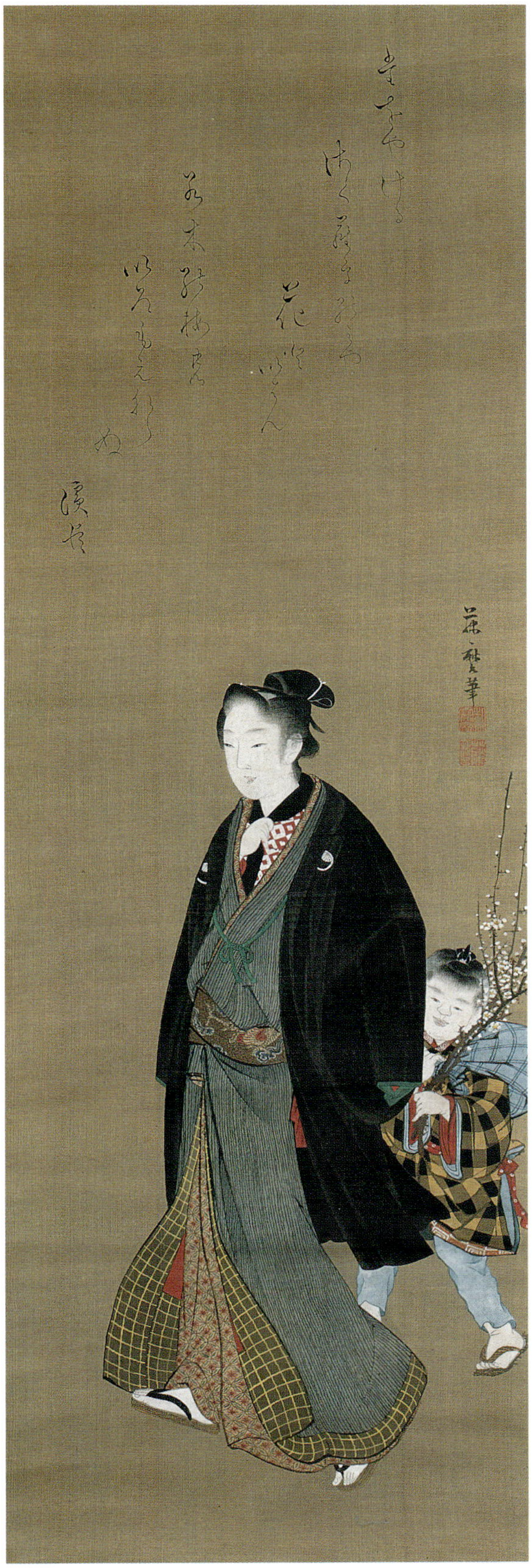

IV-4

IV-5

Ichikawa Gakuzan (dates unknown)

***Shirandō shingenkai no zu*, "Picture of the New Year's Party at the Shirandō"**

1795

Hanging scroll; ink on paper; 140 x 127

Signature of artist (Ise [?] Ichikawa Yō) at end of inscription at lower left

Waseda University Library

A party quite unlike any of the others depicted in this exhibition is shown taking place in one of the rooms of the Shirandō, a Dutch language school operated by Ōtsuki Gentaku in the Kyōbashi district of Edo. Twenty-eight guests are present, seated on the floor around three tables that have been pushed together for the occasion. The host, wearing Dutch clothes (including a hat), presides over the proceedings from a European-style armchair in the corner. Obviously this is no ordinary party. Though the guests—in contrast to the host—are seated in Japanese fashion on the floor, the fact that they are gathered around tables is unusual: traditionally in Japan, each guest at a party receives his own individual food stand or *zen* (see Catalogue no. II-36). Moreover, the tables are set with knives, forks, and glasses rather than with chopsticks

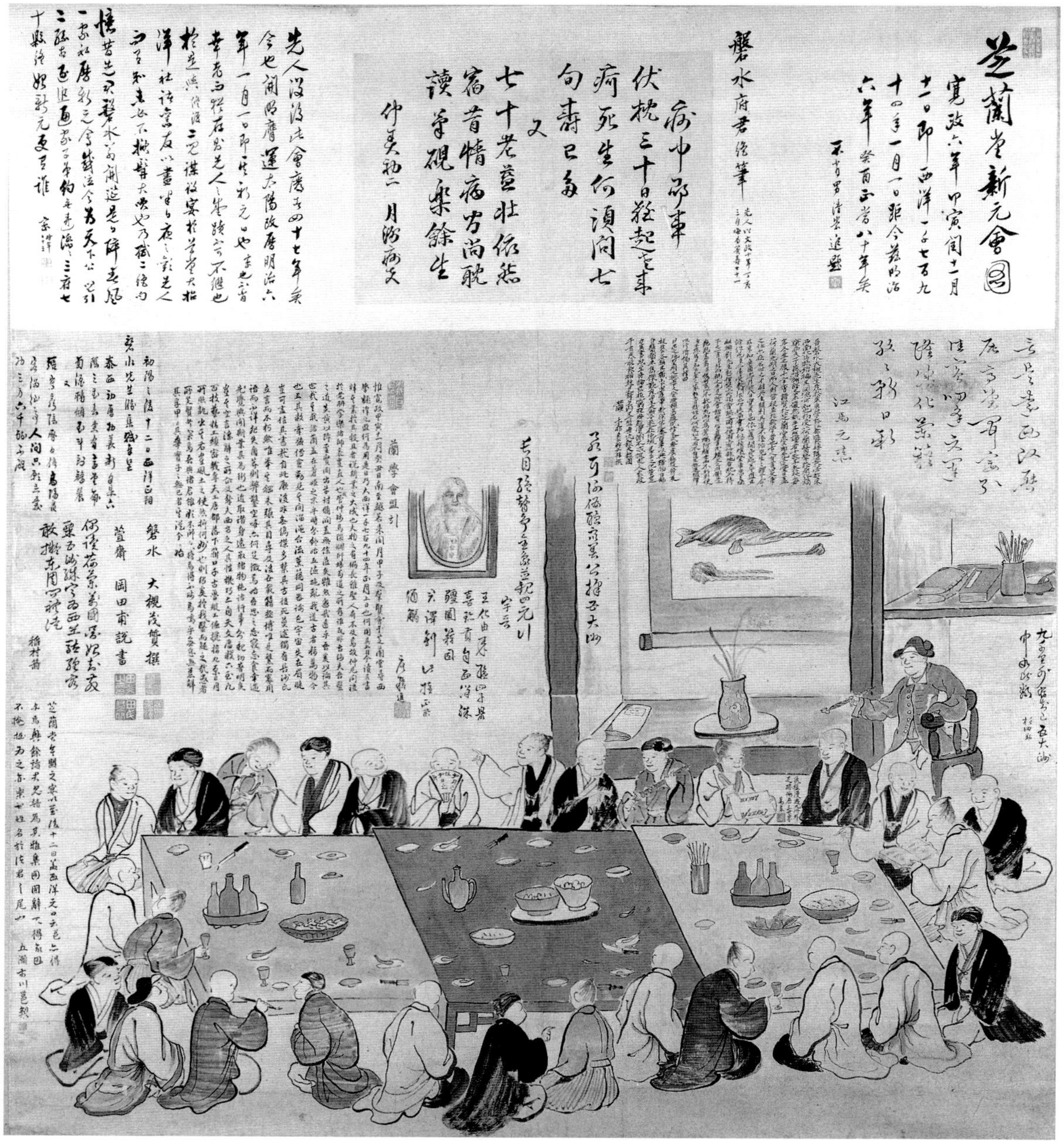

IV-5

and lacquer sake cups. Adding to the oddity of the occasion, one of the guests (seated in front of the *tokonoma*) displays a piece of paper on which he has just written two words in a European alphabet with a quill pen.

The inscription at the upper-right corner of the scroll tells us that the picture shows a party held to celebrate the Dutch New Year's. The date in question coincided with the eleventh day of the eleventh intercalary month of Kansei 6 in the Japanese calendar. Though the inscription states that the year in the western calendar was 1794, it was actually 1795. Records show that similar parties were held at the school every year thereafter through 1837.[*]

The guests were all men who had been involved in one branch or another of *rangaku*, or "Dutch learning," as any study of European art or science was then called.[†] Among the guests were Sugita Gempaku and Maeno Ryōtaku, who had translated a Dutch book on anatomy, and Katsuragawa Hoshū, one of the house physicians to the shogun, and his brother, Morishima Chūryō. Chūryō (1756-1810), who wrote kibyōshi under the pseudonym of Shinra Banshō, was a close friend of Ōta Nampo and the organizing spirit behind some of the more inventive literary parties held during the Temmei era. His presence at this particular party is the main reason for the work's inclusion in the exhibition. Chūryō was one of several gifted men of samurai background who were active in both the Floating World and *rangaku*. Another was the brilliant but ill-fated Hiraga Gennai. For men of their background, European studies, while encouraged (to a point) by the authorities, were considered unorthodox, if not actually suspect. Involvement with the Floating World was deemed even more inappropriate.

IV-6

Torii Kiyonaga (1752-1815)

Three Drunken Women

Circa 1785

Hanging scroll; ink and colors on paper; 32.7 x 52.7

Signature (Seki Kiyonaga ga) and seal (indistinct; probably Kiyonaga) of artist at lower right

Honolulu Academy of Arts

Three women cavort in three states of drunkenness. In keeping with the subject matter, the

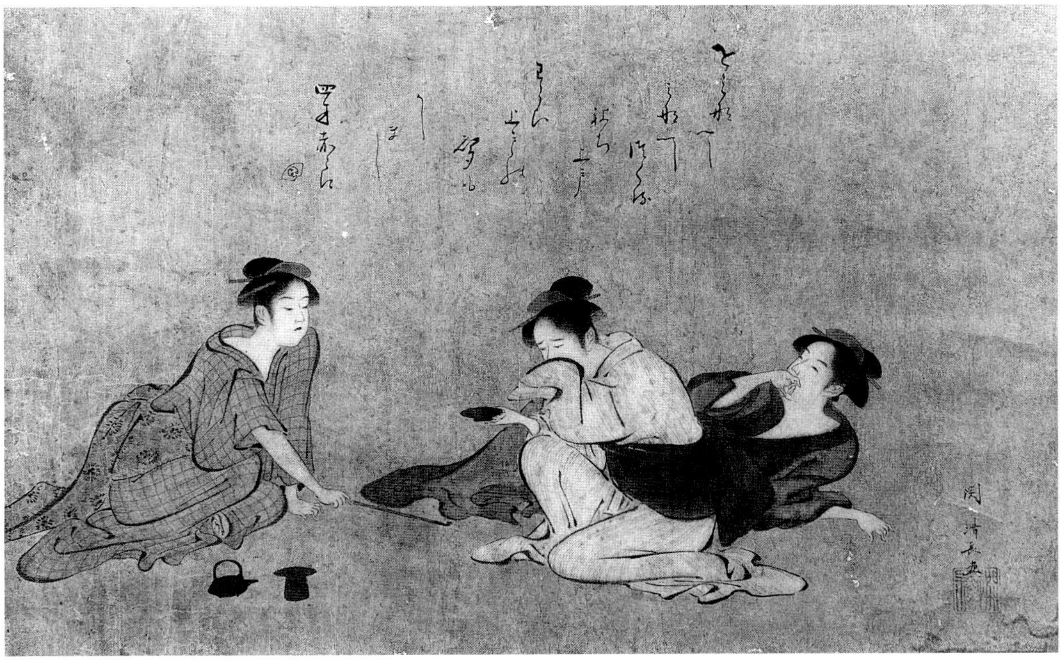

IV-6

* Jimbo Kazuya, Kobayashi Tadashi, and Kitahara Susumu, eds., *Kyōden, Ikku, Shunsui. Zusetsu Nihon no koten* (Tokyo Shūeisha, 1989), 18: 206.

† The seclusion policy, in effect through most of the Tokugawa Period, forbade any contact with Europeans other than the Dutch, and even that contact was minimal. This meant that the only access the Japanese had to European knowledge was through Dutch sources.

painting style is loose and playful. The light-handed brush strokes may be contrasted with the style Kiyonaga used in the depiction of actors (Catalogue nos. V-1, V-2, V-11, and V-12) and in illustrated books (Catalogue nos. I-11 and I-12).

On the left side, a woman in a black-and-blue checked *yukata* belligerently strikes the tatami with her *kiseru*, as if emphasizing her argument with the woman in the center, who weeps into her sleeve. On the right, a reclining woman laughs, possibly at the humor she finds in the ranting of the other two.

Balanced above the figures is a kyōka by Yomo no Akara (Ōta Nampo) bearing his *ogi ni tomoe* (comma pattern on fan) seal: *Omina e shi mina e shi tsukuru ne chi jōgo / warai jōgo no koe mo kashimashi* (The irate drunk forces herself on the other women, the laughing drunk adds her voice to the clamor).

Further meaning is to be derived from clever plays on words and layerings of words, and on the Chinese characters that form them. For instance, the word *kashimashi*, which means "boisterous," is actually a *kanji* made up of the character for "woman" written three times. Since it is written only with *hiragana* here, the viewer can contemplate that the "three women" are painted instead of written—a sort of visual pun.

Reading the words as a delightful rhyme: *omina eshi / mina eshi*... gives yet another meaning. *Omina* may be translated as "old women," while *omina-eshi* is a type of flower. Familiarity with classical poetry and contemporary songs would provide further insight to the nuances.

In the *Ehon monomi ga oka*, composed at the end of Temmei 4, there is evidence of the friendship between Nampo and Kiyonaga, as well as Kiyonaga's fondness for kyōka. No doubt the *Three Drunken Women* is also from that time.

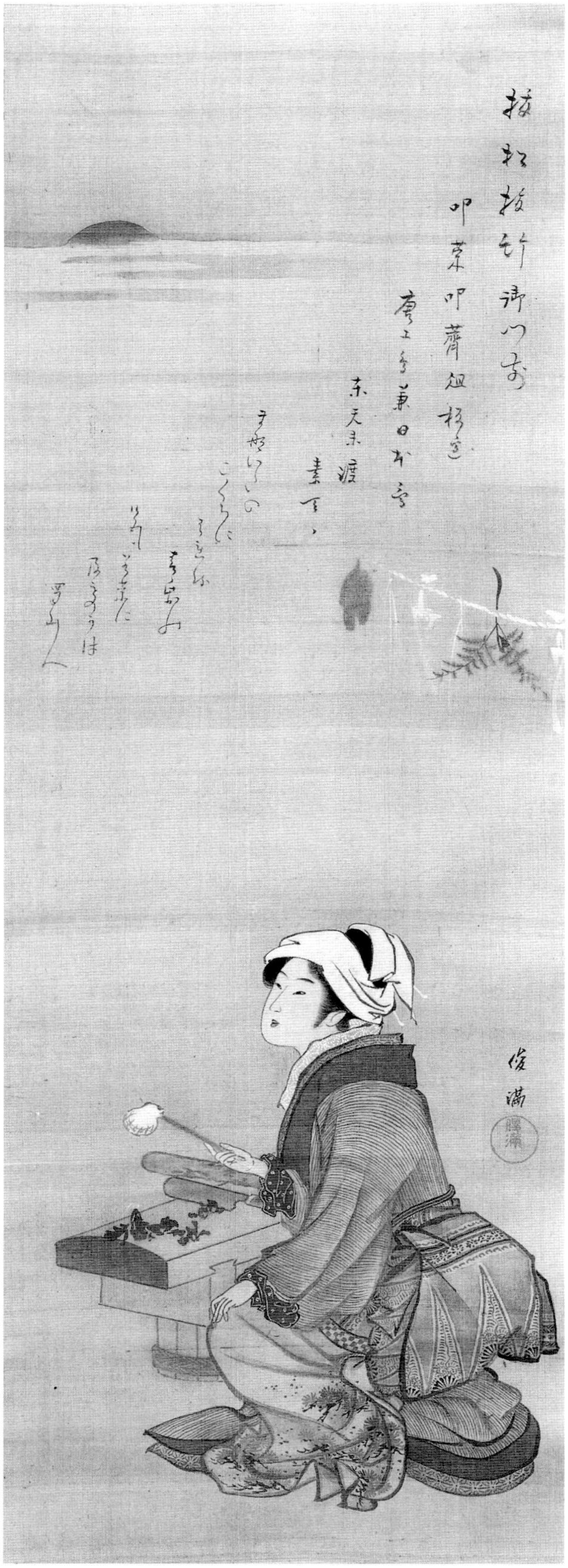

IV-7

IV-7

Kubo Shumman (1757-1820)

Preparing for the *Nanakusa*

Circa 1796

Hanging scroll; ink and colors with gofun on silk; 85.6 x 30.5

Signature (Shumman) and seal (Shumman) of artist at lower right

Minneapolis Institute of Arts, Bequest of Richard P. Gale

Shumman's lyrical painting style evokes a mood of quietude and grace in this scene of a woman chopping fresh herbs at daybreak. The celebration of the "seven herbs" (*nanakusa*) is held on the seventh day of the new year, when holiday decorations are taken down and a hearty soup made with seven fresh greens is served. The references to New Year's decorations, such as the pine branches on the woman's kimono and the rope hung with ferns and paper streamers (*gohei*), further point to the significance of the day.

The first poem on the painting (probably written by Shumman) reads like a song to accompany the preparation of the soup's ingredients, at so early an hour that the birds have yet to appear. It may be translated as follows: Taking down the pine, taking down the bamboo in front of the gate, chopping the greens, chopping the shepherd's purse on the edge of the chopping board, the birds of China, the birds of Japan have not yet crossed the eastern sky, tra la la.

The second poem was written by Shokusanjin (Ōta Nampo). The calligraphy has been so abstracted that it is quite difficult to read; nevertheless we offer the following as a possible interpretation: *Manaita no / kokuchi ni / hareru / ao kami no / o-iro mo wakakusa ni / oyobu mono ka wa* (Could the color of the green paper on the rim of the cutting board possibly rival that of the young greens?).

IV-8

Various artists

***Sekiga* (Party Scroll)**

1820

Hanging scroll; ink and colors on silk; 79.4 x 59.4

The Metropolitan Museum of Art, The Harry G. C. Packard Collection of Asian Art, Gift of Harry G. C. Packard, and Purchase, Fletcher, Rogers, Harris Brisbane Dick and Louis V. Bell Funds, Joseph Pulitzer Bequest, and The Annenberg Fund, Inc., Gift, 1975

Given its relatively late date, this party scroll would seem to fall outside the focus of this exhibition. Moreover, many of the artists—perhaps the bulk of them—were pupils of Edo's leading *bunjinga* (or *nanga*) painter, Tani Bunchō (1763-1840), and their contributions are quite different stylistically from most of the other work in the exhibition. Several familiar names, however, are among the sixty-odd contributors. The scroll is worth looking at, also, precisely because of some of the ways in which it differs from earlier *sekiga* such as Catalogue nos. II-13, III-5, and III-6.

Two differences stand out. One—the most obvious—is in the sheer number of contributors; the other is in the diversity of their contributions. The other *sekiga* in this exhibition all seem to have been created at more intimate gatherings and by men clearly sharing a common sensibility. That common sensibility is probably their most significant element. As Haruko Iwasaki points out in her essay in this catalogue, several of Nampo's parties of the

IV-8

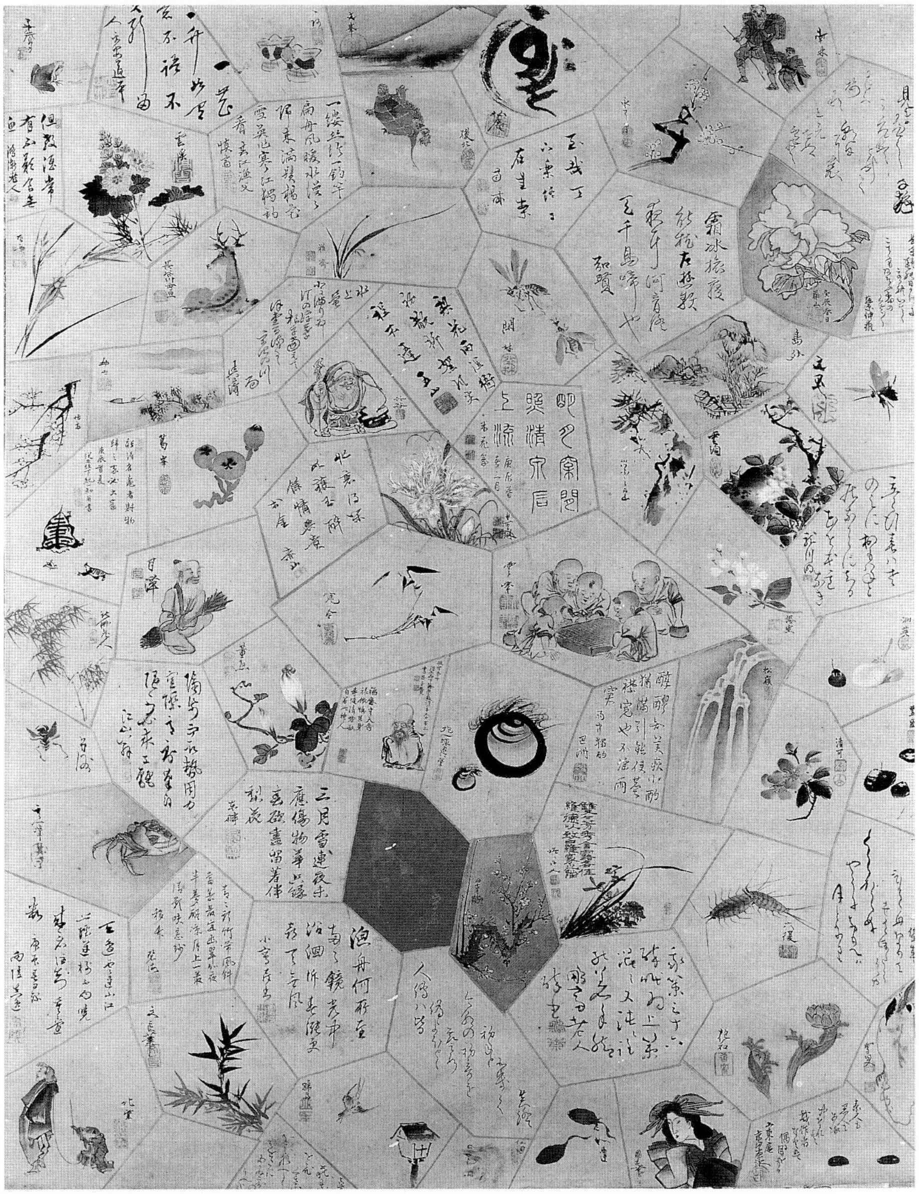

1780s attracted even more than sixty guests; however, the works of art chronicling these parties (works that were not *sekiga* in any case) followed a common theme and reflected a shared point of view.

Since many of the sketches in this scroll are by pupils of Tani Bunchō, they reflect his somewhat eclectic interest in Chinese-derived subject matter. The style Bunchō espoused was loosely based on Ming Dynasty Chinese literati painting, or *wenrenhua* (*bunjinga* in Japanese).

The inscription in the bottom-right corner of this scroll is by Santō Kyōden's younger brother, Kyōzan (1769-1858). Kyōzan, a seal carver by trade, was also a prolific author and kyōka poet in his own right. The sketch of a woman immediately to the left of Kyōzan's inscription is by a pupil of Toyokuni, and the drawing of a monkey trainer in the lower-left corner of the scroll is by a pupil of Hokusai. A bit farther up along the left side is a sketch of a crab by the Rimpa painter Suzuki Kiitsu (1796-1858). The real surprise in the midst of all these sketches and inscriptions, however, is farther up and just to the right of the middle. It is a quick ink drawing of a section of a pine tree by Chōbunsai Eishi, who is represented by numerous works in this exhibition (including Catalogue nos. I-3, II-5, II-6, and II-7). It is drawn in the Kanō School style in which he received his early training.

IV-9

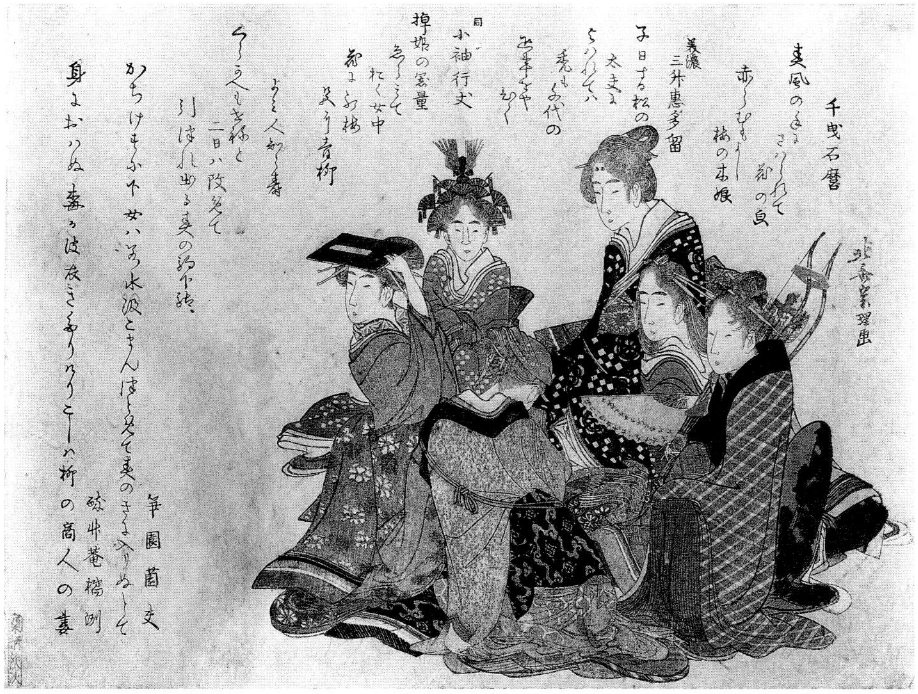

Dates on several of the sketches and inscriptions indicate that the scroll was created during the late spring or early summer (*shuka*) of the "Dragon Year" (*kanoe tatsu*) of 1820 (Bunsei 3).

IV-9

Katsushika Hokusai (1760-1849)

The Six States of Woman

1798

Calendar print (egoyomi); colors on paper; 19.2 x 25.5

Signature of artist (Hokusai Sōri ga) and signatures of kyōka poets; seal at lower left may be that of publisher

Arthur M. Sackler Museum, Harvard University Art Museums, Duel Collection

The picture (*e*) calendar (*koyomi*) was generally a privately commissioned print presented to friends as a New Year's gift or composed by a poetry club to commemorate the new year.* In this calendar print, the calendar itself appears in the fan held open in the midst of the six women. It is inscribed with the long (*dai*) and short (*shō*) months of the year 1798 (Kansei 10), which was a Year of the Horse. The print is inscribed with six kyōka poems, which correspond to the six women portrayed. All the kyōka concern New Year's, which occurred in early spring, the season associated with plum blossoms.†

Harukaze no / te ni sawararete / hana no kao / akaramu mo yoshi / ume no ki musume (Daughter of the plum tree, blushing sweetly, her blossom face tinged by the spring breeze)
—Chibiki Ishimaro

The next poem puns on the word *matsu*, which means "pine" (a symbol of the new year) and "waiting."

Ne no hi suru / matsu no tayū ni / yobarete wa / kamuro mo chiyo no / henji o ya-hi-ku (When beckoned by the awaiting courtesan playing "uproot the pine," the *kamuro* gives her eternal response, "I'm coming")
—Mimasu Etaru, from Hino

* Matthi Forrer, *Egoyomi and Surimono* (Uithoorn: J. C. Gieben, 1979), 4.

† The transliteration of these poems is taken from Theodore Bowie, *Art of the Surimono* (Bloomington, Indiana Universtiy Art Museum, 1979), 152-53.

Saohime no / kiryō erabite / okujochū / hana ni kōbai / iro ni aoyagi (The daimyo's handmaid, choosing the beauty of the goddess of spring, picks the red plum for her flower, the green willow for her color)
—Kosode Yukitake, from Hino

Subtle references to the Year of the Horse appear in the *kanji* for certain words in this poem.

Kuragae mo / sento futsuka wa / aratamete / hikitsure izuru / haruno komageta (Even though she changed houses, she goes out, once again, on the second day of the new year to pay her respects in her springtime clogs)
—Yomibito Shirazu

Kajikezu ni / gejo wa wakamizu / kumi koman / tsutomete haru no / ki ni iri nu tote (Not feeling the cold, the maid draws the first water on the morning of the new year, diligently, for her favorite master—spring)
—Sōen Sono-o

Mi ni owanu / ume ga hagoromo / kitaru nari / koshi wa yanagi no / akindo no tsuma (Shopkeeper's wife—were she to envelop herself in a plum-blossom cloak of feathers, her waist would be willowy)
—Suichiku-an Kisshū

Compositionally, the print is a play on the *rokkasen* theme—a contemporary rendering of the six immortals of poetry. Through symbols that were immediately associated with the classical poets, this *mitate* likens each of these ordinary women to a classical literary figure. In depicting the poets as women from different walks of life, this print is similar to *Nine Women Playing Kitsune-ken* (Catalogue no. II-1), while in the *rokkasen mitate* device, it resembles the Fujimaro scroll (Catalogue no. IV-3) and the Utamaro print (Catalogue no. IV-11). As in these other works, a quiver of arrows identifies Ariwara no Narihira, who is played by a merchant's wife. A courtesan, as Ono no Komachi, holds the fan with the calendar; Otomo no Kuronushi is represented by a daimyo's maid; Sōjō Henjō is acted by a *kamuro*; Bunya no Yasuhide's role is performed by a geisha; and Kisen Hōshi, seen from the back, is played by a maidservant.

IV-10

Kubo Shumman (1757-1820)

Poet and Companions Viewing the Moonrise over the Sumida River

Mid to late 1790s

Surimono; 41.6 x 56.1

Seal of artist (Shumman) at left under bridge

The Chester Beatty Library and Museum of Oriental Art

A man and four women gaze at the rising moon from the balcony of a restaurant or teahouse overlooking the Sumida River. It is autumn, and horizontal bands of mist are visible along the opposite shore and over the bay opening out to the right. The cool, stable weather and clear skies typical of the season made it ideal for moon viewing. (The exhibition includes another picture of a moon-viewing party at the same time of year [Catalogue no. II-25]. That party, however, takes place in a more bucolic setting, a balcony overlooking the paddy fields surrounding the Yoshiwara.)

This is the farthest downstream of all the views of the Sumida River in this exhibition. The Eitai Bridge, just visible at the upper-left corner of the print, was the last of the four large bridges to cross the river, and the rooftops and fire tower shown in silhouette on the other side were in the southernmost section of Fukagawa. Tsukuda Island, seen off the balcony of the teahouse at the right, was in the bay near the river's mouth. There was a fishing village on the island, and at this period it was invariably shown, as here, with boats moored around it.

As surimono grew in popularity, Shumman, who was an avid kyōka poet and, from the mid-1790s on, the leader of a kyōka club of his own, seems to have given up designing other kinds of prints to concentrate on the new genre. Already in his earlier work he had shown a predilection for poetic and atmospheric effects that would serve him well when applied to the new form.

Twenty-one poems are printed on the lower half of this surimono, together with a notation to the effect that they were composed at one or the other of two moon-viewing parties, one on the fifteenth day of the eighth month and the other on the thirteenth day of the ninth

IV-10

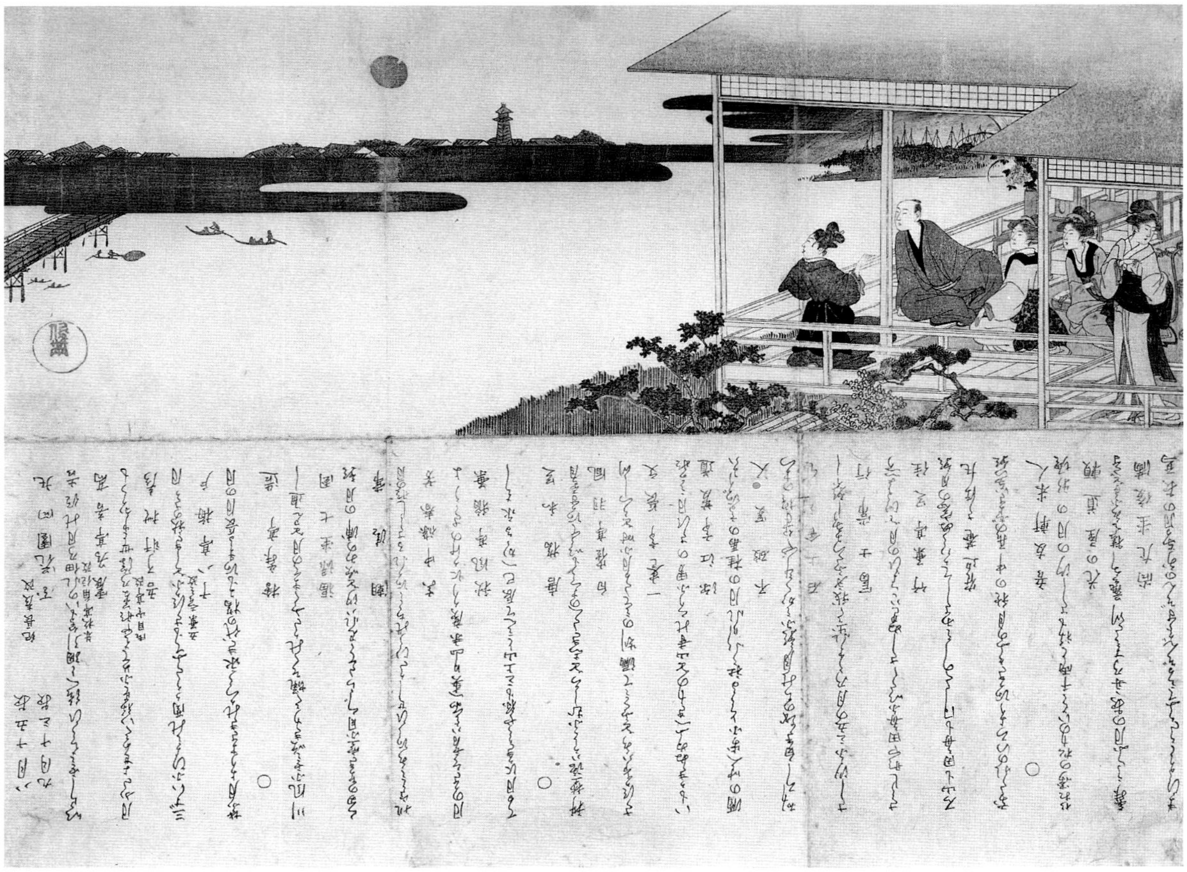

month of an unspecified year. It seems likely that all of the poets were members of Shumman's kyōka club, the Bakurōgawa.

IV-11

Kitagawa Utamaro (1753-1806)

Women Mimicking the *Rokkasen*

Circa 1792

Woodblock print: ōban diptych; 39.5 x 24.5 (right panel); 38 x 25.1 (left panel)

Signature of artist (Utamaro ga), kiwame seal, and trademark of publisher, Tsutaya Jūzaburō, on each panel

Portland Art Museum, Mary Andrews Ladd Collection

Those who have seen Catalogue no. IV-4 by Fujimaro and Catalogue no. IV-9 by Hokusai will recognize this diptych at once as another *rokkasen mitate-e*. This is unquestionably the earliest of the three examples, however, and it also differs from the others in that the six women mimicking the *rokkasen* are identified by name. They were all, it seems, real women associated with teahouses or other popular entertainment spots of the time. Three of them—the second figure from the right, Takajima O Hisa, the fourth figure from the right, Tomimoto Toyohina, and the sixth figure from the right, Naniwa O Kita—seem to have been particular favorites with the Edo public, and appear in numerous other prints by Utamaro, most of which may be dated to the early 1790s.

Many of the devices used in the other two works to represent the attributes of the different *rokkasen* are already evident in this earlier version. Ono no Komachi's fan (in this case actually a sheaf of love letters) and Narihira's bow and quiver were, of course, essential for any portrayal of these two poets; but the book used to represent the tall court hat of Bunya no Yasuhide and the kerchiefs used to mimic the shaven pates of the two priest poets, Sōjō Henjō and Kisen Hōshi, though much more far-fetched, also appear in both later works.

We will not take the time to set down or translate any of the six kyōka inscribed in the cloud-like form arching above the figures. Suffice it to say that each is a rather obvious parody of a well-known poem by the Immortal of Poetry represented immediately below. Several of the poems—the originals, not the parodies—figure in other works in the exhibition (e.g., Catalogue nos. II-17 and II-22).

The names of the women forming this tableau are enclosed in small rectangles placed at the start of each verse, and the names of the kyōka poets are also given. Yashoku Katamaru, the author of the first kyōka at the right, is included in Hokusai's *Isuzugawa kyōka guruma* of 1802 (Catalogue no. IV-13).

IV-12

Kitagawa Utamaro (1753-1806)

A Poet's Success

Circa 1786

Woodblock print; ōban diptych; 39.1 x 26 (each panel)

Signature of artist (Utamaro ga) at far right and lower left, and trademark of publisher, Tsutaya Jūzaburō, at lower left

The British Museum

A sizable party, mainly of women, has just arrived at a bayside beach with a view of Mt. Fuji off to the right. A prosperous-looking man holding a pipe prepares to alight from his palanquin as a courtesan in a second palanquin arrives to join him. The other women in the party, most of whom wear broad-brimmed straw hats and seem to have come on foot, look inquiringly at one another as though uncertain about what to do. One woman, probably a maid, bends down toward the man to show him an open book. A boy with a rolled-up straw mat on his back approaches the courtesan with a dipper of water.

The pine-covered sandbar in the middle distance indicates that the outing is taking place at Miho no Matsubara, the site of the *Hagoromo*, "Cloak (or Robe) of Feathers," legend. According to the legend, which became the basis for a famous No play, a heavenly being once left her cloak of feathers hanging in a tree at this spot when she stopped here to bathe. The cloak was found by a fisherman who refused to give it back unless the beautiful creature promised to marry him. Since she could not fly without the cloak, she was completely at his mercy. Ultimately, however, he relented when she promised to dance for him.

The inscription on the right-hand panel by Yomo no Akara (Ōta Nampo) explains that this

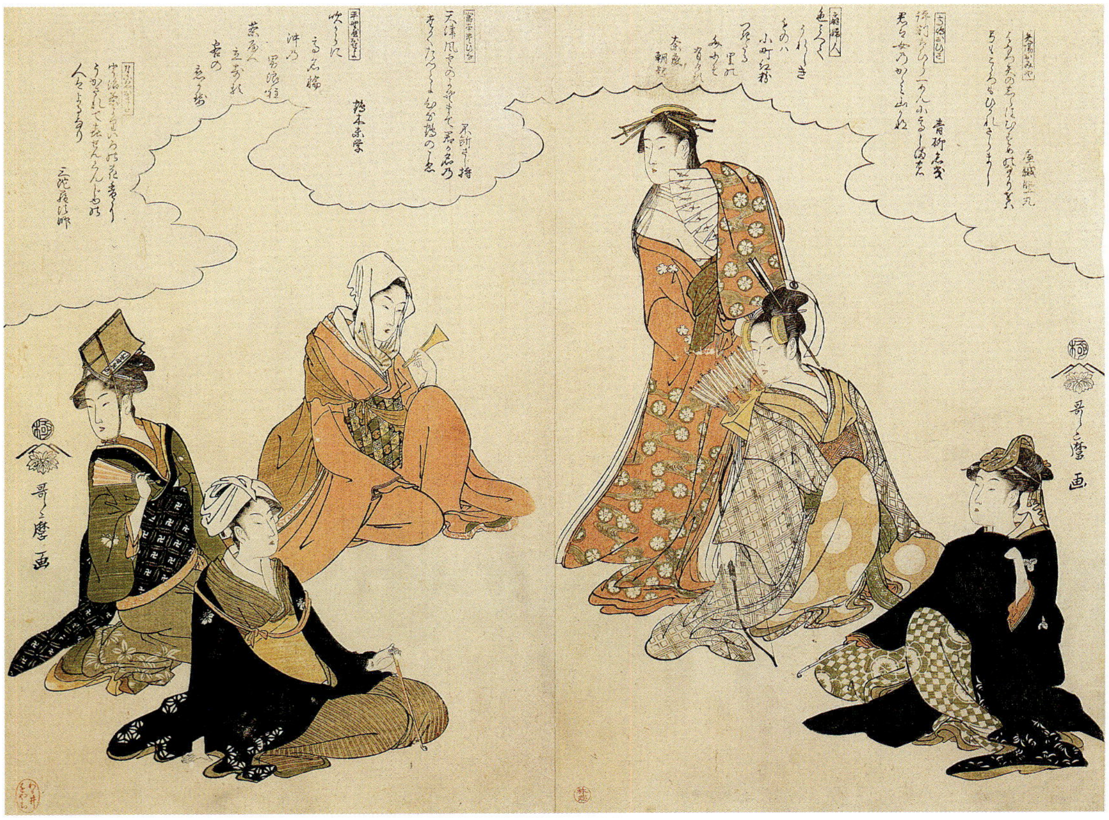

IV-11

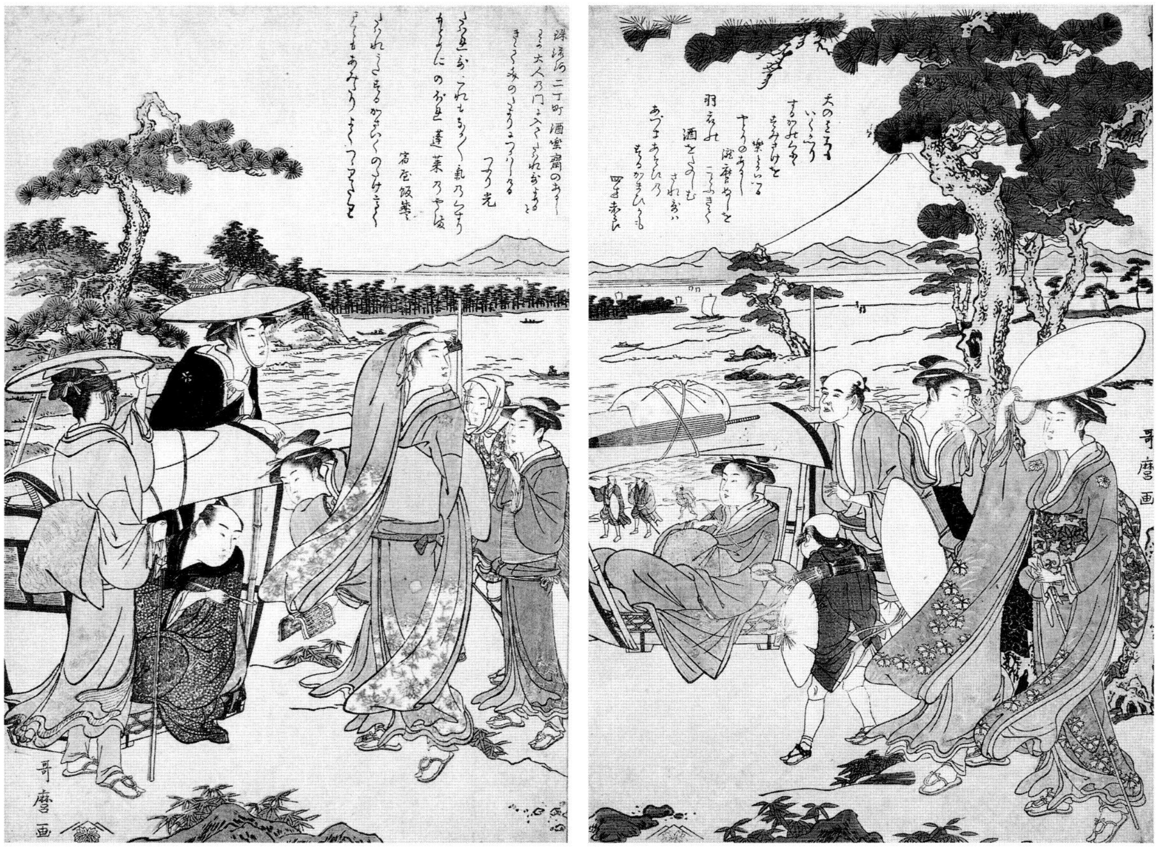

IV-12

diptych was published to celebrate a certain Shūrakusai Takimaro's acceptance into Akara's kyōka group. Shūrakusai (literally, "Delight in Drink Studio") was the proprietor of a lodging house in Sumpu (present-day Shizuoka), which was close to Miho no Matsubara. His acceptance at such a relatively early date into Akara's kyōka circle is an indication of the extent to which the taste for Edo-style kyōka had already begun to spread to the provinces. Later, Shūrakusai seems to have become quite well known in the capital. He contributed a kyōka to Tsutaya's *Ehon mushi erami* of 1787 (part of the same series as *Momochidori kyōka awase* [Catalogue no. IV-15]) and was mentioned in two different kibyōshi by Santō Kyōden. He died in 1798.

Akara's inscription includes a kyōka that reads: *Hagoromo no / sake o tanoshimu / zareuta wa / Azuma asobi no / suru kamai ka mo* (Humorous poems that take pleasure in "Cloak of Feathers" sake—Is this not an entertainment in true Azuma [i.e., Edo] style?).

The inscriptions on the left-hand panel include kyōka by Tsuburi no Hikaru and Yadoya no Meshimori. (The latter compiled the verses for *Ehon mushi erami,* mentioned above.) Hikaru introduces his poem with another brief mention of Shūrakusai's entry into the group. The poem itself reads: *Tawareuta / kore mo nakanaka / ki no kusuri / motome ni nobore / Hōrai no yama* (Witty verses, let them also rise in response to the happy requests—Mt. Hōrai). Mt. Hōrai was a fabled island peak inhabited by immortals. Meshimori's verse involves so many plays on words that we will not seek to translate it here.

IV-13

Katsushika Hokusai (1760-1849)

***Isuzugawa kyōka guruma*, "A Wagon of Kyōka from Isuzugawa"**

1802

Illustrated book; 26.7 x 18.1

Signature of artist (Hokusai Tatsumasa ga) and name of publisher, Tsutaya Jūzaburō, in colophon

Spencer Collection, New York Public Library

This book contains the portraits of fifty kyōka poets, all of whom were pupils of the compiler, Senshūan Sandarabōshi (1731-1814). As was the

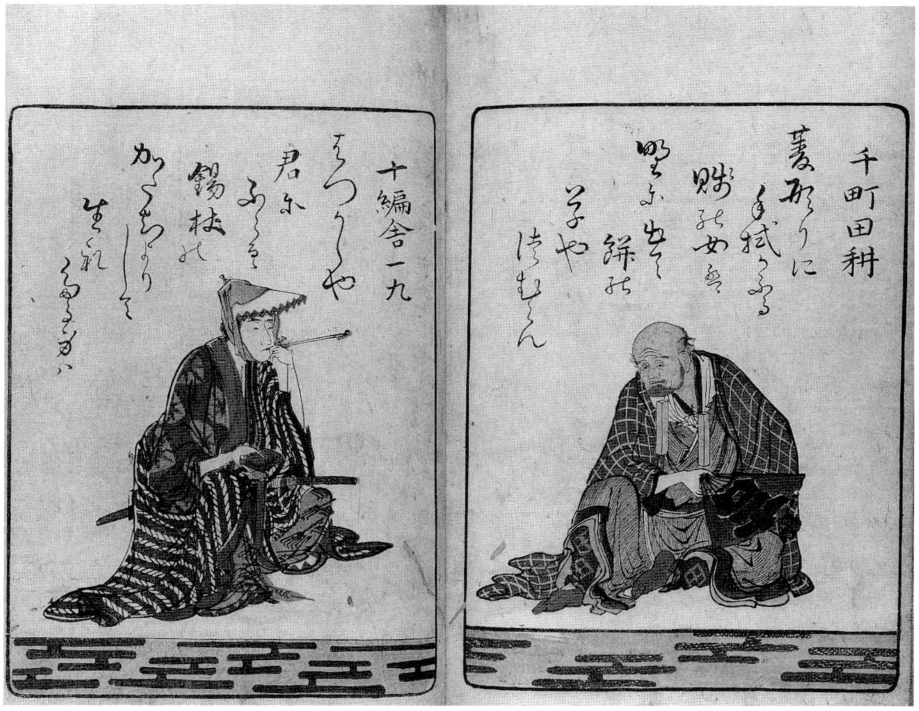

IV-13

custom with books of this kind (a custom that, as was pointed out in connection with Catalogue nos. III-10 and III-11, goes all the way back to classical poetry scrolls), the name of the poet and one of his poems is inscribed above each portrait.

Sandarabōshi was one of the leading kyōka masters of the time and a much sought-after judge for poetry contests. He moved in many of the same circles as Ōta Nampo, and he was a contributor, with Nampo, to two of the *sekiga* in this exhibition (Catalogue nos. II-13 and III-5). His name—or rather, the name he took on in his role as a kyōka poet, Sandarabōshi—sounds Buddhist at first hearing (*bōshi* means "priest"), but, as was common with many such *kyōmei*, it could be given another, more humorous, reading. Written with other characters, *sandarabōshi* meant the covers at the top and bottom of a rice bale.

Humor, of course, was what kyōka was all about. Unfortunately, as we know, much of the humor found in kyōka depends on puns and allusions that are next to impossible to convey in translation. The spirit of fun animating the portraits in this little book, however, needs no translation. It is immediately apparent to anyone. In the reproduction here, for instance, the figure at left appears to be deliberately "hamming it up." He has covered his head with a half-open folding fan tied down with a kerchief, and puffs a pipe at a jaunty angle while holding out a tobacco pouch in his right hand. Even his colorful, ill-matched clothing appears to have been chosen expressly with the role of the buffoon in mind, and his formal samurai sword, which in other circumstances might have added dignity to his appearance, looks so out of place that it merely adds to the comic effect.

This amusing figure is Jippensha Ikku, whom we have already met as the author of the text to Utamaro's *Seirō ehon nenjū gyōji* (Catalogue no. II-34), and who is best known not as a kyōka poet but as the author of enormously popular *kokkeibon* ("funny" books) about two rascally Edokko, Kitahachi and Yajirobei. Ikku came by his sword legitimately; he was the son of a minor city official in Suruga Fuchū. Like many young men of samurai background, however, he gave up his inherited position to pursue a more exciting life in the Floating World. For several years during the 1790s, while getting started as a writer, he worked in Tsutaya Jūzaburō's book and print shop, but by 1800 or shortly thereafter he was already making enough to be able to live solely from the proceeds of his writing. He was one of the first in Japan to be able to do so. The size of the reading public grew dramatically after 1800, and Ikku (like his contemporaries Bakin and Shikitei Samba) was able to capitalize on this growing market in a way that would never have occurred to Kyōden or Nampo.

We know next to nothing about the figure at right, not even how to pronounce his name with certainty; it may be read either in sonorous, pseudo-Chinese fashion as *Senchō Denkō*, or, in more native Japanese style, as *Chimachi Tatagayashi*. With his wrinkled forehead and older, more careworn features, he cuts a very different figure from that of Ikku. He wears what look like two clappers or sounding blocks *(hyōshigi* or *tsuke*) suspended from a cord around his neck and holds out a fan emblazoned with the character *kichi* (good luck or congratulations). The character *ta* (or *den*), which forms part of his name, is visible on one of his underkimono showing around his ankles.

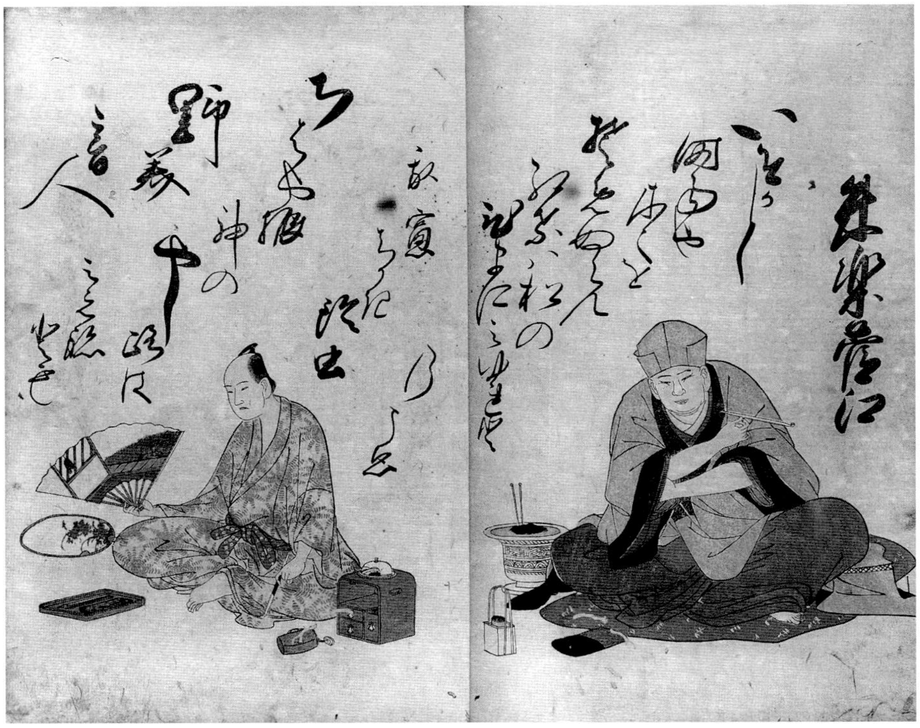

IV-14

IV-14

Utagawa Toyohiro (1773-1829)

***Ehon Michinokugami*, "Picture Book of Paper from Michinoku"**

1793

Illustrated book in one volume; 30.5 x 21

Signature and seal of artist (Ichiryūsai Utagawa Toyohiro ga) and address and name of publisher (Shiba Shimmeimae, Fuyōdō, Takasu Sōshichi han)

Spencer Collection, New York Public Library

Michinoku was the old name for the northeast provinces of Honshu (the main island of Japan), an area now known as Tohoku. During the Edo Period, the region represented everything that was remote and rustic, but it was also the source of a fine crepe paper, the *Michinokugami* of this book's title.The name was probably chosen for its connotations of something precious coming from an unlikely quarter.

This little volume reproduces the portraits of twenty-six kyōka poets, together with representative verses by each. The verses are written in a bold, highly eccentric hand that is difficult to decipher. The book begins with a two-page preface by Gouchō Ayabane and concludes with a colophon by Machiawase Kuji, both of whom contributed poems and are portrayed in the book. The authors of this catalogue have been unable to discover any information about these men. They appear to have been unknown, at least under the names used here, to either Ōta Nampo or Yadoya no Meshimori—who, however, had both temporarily retired from kyōka at the time this book was published. It is all the more surprising, therefore, to find such a staunch member of the Nampo-Meshimori circle as Akera Kankō included among the poets selected.

Kankō's portrait is reproduced here at right. Balancing a pipe in one hand, his arms folded in concentration, he gazes unseeingly ahead, apparently giving his full attention to the lines he is about to create. His hat looks as though it could have belonged to a Chinese scholar, and Toyohiro invests him with the same kind of massive dignity with which he is portrayed in Catalogue nos. III-10 and III-11.

Yami no Kotobito (?), the poet depicted on the facing page, presents a much more casual figure, as, wearing a light summer kimono (*yukata*), he stares down at the *suzuribako* in front of him, holding an open fan in one hand and a pipe in the other. There is something enigmatic about the scene painted on the fan: an empty veranda with steps leading down into a garden and a section of wall with a latticed window in which hangs a small bell or wind chime. The scene is probably intended as a rebus to be used in interpreting the poem. The poem refers, among other things, to the voice of the *suzumushi*, or "chime bug"—so called because it made a sound like a chime. The rebus was a popular device in prints of the mid-1790s.

IV-15

Kitagawa Utamaro (1753-1806)

***Momochidori kyōka awase*, "A Kyōka Contest of Hundreds and Thousands of Birds," or "A Chorus of Birds"**

Circa 1790

Gajō (folding album) in two volumes with illustrations; 25 x 19

Published by Tsutaya Jūzaburō, with prefaces to each volume by Akamatsu Kinkei

The Art Institute of Chicago

If any one person may be credited with inventing the illustrated kyōka book, it is the publisher Tsutaya Jūzaburō. From 1786 to 1791, his imprint appeared on every innovative publication in the genre, including an extraordinary group of albums designed by Utamaro that pushed the expressive potential of the woodblock medium to new limits. *Momochidori kyōka awase* is one of these. It is related to two other, earlier albums, also designed by Utamaro: *Ehon mushi erami* and *Shioi no tsuto*, often called "The Insect Book" and "The Shell Book," respectively. In fact, the relationship is close enough to make it seem likely that the three albums were conceived as a series, even though they were never explicitly so linked. All three albums, for instance, are actually witty parodies of the classical *jūgoban uta-awase* genre, in which fifteen pairs of poets were presented, along with their verses, in the guise of contestants in a poetry contest. The albums are also linked thematically in that they represent three of the four standard categories—*shisho* (birds, insects, sealife, and animals)—traditionally used for classifying living creatures in Japan. This latter fact has given rise to speculation that the series—if series it is—was originally intended to include a fourth volume.

One's enjoyment of this album may be considerably enhanced when it is seen, as Utamaro (and Tsutaya) clearly intended, as a parody of a classical *uta-awase* in which portraits of poets appeared on facing pages. The birds then become substitutes for the poets, which puts an entirely different light on how we interpret the way they interact (or fail to interact) with one another. Seen in this light, the pages showing a winter wren chirping away at a pair of cranes, which seem totally indifferent to its singing, become a kind of witty commentary on human behavior. The same is true of the scene showing an owl about to fly off in one direction while a jay, sitting on an adjoining branch, stares resolutely in the opposite direction. None of this prevents us from appreciating these designs as nature studies as well, however, which again was surely what was intended. Much of the richness of the work is a result of the many different levels from which it can be viewed and enjoyed.

Another of these levels is provided by the poetry. Here, unfortunately, most of us are at a disadvantage. Even most present-day Japanese find these kyōka, with their multiple allusions and hidden puns, difficult to decipher. Suffice it to say that they all deal with love affairs or the gossip and complications attending them, and in every case at least one reference, direct or indirect, is made to the birds depicted. In a few instances, the poem is phrased as though a bird itself had uttered it; more often the birds are merely used as a basis for similes or puns. In any case, the variety of conceits and the sheer amount of wordplay—all relating to birds—is astonishing. Most previous writers who have discussed these albums have tended to dismiss the poems as being little more than doggerel, and admittedly they would not have much weight standing on their own, but when read in the context for which they were designed, they display a wit and deftness that can be quite captivating.

Of the three albums mentioned above, this one seems the most appropriate thematically to Edo, since one of the poetic phrases (*makura kotoba*) traditionally associated with Azuma—that is, the East or Edo—is *tori ga naku*, "where the birds sing." The avian theme is played to the hilt by the compiler, Akamatsu no Kinkei, in his prefaces to both volumes. Even his *kyōmei* (name as a kyōka poet), which actually means

IV-15

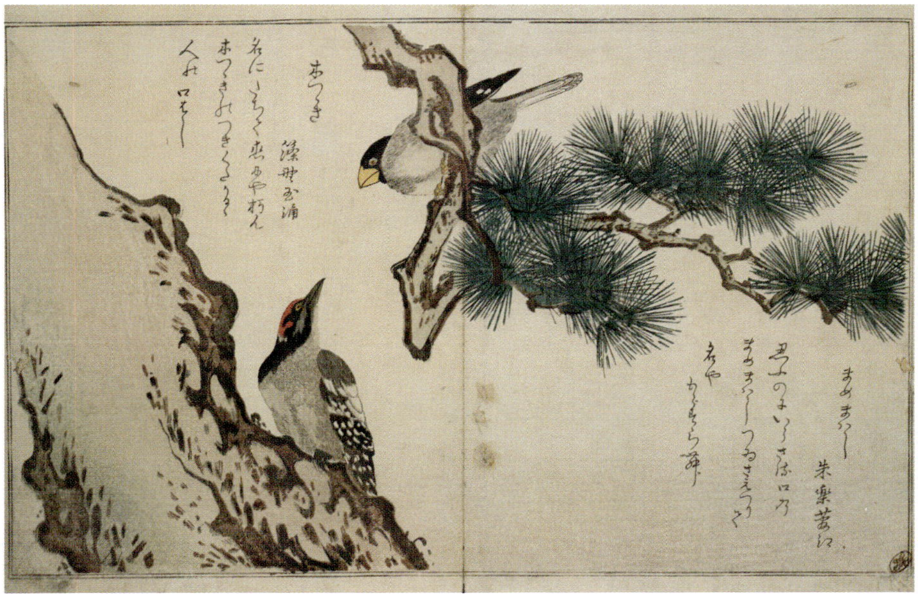

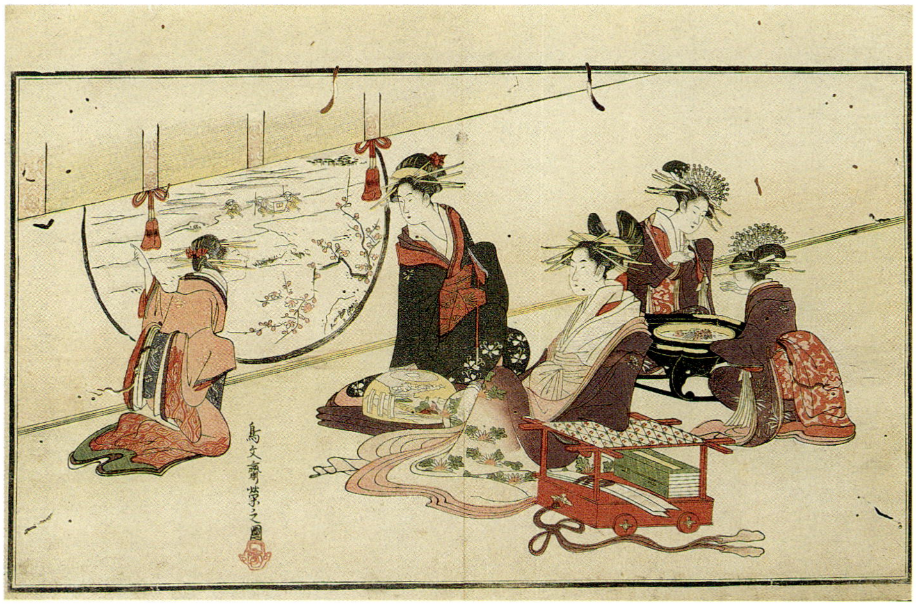

IV-16

"Golden Cockerel of the Red Pine," and the type of paper on which the album is printed, *tori no ko* (literally, "chick" paper) seem ideally suited to the enterprise. Yet Kinkei, apparently feeling that the project needed some of the aura of the past as well, also claimed that the verses had been composed on the theme of Asuka, the ancient capital "of the flying bird"—a claim that does not seem to be borne out by the poems themselves.

Artistically, this album is every bit the equal of its two predecessors. The birds are observed with a naturalist's attention to detail but with enough humor and whimsy added to give the designs an unusual sense of animation. The colors are rich, though relatively subdued, and are played off effectively against the warm ivory of the paper. Special effects, such as gauffrage and overprinting, are used sparingly but successfully to capture the gloss or brilliance of plumage. One of the most memorable designs is one that at first glance may seem understated to a fault but that is actually something of a tour de force. On one side it shows a black cormorant with its tail above the water and the rest of its body dimly visible below the surface, while on the other it shows two standing cranes, their long, white feathers rendered in gauffrage.

IV-16

Shigemasa, Ekigi, Eishi, Utamaro, Hokusai, and Tōrin

***Otoko dōka*, "The Stamping Sound of Men"**

1798

Kyōka book with illustrations; 25.4 x 18.9

Signatures and seals of artists on each illustration; date (Kansei tsuchi no e uma), address, and name of publisher, Tsutaya Jūzaburō, on last two pages; preface by compiler, Sensōan Ichindō

Robert Ravicz

There are only six illustrations in this relatively thick book, and, unlike the illustrations in kyōka albums such as *Momochidori kyōka awase*, none of them are inscribed with verses. The bulk of the book consists of page after page filled with narrow columns of kyōka and the names of the poets who had written them. The poems, most of which relate to early spring, came from kyōka clubs all over the country, and the submissions from each club are grouped together. In the midst of these relatively dense pages of text, the illustrations, which are inserted at only irregular intervals, come as a delightful surprise, adding freshness and color to what might otherwise seem too claustrophobic a format.

The cataloguer has not been able to make the kind of close reading that would be required to determine whether any of the illustrations were intended to relate to specific poems. It seems more likely that their function was more general, to add an air of elegance and visual poetry to the book as a whole. Their relative independence from the text seems to have encouraged unscrupulous dealers to remove them from the book and pass them off as single-sheet prints, since they could make more money that way than by selling the book intact. This would explain how the illustrations crop up so often masquerading as prints in print collections.

Of the six illustrations, it is Eishi's that most effectively evokes the spirit of the Floating World. It depicts a Yoshiwara courtesan seated in her spacious private apartment, surrounded by her attendants. The furnishings in the room are few but elegant: a charming little book cart filled with books and poem slips, a lacquer hand warmer decorated with a scene from *The Tale of Genji*, and a wooden hibachi in Chinese style.

It is a cold, early spring day, and the hand warmer sits on the floor between the courtesan and an older attendant while the hibachi is shared by the courtesan's two *kamuro*, who hold their hands out over its coals. Bamboo curtains extend along one wall of the room, covering the top of a large round window that looks out past a flowering plum branch toward the Nihon Dike and the surrounding countryside. A palanquin is being carried along the dike, and a maid, perhaps knowing that it is bringing a lover or a favored customer, draws the courtesan's attention to it.

The other five illustrations vary widely in subject matter and style, and several of them do not even touch on the early spring theme of the book. This is not the case with Utamaro's, however, which shows the women and maids of an upper-class household bringing a caged bird—almost certainly an *uguisu* (the warbler traditionally associated with spring and plum blossoms)—out onto a veranda where they are preparing to grind seeds for it. One of the maids titters as she shows a pestle to another maid, who seems equally amused—presumably at the pestle's resemblance to a phallus. A plum tree growing at the edge of the veranda is in full bloom, further underscoring the seasonal theme.

We will not take the time to describe the other illustrations in detail. Hokusai's is a country scene showing three women crossing a bridge near a village teahouse, and Shigemasa's depicts a detail from a court festival. The other two illustrations are by relatively obscure artists, and it seems strange to find their work linked in this book with that of their so much better-known contemporaries. Their contributions more than hold their own, however. Ekigi's picture of a court lady at a window admiring a flowering plum tree plays off the strong, curving diagonal of the tree trunk against the lady's billowing robes and long, flowing hair in admirable fashion. Tōrin's illustration, which seems to be closer in spirit to the Maruyama-Shijō School of Kyoto than to Edo ukiyo-e, shows a woman making her way through a downpour to an open room where two men are absorbed in a game of *go*. The contrast of the dense rain outside and the quiet in the open room is extremely effective.

The title, *Otoko dōka,* comes from the name of a ritualized folk dance that had been performed at the court in Kyoto until the sixteenth century. The dance was traditionally performed on the fifteenth day of the first month, which, following the old lunar calendar, made it a spring observance. It was this association with early spring that Sensōan must have had in mind when he chose the name of this long-since-discontinued dance for his title. An esoteric allusion of this sort would have fit right in with the playfully pedantic spirit of Edo kyōka.

IV-17

Various artists

***Shokusanjin enjo meisekishū,* "Master En's Collection of Shokusanjin Memorabilia"**

Circa 1804

Gajō (folding album) of letters, paintings, sketches, and poems; 40.3 x 24

Azabu Museum of Arts and Crafts

The collection of memorabilia in this album probably illustrates better than anything else in this exhibition the kinds of relationships and the mix of literary and artistic interests at the heart of the Floating World. The album con-

IV-17

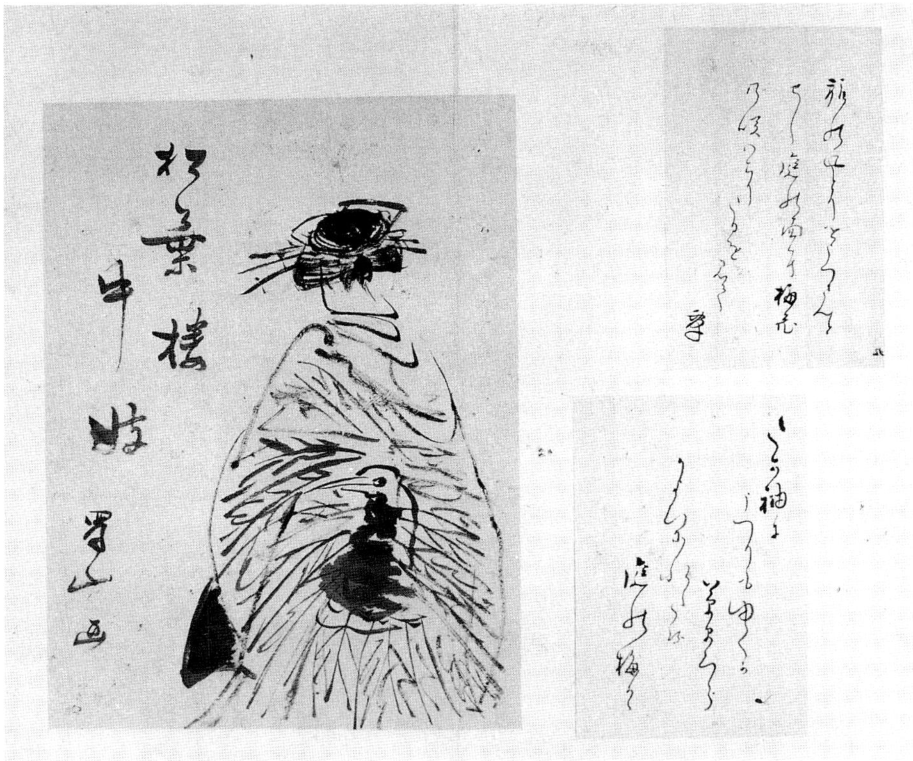

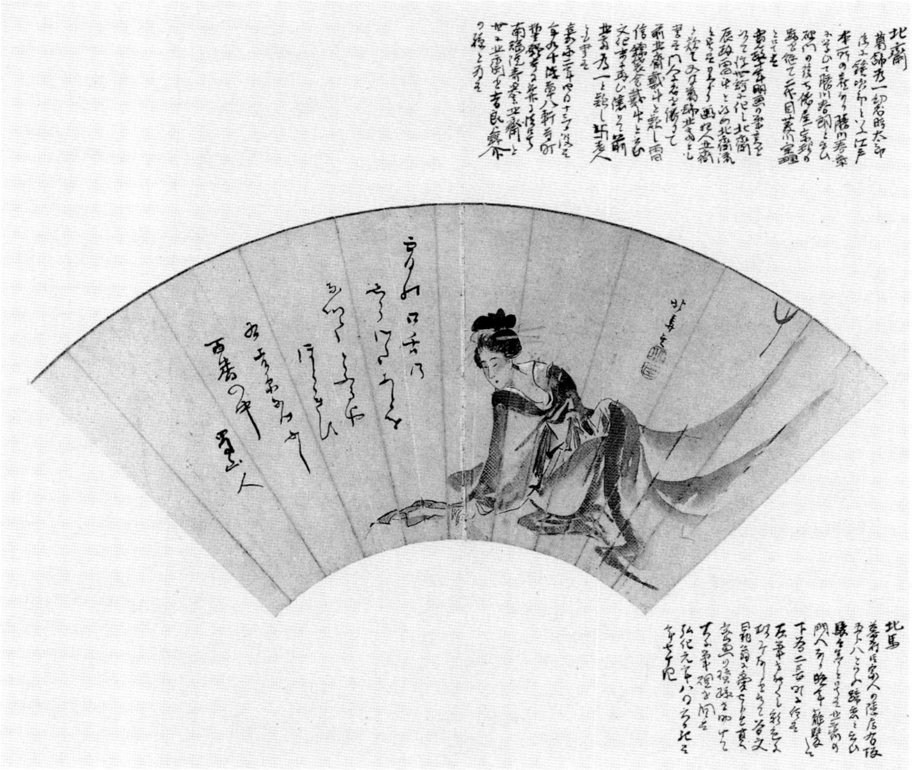

IV-17

tains a fascinating variety of work mounted, in no particular order, on forty-one double pages, with the items differing markedly from one another in size, format, and finish. The only unifying thread is provided by the fact that every item included relates, in one way or another, to Ōta Nampo, or, as he called himself when the papers were put together, Shokusanjin.

Though no one knows for sure when the materials were mounted in their present form, it is clear that they all originally belonged to Nakamura Sakugorō (whose *gō* was Kien), a friend of Nampo who lived in Nagasaki. Also, most, if not all, of the items seem to have some connection with Nampo's tour of duty to Nagasaki, which took place in 1804-05. It is now assumed that Nampo brought many of the paintings and poems with him to Nagasaki, as mementos, that he added other papers to the collection while he was there, and that he then, or subsequently, presented the entire collection to his friend.

The materials preserved in this folding album are too rich and extensive to be described in detail in this catalogue. Those who can read Japanese and would like to know more about the contents may refer to Shibata Mitsuhiko's article in *Bulletin of the Azabu Museum of Art*, no. 2, in which each item is thoroughly catalogued and discussed. Others will have to be content with what information we are able to provide here.

The collection includes poems (many by Nampo himself), paintings, sketches, letters, and occasional notes. Some of the poems are written on *tanzaku* (specially prepared poem slips); others are inscribed on fans; yet others are merely jotted down on scraps of paper. All of them convey a sense of having been composed and set down in a relaxed, impromptu manner. The same seems to be true of the paintings, which are all in the form of fans, with the exception of a particularly lovely brush drawing by Hokusai, which is on a rectangular sheet of paper.

Two ink sketches by Nampo himself are included among the pictures in the album. One is of a courtesan seen from behind; the other is of geisha, also seen from behind, playing a *shamisen*. The courtesan almost seems to have been drawn with a pen, in a rapid scribble of lines that manages to hold its own against the purposeful ungainliness of the accompanying calligraphy. The sketches are not masterly works of art, but they are lively and show that Nampo could easily come up with the kind of impromptu drawing that could prove useful at a party. His choice of subjects suggests that the pleasure quarters had not lost their fascination for him.

Among the other pictures in the album, several deserve particular mention. One of these is the brush drawing by Hokusai depicting a young samurai, his head not yet shaven, wearing his two swords and dressed in the formal attire befitting his rank. There is a tentative air about the young man, who gazes off to the left at something the viewer cannot see. His garments are rendered in deft washes of color—pale blue-green for his *hakama* and a grayish-purple with a touch of light brown showing through underneath for his jacket. The young man's attractiveness is underscored by the poem Nampo has added, which has unmistakable homoerotic implications.

A fan painting by Hokusai's pupil Hokuba is mounted on the following page. It depicts a courtesan about to slide under the curtains of a mosquito net. The bright red of the courtesan's undergarments showing at her shoulders, matched by the equally vivid red of the hem of the mosquito net, present a striking contrast to the delicate palette in the Hokusai drawing.

The inclusion of two Chinese-inspired fan paintings, one a *Nanga*-style landscape by Harugi Nammei, the other an amusing picture of the drunken Li Po by Unshitsu Dōjin, shows that Nampo's interests in art were not restricted to ukiyo-e. The artists were both residents of Edo but had both also studied in Nagasaki, which was noted for the closeness of its contacts with China.

IV-18

Brush Holder

Chinese origin; late Ming Dynasty (1570-1644)
Carved bamboo; 14.4 x 14.9 x 8.3
Portland Art Museum, Purchased with funds donated by Mr and Mrs. Bruce M. Stevenson

For centuries intellectuals in Japan had looked to China as the pinnacle of civilized philosophy, language arts, painting, and technology. This was increasingly so for the under-employed samurai of the Edo Period. Educated in classical Chinese studies, the intelligentsia, epitomized in this exhibition by Ōta Nampo, idealized the lives of the scholars living in China during the late Ming Dynasty (the roughly one-hundred-year period before the fall of the Ming in 1644).

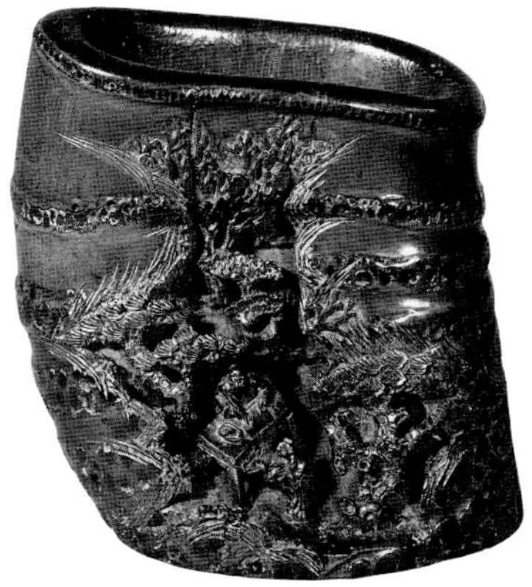

IV-18

The Chinese literati had pursued lives set apart from the workaday world, choosing remote and beautiful surroundings where they were free to ponder and philosophize. In contrast, the Edo intellectuals were captives in their own city, unable to extricate themselves from duty to their overlords. In their studies at their desks, however, they were able to exercise a degree of freedom, and could surround themselves with accoutrements representing a life dedicated to scholarly pursuits. Their intellectual endeavors often transported them to China, the meter of their poetry harkened back to the Chinese, and the implements they cherished were likewise Chinese, either in origin or in derivation.

This brush holder is embellished with an intricately carved scene of a calligrapher inscribing a scroll at his desk. Another man stands in the foreground, holding a bird. Trees rise to the side and behind, suggesting the isolated grove where these refined scholars dwell. The bamboo retains its strongly delineated growth bands, and is of an unusual tilted shape—the sort of natural irregularity that is particularly valued in the Japanese aesthetic.

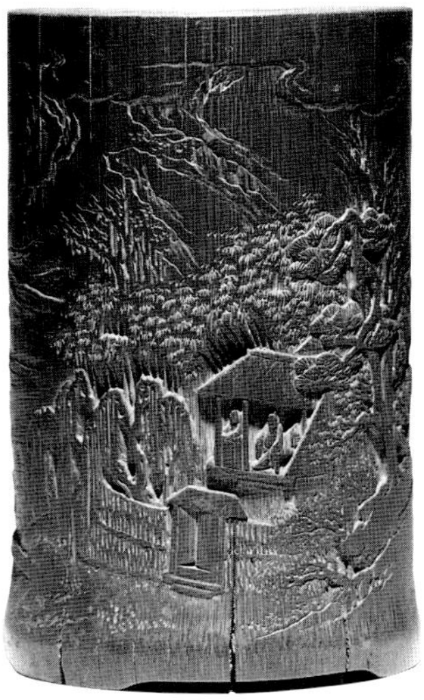

IV-19

IV-19

Brush Holder

Eighteenth century
Carved bamboo; approx. 13 (h) x 8 (diam.)
Peabody Essex Museum

Many scenes of men and women in the act of writing appear in this exhibition, providing numerous glimpses of the implements and accessories that would typically adorn a desk. We are shown examples of the inkstones and ink sticks used for grinding a rich writing fluid; highly decorated paperweights to keep the paper smooth; fanciful water droppers; ornate boxes for storing utensils; and brush holders for keeping animal-hair brushes of varying thicknesses in easy reach.

This bamboo brush holder has been intricately carved and engraved with a Chinese poem. The landscape depicts two figures crossing a bridge toward a clearing among the trees. One figure is carrying a walking stick and wears a long robe. Rocks and pine trees border the area, and a fence with a door and covered entrance encloses the clearing. Inside the gate is a small, simple pavilion where there are two people. The poem reads: "Under the moonlight we came across the bridge to hear the music of the harp."

These Chinese images were highly esteemed by the cultured Edo intellectuals. The literati of the late Ming were especially fond of the harp (or zither) for its associations with early scholars, who considered music to have a salutary effect and were inspired to compose poetry under its influence.

IV-20

Nested Incense Boxes (*kōjūbako*)

Eighteenth century (?)

Gold lacquer wooden box on four low feet; overlapping lid and two interior tiers of decorated lacquer boxes; 6.8 x 12.3 x 8.5

Walters Art Gallery

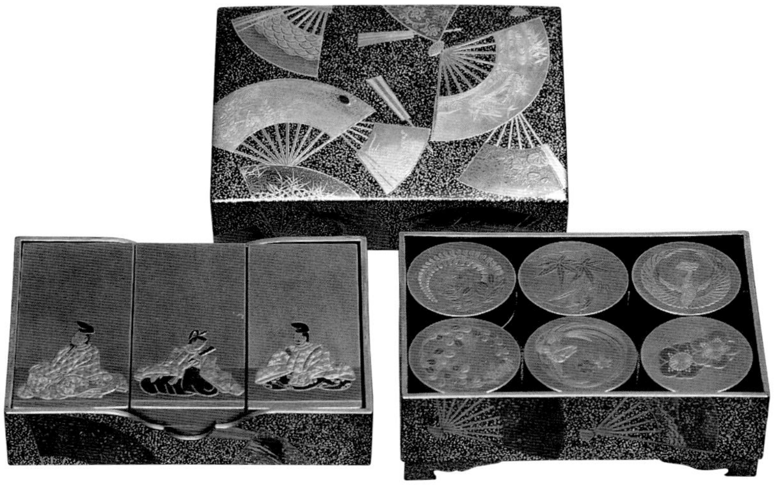

IV-20

The references to poetry in the decoration of this set of incense boxes make this an object of particular interest in this exhibition. The lids of the three rectangular boxes nested in the upper tier are adorned with *taka maki-e* portraits of three noblemen who appear to be classical poets.

In the Edo Period, incense boxes were used to store the fragrant wood fragments and pressed powders that set the scene for the incense game. This delicate pastime was popular in literary samurai circles in much the same way that the shell game and poetry contests were. On the surface, these pursuits may appear simply charming; in practice, they required an intimate understanding of classical art, literature, and poetry. The players exposed the depth of their learning through their skill in the game, and adhered to a formal etiquette that recalls the studied ritual of the tea ceremony. In essence, the game consisted of finding literary associations for ten varieties of incense, whose fragrances had to correspond to the season in which the game was played.

The utensils for handling the incense and coals, as well as the boxes for storing them, were themselves important aspects of the game, and conveyed a mood of beauty. It should be noted that the expense of these implements and the high cost of the treasured incense limited practice of the game to the wealthy.*

The lid and the exterior of this set of boxes are decorated with gold lacquer fans on a gold-dusted background. The fans, in turn, are embellished with floral elements, butterflies, a rabbit, and a boat. The six circular boxes in the lower tier are covered with emblematic designs of flowers and birds in relief (*taka maki-e*) on a matte, gold background.

---

*Gerd Lester, "Kodo—the Japanese Incense Game," *Arts of Asia* (January-February 1993), 70-75.

IV-21

Inkstone (*suzuri*)

Early nineteenth century

Engraved stone with wooden lid; 2.4 x 12.0 x 10.3

Portland Art Museum

Prized by connoisseurs for the smoothness of the stone, the *suzuri* served an important func-

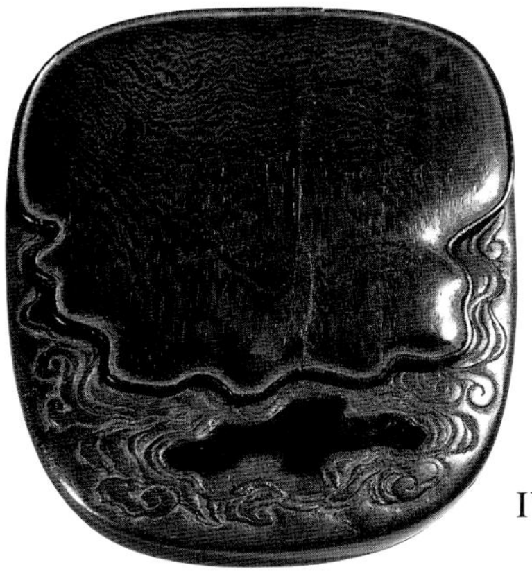

IV-21

tion on the scholar-calligrapher's desk: it was where the ink was ground. The stone needed to have a certain abrasiveness to break down the ink, while at the same time an even texture was required to prevent damage to the fragile bristles of the brush tip. Ideally, the grinding of the ink would be a silent, even meditative, process; a coarsely textured stone would cause the ink stick to squeak annoyingly. Moreover, the stone had to be nonporous to keep the ink from drying too quickly.

The shape of the stone was likewise important. It had to be flat to provide a surface for grinding the ink stick with a few drops of water, and it needed to have a well at one end into which any excess liquid could flow. The smoother the stone, the more luxuriant the ink and the lighter the abrasion against the brush.

The inkstone shown here resembles the one shown in Eishi's portrait of Shokusanjin (Catalogue no. IV-1). The stone is carved in a stylized and perforated water design, and the wooden lid, which would cover the stone when not in use to protect it from abrasive dust, is scalloped at the edges. There is a small indented margin all around, and a highly visible wood grain.

IV-22

Writing box (*suzuribako*)

Early nineteenth century.

Gold lacquer on wood; 24 x 22 x 4.7

Walters Art Gallery

Perhaps no other personal possession is as symbolic of Japan's literary civilization as the writing box. Not a showy ornament or an image booster, the *suzuribako* was a private luxury, bespeaking the owner's delight in writing. Moreover, it functioned as a convenient desk organizer that held all the utensils needed for writing—inkstone, ink stick, water dropper, brush. The degree to which these implements were cherished is evident in the extraordinary craftsmanship displayed in the boxes themselves.

It is important to remember that the room in which such a box would have been kept was probably not highly decorated. The walls were a neutral tone, the floors were tatami mats, and the windows were shaded with plain paper shoji screens. Usually, the only painting embellishing the walls would be a scroll hung in the *tokonoma* alcove, and possibly painting on the *fusuma* screen doors. Although furnishings during the Edo Period were usually ornate, they were used sparingly. Closets and cabinets were not normal features of Japanese interior design; shelves and chests were kept to a minimum because of the amount of living space they would consume. Hence, boxes and handy containers proliferated as places for storing things and imposing order on them.

Lacquered wood was a favorite material for such containers because of its resistance to mildew—in fact, lacquerware needs a humid environment. Thus, there is a natural relationship

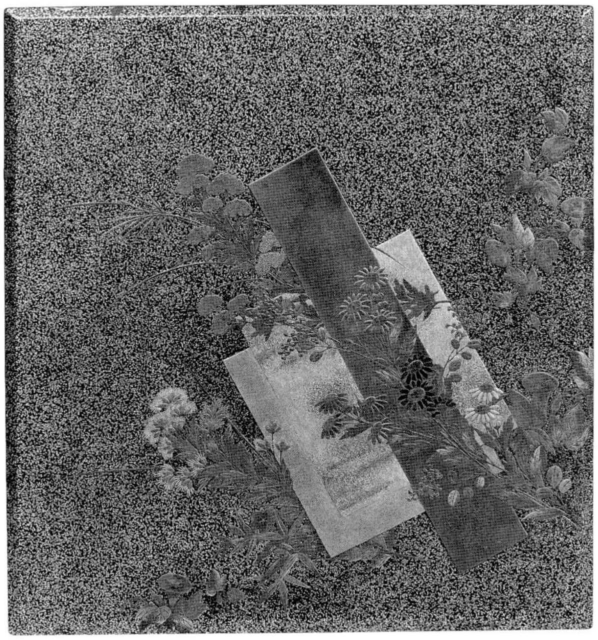

IV-22

between Japan's wet springs, muggy summers, stormy autumns, and damp winters and these receptacles.

The decoration on the lid of this box is specifically literary. Depicted in gold and silver *hira maki-e* on a *nashiji* background are a long, narrow *tanzaku* and square *shikishi*.* They lie amongst an autumnal bouquet of *kikyō* (bell-flowers), *kiku* (chrysanthemums), *ominaeshi* (scabiosa), *asagao* (morning glories), *nadeshiko* (pinks), and *suzuki* (pampas grass). The design extends to the sides, the lid interior, and one interior tray. Inside the box are two interior trays and a frame holding an inkstone and water dropper.

---

* *Hira maki-e*: "Flat gold-dusted picture" made by blowing fine gold powder through a bamboo tube onto the still-damp lacquer. The design is slightly raised above the ground by layers of lacquer. *Nashiji*: "Pear skin," because of the golden glint and grainy texture. Irregularly shaped gold flakes are strewn on the still-damp lacquer to form a background.

IV-23
***Inro* clock**
Circa 1800
Brass case, brass with silver and gold alloy ojime with kneeling figure and kettle, sundial netsuke; 6.9 x 5.6 x 2.5
Albert L. Odmark

IV-24
Pillar clock (*shaku-dokei*)
Circa 1800
Shitan wood cabinet, brass corner pillars, circular movement, adjustable silver numerals, basket of flowers in openwork front plate; 35.1 x 5.4 x 4.5
Kazue and Mearl Snell

IV-25
Standing clock (*dai-dokei*)
Late eighteenth century
Cabriolet legs and stand of shitan wood, shitan hood, brass casing and gilt-fired mechanism, brass front plate with scroll-like flowers in openwork showing traces of gold plating. The clock is furnished with a single calendar that indicates short (shō) or long (dai) months. Circular escapement with shallow bell; 67 (h)
Kazue and Mearl Snell

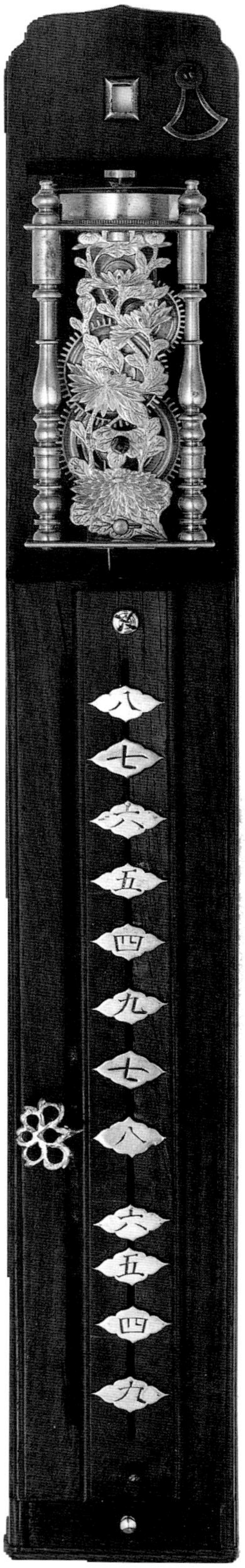

IV-24

A Note about Time-Keeping

In 1549 the Portuguese Jesuit missionary Francesco Xavier landed at Kagoshima and a year later sought permission to establish a mission, presenting a clock to the local magistrate. It was the first mechanical clock in Japan. Other missionaries subsequently brought many such clocks into Japan, though most of them have not survived. The earliest remaining clock bears the date 1581, and was presented to the shogun, Tokugawa Ieyasu, by the Spanish governor of Mexico.

Besides evangelizing, the missionaries taught the principles and procedures for making printing presses, organs, clocks, and astronomical devices at their *seminarios* in Kyoto and Kyushu. It seems safe to assume that, until 1624, when the Spaniards were expelled, most early Japanese clockmakers came by their knowledge through these missionary schools.

Tsuda Jōzaemon of Kyoto was given the task of repairing Ieyasu's clock, which he used as a model for devising a new one. Presented with such workmanship and ingenuity, Ieyasu put Tsuda into his service, and in 1598 made the Tsuda family the official clockmakers for the Tokugawas.

Many daimyo were also interested in clocks, and the clockmakers who came to serve them began producing timepieces as elaborate works of art. Because of the isolationism during the Edo Period, it was almost impossible for new

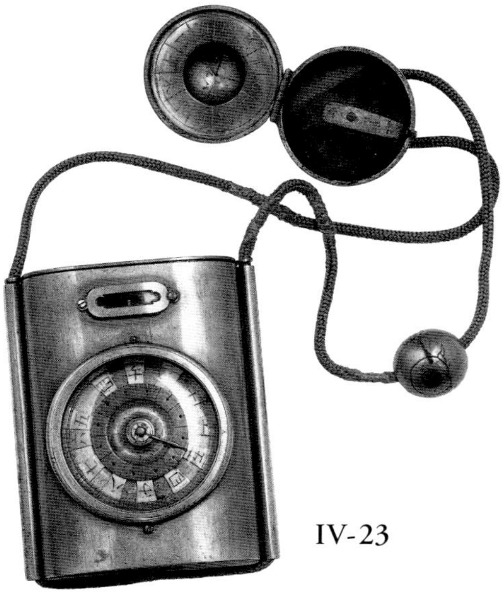
IV-23

European technology to be introduced to Japan. In its absence, Japanese clocksmiths devoted their efforts to reconciling their regulated timepieces with the Japanese system of keeping time.

Once mass-produced chiming clocks began to be imported in the Meiji Period, after Japan had adopted the western time-keeping system in 1873, the old system of keeping time quickly fell into disuse.*

There are three main classifications of Japanese clocks. Tower clocks (*yagura-dokei*), so called because Ieyasu had placed his in the tower of Fushimi Castle, were driven by weights, and either placed on stands or mounted on the wall (see the Suspended Lantern Clock, Catalogue no. II-35). Pillow clocks (*makura-dokei*), because the shape resembled a pillow, were driven by springs. Their compact cases enabled them to be placed on a writing table or shelf. Usually the cases were wood (*shitan*, persimmon, or mulberry), though occasionally they were lacquered or decorated with mother-of-pearl. Pillar or ruler clocks (*hashira-kake* or *shaku-dokei*) were intended to be hung on the wall. There were also many unusual forms, such as the *inro* clock, in which clockmakers joined their skills with those of other artisans.

Clocks were viewed as exquisite novelties rather than as practical objects. The clocks included in this exhibition were most likely owned by regional lords who may have commissioned them from craftsmen; intellectual samurai, such as those attending the Shirandō New Year's party (Catalogue no. IV-5), who were intrigued with western science and technology; or wealthy merchants who would have had the means to acquire one.

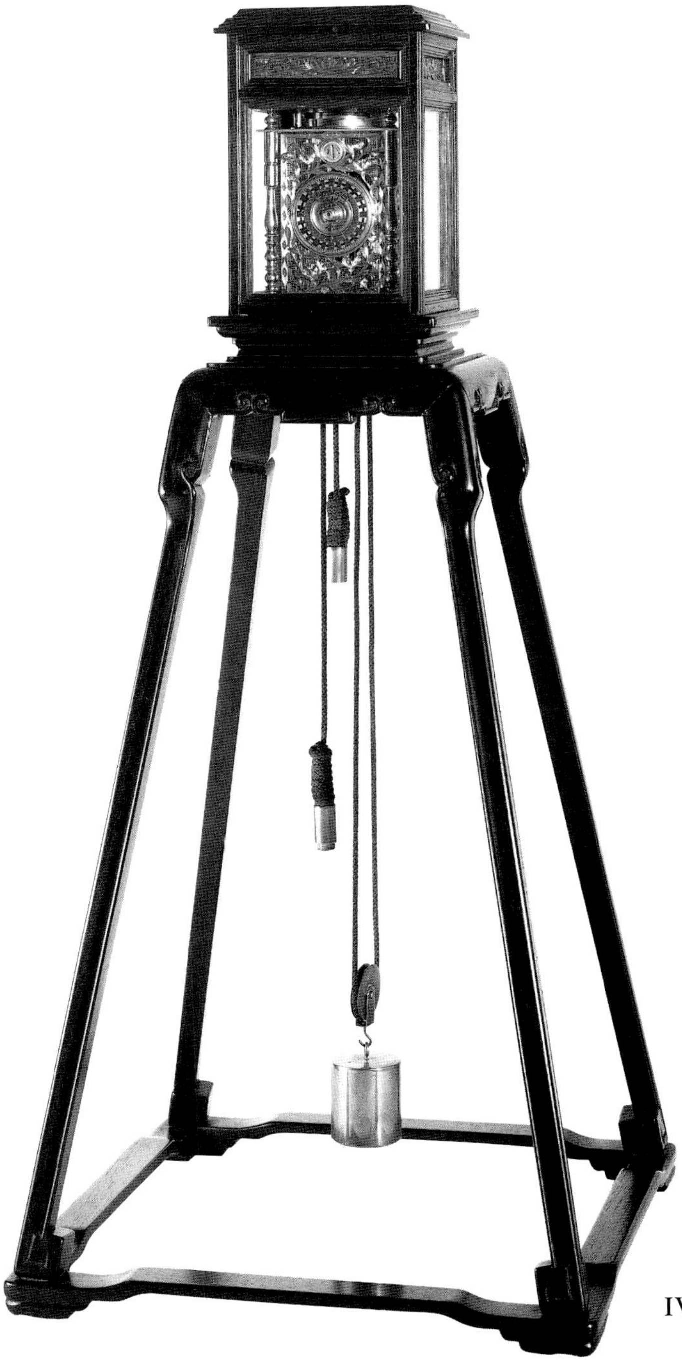

IV-25

* Kagaku Hakubutsukan Kōenkai, *Zūroku Wa-dokei* (Tokyo: Zaidan Hōjin Kagaku Hakubutsukan Kōenkai, Showa 59), vol. 2.

Catalogue Section V: Kabuki and Ichikawa Danjūrō V

Edo's theater district centered around Fukiyachō and Sakaichō, the former site of the Yoshiwara—an area that had been nothing but swampy marsh when the licensed quarter was first designated in 1618. After the horrendous fire of 1657 that destroyed the brothels, the Yoshiwara moved to the paddy fields north of Edo, but the old neighborhood kept its associations with entertainment, merely changing its focus from courtesans to actors. Two of the great Edo theaters were near one another there: the Nakamura-za in Fukiyachō and the Ichimura-za in Sakaichō. They were surrounded by smaller theaters, many of which offered puppet dramas (*bunraku*), while nearby were eating establishments, teahouses, and actors' homes. The other leading Edo theater, the Morita-za, was about two and a half kilometers to the south, in the neighborhood of Kobikichō.

The Edo public adored the theater for its diversion, its innovation, and its style. Actors were celebrities and trendsetters. In this exhibition, we see how the actor Ichikawa Danjūrō V (1741-1806) not only epitomized his art but became a symbol of the Edokko, the city's native son.

The first Ichikawa Danjūrō (1660-1704) is said to have originated the *aragoto* acting style of exaggerated poses and intense emotion that became the legacy of subsequent generations of the family. This powerful performing style remained popular, but by 1776 Danjūrō IV had already begun to move toward a more realistic portrayal of character with his performance of Matsuomaru, in a departure that probably reflected the changing social tendencies. Danjūrō V continued the trend so as to keep the theater relevant to his audiences. As we see throughout this exhibition, the late eighteenth century was a time of innovation and change in Edo, and a great deal of new writing and stagecraft (sometimes in response to new government laws) was changing kabuki theater. In the course of his 140 performances, Danjūrō V used a wider range of styles in his enactment of heroes.

Theater managers, meanwhile, were aggressively promoting new plays, and audiences were filling the houses to see them. Actors themselves performed many types of roles, rather than being identified with a single type of character, as they had been in the past. Danjūrō V proved to be a master of many roles (*kaneru yakusha*), and thereby gained an extraordinary following. Like all leading actors then and now, he was the object of insatiable public curiosity about his personal life as well as his stage career.

The burgeoning publishing industry contributed to this public hunger for "images"—models for people to imitate in dress, speech, and behavior. We have seen how this was true of the Yoshiwara beauties; it was likewise true of the great actors. People idolized them, clamored for pictures of their behind-the-scenes lives, bought books that gossiped about them, and gained prestige by using things that carried their family crests or names—a phenomenon that resulted in part from the increased flow of money into the merchant class, in part from the strength of the performances the actors brought to the stage.

While it is easy for us to understand the dynamics of stardom and to analyze the economics of show business, it is perhaps more difficult for us to imagine the richness of the Edo actor's art. Growing up in an acting family, an actor was imbued with generations of acting philosophy and style. Ichikawa Danjūrō I and II had bequeathed to their descendants artistic instructions, which included technique as well as meditations on how the actor should cope with fame, pride, and personal life. Danjūrō V encountered these issues daily, in an immersion that may be assumed to have given much depth to his performances, and to have led him to reflect on the distinctions between life on stage and off. Writing poetry—a traditional Ichikawa family pastime—may have helped him express these complexities.

In 1791 Danjūrō V gave a lengthy prologue (*kōjō*) for the *kaomise* in which his son, Danjūrō VI, was appearing. The prologue contained numerous kyōka, written by Danjūrō V, who was an accomplished poet in conventional *waka* as well as comic verse, and was known by a number of poetry names (Mimasu, Hakuen, Hogoan, and, for kyōka, Hanamichi no Tsurane). As we have already seen, the kyōka movement was at its peak in the late eighteenth century. Its leading proponents, Ōta Nampo (Yomo no Akara) and Akera Kankō, were eradicating the snobbish Kyoto-centered image that verse composition carried and placing it within reach of commoners. Danjūrō V himself was closely allied with Ōta Nampo, Shikatsube no Magao, and Tatekawa (or Utei) Emba in the kyōka movement.

Though Danjūrō V apparently did not seek publicity, his training allowed him to bear it casually while following his own interests and enduring his own tragedies. Through the traditions in which he was steeped, he introduced a new spirit to the stage, mesmerizing audiences who regarded him as the perfect embodiment of the Edokko, born and bred in the heart of town, and proud of it.

V-1

Attributed to Torii Kiyonaga (1752-1815)

Billboard for a Performance of "Junshoku Yaoya O-Shichi"

Circa 1793

Mounted as a four-panel screen; colors on paper; 160.5 x 254

No signature

Tsubouchi Memorial Theater Museum, Waseda University

Considerably larger than posters of today, billboards of this type were displayed in front of theaters during the late Tokugawa Period and were produced almost exclusively by the Torii School. Since they were expected to be taken down (and destroyed) once the performance being billed was over, the paints used for them were of poor quality. Posters that have survived have not aged well—the paint used on this one has started to peel. The poster was mounted as a four-panel screen about forty years ago.

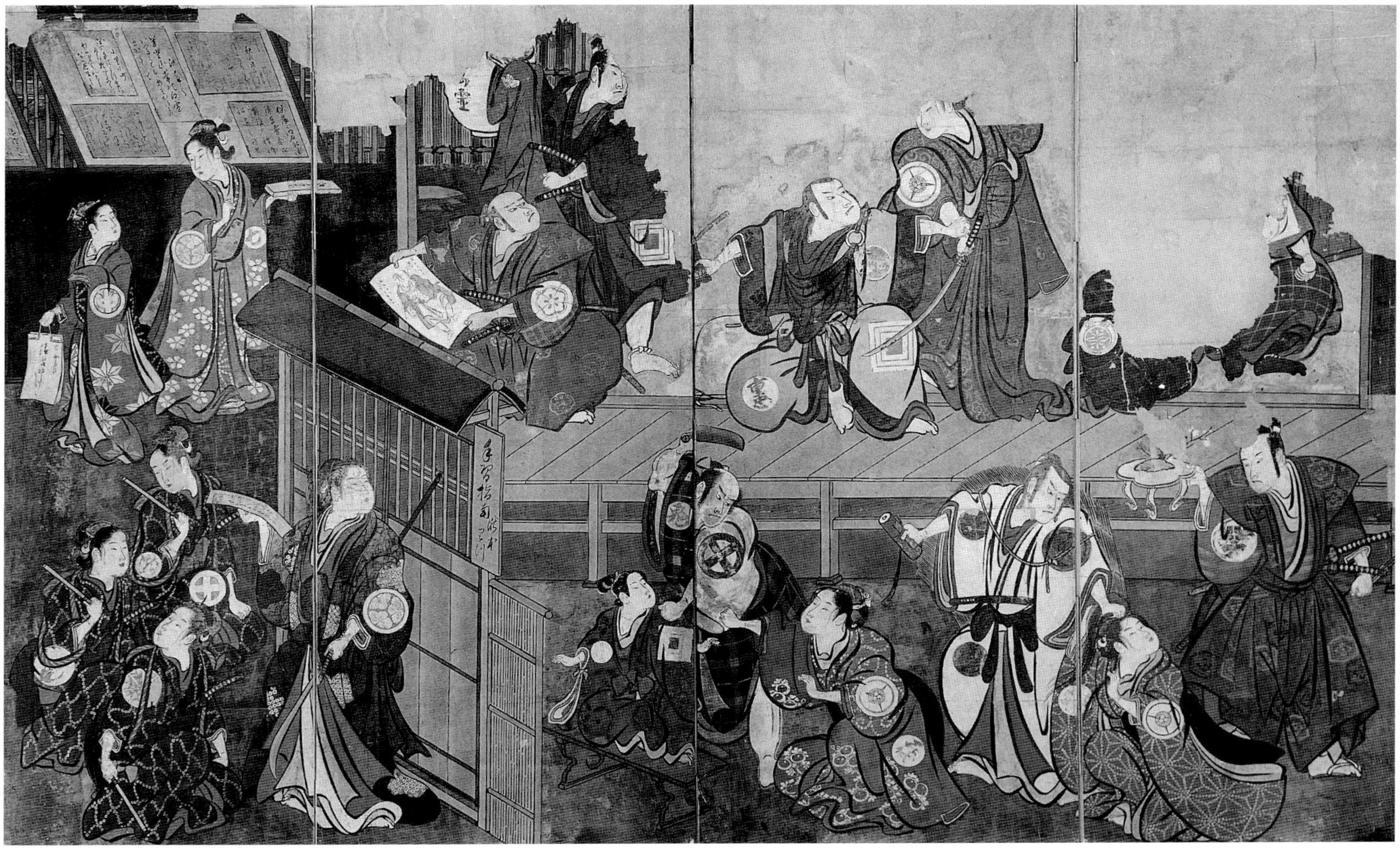

V-1

The billboard announces a performance of *Junshoku Yaoya O-Shichi* at the Kawarazaki-za theater in the seventh month of Kansei 5 (1793). This was to be a three-part, daylong performance. The poster depicts scene 2, part 3, "Mizakidera koya." Program notes for the *Junshoku Yaoya O-Shichi* explain that the play is a continuation of the *Yaoya O-Shichi* performance of the fifth month, which had been a great success. Because no program remains from that performance, the playwright cannot be identified with certainty, but the names of Masuyama Kinpachi and Kimura Enji appear in the *kaomise* program of Kansei 4 and program albums of Kansei 5, so it is safe to assume that they were the writers.

The actors can be identified by the crests on their costumes: in the lower-right corner of the right-most panel of the screen stands Bandō Mitsugorō II, while the *onnagata* to his left is Iwai Kamesaburō. On the right of the section that has peeled is Bandō Zenji; to his left is Nakamura Yodonosuke. In the second panel of the screen is Sawamura Yodogorō, in white, pulling the hair of the woman; above, the woman holding the sword is Iwai Heishirō IV. To her left is Ichikawa Ebizō (Danjūrō V). The woman below the platform is Nakamura Kiyotarō, and Ōtani Hiroji is the actor wielding the hatchet at the edge of the panel. Playing the child sitting at the desk is Ichikawa Kiyosaburō. The man in the black *haori* in the top section of the third panel is Ichikawa Omezō; below him, unfolding a "wanted" poster, is Mikoku Fujigorō. Outside the gate, the woman holding the halberd is Kosagawa Tokoyo. Three young girls stand to her left: Ōtani Takijirō and two Nakamuras, Manyo and Fujitaki, from the famous family of *onnagata* actors. Above them are Kosagawa Shichizō and Nakamura Yahachi, playing two calligraphy students.

It was during this theater season that Ichikawa Ebizō broke down backstage and divulged to Santō Kyōden his intention to retire, as described by Laurence Kominz in his essay in this catalogue.

Although it is not signed, the poster gives

many clues that point to Kiyonaga as the artist. Principally, there are the characteristically round faces of actors in women's roles, as well as the calligraphy in the copybook and on the wooden plaque, which resembles Kiyonaga's signature style. The composition, flowing lines, and somber colors with prominent reds lend further credence to the premise that the work came from Kiyonaga's brush.

It is also known that Kiyonaga returned to the profession of billboard production when his mentor, Torii Kiyomitsu (1735-1785), began to ail. In contrast to printmaking, the job of painting theatrical posters at least paid a living wage. It was, moreover, the profession of the Torii family, and thus it became Kiyonaga's duty to continue the tradition after Kiyomitsu's death.

V-2

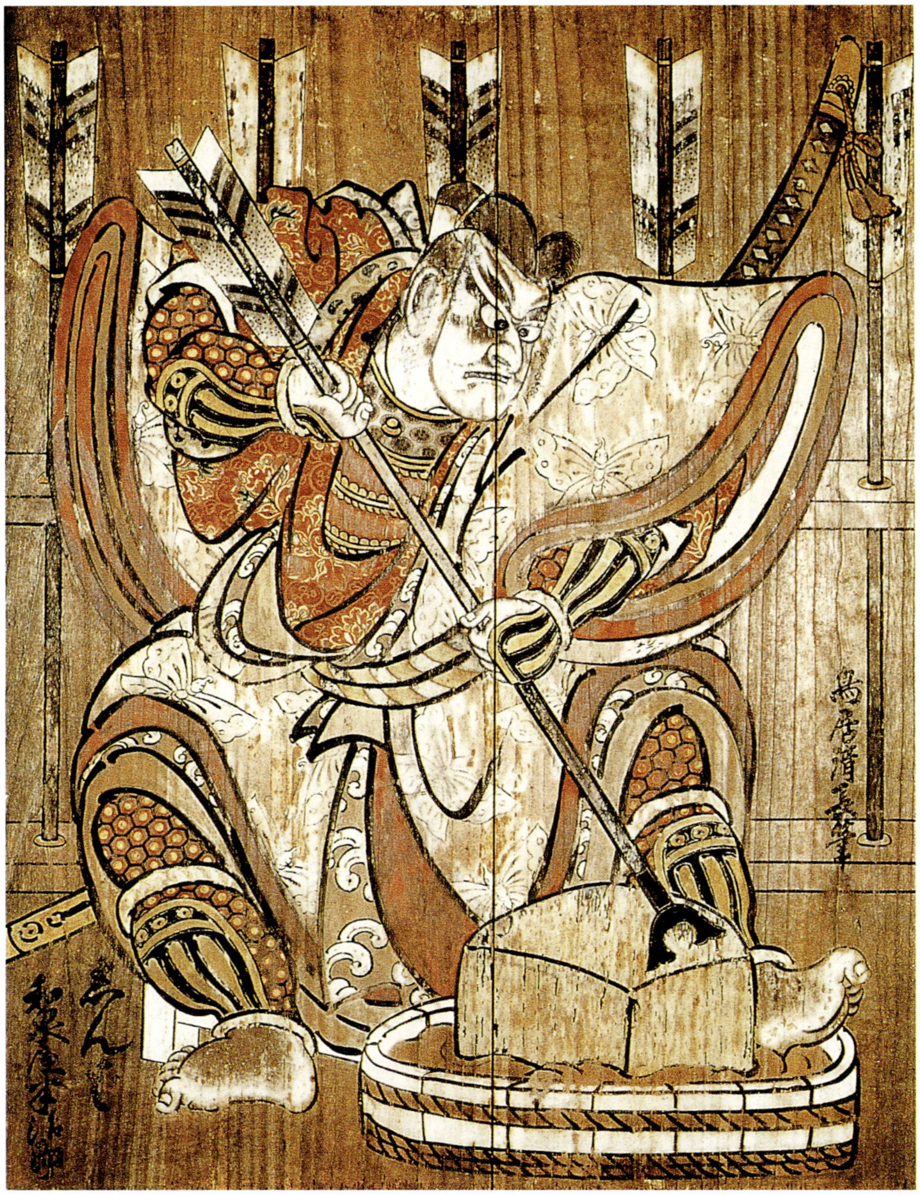

V-2

Torii Kiyonaga (1752-1815)

Danjūrō V as "Ya no ne" Gorō

Donated in 1810

Ema; colors on wood; 91 x 116

Signature of artist (Torii Kiyonaga hitsu)

Takoyakushi Jōjuin

In contrast to the decorative prints and paintings on paper and silk that form the greater part of this exhibition, this work, painted on a wooden plaque, was made specifically to be displayed at a temple. Such votive paintings were generally commissioned by worshippers and then presented to the temple out of gratitude or devotion, or to fulfill a vow.

"Ya no ne" (The arrowhead) was one of the eighteen signature scenes in the Ichikawa Danjūrō repertoire, acted in characteristic *aragoto* style. Several poses and moments of emphasis allow the actor to display his skill in flamboyant style while biting humor weaves through the lines, making the play a favorite with audiences. Without a strong plot line, it loosely recounts the story of the Soga brothers, and is replete with New Year's customs and vocabulary familiar to Edo-period audiences. These devices tighten the tale's conventionally weighty tone and bring the legendary hero, Soga Gorō, closer to the lives of ordinary people.

The *ema* was donated by Izumiya Chūbei and Izumiya Hanjirō; the inscription on the lower-left side of the plaque reads: Shinba / Izumi Chūbei. Shinba was a merchant section of Edo assigned to stores specializing in prepared foods such as packaged sweets and boxed dried fish. Such things were popular as gifts from kabuki fans to their favorite actors. Izumi Chūbei reportedly ran the Izumiya shop; he may have been a Danjūrō fan or perhaps found that his prosperity was closely linked with the success of famous actors. The *ema* was donated to a popular temple, Takoyakushi Jōjuin, three years after Danjūrō V's death, and is believed to depict him, since Danjūrō VII had not yet appeared in the "Ya no ne" Gorō role at that time.

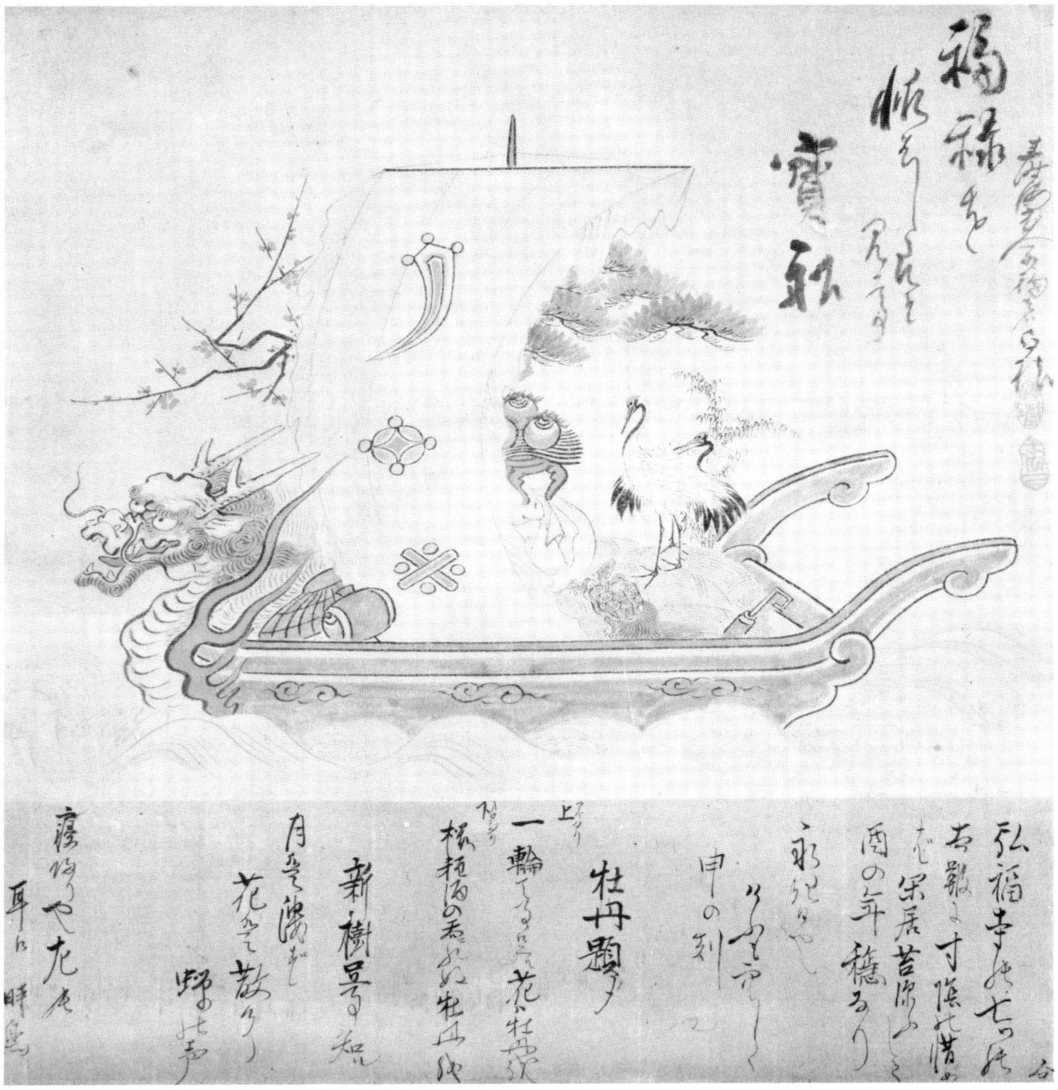

V-3

The depiction, however, is neither a portrait nor representative of Kiyonaga's naturalistic painting style: the *ema* was painted in the traditional Torii style for theatrical billboards (see Catalogue number V-1), which emblemize the characters more than the actors. It shows Gorō sharpening his arrows in preparation for his revenge on his father's murderer, and is in a sense a metaphor for the sharpening of martial skills and spiritual focus that Gorō needed to accomplish his mission. This resolution of purpose was believed to include spiritual devotion, and therefore made the scene appropriate for an *ema*.

V-3

Ichikawa Danjūrō V (1741-1806) and Danjūrō VII (1791-1859)

Treasure Boat and Haiku Verses

Circa 1801 and later

Hanging scroll in two parts; ink on paper

Signature of artist (Jukairōjin kobukusha Hakuen, "The White Monkey blessed with many children by the god of longevity")

Tsubouchi Memorial Theater Museum, Waseda University

This curious scroll has been assembled from two preexisting works, a painting of a treasure boat with a haiku written by Danjūrō VII at top and a manuscript with five haiku by Danjūrō V at bottom. The picture of the treasure boat itself is somewhat unusual. Most nineteenth-century representations of treasure boats were more realistic, and carried tangible cargoes of goods like rice and money. This one is patterned after the fanciful dragon boats found in medieval Japanese handscrolls, and its cargo is strictly symbolic. The "treasures" are represented by the three emblems on the sail and objects like the hammer and conch shell in the bow of the boat and the two "pearls" on the stand near the mast. A crane, symbolizing longevity, and a branch each of pine, plum, and bamboo, the so-called "three friends of winter," extend the roster of auspicious symbols even further. Danjūrō VII's verse reads: *Fukuroku o / nobashira to mite / takarabune* (With [the god of] wealth as its mast, the treasure boat!).

Danjūrō V's verses are preceded by an inscription indicating that they were written during an idle moment at Kōfukuji Temple in the Year of the Cock (probably 1801). Kōfukuji was in Mukōjima, where Danjūrō had retired to write poetry after leaving the stage, and was one of the stops on a mock pilgrimage to the seven gods of good luck invented by Shokusanjin (Ōta Nampo) and his friends some time in the early 1800s. Danjūrō's haiku often take the peony as their subject. We will transcribe and translate only two of them: *Ichirin de / kototaru hana wa / botan kana* (With the peony, one flower alone will suffice); *Negaeri ya / hidari no mimi ni / hototogisu* (Turning over in my sleep, I heard a cuckoo's call in my left ear).

It is not known when Danjūrō VII's verse was written or when the two works were mounted together in their present form.

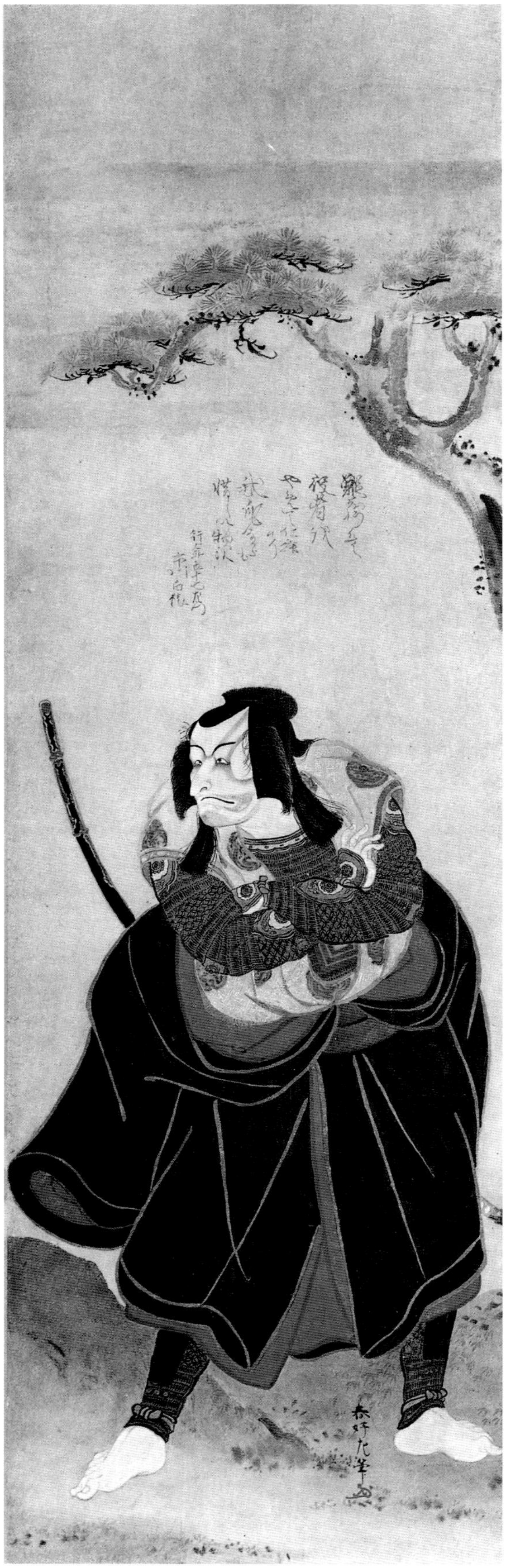

V-4

V-4

Katsukawa Shunkō (1743-1812)

Ichikawa Ebizō IV (Danjūrō V)

1797

Hanging scroll; ink, colors, and gofun on paper; 85.7 x 27

Signature of artist (Shunkō sahitsu, "painted with the left hand") followed by hand-painted seal (kakihan or kao)

The Minneapolis Institute of Arts, Bequest of Richard P. Gale

Ebizō (or Hakuen, as he called himself after 1796) strikes a characteristic pose, legs apart, arms folded, glaring balefully off to the left. He has freed his arms and armor-clad upper body from his outer robes, which hang down around his hips, held in place by his obi. When a hero freed his arms in this way, it was usually a sign that he was about to do battle, but here he has still not unsheathed his sword, perhaps feeling that he can vanquish his opponent with nothing more than the malevolence of his stare.

Above, written in Hakuen's distinctive hand, is a poem beginning with the words *Ebizō wa / yakusha o yamete* (Ebizō, having given up being an actor), and signed *gyōnen gojūshichi sai no Ichikawa Hakuen* (The White Monkey Ichikawa at age fifty-seven). Hakuen had actually retired from the stage in 1796, and it is assumed that this picture represents him playing Kagekiyo prior to that. Danjūrō VI, his son, played the son of Kagekiyo in a Soga play performed at the Miyako-za during New Year's of 1797.

Hakuen's *mimasu* (rice-measure) crest is only partially visible under his folded arms, but appears again, in the scroll's present mounting, in the two vertical strips of brocade bordering the actual painting.

Shunkō is thought to have lost the use of his right arm through paralysis some time between 1787 and 1788, but he trained himself to use his left hand and continued to paint with no discernible loss of skill.

V-5

Katsukawa Shunshō (1726-1792)

Danjūrō V in a "Shibaraku" Role

Circa 1788

Hanging scroll; ink, colors, and gofun on silk; 49.1 x 24.8

Signature of artist (Katsu Shunshō) with red kakihan

The Minneapolis Institute of Arts, Bequest of Richard P. Gale

"Shibaraku" scenes, an Ichikawa family specialty, had been a popular feature of Edo kabuki since Danjūrō I first performed one in the late seventeenth century. As Laurence Kominz points out in his essay in this catalogue, Danjūrō V invariably included a "Shibaraku" scene in his annual *kaomise* appearances, and they never failed to be crowd pleasers.

Given its inherent drama, the subject was a favorite with ukiyo-e artists as well. Most prints and paintings dealing with the subject (including Catalogue nos. V-7 and V-16), however, depict the moment when the hero first calls out *"Shibaraku!"* from the *hanamichi*, and all action comes to an immediate halt. Shunshō has broken with this convention and chosen the moment, closer to the scene's finale, when the hero

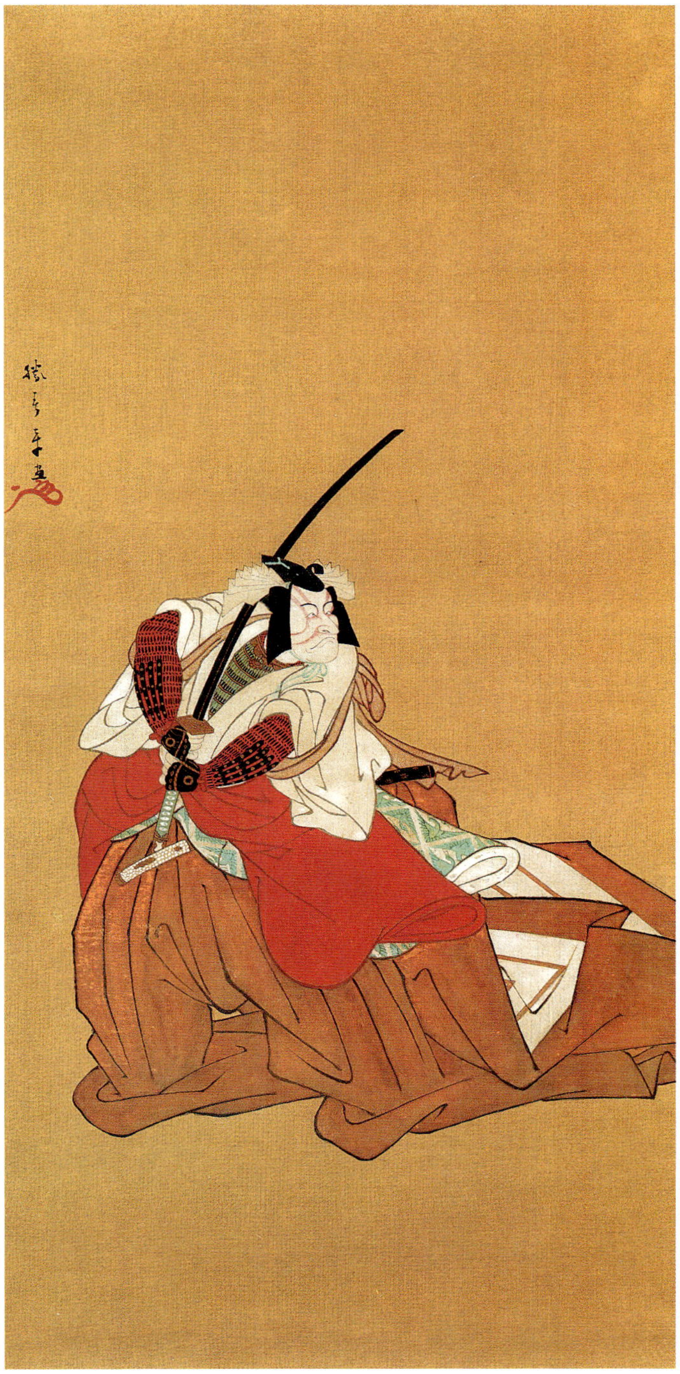

V-5

has already drawn his seven-foot-long sword and turns to face his adversaries, whose heads he will soon lop off in a single sweep. The change in timing is crucial. Most other depictions show the actor glowering but motionless, virtually encased in his ponderous robes. These engulfing robes posed a problem for Shunshō. He solved it by using the long curve of Danjūrō's sword as a pivot around which to draw vigorous lines animating the hero's costume. Danjūrō has already removed his arms from the sleeves of his brick-red outer garment, and the lowered sleeves swing out from his body as he turns. The actor's stony face provides the only other point of stillness (besides the sword) in this otherwise highly energetic composition. Even Shunshō's *kakihan* seems to share in the general sense of movement. It could almost be a mirror image, in calligraphic form, of the actor's figure. The energy Shunshō has managed to convey in this painting seems the more impressive given the work's relatively modest size.

V-6

Anonymous, Katsukawa School

Danjūrō V as Matsuomaru

1789-90

Section of a handscroll mounted on board; ink and colors on paper; 18.5 x 19.9

No signature

The British Museum

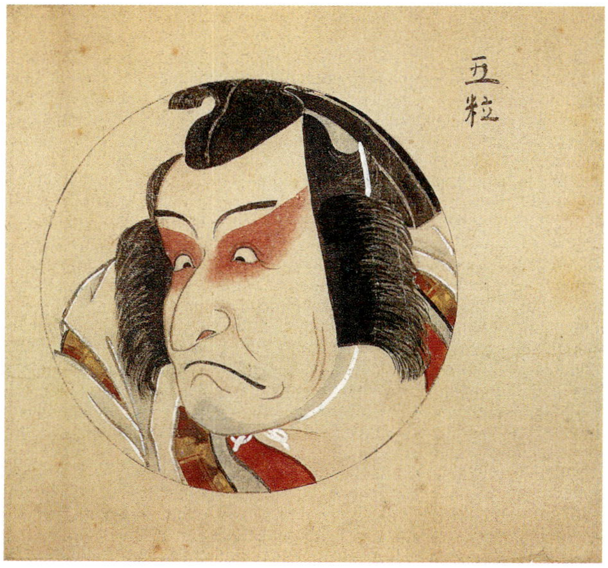

V-6

This is one of the surviving sections of a handscroll of portraits of kabuki actors in round windows. Two longer sections of the scroll, each portraying two actors, are also preserved in the British Museum. Each of the portraits is identified with one or more of the actor's names: his *haimyō* (haiku poetry name), *yagō* (house name), or standard acting name. In this case, the only name given is Danjūrō's *haimyō* of the time, Goi. He only later adopted the *haimyō* encountered most frequently in this exhibition, Hakuen.

The Freer Gallery of Art, in Washington, D.C., has a full-length painting by Katsukawa Shunkō of Danjūrō in the same role, in which the face is almost identical, detail for detail, with this portrait.* It is thought that the Freer painting records Danjūrō's performance in a play at the Kiri-za in 1788. Based on the names of the actors depicted on the other sections of the scroll, this portrait could have been painted only a year or so later at most. Whether or not it is by Shunkō, as the resemblance to the Freer painting suggests, there can be no question that it is by a Katsukawa School artist and, judging by the spontaneity and sureness of the drawing, one of considerable talent and maturity.

Matsuomaru was one of the three heroes of the popular kabuki play *Sugawara denju tenarai kagami*, first performed in 1746. The play was a great showpiece for *aragoto* acting, which was a specialty of succeeding generations bearing the Danjūrō name.

* The entire painting and a detail of the head are reproduced in Harold P. Stern, *Ukiyo-e Painting* (Washington, D. C.: Smithsonian Institution, 1973), 184, 187.

V-7

Rekisentei Eiri (active 1790-1800)

"Shibaraku" Scene

Circa 1796

Woodblock print: horizontal ōban; 26.7 x 38.4

Signature of artist (Rekisentei Eiri ga) and name and address of publisher (Shiba Shimmeimae, hammoto Izumiya) with title in panel at right

Arthur M. Sackler Museum, Harvard University Art Museums, Duel Collection

A capacity crowd has gathered in one of the great theaters of Sakaichō to see Danjūrō V per-

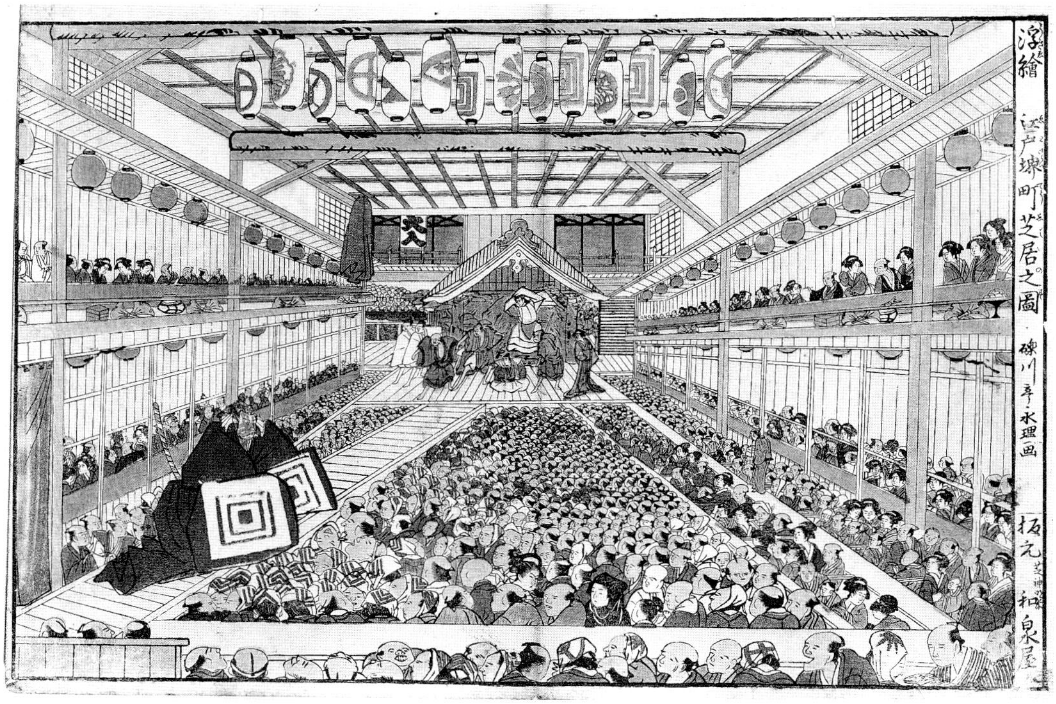

V-7

form his famous "Shibaraku" scene. The audience is packed so tightly that there is no room to move, and additional tiers of seats have been set up behind the stage, creating a so-called *rakan* gallery.* A banner hanging above the stage at left declares the obvious, *ō-iri*, "full house." Danjūrō has just made his appearance on the *hanamichi*, and all eyes are riveted on him. His face is painted with red-and-white striped *kumadori* makeup, and he is wearing the stiff crimson robes emblazoned with the family crest that were the standard costume for the scene. Action on the stage itself has come to a stop as he launches into a monologue of his own creation. A cluster of onlookers wearing kerchiefs with the Ichikawa crest—clearly members of one of the actor's enthusiastic fan clubs—have stationed themselves at his feet.

Though the focus of this print is definitely on Danjūrō, other aspects of the scene are not neglected. Different classes of playgoers are distinguished clearly by their clothing and behavior, and features of the building, like the clerestory windows above the boxes and the roof over the stage, are carefully delineated. Note the row of paper lanterns hanging overhead toward the back of the theater. These bore the crests of the leading actors. Significantly, three of them are emblazoned with the Ichikawa *mimasu* crest. Danjūrō (actually then going by the name of Ebizō) performed one of his most memorable "Shibaraku" scenes as part of the *kaomise* of 1796. It is tempting to think that this is the performance commemorated here.

Since the title given to this print on the panel at right is *Edo Sakaichō shibai no zu* (A picture of a play in Sakaichō, Edo), we know this must be either the Nakamura-za or the Ichimura-za, because the only other great kabuki theater in Edo, the Morita-za, was in another part of town.

Uki-e, "perspective pictures" of theater interiors, occur often enough in ukiyo-e, and share enough features in common, to be considered a category of their own. The earliest known prints of the type date from the 1740s, but they continued to be popular, and there are two other examples in this exhibition alone (Catalogue nos. V-7 and V-16).

* The name derived from the resemblance to the tiers in which images of *rakan* (sainted Buddhist ascetic monks) were arranged in temples such as Edo's Rakanji.

V-8

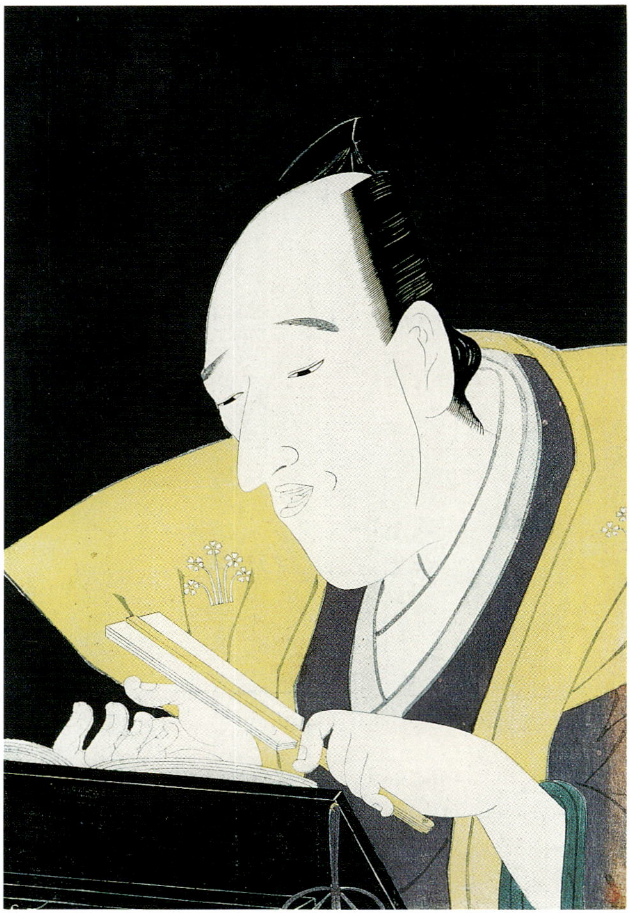

V-8

Chōkyōsai Eiri (active 1790s)

Portrait of Tomimoto Buzendayū II, or *Edo no hana Yanagibashi natori*, "The Flowers of Edo—The Master of Yanagibashi"

Circa 1795

Woodblock print; ōban; 36.8 x 25.2

Signature of artist (Eiri ga) at upper right, at left of title

The Mann Collection

Eiri has caught the great exponent of *tomimoto bushi*, Buzendayū II (1754-1822), as he intones one of his popular chants from a book on a lectern in front of him. Beating time with a folded fan in one hand, he carefully keeps the book open to its place with the other. Every design element in the composition—the tilt of Buzendayū's head, the downward slope of his shoulders, the concentration of mass in the bottom two-thirds of the picture—emphasizes the master's total concentration on his performance. It is as though the print is saying, "*This* is what Buzendayū is all about; *this* is what gives him his fame." A comparison with Eiri's portrait of Santō Kyōden (Catalogue no. III-7), which was designed as part of the same set, is instructive. Though Kyōden, too, is shown together with articles relating to his profession—an inkstone, and fans waiting to be written on—he is not shown in the act of writing. Instead, the hint of a smile plays across his face as he gazes pensively ahead, perhaps thinking of some witticism appropriate to his task. In both instances, Eiri was clearly intent on capturing his subjects at a characteristic moment. Equally clearly, he was also interested in capturing whatever was most distinctive in their appearance. Kyōden's handsome, manly features presented no problem. Buzendayū's "horse face" (as it was called at the time), however, posed a serious challenge. With his low forehead, prominent nose, and massive jaw, he would have been only too easy to caricature. Eiri comes dangerously close to doing so, but is saved by his obvious respect for his subject. One cannot help being impressed by Buzendayū's loving absorption in his work.

Several unusual features about this print suggest that it and its companion piece (the portrait of Kyōden) may have been issued privately. Both prints are extremely rare (this one especially so; only one other impression, now in the Musée Guimet, has ever been recorded); both are printed with the finest pigments (the particular yellow of Buzendayū's *kataginu* appears on only one other print of the period); and—even more telling—neither print bears a publisher's trademark or a *kiwame* seal.

Many scholars now feel that Chōkyōsai Eiri is not the same person as Rekisentei Eiri. If that is the case, he is another of those mystery artists, like Sharaku, who crop up so frequently in ukiyo-e. Apart from the two portraits in this exhibition, only one other major work, a triptych, bears his signature.

V-9

Katsushika Hokusai (1760-1849)

Nesting Cranes in a Pine Tree

Circa 1805

Surimono, 38.8 x 52.3

Signature of artist (Gakyōrōjin Hokusai ga, "Drawn by Hokusai, the Old Man Mad About Painting") at lower right

Spencer Museum of Art, The University of Kansas (William Bridges Thayer Memorial)

A crane watches over three nesting fledglings in a pine tree while its mate soars overhead in front of the rising sun. Bands of mist partially obscure the sun's red disk, which emerges from a sea of embossed waves. The rising sun, the cranes, and the pine are all symbols of longevity usually associated with New Year's. The actual occasion for the commemoration of which this print was issued, however (which may or may not have taken place on New Year's), was Ichikawa Hakuen's granting of a new name, Sansuke, to one of his pupils, formerly called Karoku. Hakuen was the *haigō*, or name used in haiku poetry, taken on by Danjūrō V when he retired from the stage. Little is known of Sansuke other than that he was one of Hakuen's protégés at the time. The character *san* is taken from the word *sanshō*, an alternate reading for the *mimasu* (rice measure) crest of the Ichikawa lineage.

Hokusai's composition is concentrated within the right two-thirds of the print, leaving ample space at the left for the five haiku written in honor of the occcasion. The contributors were Hakuen; two of the leading actors of the day, Bandō Mitsugorō III (1773-1831) and Iwai Hanshirō V (1776-1847); another of Hakuen's students, Sankō; and the recipient of the new name, Sansuke. The latter's poem works particularly well with Hokusai's imagery. It reads: *Matsu ni soute tatsu ya kasumi no hi no megumi* (It rises with the pine, the blessing of the mist-swathed sun!). Hakuen uses another symbol associated with the new year in his verse: *Negau*

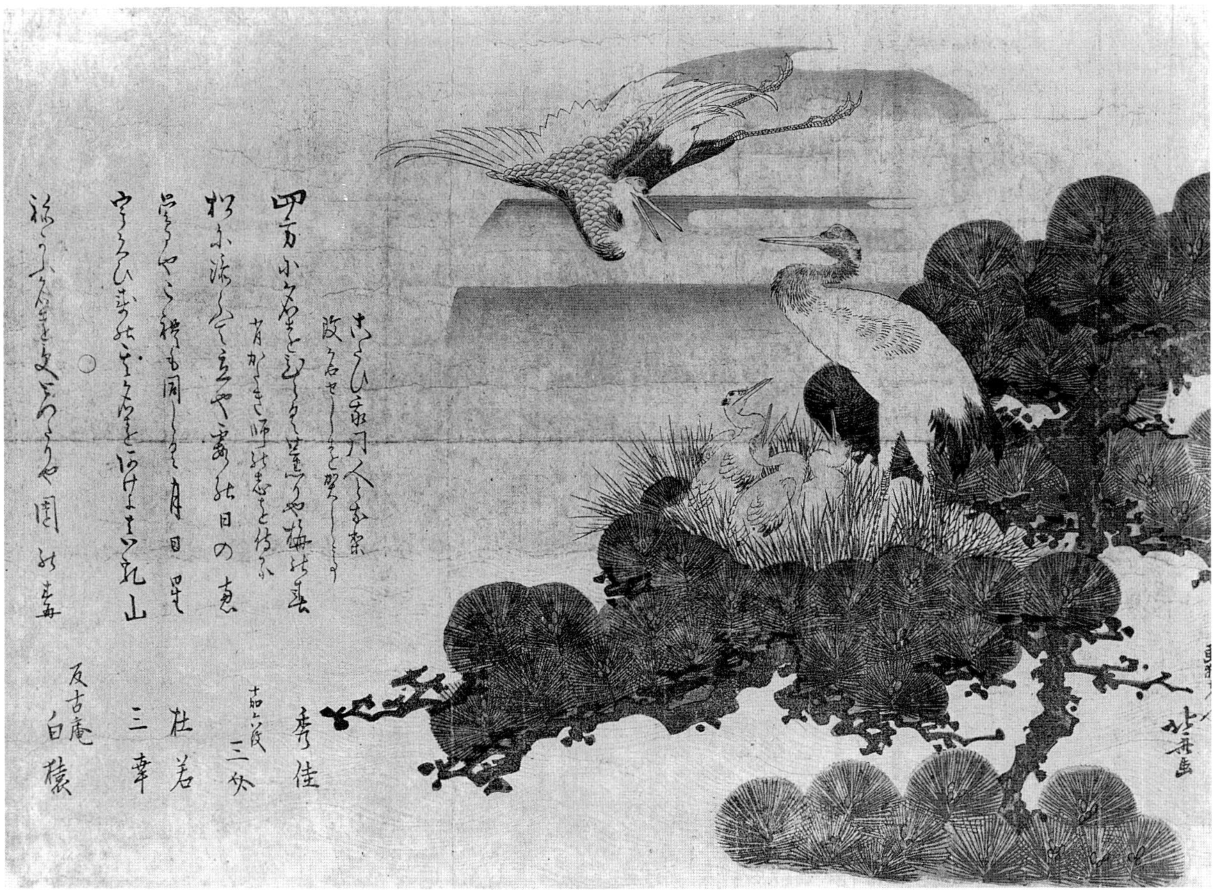

V-9

na o kaetottari ya sono no ume (It received the name it wanted: the plum tree in the garden).

This is the only known impression of this splendid print. The design has a grandeur—apparent even in its present worn and somewhat soiled state—that is unusual among Hokusai's surimono of this period, most of which were more intimate in feeling. As Roger Keyes points out in his catalogue of the surimono in the Spencer Museum, the print may be dated to 1805 with a fair degree of certainty, since Hokusai did not call himself "the *Old* Man Mad About Painting" before the spring of 1805, and Hakuen died the following year.*

* Roger Keyes, *Surimono, Privately Published Japanese Prints in the Spencer Museum of Art* (Tokyo: Kodansha International, 1984), 70.

V-10

Katsukawa Hokusai (1760-1849)

Women Folding a Kimono

1803

Surimono; 18.5 x 51.2

Signature of artist (saki no Sōri Hokusai ga, "Painted by Hokusai, formerly Sōri") at far right

Indiana University Art Museum

This print is included in the exhibition primarily because of the bold inscription at left, which almost certainly replicates the handwriting of Ichikawa Hakuen (Danjūrō V). The inscription consists of a New Year's verse by Hakuen, followed by his signature and a notation of his age. The poem, a haiku, reads as follows: *Nenrei ya / warau kado ni wa / fukujusō* (It is time for New Year's visits; in the smiling doorway is an adonis plant).

The adonis, which blooms as early as January or February in Japan, was often grown as a potted plant to be used in New Year's decorations. It not only bloomed before anything else, but its long-lasting yellow blossoms, resembling miniature sunflowers, were considered particularly auspicious. The Japanese name means "plant of prosperity and longevity."

Hokusai's contribution to the surimono is a domestic scene in which only the opulent kimono being folded up and packed (or is it being unpacked for the holiday?) hints at the festivity of the season. The kimono, with its rich peacock-feather design, is clearly a treasured object, but everything else in the room speaks of routine daily life. Strewn about the floor are a hibachi, a brass kettle, an ironing vessel, a pipe, and a tobacco pouch. Perhaps Hokusai's point is that just such tranquil domesticity is at the heart of a smiling house.

Surimono of this width were often twice as tall, with another horizontal panel filled with verses underneath. The exhibition includes two examples of such full-sheet surimono (Catalogue nos. III-9 and IV-10). It is impossible to say whether this particular print was designed from the start in the half-sheet format or whether, as often happened when surimono were brought to the West, the lower half was cut off.

Hakuen's signature reads *Gyōnen rokujū-ni sai Ichikawa Hakuen* (The sixty-two-year-old

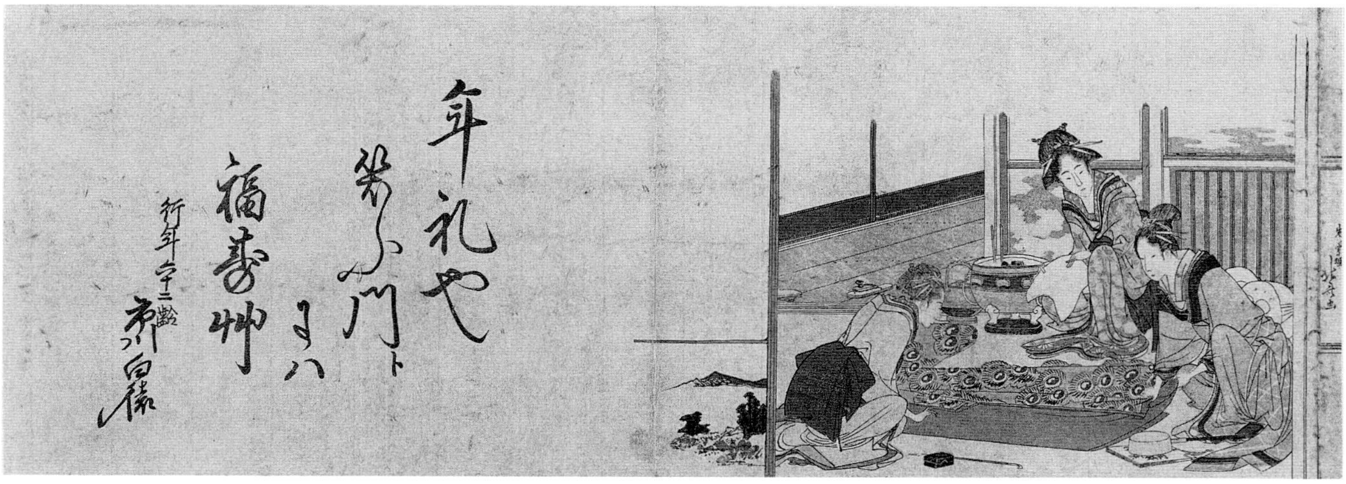

V-10

Ichikawa Hakuen). Since we know that he was born in 1741, the print may be dated precisely to 1803.

V-11

Torii Kiyonaga (1752-1815)

***Degatari* Scene Featuring Ichikawa Monnosuke and Segawa Kikunojō**

Circa 1783

Woodblock print; ōban; 37.7 x 24.9

Signature of artist (Kiyonaga ga), seal of publisher (Eijudō Nishimura-ya) on left-hand side, and seal of collector (Hayashi Chū)

Portland Art Museum

Degatari refers to the scenes in kabuki plays in which the chorus and musicians appear onstage with the actors. In the late eighteenth century, this represented a new departure, since musicians had previously sat behind the scenes, out of view. This particular print has been included in the exhibition to point out the prominent position that music held in the Temmei theater, depicted here by Kiyonaga at the peak of his career.

Easily identifiable by their crests in this print are Segawa Kikunojō III, in the lower left, playing a woman's role, and Ichikawa Monosuke II, holding the fan in the center. The actor playing the villain, crouching on the right, may be Nakamura Nakazō I.

Above the actors sit three musicians. On the right, the *shamisen* player, Namisaki Tokuji, is shouting a musical cue (*kakegoe*). The chanters are singing the story and the actors are dancing to their accompaniment. The central musician is Tomimoto Buzendayū (see also Catalogue no. V-8), the premier *jōruri* vocalist of his day. His particular brand of chanting was called *tomimoto bushi*, which derived originally from the *jōruri* narrative music used in the puppet theater (*bunraku*). Seated beside him, on the left of the print, is his disciple Tomimoto Itsukidayu, who later started the *kiyomoto* music style that eventually eclipsed the genre of his mentor.

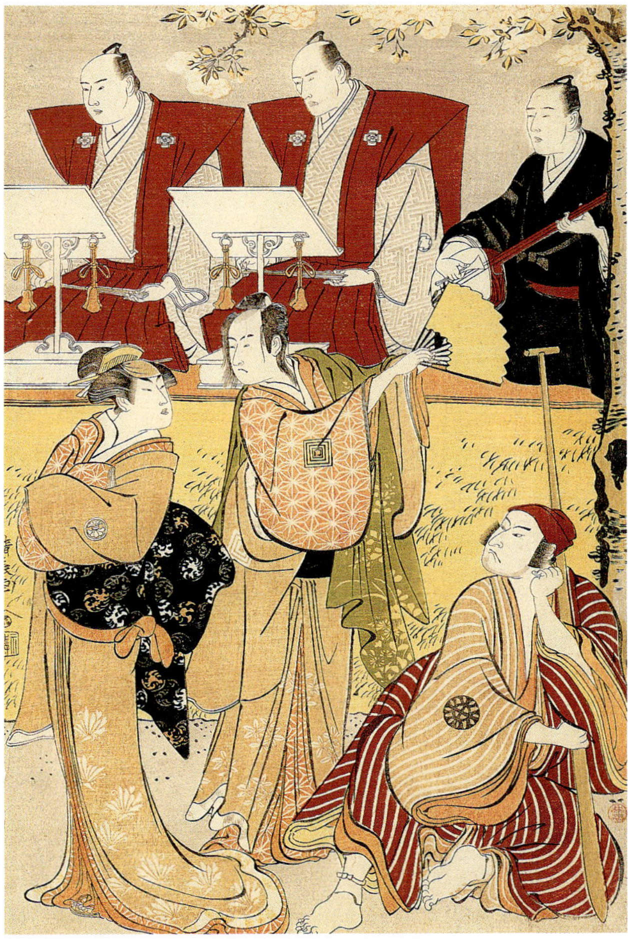

V-11

V-12

Torii Kiyonaga (1752-1815)

Ichikawa Danjūrō V Out Walking with His Family

Circa 1783

Woodblock print, ōban; 39.6 x 26.4

Signature of artist (Kiyonaga ga) at upper right

The Mann Collection

This portrait of Ichikawa Danjūrō V and his family out for a stroll may well have been commissioned during the height of the actor's fame, when fans clamored for behind-the-scenes glimpses of their hero. Shunshō's dressing-room portrayal and illustrated book (Catalogue nos. V-19 and V-22), as well as Toyokuni's illustrated book (Catalogue no. V-23), also fit into this category.

This particular print brings us face-to-face with a turbulent chapter in the life of Edo's leading actor. At this point, he had witnessed the death of his eight-year-old son, Momotarō,

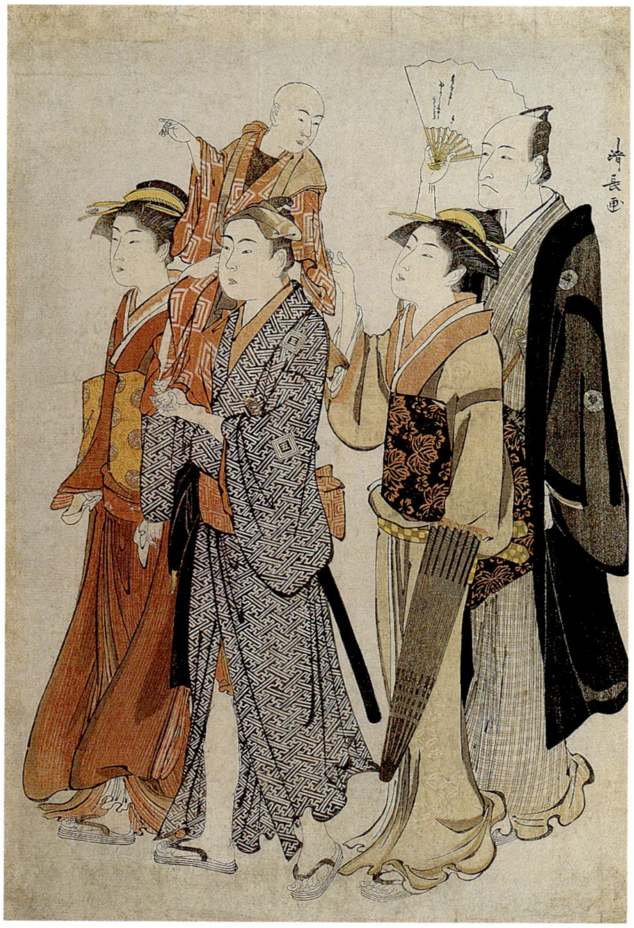

V-12

in 1777; separated from his wife, Okame; engaged in an affair that produced the illegitimate son being paraded here; and then become reconciled with his wife. He walks at the rear of the group, holding up a fan to shield his face from the summer's sun. The crest on his transparent linen *haori* may be one of his alternate crests (*kaemon*). The boy riding on the shoulders of a Danjūrō disciple is Tokuzō, Danjūrō's son by another woman, who was formally adopted into the actor's family in 1782 when he was four years old. The child's clothing bears Danjūrō's family crest. The man on whose shoulders he is riding also bears the crest on his obi, while the character for "five" on his kimono is bordered by *mimasu*-like squares. Unfortunately, we are unable to identify this man further, and can only surmise that the woman by his side is possibly one of Danjūrō's daughters, while the woman on the right may be Tokuzō's nurse.

V-13

Tōshūsai Sharaku (active 1794-1795)

Ichikawa Ebizō IV (Danjūrō V) as Takemura Sadanoshin

1794

Woodblock print; ōban; 37.5 x 24.7

Signature of artist (Tōshūsai Sharaku ga), kiwame seal, and trademark of publisher, Tsutaya Jūzaburō, at left

The Minneapolis Institute of Arts, Bequest of Richard P. Gale

In his dramatic, "large-head" actor portraits of 1794-95, Sharaku focuses on his subjects' faces with an intensity that even today viewers sometimes find disconcerting. Yet this effect is achieved with the simplest of means—a few judiciously placed lines and a minimum of color. Most of the portraits are unflattering to the point of caricature—Sharaku did seem to have the caricaturist's ability to capture a likeness by concentrating on a few telling details—but there is a psychological dimension to them as well that sets them apart from almost anything else done in ukiyo-e at the time.

One is not always certain whether these psychological overtones have to do with the actor himself or with the personality he is playing. Here, for instance, Ebizō is playing the part of an aging retainer whose daughter has committed a grave offense against the family he serves; the wheedling, obsequious way in which he wrings his hands and the panic that seems to lurk behind his eyes almost certainly relate to his role. Yet Sharaku has also picked up on a certain slackness in Ebizō's features, a hint of weariness, that may well have reflected something of the actor's own inner feelings at the time. As Laurence Kominz points out in his essay in this catalogue, Ebizō (Danjūrō V) had already begun to think about retirement several years before. In the play, the character Ebizō portrayed commits suicide in an attempt to expiate his daughter's guilt. The play was performed at the Kawarazaki-za in the fifth month of 1794.

Sharaku is one of the great mystery figures of ukiyo-e. Though he has been the subject of intense speculation and all sorts of theories as to his "true" identity have been put forward, virtually nothing is really known about him. The few contemporary references to him that have come to light are more tantalizing than revealing. They tell us little more than that he served as a No actor in the household of a daimyo, that his portraits were unpopular because of their excessive realism, and that he designed prints for only a short time. In fact, he seems to have worked for only ten months, during which time he designed some 150 extraordinary portraits, all of which were published by Tsutaya Jūzaburō.

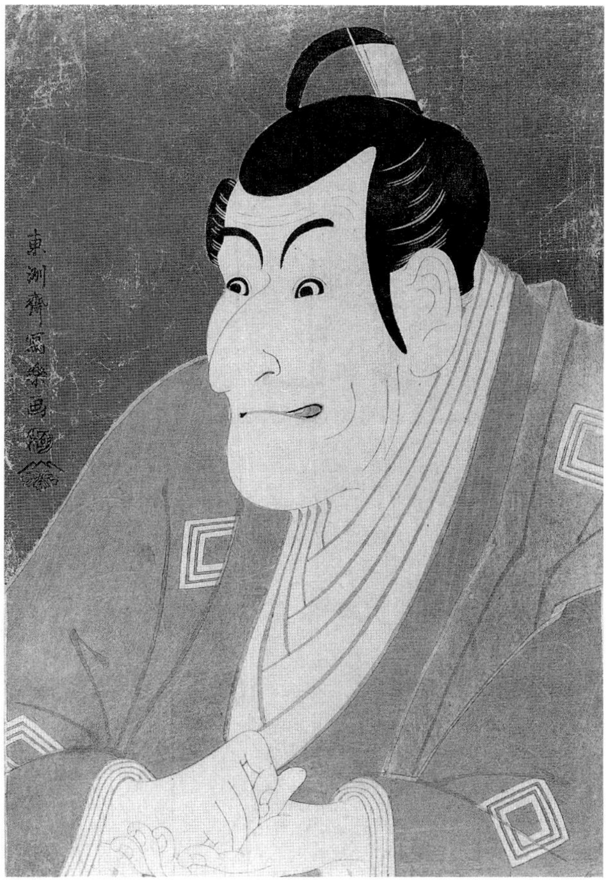

V-13

V-14

Katsukawa Shun'ei (1762-1819)

Congratulations on a New Name

Circa 1796-1800

Surimono; 18.9 x 50.3

Signature of artist (Shun'ei ga) on banner

The British Museum

In Japan, the granting or taking on of a new name was a significant milepost in the life of anyone associated with the arts, and would often —increasingly from the 1790s—be announced by the issuing of a special surimono like this for the occasion. Curiously, in this instance the name of the recipient is not specifically mentioned. That it was a male, and probably a young boy, is indicated by the various Boys' Day emblems that make up the design: a *koinobori* (carp streamer); a banner depicting the Chinese hero Shoki the Demon Queller; and a doll representing Danjūrō in the role of the fiercely masculine "Ya no ne" Gorō. In a society as heavily influenced by Confucianism as Edo-period Japan, it should come as no surprise to learn that Boys' Day was considered a particularly auspicious holiday. Its positive associations were clearly in the minds of those who commissioned the surimono. The point is underscored by the character *fuku*, "happiness" or "good fortune," which forms the repeat pattern on the purple

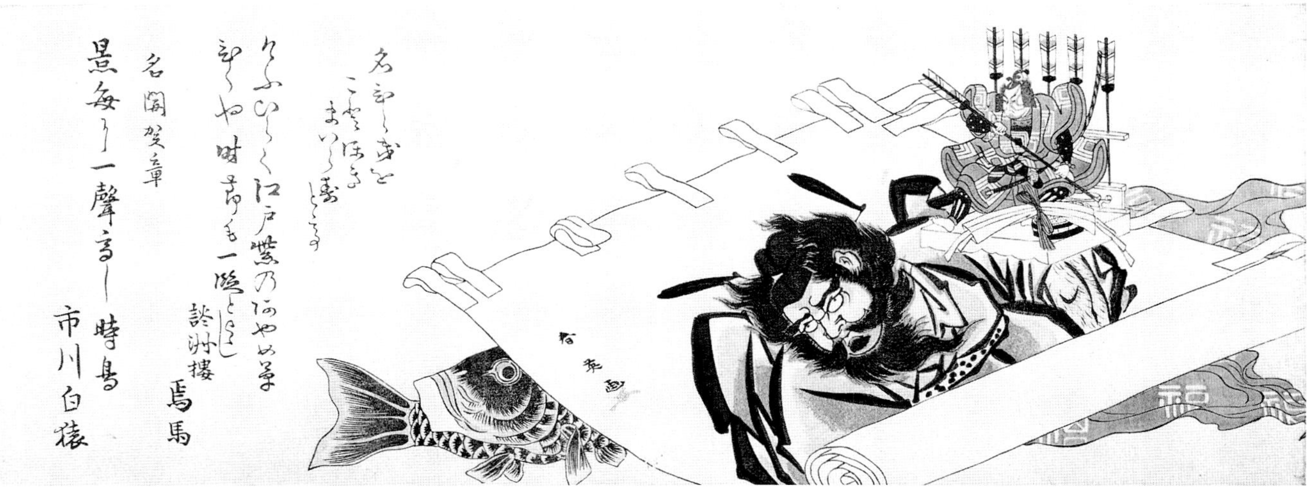

V-14

cloth showing under the banner at right.

There are two congratulatory verses, a *waka* by Danshūrō Emba and a haiku by Ichikawa Hakuen. Emba's verse reads*: Kyō hiraku / Edo murasaki no / ayamegusa / hira ya jisetsu mo / isshun to gotoshi* (Today's blooming of the sweet flag of Edo purple is announced, and the season seems but an instant). Hakuen's haiku reads: *Kei goto ni / hitokoe takashi / hototogisu* (The cuckoo, with every successive view its voice is higher). Emba's verse is full of allusions. Purple cloth (*Edo no murasaki*) was an Edo specialty; it was also associated with several roles traditionally played by the Ichikawa (Naritaya) family. One of the customs connected with Boys' Day was inserting sweet flag (*ayamegusa*) into thatched eaves. The plant was quite fragrant and was supposed to ward off colds.

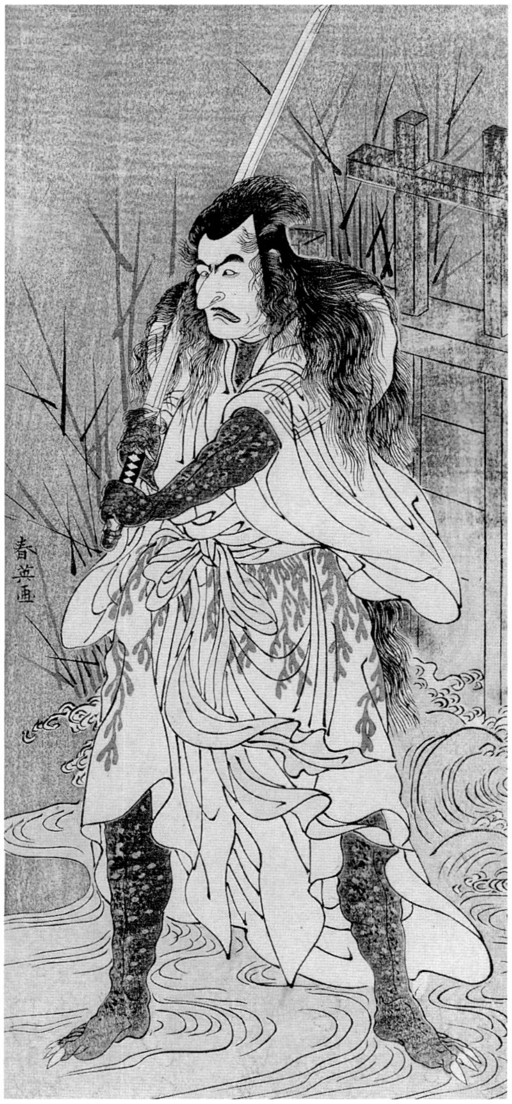

V-15

Hakuen (literally, "White Monkey") was the *haimyō* (name used for writing haiku) taken on by Danjūrō V in Kansei 3 (1791) when he changed his stage name to Ebizō. Danshūrō—obviously a playful variant of Danjūrō—was one of the many names used by Tatekawa (or Utei) Emba (1743-1822), a fascinating character who made his livelihood from carpentry but whose gift for storytelling had endeared him to some of Edo's more influential literati such as Ōta Nampo. An ardent fan of Danjūrō, he became a virtual promoter of his idol's interests. His association with Danjūrō and his love of the stage led him to write the first real history of kabuki, *Hana Kōto* [or *Edo*] *kabuki nendaiki*, which was published in 1811. Emba is also considered to be the founder of the comic storytelling genre now known as *rakugo*, which remains popular to the present day.

In the past it has been assumed that the recipients of the new name(s) announced in this print were Emba and Hakuen. Normally in surimono of this kind, however, others besides—or at least in addition to—the recipients of the new name(s) would have contributed the congratulatory verses. Moreover, if the assumption were correct, the date of the print would have to be 1791 (since this is when Danjūrō V first called himself Hakuen), but such an early date seems improbable, given that surimono in this format became popular only in the late 1790s. A more likely candidate for the recipient would be Danjūrō VII, who received that name in 1800, when he was still a child.

V-15

Katsukawa Shun'ei (1762-1819)

Danjūrō V as Tokubei the Frog Man

1787

Woodblock print; hosoban; 33 x 15.2

Signature (Shun'ei ga) at left

The Minneapolis Institute of Arts, Bequest of Richard P. Gale

Standing with feet apart and grasping a naked sword in both hands, Danjūrō, in the role of Tokubei, glares at an unseen adversary outside the frame of the picture at left. The actor's long, loose hair streams over his shoulders, and the

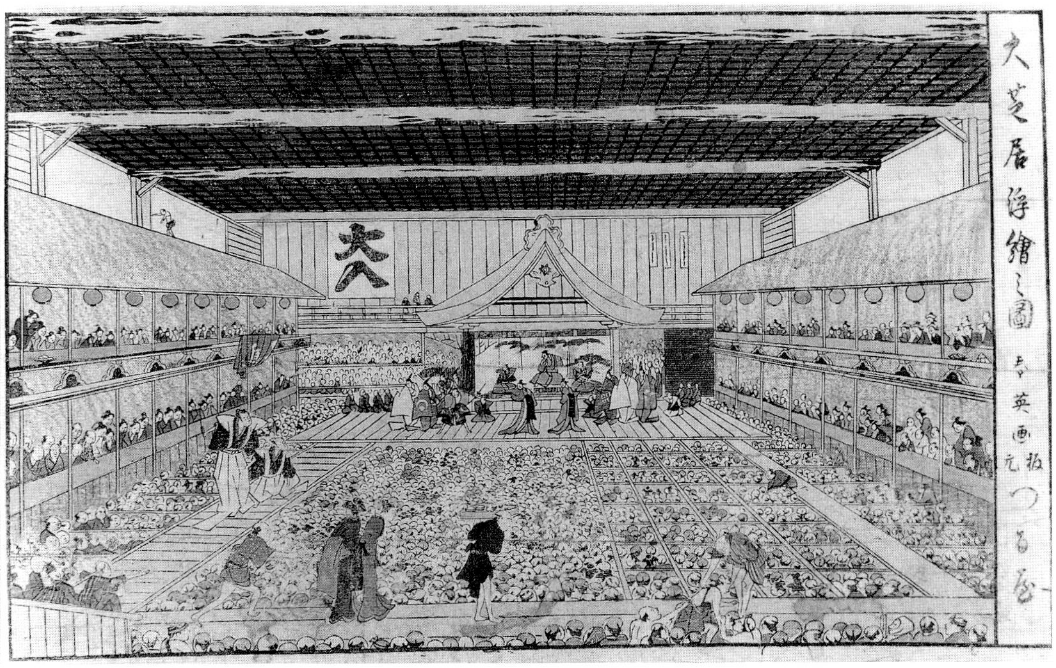

V-16

skin of his arms and legs is purple and mottled, resembling a frog's. His white kimono is decorated from the waist down with a design of green seaweed. Water (originally blue but now faded to buff) pours from the orange sluice gate behind him.

Danjūrō played the role of Tokubei in the play *Tenjiku tokubei kokyo no torikaji*, performed at the Kiri-za in the ninth month of 1787. Tokubei was a legendary character who could turn himself into a frog by magic.

As small as it is, a print like this still manages to convey some of the forcefulness of Danjūrō's stage presence. His face, with its prominent aquiline nose, broad mouth, and curved eyebrows, was particularly well suited for the scowls and grimaces of the more ferocious roles in the kabuki repertoire.

V-16

Katsukawa Shun'ei (1762-1819)

***Dai shibai uki-e no zu*, "Perspective View of a Theater Interior"**

Circa 1795

Woodblock print; horizontal ōban

Signature of artist (Shun'ei ga) and trademark (illegible) of publisher in title panel at right

Tsubouchi Memorial Theater Museum, Waseda University

At first glance, this print seems quite similar to the print of a crowded theater interior by Eiri (Catalogue no. V-7), but closer examination soon reveals numerous, quite significant differences. To begin with, Shun'ei seems to be much more comfortable with western-style perspective. Where the side walls of the theater in Eiri's print telescope sharply toward the stage, here they remain farther back, and as a result the stage seems wider and the entire theater more spacious. Shun'ei also seems to handle relative scale more effectively. The figures here gradually diminish in size in relation to one another, unlike the actors on the stage in Eiri's print, who seem much too large compared with the surrounding figures. The two prints also differ in other, less basic, ways. Here, for instance, no crest-emblazoned lanterns hang from the ceiling's cross-beams and no curtain is shown above the stage. Were they left out because they were missing in the actual theater or because they would have detracted from the sense of spaciousness for which the artist was striving?

The scene portrayed here is the so-called "confrontation scene" from one of the plays featuring the Soga brothers, traditionally performed at New Year's. Though the plots of these plays changed considerably from year to year, the culminating confrontation scene always remained more or less the same. The story

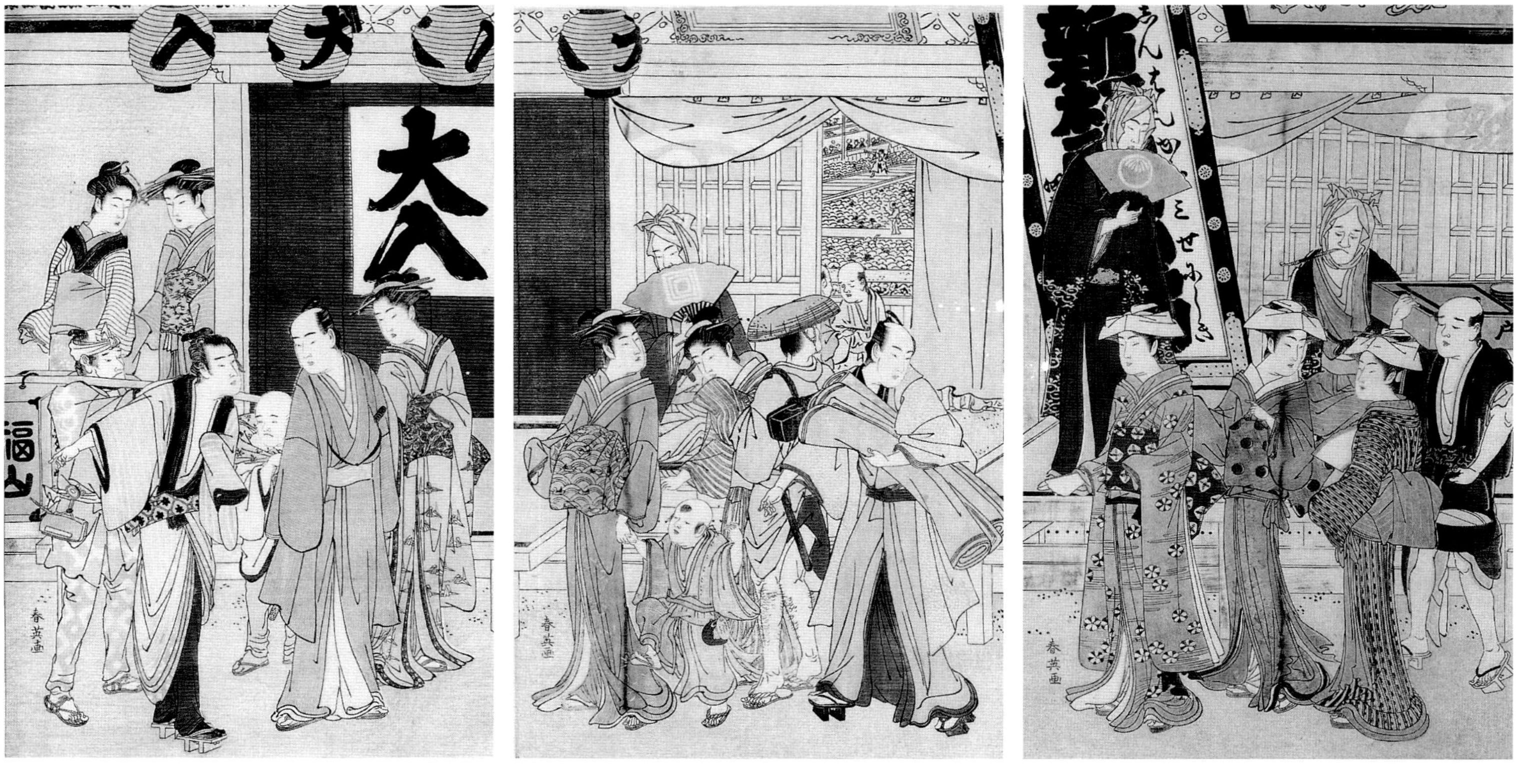

V-17

behind any Soga play involved the brothers' determination to seek revenge for their father's murder at the hands of Lord Kudō no Suketsune. In the final scene, the brothers are persuaded to attend a New Year's party at the lord's residence. When they actually see their enemy face to face, the impetuous younger brother, Soga no Gorō, dashes the cup of sake offered to him to the ground and threatens to kill Kudō on the spot. However, he is restrained from doing so, and the contemptuous lord offers to give them another chance to kill him at a hunt he has planned for the spring. Vowing to take him up on his offer, the brothers depart.

Stated thus baldly, the scene's inherent drama is quite evident, but by at least the late eighteenth century these annual performances of the scene had become ritualized as a kind of institutional invocation of good luck for the coming year. As a result, ceremony and spectacle often overshadowed much of the tension one might have expected from a confrontation between mortal enemies. Some of this more ceremonial aspect of the scene is apparent here, as the Soga brothers make their entrance along the *hanamichi* and the rest of the actors form an elaborate, highly stylized tableau on the stage.

V-17

Katsukawa Shun'ei (1762-1819)

Outside a Kabuki Theater

Circa 1795

Woodblock print; ōban triptych, 38 x 25 (each panel)

Signature of artist (Shun'ei ga) in lower-left corner of each print

The British Museum

A procession of various Edo types moves past the front of a kabuki theater where a play is in progress. The performance has been sold out, and the theater trumpets the fact with a row of paper lanterns and a sign, posted on the bamboo blinds at left, with the characters *ō-iri*, "full house." A partially open sliding door and parted curtains afford a glimpse of the tightly packed crowd inside watching an actor strike a pose on the *hanamichi*.

The blue curtains hanging over the sliding doors have faded to a pale tan. They have been drawn up to reveal only a part of the theater's crest, which seems to be the *tachibana* (mandarin orange flower) crest of the Ichimura-za (operating under its alternative license as the

Kiri-za at the time). Two hawkers or doormen with kerchiefs tied around their heads are stationed on either side of the entrance, holding fans in front of their mouths (a third sits at the far right, smoking a pipe). The fan held by the hawker standing to the right bears the crest of Sawamura Sōjūrō III (1753-1801); the other hawker's fan is decorated with the *mimasu* crest of the Ichikawas. A framed sign behind the hawker at right reads *Shinhan kaomise nishiki* (A newly published brocade [print] of the *kaomise*), and is obviously intended to serve as the title of the triptych.

Among the people passing in front of the theater is a party of three women, probably all merchants' wives, wearing white caps (*agebōshi*) to protect their oiled hair from dust. In front of them is a motley group consisting of a young man carrying three rolled-up rugs, a bare-legged monk with a straw hat who turns to stare through the open door of the theater, a courtesan leading a little boy by the hand, and a woman who raises her sleeve to her mouth as though shocked by the boy's behavior. Next come a samurai and his wife, followed by a young servant carrying a box on his back. The samurai is being addressed by a young man pointing to something off to the left. At the far right, a deliveryman carries a rice bucket and a box full of trays and bowls, while at the far left, two women standing on the porch of the theater look down at a laborer carrying a box slung from a pole.

V-18

Katsukawa Shunkō (1743-1812)

Ichikawa Danjūrō V as Kazusa no Gorobei Tadamitsu

1780

Aiban; 32.2 x 22.5

Signature of artist (Shunkō ga) at center right

The Art Institute of Chicago, Clarence Buckingham Collection

Danjūrō, his face painted in *sujiguma* makeup, stares out from under an open "snake's eye" umbrella. He has planted his chin on his fist and his eyes are crossed in determination (one of the standard kabuki conventions). The long sideburns of his wig bristle like stiff wings from the ends of the red "strength lines" of his makeup; his purple kimono is decorated with wave roundels and has the Ichikawa family *mimasu* crest on its sleeve.

This print portrays Danjūrō in act 3 of the play *Kitekaeru nishiki no wakayaka* (Returning home in splendor), performed at the Nakamura-za in the eleventh month of 1780. It probably depicts him just before the nighttime "silent encounter" (*dammari*) scene in which he struggles for possession of a sacred bow with Nakamura Nakazō in the role of Chinzei Hachirō Tametomo. Nakazō, as Laurence Kominz explains in his essay, was another of the lions of the kabuki stage at the time.

Shunkō has moved in so close to his subject that the image fills more than three-quarters of the paper. This allows him to concentrate on the intensity of Danjūrō's gaze and the ferocity of his scowl. Every other compositional element in the print—such as the upward thrust of the actor's fist or the diagonal of the umbrella handle—only serves to draw additional atten-

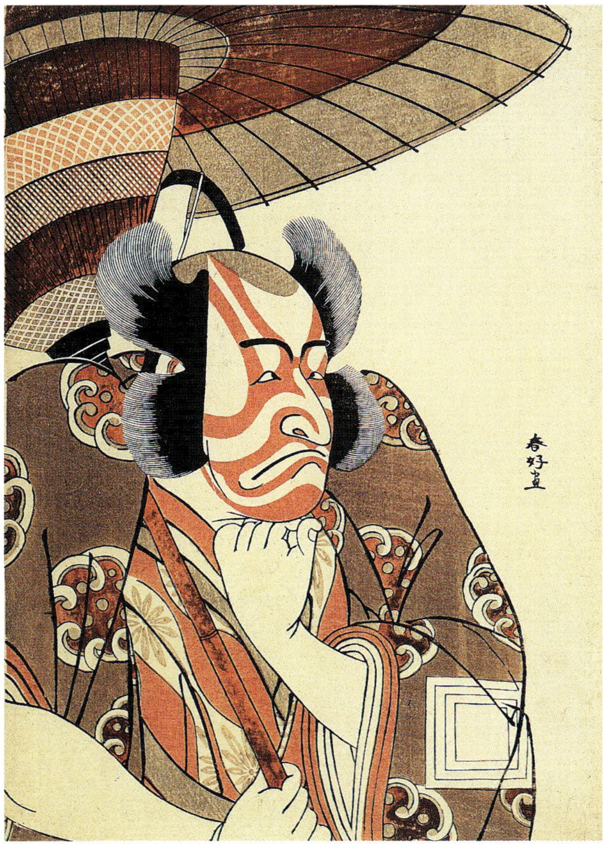

V-18

V-19

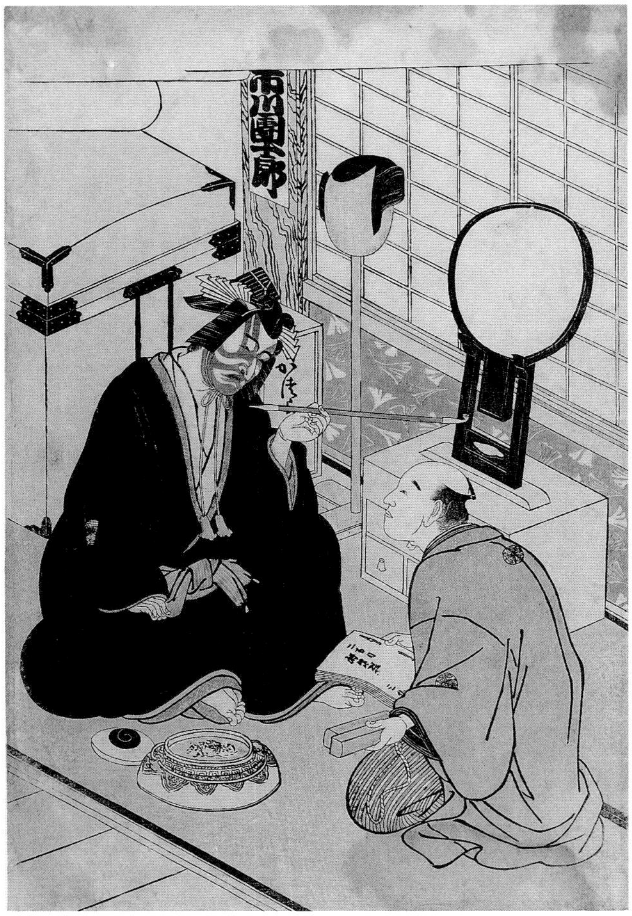

tion to this primary center of interest.

Before 1780, all actor prints depicted the entire figure. This splendid image, in mint condition, is one of the first close-up actor prints to have been published; as such, it may be viewed as a prototype for the dramatic bust portraits, such as Catalogue no. V-13, that appeared in the 1790s and are now considered one of the glories of ukiyo-e.

V-19

Katsukawa Shunshō (1726-1792)

Ichikawa Danjūrō V in His Dressing Room with the Program Announcer

Circa 1781

Woodblock print; ōban; 38.5 x 25.7

Unsigned

The Art Institute of Chicago, Frederick W. Gookin Collection, 1939

Danjūrō is shown relaxing in his dressing room, chatting with the program announcer. He is wearing the ferocious-looking red-and-white makeup (*kumadori*) and tiny black cap with folded paper "wings" used for a "Shibaraku" scene of the kind that had become an Ichikawa family specialty, but he has not yet put on the cumbersome brick-red robe that would engulf him when he made his appearance on the *hanamichi*.

The contrast between Danjūrō's manner and the more subservient posture of the program announcer is marked. Danjūrō sits back, casually balancing his *kiseru* as he seems to ponder something, while the announcer leans forward attentively, holding program notes in one hand and a pair of wooden clappers (used to signal scene changes) in the other. A portable brazier with hot coals for lighting a pipe sits on the floor between the two men. Everything else in the room relates directly to costuming and makeup. The large chest behind Danjūrō was used for storing robes. The small box beside it, under the plaque with Danjūrō's name, is a wig box, and beside it is a wig stand with wig. The most important pieces of furniture in the room by far, however, were the dresser and mirror stand at the actor's left. It was in front of these that he would have applied the grotesque *kumadori* makeup that was associated with so many of his most celebrated roles.

Though Shunshō was an enormously successful print artist and had many pupils, nothing is known about the circumstances of his birth. His earliest actor prints, which date from the mid-1760s, departed from previous conventions in giving their subjects recognizable features (earlier artists had simply used generic facial features). Largely on the basis of this innovation, he quickly became the dominant actor-print artist of his time, remaining so well into the 1780s.

Prints showing actors offstage are relatively rare in Shunshō's extensive oeuvre. The series to which this print belongs is unusual not only in that respect but also because of its *ōban* size (most of his actor prints are in the smaller *hosoban* format). He may have got the idea for this series while he was working on his illustrated book, *Yakusha natsu no Fuji* (Catalogue no. V-22), which was published in 1780.

V-20

Utagawa Toyokuni (1769-1825)

Inside a Kabuki Theater

Late eighteenth century

Woodblock print; ōban triptych; 37.7 x 24.9 (each panel)

Signature of artist (Toyokuni ga) on each panel and seal of publisher (Eijudō Nishimura-ya)

The British Museum

This perspective print (*uki-e*), with the floorboards of the stage slanted toward the center, clearly details all the elements of the Edo theater.

The kabuki stage was designed to provide both indoor and outdoor settings by means of the No-inspired roof, which is the focal point in this Toyokuni triptych. Indoor scenes were performed on the raised platform under the roof, in front of painted backdrops. Outdoors is represented by the forestage, which here has been decorated with props indicating a rough terrain—the actors are posed for a confrontation.

The balcony behind the stage, with painted panels of bamboo, was purely decorative. Banners are hung with the actors' names and roles on them, while the bamboo scenery reminds the audience of the early days of the theater, before 1720, when the stage was open to the elements. Also prominently displayed on the rear balcony is the bold-faced *o-iri* banner proclaiming a full house.

The attention of most of the audience is drawn to the stage for the significant moment about to unfold. In the panel on the left, spectators in the *rakandai* (first-story "peanut gallery") and *yoshino* (second-story gallery, where the seats were even cheaper) are leaning as far as they can to get a clearer view. The main floor below the stage (*doma*, or "earthen floor," as it was originally) is partitioned into box sections (*masu*, or "rice measures") where seven people could sit. Small tables have been provided so that the spectators could eat as they watched. Since kabuki performances often went on all day, people made a party of it, visiting amongst themselves—or brawling, as we see in the *rakandai*.

The walls of the *masu* rise flush with the stage floor to form aisles. Lining the sides of the theater are the box seats (*sajiki*) where samurai and wealthy townspeople sat. The pillars between the *sajiki*, incidentally, display signs that caution against fire (*hi no yōjin*)—a significant concern, since conflagrations (euphemistically

V-20

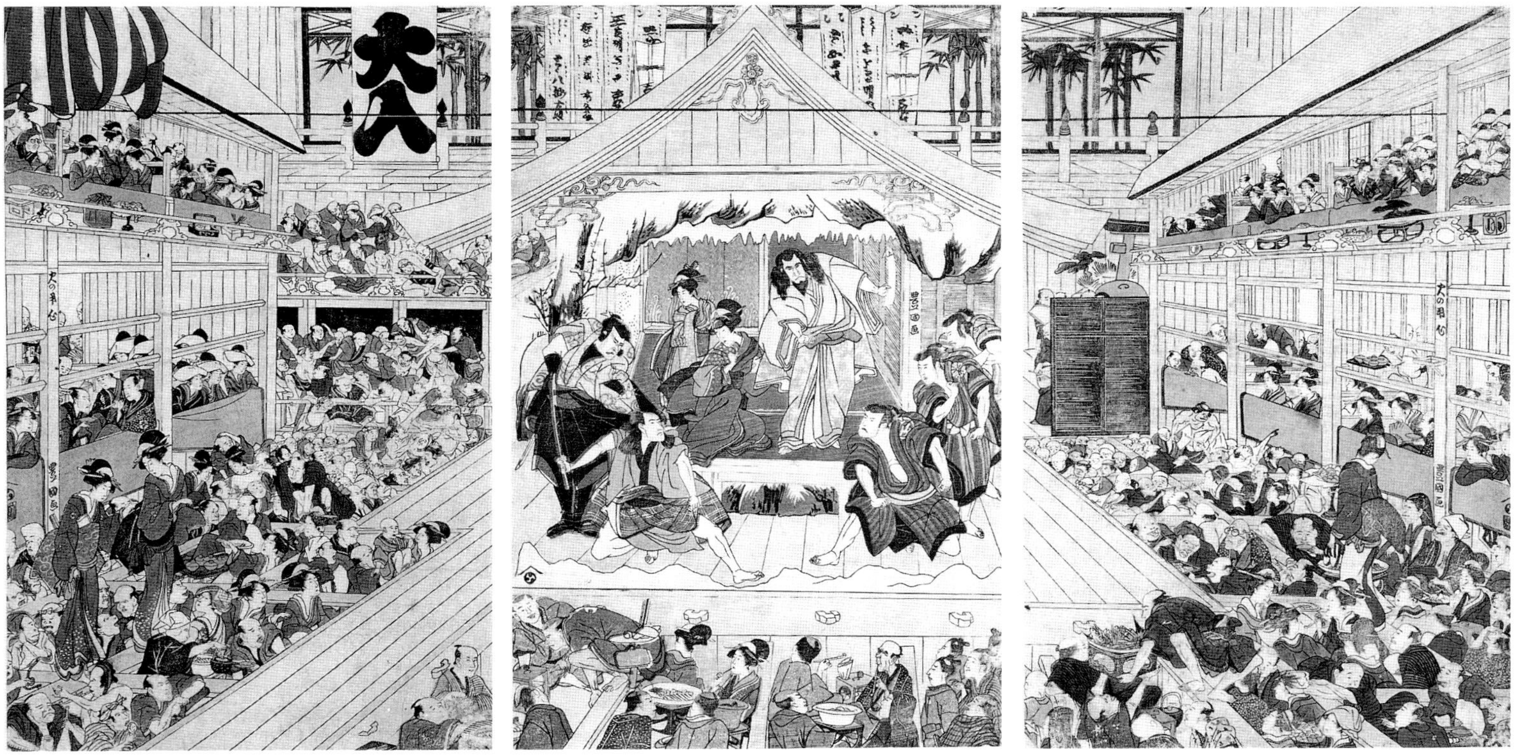

V-21

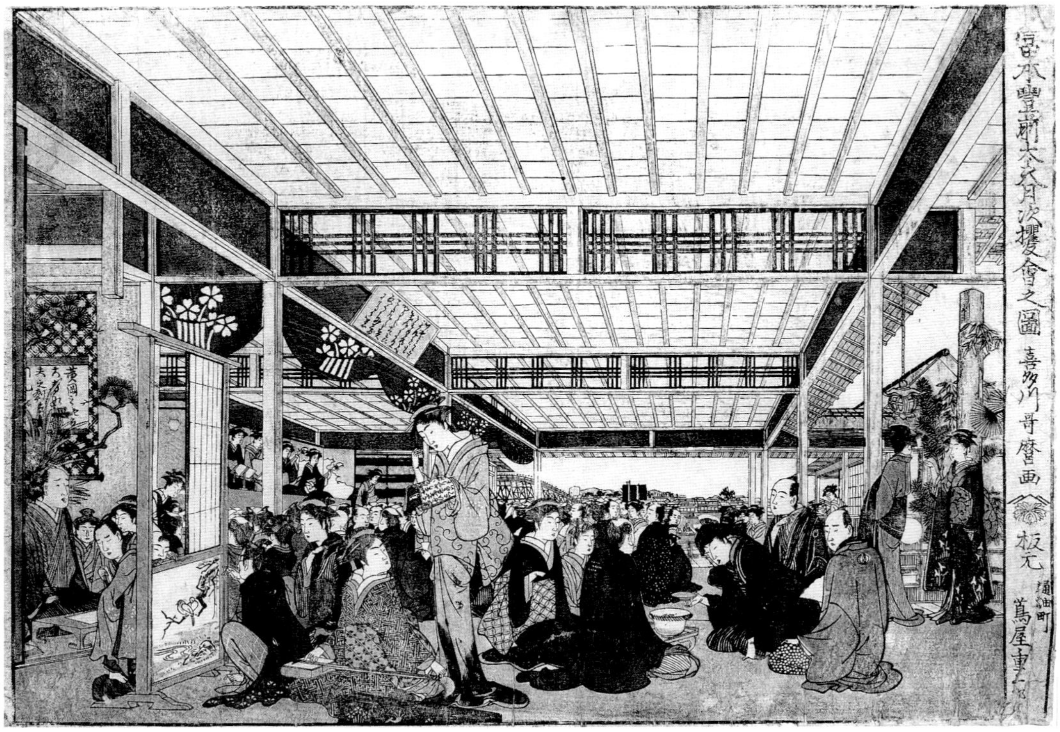

called "flowers of Edo") occurred so frequently, and, in fact, provided the government with ample pretext for regulating the construction, layout, and location of theaters.

Wide platforms surround the stage. On the right of the stage (left panel of the triptych) is the *hanamichi*, which extends the length of the theater, and is where the actors made their entrances, often pausing for dramatic scenes, monologues, and character-defining poses. The dimensions and functions of the platforms around the stage gradually changed throughout the history of kabuki. The periodic demolition of the theaters because of fire was partly the cause, and fostered a sense of impermanence and change that kept the theater vibrant.

Toyokuni has cleverly incorporated his signature into the design of the print, placing it on the pillars below the fire warning signs, and on one of the pillars supporting the No roof. Such interior roofs, by the way, fell into disuse after 1796.

V-21

Kitagawa Utamaro (1753-1806)

Buzendayū's Monthly Recital

Circa 1790 or earlier

Horizontal ōban; 30.9 x 43.8

Signature of artist (Kitagawa Utamaro) and trademark, address, and name of publisher (Hammoto, Tsutaya Jūzaburō, Tōri Aburachō) in title panel at right

City of Genoa, Museo d'Arte Orientale Edoardo Chiossone

A crowd has gathered in a large room presumably belonging to a restaurant. The shoji have been removed from two sides of the room, so that one can look out at the courtyard at right and over the Sumida River to the hills beyond at the back. It is unclear whether the recital has actually begun, though a row of geisha have already taken their place on a platform toward the back of the room. Buzendayū himself, his long "horse face" unmistakable, is seated in the place of honor in front of the *tokonoma*, decorated with a calligraphic scroll and a formal flower arrangement, at left. A curious piece of furniture, resembling both a *tsuitate* and a portable shoji, screens him from the bulk of the crowd. In the center foreground, several actors, some clearly identifiable by their *mon*, are seated around a hibachi, conversing with a gentleman, probably a samurai, whose back is turned to us. No one seems to be paying much attention to the geisha on the platform, which may or may not be an indication that the recital has yet to begin. Contemporary prints of kabuki performances often show audiences equally oblivious to the action onstage.

The low hills visible across the river would have been in the direction of Surugadai and Yamanote, that is, to the west; which means that the restaurant would have been on the east side of the Sumida, probably in Fukagawa or Honjo. The large bridge partially glimpsed through the open shoji at the back was probably Ryōgoku.

Buzendayū was another name for Tomimoto Buzennojō II (1754-1822), the master of a style of *jōruri* (narrative) music known as *tomimoto bushi*. He appears in this role in the *degatari* scene by Kiyonaga (Catalogue no. V-11).

Perspective prints like this are extremely rare in Utamaro's oeuvre. Shibui lists only two examples (not including this one) in his *Ukiyo-e zuten*. During the years covered by this exhibition, the genre is most often associated with Utagawa Toyoharu (1735-1814).

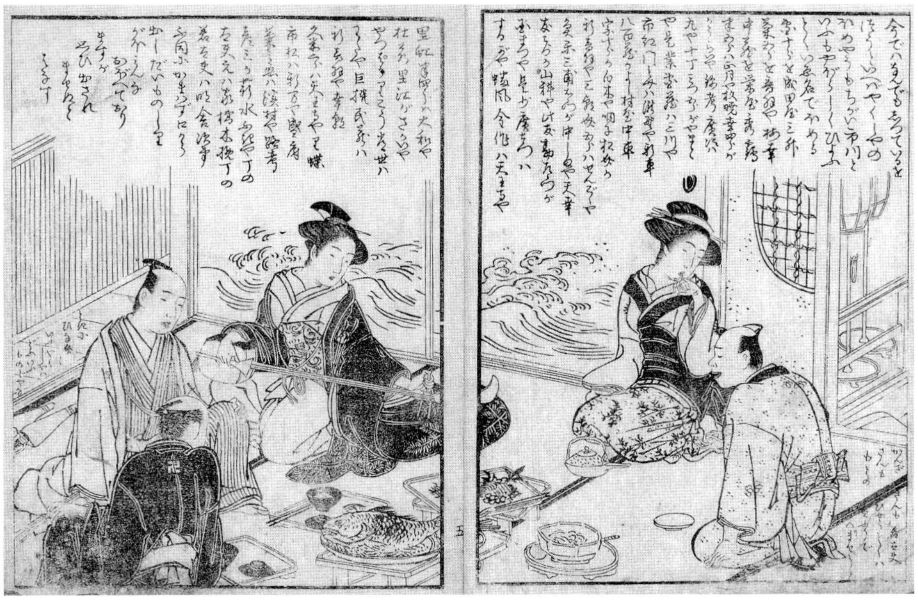

V-22

V-22

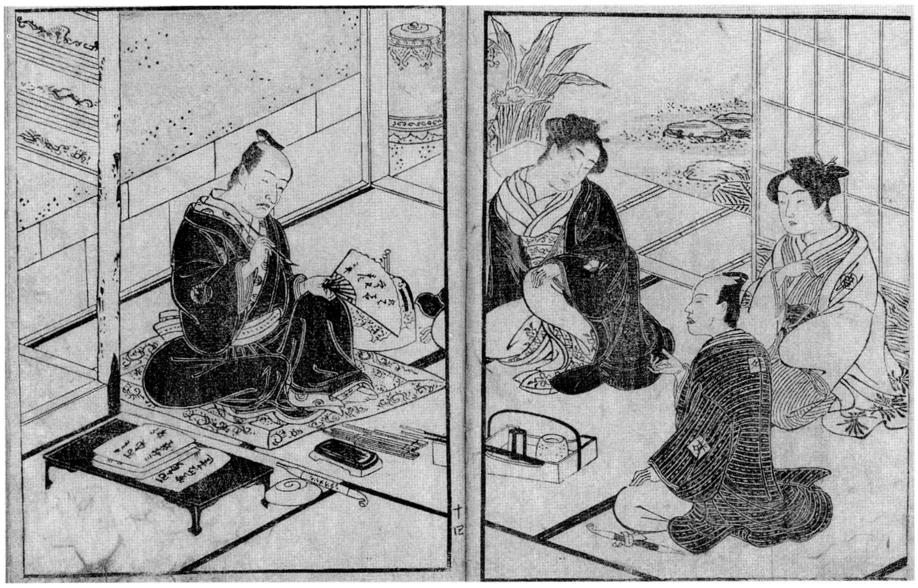

V-22

Katsukawa Shunshō (1726-1792)

***Yakusha natsu no Fuji*, "Actors as Fuji in Summer"**

1780

Illustrated book in one volume; 21.5 x 15

Name of artist (Gakō Katsukawa Shunshō), date of publication (Kanoe ne An'ei 9), and names of publishers (Okumura Genroku and Matsumura Yahei) in colophon

The Art Institute of Chicago

The curious title of this book is based on a rather fanciful analogy between Mt. Fuji in summer, when it is without snow, and actors offstage, when they are without wigs or makeup. The book was one of the first (if not *the* first) to offer—or at least purport to offer—glimpses of the private lives of some of the most popular actors of the day. Books offering the same kind of behind-the-scenes glimpses of the lives of celebrated courtesans had already appeared some years earlier. Shunshō himself had collaborated in designing one of these, *Seirō bijin awase sugata kagami*, "A Mirror Comparing the Forms of Beautiful Women of the Green Houses," which had been published in 1776 (Catalogue no. II-33 is another, later, example of the same genre). On the whole, works depicting the private lives of courtesans seemed to be more popular than similar works about actors.

The first five illustrations, which serve as a

kind of lead-in to those that follow, deal with the public side of kabuki, particularly with the public's infatuation with actors. One, for instance, shows a group of women poring over a playbill; another depicts a crowd outside the stage door of a theater; yet another shows a theater interior. Each of the five is accompanied by an explanatory text. The rest of the book is devoted to illustrations of actors offstage, as the title promises. There are twelve of these, all without text.

We reproduce two illustrations here. The first, from the introductory section, shows a wealthy patron, seated at left, being entertained in a teahouse between acts. A meal of almost banquet-like proportions is laid out on stands and trays in front of him, and a musician tunes up her *shamisen* in readiness to play. Scraps of conversation are included, kibyōshi-style, behind the patron and the somewhat sycophantic-looking figure across the room with whom he is conversing. The topic, judging from the text inscribed above the scene, seems to be the proper name to use when shouting out approbation of an actor's performance. The proper name to use for Danjūrō, for instance, would be his *yagō*, Naritaya Sanshō. To call out anything else, the text suggests, would be *yaborashiku*, "boorish."

The second illustration shows Danjūrō V inscribing a poem on a fan as a guest and two women from his household look on. Three other fans, still folded, lie on the tatami in front of him, beside his inkstone and in front of a shallow *tabako-bon*, while to his right, on a low lacquer table, lie four of his books. Open shoji afford a view into a garden behind the two women, and a *tokonoma* projects into the room on the other side. Danjūrō's interest in poetry has been alluded to frequently in this catalogue. When he retired in 1796, it was with the stated intention of devoting himself exclusively to his literary pursuits. Shunshō's portrayal of him here shows that poetry already was an important part of his life sixteen years earlier.

This copy is from the second edition of the book, which is thought to have come out in 1781 or 1782. The only difference between it and the earlier edition is in the final illustration, which (among other changes) depicts an actor who did not come to Edo until 1781.

V-23

Utagawa Toyokuni (1769-1825)

***Yakusha sankai kyō*, "Amusements of Actors on the Third Floor"**

1801

Illustrated book in two volumes; 21.5 x 15.5

Signature of artist (Utagawa Toyokuni ga), name of publisher (Nishimiya Shinroku), and date (Kansei 13) in colophon

The Art Institute of Chicago

The second half of the title of this book, *sankai kyō*, is identical in sound—though not in the characters with which it is written—with the title of an ancient Chinese work on natural history in which *san* meant "mountain," *kai* meant "sea," and *kyō* meant "book" or "classic." Here the title is written with characters that mean "third floor" (*sankai*) and "amusements" (*kyō*). Titles incorporating esoteric puns of this sort were not at all unusual in Japanese books of the late eighteenth and early nineteenth centuries.

The third floor of the title refers to the part of a kabuki theater that housed the actors' dressing rooms. The implication was that the book offered a behind-the-scenes look at the lives of actors in their dressing rooms or off the stage, and most of the illustrations do (or at least purport to do) just that. There are views of famous actors of the day at banquets, on outings to various scenic spots around Edo, in the privacy of their homes (one picture shows Ichikawa Hakuen [Danjūrō V] inscribing a paper lantern for a fellow actor in his study, for instance), and so on. There are also several backstage scenes in theaters, one of which, depicting a nighttime rehearsal (notice the burning candles), we reproduce here. It is probably the most crowded scene in the book, with actors, musicians, and directors all present. In the middle of the room, four actors run through their lines while three others sit looking on, and four men, presumably writers and/or directors, discuss whether to make any changes. One of the men gesticulates with his pipe, while another (the third from the left) keeps a brush and inkstone ready to jot down any modifications in the script that are decided on. Two of the actors, including the one standing in the center of the room, wear the

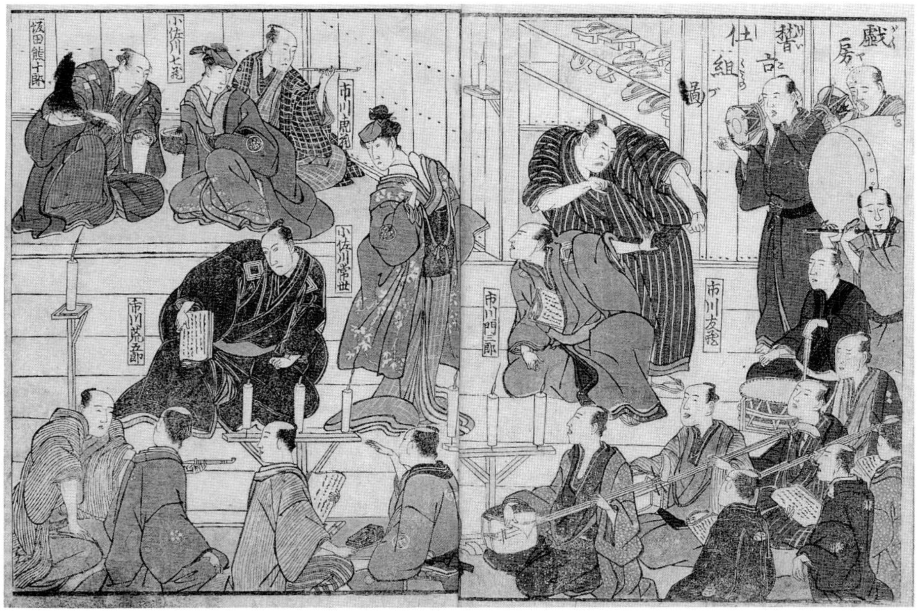

V-23

purple kerchiefs that identify them as *onnagata* (performers of female roles).*

Strictly speaking, no building in Edo was supposed to be more than two stories tall. Kabuki theaters, which typically had a third story at the back for dressing rooms, got around this restriction by calling the third story the *hon nikai* (the main second floor) and the second story the *chū nikai* (the middle second floor). This is yet another instance of the stratagems used by the people of Edo to get around annoying government regulations, and is reminiscent of the way in which the brothel owners of the Yoshiwara managed to keep open for business after the official closing time.

The preface to this book was written by Shikitei Samba (1776-1822), a comic writer who would become famous with the publication in 1809 of *Ukiyoburo* (The bathhouse of the Floating World).

---

* These kerchiefs covered the actors' shaven pates, which would otherwise destroy the illusion of femininity it was so important for them to project. During the Edo Period, all mature men were expected to shave the tops of their heads.

Contributors

Haruko Iwasaki
Ph.D., Harvard University
Associate Professor of Japanese Literature, University of California at Santa Barbara

Lynn Jacobsen-Katsumoto
Research Assistant, Portland Art Museum

Donald Jenkins
Curator of Asian Art, Portland Art Museum

Tadashi Kobayashi
Ph.D., Tokyo University
Professor of Art History, Gakushuin University

Laurence Kominz
Ph.D., Columbia University
Associate Professor of Japanese, Portland State University

Henry D. Smith II
Ph.D., Harvard University
Professor of Japanese History, Columbia University

Glossary

ageya. House of assignation used for high-ranking courtesans and their clients.

aiban. Intermediate paper size for woodblock prints, approximately 34 x 22 cm.

aragoto. Literally, "rough stuff," a type of flamboyant kabuki acting developed by Danjūrō I (1660-1704) for heroic roles, characterized by posturing and displays of superhuman strength; contrasted with *wagoto.*

bakufu. Military government of the shogun in Edo.

bijin. Beautiful woman.

bunjin. Literati.

bunraku. Puppet theater.

chō. Basic unit into which a city was divided; a block that usually meant the area along both sides of a street from one intersection to the next.

chokibune. Small boat with a single oarsman, used, among other things, for transporting passengers to the Yoshiwara on the Sumida River.

chōnin. Townspeople; the artists and merchant class in the cities, residents of *chō.*

chūsan. Highest-ranking class of courtesans, among whom were the *yobidashi.*

courtesan. Term usually employed when referring to higher-ranking prostitutes of the Edo Period.

daimyo (daimyō). Feudal lords, fiefed in provinces (domains) by the shogun.

Daruma. Founding patriarch of Zen Buddhism; also (eighteenth-century Edo slang) "prostitute" and "*haori.*"

degatari. Scenes in kabuki plays in which the chorus and musicians appear onstage with the actors, instead of sitting out of view.

dōchū. Parade; the evening promenade of high-ranking courtesans and their attendants.

Edo Period. Period of the Tokugawa family regime, between 1603 and 1868; also called the Tokugawa Period.

Edokko. Literally, "child of Edo"; native citizen of Edo.

ehon. Picture book.

ema. Votive pictures, dedicated to shrines and temples.

emaki. Handscroll.

fu dogs. Pair of guardian figures (usually lions) at the entrance to a Buddhist temple, often referred to as "dogs."

furisode. Kimono with long "swinging sleeves," worn by children, unmarried girls, and apprentice courtesans.

fusuma. Sliding screens covered with thick paper on both sides, frequently decorated with paintings or calligraphy; used as partitions to divide a large interior space into smaller units.

geisha. Literally, "accomplished person"; entertainers who dance, play music, sing, and converse with guests.

gesaku. Literally, "playful composition"; term for light literature composed from about 1770 to 1870.

geta. High wooden sandals or clogs.

gō. Art name or studio name; pen name.

gofun. White, gesso-like pigment made from baked shells.

gōkan. "Combined volumes"; genre of popular literature.

gohei. Paper streamers associated with Shinto shrines or festivals.

green houses. Translation of the Japanese word *seirō*; Edo-period term for houses of prostitution.

haikai. Casual form of linked verse derived from medieval linked verse known as *renga.*

haiku. Term invented in the late nineteenth century to designate a poem that is complete in seventeen syllables and is not part of a sequence.

hakama. Full, trailing trousers resembling a divided skirt.

hanamichi. Raised walkway through the audience to the stage of a kabuki theater.

haori. Three-quarter-length garment worn like a jacket.

hari. Vivacious, independent spirit; the hallmark of a Yoshiwara courtesan.

harimise. Public display of lower-ranking courtesans behind a latticed, cage-like window in full view of passersby.

hatamoto. Literally, "bannermen"; knighted samurai under the direct command of the shogun.

hiragana. One of the two phonetic Japanese scripts or syllabaries, a type of *kana.*

hyōbanki. Books containing evaluations of actors and courtesans.

iki. Sense of sophistication; fashionable refinement.

jōruri. Narrative musical form accompanied by the *shamisen*, associated with kabuki and puppet theater.

kamuro. Child-attendant of a high-ranking courtesan.

kana. Japanese syllabary.

kaneru yakusha. Versatile actor; actor who plays a wide variety of roles.

kanji. Chinese character used in written Japanese.

Kanō School. Traditional school of Japanese painting specializing in Chinese-style ink landscape painting.

Kansei Reforms. Edicts issued from 1787 to 1793 by the chief councilor of the *bakufu*, Matsudaira Sadanobu, that were intended to restore the social order through sumptuary laws.

kao. Hand-painted (rather than stamped) seal or cipher (also known as *kakihan*).

kaomise. Literally, "face showing"; annual performance sponsored by the prominent kabuki theaters to preview actors hired for the next year.

kasuri. Splash-pattern with design produced by tie-dye in warp and woof threads before weaving; white geometric patterns on navy-blue ground are most common.

katakana. Angular, phonetic Japanese script, a type of *kana.*

kibyōshi. Form of *gesaku* literature popular at the end of the eighteenth century featuring illustrations and text, often depicting recognizable people or their attributes that a contemporary reader would find amusing, identified by the books' yellow (*ki*) covers (*hyoshi*).

kido. Wicket gates that set off one *chō* from another; also, the entrance to a theater.

kiseru. Long-stemmed pipe with a small bowl, for smoking tobacco.

kitsune-ken. Hand game played at parties.

kiwame. Literally, "investigated" or "reviewed"; meaning that a print had received official approval for publication.

kōjō. Speech delivered to the audience by a kabuki actor wearing standard dress and little makeup.

komageta. Lacquered wood sandals (*geta*) on high platforms worn by courtesans.

kotatsu. Framed foot-warmer.

kukurizaru. Small cloth charms in the form of stylized monkeys, popular in the Yoshiwara for their imagined efficacy in attracting clients.

kumadori. Kabuki's most distinctive makeup technique, which emphasizes the movement of the facial muscles, said to have been created in 1673 by Ichikawa Danjūrō I; a specialty of the Ichikawa line of actors.

kyōka. Literally, "crazy verse"; poems that usually transform or parody classical poetry by means of wordplay.

meisho-e. Pictures of famous scenic places.

mie. Dramatic pose in kabuki theater.

miso. Soybean by-product used as salty flavoring.

mitate. Form of visual and literary parody.

mitsubuton. Three-layered cushions considered symbols of Yoshiwara luxury.

mon. Family crest.

nagauta. School of narrative music (*jōruri*) usually associated with kabuki.

Nakanochō. Main street in the Yoshiwara.

Nanga. Japanese school of painting based on Ming Dynasty Chinese models.

nishiki-e. Literally, "brocade pictures"; polychrome prints.

No (nō). Classical, masked drama of the pre-Edo Period, often influencing kabuki; maintained as official entertainment by the military ruling class in the Edo Period.

noren. Shop curtain.

ōban. Standard-size print, approximately 37.5 x 25.5 cm.

obi. Long sashes of various widths wound around the waist or hips to fasten garments in place.

oiran. General term used after the mid-eighteenth century for high-ranking courtesans.

ō-kubi-e. Literally, "large-head pictures"; close-up portraits emphasizing the head.

onnagata. Male actor specializing in female roles in kabuki.

renga. Art of linked verse.

Rimpa. Edo-period school of Japanese painting emphasizing decorative effects.

rokkasen. The six immortals of poetry.

rōnin. Masterless samurai.

ryō. Largest monetary unit of the Edo Period, roughly equivalent to $450 in 1993 U.S. currency.

sankin kōtai. Legislation that obliged all daimyo to reside alternately in their provincial domains and in Edo.

sekiga. Impromptu collaborations by artists and poets; "party pictures."

senryū. Comic verse form written in 5, 7, 5 syllables, usually poking fun at human foibles.

shamisen (samisen). Three-stringed musical instrument popular since the sixteenth century.

sharebon. Form of *gesaku* fiction generally devoted to describing the licensed quarters.

shikishi. Squares of tinted or decorated paper used for inscribing poetry.

shinzō. Attendants of high-ranking courtesans; apprentices.

shogun. Military dictators of Japan, from 1185 to 1868.

shogunate. Military government headed by the shogun.

shoji (shōji). Sliding screens made of heavy translucent paper mounted on a wooden frame for the exterior of the house.

shumei. Assumption of a new name.

surimono. Privately commissioned prints intended for use as gifts, announcements, and mementos of special occasions, often elaborately printed.

suzuribako. Box containing writing utensils.

tabako-bon. Smoking kit.

Tanabata. One of the five principal festivals of Japan, occurring on the seventh day of the seventh month; in celebration, poems were written on *tanzaku* and hung on bamboo branches.

tanzaku. Narrow strip of tinted or decorated paper used for inscribing poetry.

tatami. Woven floor mats, rectangular in shape and approximately one by two meters in size; the size of a room is generally expressed in terms of the number of tatami mats it contains.

tokonoma. Alcove with a raised floorboard used for the display of hanging scrolls and important articles such as vases, incense burners, or candle stands.

Tokugawa Period. Period of the Tokugawa family regime, between 1603 and 1868; also called the Edo Period because the Tokugawa's capital was Edo.

torii. Symbolic gateway leading to a Shinto shrine.

Tosa. Leading traditional school of Japanese-style painters.

tsū. Sophistication or connoisseurship; also, a person who was elegant, intelligent, witty, and urbane.

tsuitate. Framed single-panel screen.

tsurane. Lengthy monologue delivered by a hero in a kabuki play, offering insight into his motives and thoughts.

uchikake. Long outer kimono.

uki-e. Prints or paintings imitating the European system of receding perspective, an innovation of ca. 1730.

uta-awase. Poetry competition in which two groups of poets were required to compose *waka* on prescribed subjects and then judge their respective merits.

wagoto. Literally, "tender business"; romantic scenes in kabuki plays, a specialty of actors from Kyoto-Osaka; contrasted with *aragoto.*

waka. Standard classical five-line poem, varying in syllables of 5, 7, 5, 7, 7.

wakaimono. Manservant in a brothel.

yagatabune. Large, roofed pleasure boats that could be rented for private parties.

yarite. Woman who trained, supervised, and assisted high-ranking courtesans.

yobidashi. Highest-ranking courtesans of the later eighteenth century.

yukata. Cotton kimono worn after bathing or during the summer.

zagashira. Production director; the highest official rank in theater administration an actor could hold.

zuihitsu. Genre of literature in which insights are recorded in the form of random jottings and essays.

Selected Bibliography

American and European-Language Publications

Binyon, Laurence, and Sexton, J. J. O'Brien. *Japanese Colour Prints*. London: Robert G. Sawers Publishing, 1978.

Bowie, Theodore, in collaboration with Kenney, James T., and Togasaki, Fumiko. *Art of the Surimono*. Exhibition catalogue. Bloomington: Indiana University Art Museum, 1979.

Brandt, Klaus J. *Hosoda Eishi, 1756-1829, Der Japanische Maler und Holzschnittmeister und seine Schüler*. Stuttgart: K.J. Brandt, 1977.

Brower, Robert H., and Miner, Earl. *Japanese Court Poetry*. London: The Cresset Press, 1962.

Casal, U. A. *The Five Sacred Festivals of Ancient Japan, Their Symbolism and Historical Development*. Tokyo: Sophia University, in collaboration with Charles E. Tuttle, Tokyo and Rutland, 1967.

Clark, Timothy T. *Ukiyo-e Paintings in the British Museum*. London: British Museum Press, 1992.

De Becker, J. E. *The Nightless City, or the History of the Yoshiwara Yūkwaku*. Rutland and Tokyo: Charles E. Tuttle, 1971.

Forrer, Mathi. *Egoyomi and Surimono*. Uithoorn: J. C. Grieben, 1979.

_____, et al. *Les objets tranquilles, Natures mortes japonaises, XVIIIe-XIXe siècles*. Exhibition catalogue. Paris: Galerie Janette Ostier, 1978.

Gerstle, C. Andrew, ed. *18th Century Japan, Culture and Society*. Sydney: Allen & Unwin, 1989.

Hall, John W., and Jansen, Marius B., eds. *Studies in the Institutional History of Early Modern Japan*. Princeton: Princeton University Press, 1968.

Hillier, J. *The Art of the Japanese Book*. London: Sotheby's Publications, 1987.

_____. *Catalogue of the Japanese Paintings and Prints in the Collection of Mr. and Mrs. Richard P. Gale*. London: Routledge & Kegan Paul, 1970.

_____. *Utamaro Colour Prints and Paintings*. London: Phaidon Press, 1961.

Itasaka, Gen, ed. in chief. *Kodansha Encyclopedia of Japan*. Tokyo: Kodansha International, 1983.

Iwasaki, Haruko. "Portrait of a Daimyo—Comical Fiction by Matsudaira Sadanobu." *Monumenta Nipponica* 38-2: 1-37.

_____. "The World of *Gesaku*: Playful Writers of Late Eighteenth Century Japan." Ph.D. diss., Harvard University, 1984.

Jones, Sumie. "Comic Fiction in Japan during the Later Edo Period." Ph.D. diss., University of Washington, 1979.

Keene, Donald. *World Within Walls, Japanese Literature of the Pre-Modern Era, 1600-1867*. New York: Grove Press, 1976.

Keyes, Roger. *Surimono, Privately Published Japanese Prints in the Spencer Museum of Art*. Tokyo: Kodansha International, 1984.

_____. *The Art of Surimono, Privately Published Japanese Woodblock Prints and Books in the Chester Beatty Library, Dublin*. London: Philip Wilson Publishers, 1985.

Kominz, Laurence. "*Ya no Ne*—The Genesis of a Kabuki *Aragoto* Classic." *Monumenta Nipponica* 38-4: 387-407.

Kornicki, Peter F. "*Nishiki no Ura*—An Instance of Censorship and the Structure of a *Sharebon*." *Monumenta Nipponica* 43-2: 133-52.

Lane, Richard. *Hokusai, Life and Work*. London: Barrie & Jenkins, 1989.

Leiter, Samuel L. *Kabuki Encyclopedia, An English-Language Adaptation of "Kabuki Jiten."* Westport, Conn., and London: Greenwood Press, 1979.

Lester, Gerd. "Kodo—The Japanese Incense Game." *Arts of Asia*, January-February 1993: 70-75.

Markus, Andrew L. "The Carnival of Edo: Misemono Spectacles from Contemporary Accounts." *Harvard Journal of Asiatic Studies* 45 (1985): 499-541.

McCullough, Helen Craig. *Classical Japanese Prose, An Anthology*. Stanford: Stanford University Press, 1990.

Meech-Pekarik, Julia, and Kenney, James T. *Utamaro: A Chorus of Birds*. New York: Metropolitan Museum and Viking Press, 1981.

Miller, J. Scott. "The Hybrid Narrative of Kyōden's *Sharebon*." *Monumenta Nipponica* 43-2: 133-52.

Miner, Earl; Odagiri, Hiroko; and Morrell, Robert E. *The Princeton Companion to Classical Japanese Literature*. Princeton: Princeton University Press, 1985.

Mody, N. H. N. *Japanese Clocks*. Rutland and Tokyo: Charles E. Tuttle, 1967.

Morioka, Heinz, and Sasaki, Miyoko. *Rakugo, The Popular Narrative Art of Japan*. Harvard East Asian Monographs, 138. Cambridge, Mass., and London: Harvard University Press, 1990.

Murase, Miyeko. *Japanese Art, Selections from the Mary and Jackson Burke Collection*. Exhibition catalogue. New York: Metropolitan Museum, 1975.

_____. *Emaki, Narrative Scrolls from Japan*. Exhibition catalogue. New York: The Asia Society, 1983.

_____. *Tales of Japan, Scrolls and Prints from the New York Public Library*. Exhibition catalogue. New York and Oxford: Oxford University Press, 1986.

Nakane, Chie, and Oishi Shinzaburō, eds. *Tokugawa Japan, The Social and Economic Antecedents of Modern Japan*. Translation edited by Conrad Totman. Tokyo: University of Tokyo Press, 1990.

Ooms, Herman. *Charismatic Bureaucrat, A Political Biography of Matsudaira Sadanobu, 1758-1829*. Chicago and London: University of Chicago Press, 1975.

Roberts, Laurance P. *A Dictionary of Japanese Artists, Painting, Sculpture, Ceramics, Prints, Lacquer*. Tokyo and New York: Weatherhill, 1976.

Rucinski, Jack. "A Japanese Burlesque—*Nise Monogatari*." *Monumenta Nipponica* 30-1: 1-18.

Sansom, George. *A History of Japan, 1615-1867*. Stanford: Stanford University Press, 1963.

Seigle, Cecilia Segawa. *Yoshiwara, The Glittering World of the Japanese Courtesan*. Honolulu: University of Hawaii Press, 1993.

Smith, Henry D., II. "World Without Walls: Kuwagata Keisai's Panoramic Vision of Japan," in *Japan and the World: Essays on Japanese History and Politics in Honour of Ishida Takeshi*, ed. Gail Lee Bernstein and Haruhiro Fukui. London: Macmillan, in association with St. Antony's College, Oxford, 1988.

Smith, Lawrence, ed. *Ukiyo-e, Images of Unknown Japan*. London: British Museum Press, 1988.

Soranaka, Isao. "The Kansei Reforms—Success or Failure?" *Monumenta Nipponica* 33-2: 151-65.

Stern, Harold P. *Freer Gallery of Art Fiftieth Anniversary Exhibition, I. Ukiyo-e Painting*. Washington: Smithsonian Institution, 1973.

Toda, Kenji. *Descriptive Catalogue of Japanese and Chinese Illustrated Books in the Ryerson Library of the Art Institute of Chicago*. Chicago: Art Institute of Chicago, 1931.

Tsuji, Nobuo. *Playfulness in Japanese Art*. The Franklin D. Murphy Lectures VII. Lawrence: Spencer Museum of Art, University of Kansas, 1986.

Vanderhoef, F. Bailey, Jr. *Oriental Lacquer*. Santa Barbara: Santa Barbara Museum of Art, 1976.

Waley, Paul. *Tokyo Now and Then*. New York and Tokyo: Weatherhill, 1984.

Waterhouse, D. B. *Harunobu and His Age, The Development of Colour Printing in Japan*. London: British Museum, 1964.

Wheelwright, Carolyn, ed. *Word in Flower: The Visualization of Classical Literature in Seventeenth-Century Japan*. New Haven: Yale University Art Gallery, 1989.

Winkel, Margarita. "Brieven van Santō Kyōden." Master's thesis, University of Leiden, 1992.

Yamaguchi, Ruji. "Japanese Clocks and Their History." *American Horologist and Jeweler* (April 1949): 71-86.

Young, Martie W., and Smith, Robert J. *Japanese Painters of the Floating World*. Exhibition catalogue. Ithaca, N. Y.: Andrew Dickson White Museum of Art, Cornell University, 1966.

Japanese Publications

Azabu Bijutsukan Shozō. *Nikuhitsu ukiyo-e meihinten.* Tokyo: Azabu Bijutsukan, 1988.

Clark, Timothy. "Nakazu no seisui." *Kokka* 1152: 7-25.

Editorial Committee of the Ukiyo-e Encyclopedia. *Sakuhin 2 Kiyonaga-Utamaro.* Tokyo: Taishukan Shoten, Shōwa 55 (1980).

Hamada Giichirō. *Ōta Nampo. Jimbutsu sōsho* series, ed. Nihon Rekishi Gakkai. Tokyo: Yoshikawa Kōbunkan, Heisei 1 (1989).

_____, Mizuno Minoru, and Suzuki Katsutada, eds. *Kibyōshi, Senryū, Kyōka. Nihon koten bungaku zenshū*, vol. 46. Tokyo: Shōgakkan, Shōwa 46 (1971).

Hattori Yukio, *Oi naru koya-kinsei toshino shukusai kūkan.* Tokyo: Heibonsha, 1986.

Iseki Masaki, et al., eds. *Museo d'Arte Orientale Edoardo Chiossone* (*Chiossone to kinsei Nihonga satogaeri ten*). Tokyo: Mainichi Shinbunsha, 1991.

Ishikawa Ichirō, ed. *Edo bungaku zokushin jiten.* Tokyo: Tōkyodō Shuppan, Heisei 1 (1989).

Japan Institute of Arts and Crafts, ed. *Edo no fuashun—Nikuhitsu ukiyo-e ni miru onna-tachi no yosōi.* Tokyo: Azabu Bijutsu Kōgeikan, 1989.

Jimbo Kazuya, ed. *Kyōden, Ikku, Shunsui. Zusetsu Nihon no koten*, vol. 18. Tokyo: Shūeisha, 1989.

Kagaku Hakubutsukan Kōenkai. *Zuroku Wadokei*, vol. 2. Tokyo: Zaidan Hōjin Kagaku Hakubutsukan Kōenkai, Shōwa 59 (1984).

Kasuya Hiroki. *Ishikawa Masamochi kenkyū.* Tokyo: Kadokawa Shoten, Shōwa 60 (1985).

Kikuchi Sadao. *Nikuhitsu Ukiyo-e. Idemitsu Bijutsukan sensho* 9. Tokyo: Idemitsu Bijutsukan, Shōwa 51 (1976).

Kobayashi Tadashi. "Kitagawa Utamaro Hitsu yūjo to kamuro zu." Kokka 996: 43-44.

Mitani Kazuma. *Edo Yoshiwara zushu.* Tokyo: Rippu Shobō, Shōwa 52 (1977).

Mizuno Minoru. *Santō Kyōden nempukō.* Tokyo: Perikansha, 1991.

Narasaki Muneshige, ed. *Utamaro. Nikuhitsu Ukiyo-e*, vol. 6. Tokyo: Shūeisha, 1981.

NHK and NHK Promotion Inc., eds. *Ō-Edo hyakkaryōran—Edo no bigaku to kōkishin.* Tokyo: NHK and NHK Promotion Inc., 1990.

Nishiyama Matsunosuke. *Ichikawa Danjūrō.* Tokyo: Kōbundō, 1960.

_____ et al., eds. *Edogaku jiten.* Tokyo: Kōbundō, Shōwa 59 (1984).

Okamoto Masaru and Kira Sueo. *Kinsei bungaku kenkyū jiten.* Tokyo: Ofūsha, Shōwa 61 (1986).

Okamoto Yumi. "Shokusanjin enjo meisekishū shozō ukiyo-e kaisetsu." *Bulletin of the Azabu Museum of Art* 2:24-25.

Ōta Kinen Bijutsukan, ed. *Edo Tokyo monoshiri zuten.* Tokyo: Ōta Kinen Bijutsukan, Heisei 2 (1990).

_____. *Shūzō ukiyo-e meihin zuroku.* Tokyo: Ōta Kinen Bijutsukan, 1988.

Santori-Bijutsukan. *Santori-Bijutsukan 100 sen.* Tokyo: Santori-Bijutsukan, Shōwa 56 (1981).

Shibata Mitsuhiko. "Shokusanjin enjo meisekishū." *Bulletin of the Azabu Museum of Art* 2: 4-5.

Smith, Henry D., II. *Ukiyo-e ni miru Edo meisho* (Tokyo: Iwanami Shoten, 1993).

Suzuki Jūzō. *Ehon to ukiyo-e, Edo no shuppan bunka no kōsatsu.* Tokyo: Bijutsu Shuppansha, Shōwa 54 (1979).

Tabako to Shio no Hakubutsukan. *Hanbon.* Tokyo: Tabako Sangyō Kosaikai, Heisei 2 (1990).

_____, ed. *Kiseru.* Tokyo: Tabako Sangyō Kosaikai, Shōwa 63 (1988).

_____. *Tabako-ire.* Tokyo: Tabako Sangyō Kosaikai, Shōwa 63 (1988).

_____. *Ukiyo-e.* Tokyo: Tabako Sangyō Kosaikai, Shōwa 59 (1984).

Takahashi Masao, ed. *Ō-Edo no nigiwai.* Tokyo: Kawaide shobo-Shinsha, 1987.

Takahashi Yoji, ed. *Edo saimitsu kogei zukushi. Nihon no kokoro* 66. Tokyo: Betsusatsu Taiyo, 1989.

Tanaka Tatsuya. "Sakuga jiki kara sakkyū suru kasanjiki no mondai." *Ukiyo-e Geijutsu* (*Ukiyo-e Art*) 103: 3-13.

Tatekawa Emba. *Hana Edo kabuki nendaiki*, ed. Masamune Tsuruo. Tokyo: Nihon Koten Zenshū Kankōkai, Shōwa 4 (1929).

Tsuji Nobuo, ed. *Nihon no Bi—Kazari no Sekai Ten.* Tokyo: NHK Service Center, 1988.

Uchida Kinzo, Kobayashi Tadashi, and Takashina Shuji, ed. *Hana no O-Edo no Erekiteru—Hiraga Gennai to sono jidai.* Tokyo: Santori-Bijutsukan, 1989.

Yamane Yuzo et al. *Fuzokuga to Ukiyo-e Shi—Gen shoku nihon no bijutsu*, vol. 24. Tokyo: Shogakukan, 1971.